Adventure Education

Theory and Applications

PROJECT ADVENTURE

Dick Prouty ✦ **Jane Panicucci** ✦ **Rufus Collinson**

EDITORS

HUMAN KINETICS

Library of Congress Cataloging-in-Publication Data

Adventure education : theory and applications / Project Adventure ;
Richard G. Prouty, Jane Panicucci, Rufus Collinson, editors.
p. cm.
Includes bibliographical references and index.
ISBN-13: 978-0-7360-6179-7 (soft cover : alk. paper)
ISBN-10: 0-7360-6179-7 (soft cover : alk. paper)
1. Adventure education. I. Prouty, Richard G. II. Collinson, Rufus.
III. Panicucci, Jane. IV. Project Adventure, Inc.
LC1038.A385 2007
371.38'4--dc22

2006029092

ISBN-10: 0-7360-6179-7
ISBN-13: 978-0-7360-6179-7

The Web addresses cited in this text were current as of November 13, 2006, unless otherwise noted.

Acquisitions Editor: Gayle Kassing, PhD; **Developmental Editor:** Jacqueline Eaton Blakley; **Assistant Editor:** Bethany J. Bentley; **Copyeditor:** Alisha Jeddeloh; **Proofreader:** Pam Johnson; **Indexer:** Bobbi Swanson; **Permission Manager:** Carly Breeding; **Graphic Designer:** Robert Reuther; **Graphic Artist:** Dawn Sills; **Photo Manager:** Laura Fitch; **Cover Designer:** Keith Blomberg; **Photographer (cover):** Kayaking photo © Photodisc; other photos by Paul Lyden; **Photographs (interior):** Courtesy of Project Adventure, unless otherwise noted; **Art Manager:** Kelly Hendren; **Illustrator:** Lyndsey Groth; **Printer:** Versa Press

Printed in the United States of America   10   9   8   7   6   5   4   3   2   1

Human Kinetics
Web site: www.HumanKinetics.com

United States: Human Kinetics
P.O. Box 5076
Champaign, IL 61825-5076
800-747-4457
e-mail: humank@hkusa.com

Canada: Human Kinetics
475 Devonshire Road Unit 100
Windsor, ON N8Y 2L5
800-465-7301 (in Canada only)
e-mail: orders@hkcanada.com

Europe: Human Kinetics
107 Bradford Road
Stanningley
Leeds LS28 6AT, United Kingdom
+44 (0) 113 255 5665
e-mail: hk@hkeurope.com

Australia: Human Kinetics
57A Price Avenue
Lower Mitcham, South Australia 5062
08 8372 0999
e-mail: liaw@hkaustralia.com

New Zealand: Human Kinetics
Division of Sports Distributors NZ Ltd.
P.O. Box 300 226 Albany
North Shore City
Auckland
0064 9 448 1207
e-mail: info@humankinetics.co.nz

CONTENTS

PART I   Exploring Adventure Education   1

PREFACE

Adventure education has been a thriving alternative to traditional classroom education for many years, and it is increasingly displacing traditional methods in modern education. The tenets of adventure education explored in this text will provide a foundation for the way education itself is visualized and designed in the 21st century. Educators are now realizing that true engagement with others, teaming up to learn and create and discover, is the primary way humans are designed to learn. This has become a major educational trend of this century. In turn, it will drive many other trends in education, therapy, leisure planning, and organizational training and development.

Understanding adventure education is a key to your future. This textbook has been created with your future in mind, functioning as a map to help you find your own path in a workplace where experiential and adventure education is practiced, probably in multiple ways and multiple locations.

As the world of experiential and adventure learning expands into new disciplines and program areas, it becomes more complex and a bit more difficult to understand. What was once a world of wilderness and outdoor experiences is now a wide spectrum of engaging and exhilarating experiences. As a result, several new jobs are being created in the world of adventure education. Whether or not you seek employment in the field of adventure education, it is likely that the leadership and team skills you will glean with the help of this text will serve you well in your future work endeavors.

To help you navigate the text, we have created a three-part structure. In part I, Exploring Adventure Education, we look at the history, philosophy, cornerstone concepts, key outcomes, and current context of adventure education through the eyes of some of the experts in the field. In part II, Defining Skills and Competencies for Adventure Practitioners, we explore the technical adventure skills, the pedagogical skills, and the processing skills needed for this type of teaching. And in part III, Planning and Implementing Adventure Experiences, we view the array of issues to consider when actually planning and realizing these kinds of programs.

One of the main attractions of this work is that it can empower many people to find meaningful roles in designing, leading, and implementing one of the fastest-growing and most effective types of education. Adventure education is well on its way to becoming one of the dominant pedagogies of the 21st century, and this book will give you a meaningful start in participating in that journey. Enjoy!

—Dick Prouty

PART I

Exploring Adventure Education

CHAPTER 1

Introduction to Adventure Education

Dick Prouty

> **❝** I regard it as the foremost task of education to insure the survival of these qualities:
> an enterprising curiosity,
> an undefeatable spirit,
> tenacity in pursuit,
> readiness for sensible self-denial,
> and, above all, compassion. **❞**
>
> —**Kurt Hahn**

Chapter Concepts

- ✦ Adventure education is an emerging field of education. Its power is rooted in human biology and social history.
- ✦ A wide variety of adventure or experiential techniques, activities, and methods are now available to help educators create high-performing learning communities where learners are in a state of relaxed alertness.
- ✦ Adventure education is well suited to address the educational needs of schools, communities, and workplaces in the 21st century.
- ✦ Adventure education embraces personal expression and involvement of all stakeholders in a learning environment, thus creating an exciting and stimulating field of education.
- ✦ Adventure education is a growing field around the world.
- ✦ Facilities-based adventure education is growing faster than wilderness-based adventure education.
- ✦ Adventure education curricula models, such as service learning, that use settings beyond the classroom can have a positive effect on the greater community.
- ✦ Adventure education is increasingly used in a wide variety of settings, including schools, agencies, and ethnically diverse communities.
- ✦ Adventure education is entering the mainstream of education in the 21st century.

This chapter serves as an overview of the exciting field of adventure education. As an emerging field, adventure education is still evolving. However, it is also the oldest form of education. For that reason, this chapter offers a broad view of the landscape from which the field emerged, the definitions and theories that inform the field, the key organizations and events that have shaped the field, and the trends that are taking us to a future in which adventure education will be much more common than it is now.

One of the most interesting things about this field is that, at its best, it merges personal growth and social skills with solid and disciplined cognitive work. Because relationships are essential to learning, this is a highly relational field, full of human interactions. It is a promising field that offers wonderful opportunities for those who are willing to pursue it seriously.

Historical Context of Adventure Education

Adventure education can be defined as direct, active, and engaging learning experiences that involve the whole person and have real consequences. **Experiential education** has a similar definition, comprising a broader umbrella that encompasses learning methods that occur in less active modes such as the classroom. The definitions of experiential education and adventure education are merging and becoming less distinguishable because the element that makes experiential education an adventure is not just how active or physically risky the activity is, but what the learner's overall state of mind is. If learners are out of their comfort zone and are actively engaged in learning, then we are increasingly likely to describe that as good adventure education, no matter where the location and how physically risky or active the mode of learning may be.

Humans are hardwired through our nervous system to learn in small groups, experientially through interaction with others, and through in-depth direct experience. For most of our history as a species, we have learned in active and engaging ways. We most often learned in groups of 10 to 20 people—hunting, farming, and making crafts. This learning involved oral communication, direct and physical learning experience, and modeling from others. Today, people of all backgrounds have strong positive experiences in adventure education precisely because this type of education fits our nervous systems and bodies so well. We are immersed in a state of learning that relaxes, stimulates, and challenges us, all at the same time.

With the rise of the industrial state in the 20th century, education changed to better prepare workers for the industrial workplace. As factories became the predominant workplace, schools became more factorylike, focusing on the skills of timeliness, literacy, and numeracy needed to be a good factory worker or industrial manager. The majority of student experiences in 20th-century schools involved note taking and performing on written individual tests.

Finding and solving problems in a team atmosphere was generally not encouraged in the schools of the last century, as it was a set of skills not generally needed in the workplace. Indeed, the overall goal of most 20th-century schooling was to teach students to be obedient, informed, yet passive workers in a school setting not unlike a large, industrialized workplace.

Yet this has not proven to be the best way for most people to learn. At most, 20 percent of the population can learn well in a setting where reading and writing are the dominant pedagogy and skill sets; the remaining 80 percent of the population in a factory school environment simply go through the motions and are ill-prepared for the workplace of today.

The educational needs of postindustrial society in the 21st century are vastly different from those of the last century. In today's information age, the main unit of added value in the workplace is the knowledge worker. The skills required by these knowledge workers are ones that adventure education is uniquely placed to address:

- Collaborative teamwork (leveraging the skills of multiple others is a necessity to learn and produce)
- Creative problem solving and product development
- Communication with passion and skill to influence others
- A sense of ethics and corporate responsibility for the greater community

These skills are the essential competencies of the emerging workplace in the information age, no matter what your field of employment. And we must do all this in a world where we are increasingly interacting with others of different backgrounds, talents, and ethnicities.

It is both ironic and fitting that the kind of 21st-century participatory education models now evolving worldwide have more in common with our preindustrial-age apprenticeship and experiential learning experiences than they do with the standardized factory classrooms of the 20th century.

The rise of adventure education has added powerful tools and procedures to our historical method of learning, as you will discover throughout this book. It should be reassuring to us that this type of education "feels so good," because this is how we were designed to learn best (Caine and Caine 1994; Wheatley 1993).

Educators can now use a variety of experiential techniques and concepts to create a classroom of orchestrated immersion (Caine and Caine 1994). When it's done well, orchestrated immersion makes students feel accepted and safe, and it produces a correspondingly high ability to take the risks necessary to grow and learn; in other words, students are both relaxed and alert. When we are in this state, our bodies and nervous systems are poised for maximum learning—we are in a flow state, where all of our senses and our whole being are engaged in the process (Csikszentmihalyi 1991).

The personal touch matters in adventure education, and it is a key part of any effective adventure program. Building a community is a personal matter because we must trust others with our personal and psychological safety (Johnson and Johnson 2002). We are finally realizing that the most effective mode of education is the adventure or experiential model, and that this model is so effective because it resonates with our biology and our history as a species.

As many of you will find out by participating in activities in the course in which you are using this book, adventure education is personal and

Adventure education helps us to discover and accept our own unique style and voice.

engaging. Adventure education helps us to discover and accept our own unique style and voice. We feel more at home in a good adventure education course because it fits us at a deeper level than we are used to (Bohm 1987). The freedom and release that many feel during their first experiences with immersion education can be traced to this feeling of finally coming home. If you are looking for a career in a field that is defined by learning to be open and trusting as a matter of social-emotional science and effective pedagogy, then this field is one you must investigate seriously.

Today, at least a small portion of many students' education is informed through the mode of adventure education, and a small but rapidly growing number of students experience the majority of their education in this form of education. Whether it be in summer camps, peak-experience field trips, experientially oriented classrooms and schools, service learning or character education programs, college classrooms and programs, agencies serving young people at risk, or after-school classrooms and programs, more and more students today are receiving key elements of adventure education and at least some of the social and emotional skills necessary to succeed in this century.

What exactly are the demographics of adventure education today? The following are conservative estimates based on my experience and conversations with key leaders in the field. These figures show the percentages of U.S. students in 2005 that have experienced at least eight hours or more of some type of adventure education activity or class:

- 30 percent of college students
- 50 percent of summer camp participants
- 20 percent of students in public schools
- 35 percent of students in independent schools
- 30 percent of participants in youth agency programs
- 30 percent of participants in programs for adjudicated youth

And, adventure education is growing 10 to 15 percent on average each year in most of these markets.

Milestones in Adventure Education

The history of adventure education begins with Kurt Hahn. His work in the first half of the 20th century has had an enormous influence on the field of adventure education. In addition, there are many others before and after Hahn who have helped the field embrace (or, more accurately, reembrace) active learning as the natural centerpiece of any good educational experience.

The following is a time line of historic milestones in the evolution of adventure education. The time line presents examples of the types of adventure education reintroduced to the educational system of Europe and the United States after the disappointing, if not disastrous, century-long experiment with an industrial model of education. A commentary on the organizations—their historical and current roles in the field—is included. Note that this is not a comprehensive list; there has been an explosion of educators and researchers advocating for a more engaged form of pedagogy. This list will serve as a guideline for an introductory exploration of adventure education.

1910 TO 1920   *Whole-Child Camping Experiences in United States*

This form of education was developed by the YMCA, YWCA, and American Youth Foundation to address needs of the whole child and included hiking, camping, swimming, and cooperative play. Youth agencies today such as the YMCA, the YWCA, and Boys and Girls Clubs are leaders in providing adventure curricula for both after-school programs and summer camps. Adventure education is often featured in their marketing material.

1916   *American Youth Foundation (AYF)*

William H. Danforth, founder of the AYF, believed that camp should be a place that addressed the fourfold aspects of a child's development: social, physical, emotional, and spiritual. After a period of expansion in the 1990s, the AYF today is consolidating its two main campuses (New Hampshire and Michigan) and developing in-depth curricula that deliver the original vision of the founder. Helping others use these researched practices is part of the AYF vision for the future (Garvey 1999a).

1920 TO 1932   *Kurt Hahn's First Schools*

The mission of the Salem Schools (Germany) and Gordonstoun (Scotland), both founded by Kurt Hahn, was to build character through education. Challenging activities and academics were equally balanced in order to develop the whole child.

Hahn developed a strong intellectual understanding of the importance of experiential education in forming character. He had the good fortune of being

CAREERS IN ADVENTURE

NAME: Jason Flesher

JOB: Experiential Programs Manager and Search and Rescue Coordinator, National Indian Youth Leadership Project (Gallup, New Mexico)

BACKGROUND: More than 20 years of working in the field of experiential education and more than 23 years as a search and rescue volunteer; has been an event administrator for REI and an experiential facilitator and wilderness instructor educating groups of all ages and backgrounds in 15 countries and around the United States; numerous certifications in wilderness education and search and rescue

I have written a community multihazard plan and two early warning and evacuation plans for the Pueblo of Zuni. I have also written numerous operational and risk management plans for wilderness-based institutions throughout the country. Developing and presenting curriculum models and training programs for alternative education, wilderness education, and team development is a passion that takes me all over the world to train facilitators, deliver keynote addresses, and design strategic programs in these areas.

WHAT'S YOUR JOB LIKE? I manage 20 staff members, oversee all their programs, and coordinate two programs myself. I am also a part of the Project Venture replication training team that travels around the United States assisting new program sites in the replication of the nationally recognized program of the National Indian Youth Leadership Project (NIYLP).

Our goal at NIYLP is to empower youths and to prepare them as healthy, capable, contributing members of their peer groups, families, communities, and nations. To continue to achieve this, we must also make sure that the staff members continue to raise their own capabilities and comforts. So my job is to make sure they are also continuously empowered and challenged, and I do this through trainings, outings, and working with them one on one and in the field with their programs.

Acting as the search and rescue coordinator for a youth and adult team is another full-time job. Though it is an all-volunteer team, I still have to manage and train 40 team members; oversee the rescue equipment caches, vehicles, and command trailer; and make sure the team responds when called upon. To juggle it all and still travel to facilitate trainings around the country, the best advice that I can give is train your staff and your volunteers as if you were training them to replace you. Find their strengths and build on them and delegate to them; find their weaknesses and work with them. Empower them and trust them and you will be amazed at how people can transform a weakness into a strength for you by you simply believing in them and showing that you genuinely care.

in a place where he could influence education in both the United Kingdom and the United States at a key historical moment. He is the author of much that is carried on today in adventure education (Flavin 1996).

1920 TO 1940   *John Dewey's Progressive Education*

Dewey's influential and oft-cited work inspired an early mode of experiential education known as the progressive education movement. Dewey advocated a balance of hands-on work with classroom work and insisted on a high level of democracy in the classroom that foreshadowed later models of participatory school practices adopted by adventure education (Dewey 1938).

1946   *Outward Bound UK*

Kurt Hahn was instrumental in the development of Outward Bound in the United Kingdom, a month-long course of intense physical, emotional, and mental challenges (Miner and Boldt 1981).

1955 TO 1965   *Wilderness Therapeutic Camps*

Campbell Loughmiller's classic book *Wilderness Road* was published in 1965. Loughmiller founded a series of wilderness camps for at-risk children in Texas that involved hiking, canoeing, and other activities. These camps proved influential in later camping programming.

1960 TO 1970   *Outward Bound USA*

Josh Miner brought a model of education based on the work of Kurt Hahn to the United States. By 1970, there were four main Outward Bound schools using the month-long course of intense challenge pioneered by Kurt Hahn in the United Kingdom.

Growing rapidly in the 1970s and 1980s to become a series of wilderness schools offering programs focused on developing personal skills in a wilderness setting, Outward Bound became the largest organization in the adventure education field, a position that it retains today. Although it is developing other nonwilderness programs, for most people Outward Bound still represents "excellence in wilderness education for personal development and growth" (Miner and Boldt 1981).

1964   *Student Conservation Association (SCA)*

The SCA has grown steadily over the years to become the largest organization recruiting youth volunteers on a systematic basis to work on natural resource conservation and environmental stewardship. The SCA is active in all 50 states and provides service opportunities, outdoor skills, and leadership training to thousands of young women and men each year.

1965   *National Outdoor Leadership School (NOLS)*

Paul Petzoldt, a seasoned mountaineer, founded NOLS in 1965 after two years of working to help found Colorado Outward Bound in 1963. His vision for NOLS was to use extended expeditions to train participants in the skills necessary for leading others in the wilderness.

The 1970s saw the rapid expansion of student wilderness trips. Instructor training was launched and became an important vehicle for developing staff and deepening the skills of wilderness instructors. International sites and other domestic sites were developed.

During the next 25 years, particularly under the direction of two effective and skilled leaders, Jim Ratz and John Gantz, NOLS solidified its leadership position in the wilderness arena by focusing on leadership skills: the technical skills needed in the wilderness and the interpersonal and judgment skills needed to lead teams in that setting.

Two initiatives started by NOLS—Leave No Trace and the Wilderness Risk Managers Conference—remain solid contributors to the field. Leave No Trace is now an independent nonprofit organization (with NOLS representation on its board) and the Wilderness Risk Managers Conference is comanaged on a rotating basis by Outward Bound, NOLS, and the SCA.

1971   *Project Adventure (PA)*

The concept for Project Adventure originated with Jerry Pieh, son of the founder of the Minnesota Outward Bound School. Jerry's goal was to make the benefits of an Outward Bound experience available to everyone. He presented this concept in his thesis at Harvard in 1969.

The Hamilton-Wenham Regional High School in Massachusetts, where Jerry was principal, received funds to develop the first integrated adventure model in 1971. The model featured a combination of interdisciplinary academic classes that used the team and leadership skills learned in a 10th-grade physical education class, a series of initiative problems, and low and high challenge courses. After a successful evaluation revealed increased self-confidence, independence of thought, and improved school climate, the federal government named Project Adventure a "program that works," and schools across the country received funds to

The Hamilton-Wenham Regional High School in Massachusetts received funding to develop the first integrated adventure model in 1971.

adopt the program. By 1980, there were several hundred Project Adventure adoptions.

Today, Project Adventure has become the leader in providing facilities-based training and development for teachers and counselors from around the world. A number of applications using the basic Project Adventure techniques have been developed and disseminated, all incorporating the PA cornerstone concepts of the full-value contract and challenge by choice.

Developing in-depth curricula (with evidence-based backing) for schools and youth agencies is the key focus of Project Adventure today.

1972 TO 1973 *Association for Experiential Education (AEE)*

The AEE was founded to promote the study and dissemination of the experiential education movement that emerged in the mid-1970s. The early incorporators were mostly either Outward Bound staff or representatives from other experiential organizations such as NOLS and Project Adventure. The AEE today remains the umbrella organization of the adventure movement, with large international attendance and with initiatives on accreditation and increased research.

1978 *Publication of* Cowstails and Cobras

This work, written by Karl Rohnke and published by Project Adventure, outlined the Project Adventure

approach to physical education and gave instructions on how to construct a ropes course at a school or camp. More than 30,000 copies were sold. As a result of the popularity of this book and the work of Project Adventure, thousands of ropes courses were constructed in the fields and woods behind schools, camps, and colleges all over the world (Rohnke 1977; Rohnke 1989a).

1979 TO 1980 *Executive Challenge*

This Boston University program was based at Sergeant Camp in New Hampshire. Using a ropes course, and with substantial penetration into corporate training settings in greater Boston, it was the first example of a facilities-based corporate training program using adventure education. Tony Langston, a Boston professor, directed this program through the 1980s.

1983 *Pecos River Learning Center*

This for-profit training company was created by Larry Wilson following his successful career in the development and sale of training programs. Pecos River combined the facilities-based approach of adventure learning, including challenge courses and initiative problems, with a systematic approach to managing change in a corporate context. At its peak in the early 1990s, this center was conducting change management training with a variety of Fortune 500 corporations, and reached estimated revenues of $30 million annually. In 1994, Pecos River was acquired by the Aon Corporation and moved to Minneapolis.

1983 *National Youth Leadership Conference (NYLC)*

Jim Kielsmeier founded the NYLC and has helped it become the single most influential program in terms of policy and advocacy for experiential education in the field of adventure education. The NYLC continues to be a leader in developing curricula templates and models of service learning through its annual conference. A large number of young people throughout the United States have benefited from the work of the NYLC.

1986 *National Indian Youth Leadership Project (NIYLP)*

The NIYLP is the principal organization doing significant and culturally appropriate adventure learning work with native peoples in the United States (Hall and Raudenbush 2005). McClellan Hall, a Cherokee, has worked for the past 20 years to make the NIYLP a model program under the rigorous evaluation methods of the Substance Abuse and Mental Health Services Administration (SAMHSA) under the U.S. Division of Health, Education, and Welfare. Project Venture, the model program, has elements of adventure learning and service learning in an after-school and summer camp format.

1986 *Publication of* **Islands of Healing**

This book, authored by Jim Schoel, Paul Radcliffe, and Dick Prouty and published by Project Adventure, introduced the term *adventure-based counseling (ABC)* to the greater adventure field and was the first book to outline a systematic methodology for an integrated approach to the use of both adventure learning and group counseling. With over 40,000 copies sold to date, it has resulted in the launch of thousands of adventure-based counseling and adventure therapy programs, the majority of which are still functioning today (Schoel, Prouty, and Radcliffe 1988; Schoel and Maizell 2002).

1992 *Wilderness Risk Managers Committee*

The Wilderness Risk Managers Committee is a consortium of outdoor schools, adventure programs, and land managers working toward better clarification, understanding, and management of risks in the field of wilderness adventure education by facilitating communication and education through an annual conference.

The committee was founded in June of 1992 at a time when risk management was gaining increasing attention from students, parents, land managers, and the media. NOLS was interested in more communication within the profession of outdoor education concerning risk management. At the same time, the NOLS community and the family of a deceased student were seeking ways to find meaning after a tragic accident. Representatives of Outward Bound, the SCA, the AEE, and other institutions collaborated to form the initiative.

Each year the fall conference draws between 40 and 50 of the industry's most influential outdoor education and risk management professionals as speakers and between 300 and 400 managers and practitioners from the wilderness adventure industry to share and practice field and administrative risk management techniques.

1994 *Association for Challenge Course Technology (ACCT)*

This trade organization was organized by challenge course vendors to both promote adventure education using challenge courses and to set industry standards in the building and use of this technology. Voting members, selected for their experience and skills, elect a board that manages the standards process and offers a conference each year. In 2005, ACCT had more than 30 voting members, and 600 people attended the annual conference.

1994 *Expeditionary Learning Schools Outward Bound (ELS)*

Through a grant from the Annenberg Foundation to develop transformative educational models, Outward Bound used a team approach to develop a comprehensive model of adventure learning. A design team that included Project Adventure, Educators for Social Responsibility, and Facing History and Ourselves developed and launched a model of an integrated and project-based adventure curricula for schools.

As of 2005, ELS is active in more than 100 schools in the United States, with a school-wide model of varying degrees of depth. Greg Farrell and Meg Campbell were the two key figures in launching ELS in the early nineties, and they remain involved today in leadership capacities.

1996 *AEE Accreditation Council*

After a five-year period of advocacy by Jed Williamson and Dan Garvey, the AEE Accreditation Council was launched in 1996 as an initiative of AEE. This is the first nationally recognized accreditation program focusing on adventure experiential programming. The program features a comprehensive review of adventure programs against a rigorous set of standards in risk management and program outcomes (Priest and Gass 2005).

The general public is served by having an easily identifiable, quality standard to choose from and an objective, independent source of information on those programs in the field that meet high standards. The field of adventure learning is served by a more detailed and comprehensive set of standards that define excellence in program management.

Key Definitions and Relationships

By now you have learned a good bit about the context and the history of adventure education. As you may have noticed, there is a significant trend to use all sorts of settings and environments to deliver the maximum learning zone we associate with adventure learning.

One way to think of this evolutionary trend in the field is to compare it with trends in a different field, the computer and software industry. The computer industry has gone from being driven by large hardware and reasonably simple software in its early days to a variety of software packages that can be delivered with many different hardware platforms.

Similarly, adventure education has gone from being driven by large programs with similar and relatively simple content delivered almost exclusively in outdoor or wilderness settings to a variety of venues, equipment, and content applications. Seen in the light of this metaphor, the famous never-to-be-modified original 26-day Outward Bound curriculum was the original large software package of the field. It was renowned for its transformative power, and the 26-day format became codified early on as necessary for "transforming power." But, this curriculum was delivered on the platform of a wilderness setting that was necessary to travel to, was costly to manage and maintain, and was expensive per individual user. This is comparable to the large computers of the 1960s and 1970s that were costly to maintain, required centralized sites that users had to travel to, and offered long but relatively simple program applications.

As you read this book, keep this trend in mind and look to see it in action. The trend toward more applications of adventure learning and more venues and equipment with a much lower cost per person is likely to continue. There will be continuing development of programs married to both innovative and traditional venues and equipment: heart monitors, bicycles, snowboarding, challenge courses, and circus apparatus are likely to increasingly comingle in educational programs set in wilderness,

The tools and techniques now available to provide experiences that engage the whole person are becoming better known and researched.

classrooms from elementary to college, and travel and edutainment companies. Just as the evolution of the computer industry has paved the way for the delivery of more powerful computing power to more and more people, so will the evolution of the adventure education field make its educational power and benefits available to growing numbers worldwide.

Adventure Education

Adventure education can be defined as direct, active, and engaging learning experiences that involve the whole person and have real consequences. This is the definition that this chapter began with, and it encompasses the trend of both hardware and software integration in the evolution of the field, so to speak. As spelled out in later chapters of this book, there is an exciting array of tools, methodologies, settings, and curricula in the 21st-century models of adventure education. The pedagogical tools and techniques now available to provide experiences that engage the whole person are becoming more known and better researched. Creative recombination of these tools combined with a corresponding feedback loop of effective research will make for increasingly powerful educational models.

Experiential Education

The following is a frequently cited definition of experiential education.

> Experiential education is the process of actively engaging students in an authentic experience that will have benefits and consequences. Students make discoveries and experiment with knowledge themselves instead of hearing or reading about the experiences of others. Students also reflect on their experiences, thus developing new skills, new attitudes, and new theories or ways of thinking. (Kraft and Sakofs 1988)

This definition covers all the experiences in the time line discussed previously, all work following Kurt Hahn's work in the United Kingdom, and all subsequent programming evolution in the field of adventure education. Some still define adventure education as a subset of experiential education. But the issue of defining the difference between adventure education and experiential education is rapidly becoming a moot point. Good experiential education engages the whole learner and thus uses a variety of techniques to involve and unite our physical, emotional, rational, and spiritual selves.

With the increasingly sophisticated framing and processing techniques that use good assessment

Photo by Paul Lyden.

Good experiential education engages the whole learner.

and sequencing methodologies for planning adventure curricula, we are entering a period where all effective curricula for learning will incorporate the techniques and methods of good adventure education. And as brain research is increasingly revealing (Caine and Caine 1994), knowledge acquisition is much more efficient in a class of engaged learners who are in the maximum learning zone of relaxed alertness.

The word *adventure* is helpful for referring to a whole range of experiential programming because it captures these techniques of involving the whole person. Just as important, the word *adventure* captures the tradition of maximizing the learning zone. We now know how a series of designed experiences can empower any teacher or counselor to get a class, no matter what the subject matter and the activity medium, to the point of maximum learning.

As you will learn in this text, the world of adventure learning is vast and rapidly evolving, and it is at the cusp of becoming a dominant mode of education in this century.

Outdoor Education

Outdoor education as currently practiced follows the guidelines of adventure education but happens primarily outdoors and through involvement with the natural environment. This definition usually covers both those environmental education programs that are conducted primarily outdoors and those adventure education programs (such as NOLS) that use a variety of activity mediums in the natural environment (e.g., camping, hiking, rock climbing, mountaineering, canoeing) (Priest and Gass 2005).

Outdoor Recreation

Outdoor recreation is a rapidly evolving field of adventure education that uses many mediums and has an outcome of personal and spiritual growth. Outcomes determine whether a particular curriculum is actually outdoor education or outdoor recreation. An Elderhostel biking trip through the Italian countryside using an adventure education process is a good example of this. Such a trip can easily provide an acceptable yet significant level of physical challenge to maximize the growth potential of participants for a specific series of recreational and spiritual outcomes. Consequently, if the purpose of the biking trip was to learn the history of leadership in Italy, there would be readings on that topic, and the facilitator could relate team and leadership skills to the reading content.

Adventure-Based Educational Programs

Programs that follow the adventure model as defined earlier are growing in breadth and depth and have a variety of settings. Types of programs include the following:

- **Physical education:** Curriculum (kindergarten through college) that uses the Project Adventure physical education model of cooperative games,

initiatives, and challenge courses or other holistic and experiential methods that challenge, motivate, teach social skills, and improve fitness.

- **Health education:** Curriculum (kindergarten through college) that uses a similar activity base as physical education but frames the activities so that students learn traditional health education content more easily and motivates students to follow healthy lifestyles.

- **Adventure in the classroom:** Academic classes (kindergarten through college) that use the adventure model as a primary instructional mode, such as ELS. Learning is more easily received and retained by a brain that is both relaxed and alert, as in good adventure learning.

- **Service learning:** A variety of schools and colleges now have service learning as a requirement, and most of the best service learning programs have all the elements of good adventure programming. Common themes are environmental stewardship, mentoring, and leadership training.

- **Character education, diversity, and classroom management:** There are many programs (kindergarten through college) that seek to change the climate of schools and help individual students achieve significant personal growth. For example, the NIYLP uses an adventure model with Native American youths in achieving these goals.

- **After-school programs:** A variety of adventure programs provide enrichment programming and seek to motivate students to achieve. Many of the key elements of adventure learning are used to engage students and accelerate learning.

- **Adventure-based counseling:** These programs focus on behavior change and integrate adventure education with group counseling within schools, youth organizations, and corporations.

- **Adventure therapy:** This type of program aims at changing dysfunctional patterns of behavior in clients who have issues severe enough to warrant either residential treatment or a more intense form of community-based treatment. Clients in adventure-based counseling or adventure-based therapy often learn new strategies for coping with personal problems and transferring these lessons to life beyond the program.

- **Organizational training and development:** Programs that aim to promote goals of organizational development such as leadership, teamwork, and a wide array of more targeted outcomes (e.g., sales effectiveness) have often used adventure education methods and curricula as an organizing principle and, in many cases, chief modality.

- **Community development:** These programs address the change of community norms such as the incidence of gang violence or alcohol and drug abuse in populations of a community across company and organizational boundaries. Such programs have used adventure education as a principal mode of change. Project Adventure, NIYLP, and many others have programs that address community-wide issues.

Trends in Adventure Education

To better understand this book, it is helpful to be familiar with the trends affecting the field of adventure education. Knowing that the following trends are growing within the field will allow you to look for them in the following chapters and in your subsequent exploration of this field. More brain research and educational studies each year reveal new rationales and methodologies within the overall trend of reembracing our experiential roots as a species.

The following seven trends are distinct, but they also interact and reinforce each other frequently.

Diversity of Settings

With the continuing rise of adventure education practices, it is a pretty safe bet that adventure education is now being employed with almost every conceivable type of educational or therapeutic grouping for people of all ages and abilities. It is being employed to maximize learning outcomes of an astonishing array.

Groups using adventure education include NASA scientists, elementary students with autism, veterans with severe physical disabilities, students at college freshmen orientation, government bureaucrats in Japan, groups of gifted and talented students in Singapore, Iraqi elementary and middle physical education students from diverse backgrounds, Kenyan college students learning about ecology and reforestation, clients in hospitals with head trauma, and U.S. Central Intelligence Agency (CIA) managers.

Although a significant percentage of adventure education programs are still found in wilderness settings, the relative market share of wilderness settings versus facility settings is changing. This is mostly a function of the relative cost of providing the same outcomes, or nearly the same outcomes,

Adventure education is now being employed with almost every conceivable type of educational or therapeutic grouping for people of all ages and abilities.

in a facilities-based program versus a wilderness setting. The model of using a local facility to host a peak experience for building community over the course of one to five days and norms for longer courses of study seem to be emerging as a strong blend of both facilities-based and wilderness adventure education.

Interdisciplinary Applications

Adventure education is studied in outdoor education fields at universities, but it is also increasingly a serious topic in the related fields of psychology and education, and it is often used in an interdisciplinary way in education programming at all levels. The fact that the approach is holistic and comes from a diverse yet coherent theory base makes it a good type of education to give coherence to divergent points of view in an academic setting.

Organizational development and training and development courses increasingly incorporate adventure and experiential techniques. The surge in corporate adventure marked by Pecos-type corporate programming (see page 9) has resulted in uneven quality in the delivery of corporate training, and a pullback to a more modest but steady delivery of this kind of training has occurred. Steady growth since then has occurred in the facilities-based approach to adventure learning as a whole.

CAREERS IN ADVENTURE

NAME: Tomoko (Tomo) Seki

JOB: Trainer and Consultant, Project Adventure Japan (Tokyo)

BACKGROUND: MS in experiential education from Minnesota State University, Mankato, Minnesota; BA in elementary school education with a minor in educational psychology from Tokyo Gakugei University, Tokyo

WHAT'S YOUR JOB LIKE? I have many job responsibilities, including program delivery and consultation as well as translation and administrative work. I work with corporate teams, teachers, youth at risk, class team building, and programs focused on intercultural awareness. Although learning through adventure experiences is still new to the Japanese people, they love it. Adventure or experiential education is beyond cultural difference.

As a college student and summer camp counselor, I saw kids changed by challenge. Following my time as a camp counselor, I had two big wake-up experiences: an AP workshop by Project Adventure in 1994 and a NOLS training experience for outdoor educators (24 days in wilderness) in 1998. I knew then that I would continue to reveal and utilize the mystery of adventure.

Working with people is so exciting and fun! Not only do I see growth in others but learn from the participants at the same time. If you are a person with an adventurous spirit, are open to discovery, and love to work with people, this is the dream job. It keeps your life spirit alive.

Credentialing Programs

As the field of adventure education grows and matures, many credentialing programs and schemes continue to develop. This trend includes the following:

- Continuing education credits (CEUs) or college credits are available from professional development programs for organizations adopting a particular adventure education program.
- Certification of different adventure education practitioner skills (e.g., wilderness first aid, challenge course leadership, canoeing) is demanded by more client-serving organizations and is rapidly evolving to serve this need.
- Undergraduate majors in adventure education are increasing.

- Master's degrees with adventure education as either a key component or the focus of the degree are an option.
- Accreditation of programs by the AEE indicates compliance with high standards set by the field's umbrella organization.

Government Recognition

Various governments at all levels are increasingly recognizing adventure education with laws or policies regulating or encouraging its establishment, such as the following:

- Several model programs of SAMHSA, a division of the U.S. Department of Health, Education, and Welfare, are adventure education models. These labels are increasingly needed to access federal money, even through state and local education agencies.

- Jim Kielsmeier successfully led a political campaign in the state of Minnesota to establish service learning using adventure elements as a requirement for school graduation.
- Park and recreation departments of many cities and towns have an adventure education program, often focused on challenge courses.
- State departments of public safety or public health are increasingly looking to regulate the field of adventure-based training and development.
- The state of Illinois recently passed a law encouraging social-emotional learning as a means of closing the achievement gap between various subsets of students.
- Many countries now subsidize adventure learning activities.

Evidence-Based Research

Evidence-based research is research that uses rigorously controlled studies to prove the effectiveness of an intervention. All educational and therapeutic programs that receive U.S. federal or state monies are required to provide an increasing level of evidence-based research supporting their effectiveness. Short lists of programs that work can be found on many government Web sites, and increasingly states and local educational and therapeutic agencies are demanding that providers meet a certain level of research validity, as outlined by the gatekeeping panels that regulate these sites.

There is a strong effort developing within the field to support gathering a body of research to meet these needs. The AEE and Project Adventure joined forces in 2004 to develop an evidence-based research agenda that will be of use to prospective researchers as well as to the greater field.

International Applications

Adventure education is proving to have universal cross-cultural appeal. While there is no disputing the fact that the spread of adventure education has historically followed a path that resembles the spread of European influence, there is now a rapid expansion that is bringing it to many non-European cultures. The international spread of adventure demonstrates that there is something in humans that resonates well with experiential methodologies.

Progression From Adjunct to Integrated Models

It is a frequent occurrence now to integrate adventure elements into educational or therapeutic settings where they are not part of an adjunct program but the primary therapeutic or educational program of the school or agency. There are many examples of this:

- ELS programs use adventure methods as their primary modality for whole-school reform.
- Project Adventure's program titled Behavior Management Through Adventure (BMTA) engages all participants in a therapeutic agency or alternative school (e.g., principal, teachers, custodians) in the understanding and management of a system of adventure therapy.
- The Reconciling Conflict Creatively (RCC) program offered by the Educators for Social Responsibility is a conflict resolution program integrated into a school's classrooms and counseling methodologies.
- The NYLC developed essential standards for service learning and helped those become more integrated into school curricula standards.

The need for this trend is reinforced by the increasing recognition that a primary agenda of educational leadership must be to develop an effective learning community of the professional staff within an organization. Managing too many unrelated interventions in an organization saps energy and can reduce the ability of the program to achieve the higher levels of evidence-based results now demanded by providers of funding (Barth 1990; Fullan 2005; Senge 1990).

The long-sought goal of reaching all students is now within the grasp of adventure education through the new focus on integrated approaches and evidence-based research.

Summary

As you work through the remainder of this text, you will find more examples of how adventure learning is exerting a powerful effect on the education of hundreds of thousands of students worldwide each year. There are many reasons why education as a whole is embracing an adventure model that engages the whole person, but the most powerful is the increasing body of accepted theory and

Web Links

Project Adventure: www.pa.org

National Outdoor Leadership School: www.nols.edu

Outward Bound: www.outwardbound.org

Wilderdom: www.wilderdom.com/research.html

National Indian Youth Leadership Project: www.niylp.org

Codman Academy: www.codmanacademy.org

Expeditionary Learning Outward Bound: www.elob.org

Association for Experiential Education: www.aee.org

Educators for Social Responsibility: www.esrnational.org

Collaboration for Academic, Social, and Emotional Learning: www.casel.org

research that documents the positive effects on learning when a student is fully engaged, mind and body. As a prospective adventure education leader, it is important that you master the techniques and methods of leading an effective adventure session, and this text will certainly assist you in that process. But it is just as important that you can articulate the reasons for the power and effectiveness of adventure education and understand how to lead a team in a collaborative setting. The ability to speak to the power and vision of adventure will give you the edge in many roles you may assume in the future. So please pursue this course and text fully engaged, knowing that doing so will help you be a better learner, a better person, and a better leader of others. Enjoy!

Review Questions

1. Define *adventure education*. Why are the definitions of adventure education and experiential education becoming hard to distinguish?

2. Who is the recognized founder of the modern adventure education movement?

3. What skills of the modern knowledge worker does adventure education address, and how?

4. Why is adventure education as old as the human species?

5. How widespread is adventure education today?

6. Why is adventure education growing?

7. Are personal growth and expression valued in adventure education today? Why?

8. Which is growing faster: wilderness-based adventure education or facilities-based adventure education? Why?

9. Name three of the oldest and most influential organizations in adventure education today. Which do you think is most influential and why?

10. What are three of the most important trends in adventure education today, and how do they affect each other?

Student Learning Activities

1. Chart three to five experiential and adventure programs within 50 miles (80 kilometers) of your campus. What are the origins, ages, and diversity of these programs?

2. Interview three classmates and ask them to define the most powerful learning experience they have ever had and why it was so powerful. What elements of adventure education were present?

3. Look up adventure programming, challenge courses, and outdoor education on a search engine such as Google and compare how different programs are described on the Web. What are the claims for these programs and the evidence for the claims given? Which programs seem interesting to you for future employment? Why?

CHAPTER 2

Philosophy and Theory of Adventure Education

Alan Ewert and Dan Garvey

> " Philosophy is . . . the front trench in the siege of truth. Science is the captured territory, and behind it are those secure regions in which knowledge and art build our imperfect and marvelous world. "
>
> **—Will Durant**

© Getty Images

Chapter Concepts

- Both philosophy and theory can guide our thinking, attitudes, and behaviors within adventure education.
- In many ways, adventure education is a subset of the broader field of experiential education.
- A number of theories in the fields of education, psychology, and sociology have connections to adventure education.
- Philosophy can influence our beliefs regarding the value of a particular subject, whereas theories can help us categorize and explain how and why something happens during an adventure experience.
- Positive outcomes related to self-systems such as self-concept and personal growth are benefits commonly associated with adventure education.
- The ultimate success of many leadership programs in adventure education is based on how generalizable the leadership training is to nonoutdoor settings.
- Adventure education has been associated with positive change in a variety of participants and groups.
- New adventure educators should be intentional about the outcomes they desire. Adventure activities are often fun and challenging, but in order for them to be educational, leaders must understand why they are doing something and what outcome they desire.

Personal philosophy and belief systems are like hidden road maps in our subconscious. They guide our thinking and behaviors because, like road maps, they tell us where we should be going and how we can get there. This chapter provides a brief overview of some of the more salient philosophical beliefs and theoretical models that inform the field of adventure education. Our goal is not only to discuss these philosophical views and corresponding theories but, perhaps more important, to help you consider how your personal beliefs and philosophies influence your own behavior in an adventure education setting.

We begin with a brief history of adventure education from three perspectives. First, we look at the historical interaction between adventure education and other historical movements. For example, it would be difficult to separate the development of adventure education programs that focus on personal growth and discovery, such as Outward Bound, from the broader context of adventure education.

Then we examine how these historical developments have influenced the emerging philosophies of adventure education. One classic example of this influence is the belief that facilities, programs, and opportunities should be accessible to all our citizens; thus, accessibility has become a concern in adventure education. Further, we examine the philosophical foundations of adventure education, looking at the role that adventure education plays in the larger context of experiential education. We also examine some of the philosophical foundations that underlie the related fields of education, psychology, sociology, and leadership, and we discuss the connection between these disciplines and adventure education.

Finally, we look at the potential outcomes typically associated with adventure education. In particular, we examine the outcomes of moral and character development, personal growth, group development, and leadership.

We examine these topics from the perspectives of both practitioner (outdoor instructor) and academician (faculty member and researcher). Within this context, we hope the reader will gain a broader view of the adventure education field in terms of both philosophy and theory.

History of Adventure Education

This section will focus primarily on the history of adventure education as it has developed in North America. We begin with the camping movement in North America and trace its evolution to its present-day form. Through this history we gain insight regarding how adventure education has developed and why colleges and universities teach adventure education in departments such as recreation, education, and physical education, sometimes separately and sometimes in a coordinated fashion.

The history of adventure education emerged, in part, from a variety of interrelated programs in both organized camping and outdoor education (see figure 2.1). Although camping paved the way for outdoor education, and outdoor education was the precursor of adventure education, it would be more useful to see each of these three approaches as connected—influenced by and influencing each other. If we are to understand adventure education, we must know something about the influence of all three movements: camping, outdoor education, and adventure education. Taken separately, each area is interesting and has its own unique history, but these three movements must be understood in relation to each other because each has helped create and expand the other.

Camping

The practice of bringing children into the outdoors has deep roots within American culture. Camp Gunnery, founded in 1861 in Washington, Connecticut, was the first organized camp in the United States. In a letter about the early days of the camp, Mary Gunn Brinsmade, wife of the founder, wrote, "When the Civil War began, the boys were eager to be soldiers, to march, and especially to sleep out in the tents. They were given opportunities to roll up in blankets and sleep outdoors on the ground" (Hammerman and Hammerman 1968). For much of the public, camping was seen as a recreational activity that was good for children because it provided a wholesome environment with supervised activities. As camping developed, it became obvious that the potential of camping far exceeded the simple recreational benefits first envisioned.

During the early 1900s, programs like the American Youth Federation (AYF) and the YMCA and YWCA began to design camping experiences that addressed the needs of the entire child. William H. Danforth, founder of the AYF, believed that camp should be a place that addressed the four aspects of a child's development: social, physical, emotional, and spiritual. Danforth used camping to not only teach children about nature but also to challenge them to be their best in all circumstances: "I dare you to be strong, think creatively, develop a magnetic personality, build character, to share" (1931).

Camping remains one of the most important activities available for children to experience the outdoors. According to the American Camp Association there are more than 12,000 day and resident camps in the United States with more than 11 million children and adults attending camp each year. The camping industry has helped develop adventure activities and also has integrated adventure activities that began in other places. Today it is common to find camps offering extended wilderness trips modeled after NOLS or Outward Bound. We might also find high and low ropes courses that were pioneered by Project Adventure. Regardless of the activities, camping continues to provide a large number of young people with extended experiences in the outdoors.

Outdoor Education

Julian Smith and his colleagues had a vision that extended beyond what most people understood to be the role of the natural world in education. Smith saw the potential usefulness of outdoor activities for a broader audience than children, and he imagined the possible connections that could be made between outdoor activities and the more traditional education offered within schools:

> Outdoor education is a means of curriculum enhancement through experiences in the outdoors. It is not a separate discipline with prescribed objectives like math and science; it is simply a learning climate that offers opportunities for direct laboratory experience in identifying and resolving real-life problems, for acquiring skills with which to enjoy a lifetime of creative living, for attaining concepts and insights about human and natural resources, and for getting us back in touch with the aspects of living where our roots were once firmly established. (Smith et al. 1963)

Smith believed outdoor education was necessary to protect people from the unanticipated negative

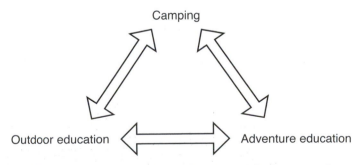

FIGURE 2.1 Camping, outdoor education, and adventure education are interrelated.

consequences of an increasingly mechanized and depersonalized society. He envisioned a complete overhaul of the educational system and a reconnection to nature:

> Outdoor education should be viewed in relation to the needs of the society in which it originated. Far-reaching changes are taking place in America, and these changes must be reflected in the schools supported by that society. A number of social influences in the present culture have provided the setting which has given impetus to education in and for the outdoors. (Smith et al. 1963)

Adventure Education

As educators like Julian Smith in North America were calling for a deeper commitment to outdoor education and a reformation of the educational curriculum, the Outward Bound program in England was being imported to America. As mentioned in chapter 1, Outward Bound was started in Britain by Kurt Hahn in order to remedy the declines he saw in young people after World War II. Hahn established a curriculum that attempted to stop the declines in

- fitness due to modern methods of locomotion,
- initiative due to the disease of spectatorship,
- memory due to the confused restlessness of modern life,
- skill due to the weakened tradition of craftsmanship,
- self-discipline due to the overuse of drugs, and
- compassion due to the haste with which life is lived (Richards 1999).

Josh Miner, an American who taught at Hahn's Gordonstoun School in Scotland during the 1950s, is credited with bringing Hahn's ideas to the United States. Upon returning from teaching in Scotland, Miner became a faculty member at Phillips Academy, a prestigious American preparatory school, and began using this new curriculum. During the next several years, Miner was instrumental in founding Outward Bound USA. He remained a visionary and guiding light for experiential educators until his death in early 2002.

Outward Bound began as a set of standard courses in which participants lived and learned in the outdoors as part of a small group, usually for 28 days. This educational offering was immediately popular because it met a need for relevance and adventure that had gone unsatisfied in American culture. Soon there were Outward Bound schools operating in six different locations in the United States and Canada.

Outward Bound can be credited with taking the concepts found in camping and outdoor education to a new level. Not only was the outdoors a place where participants could learn about nature as in camping, it also could be a vehicle for understanding human nature and a variety of subjects closely connected with traditional education.

Moreover, inherent in adventure education is the inclusion of activities and experiences that often include elements of danger or risk and uncertain outcomes. As a result of these dimensions, adventure education can offer participants a broad spectrum of psychological, physical, and emotional outcomes that are not often readily achievable in more traditional forms of education.

The outdoors is both a place where participants learn about nature and a vehicle for understanding human nature.

This connection between adventure education and traditional education became the intersection that helped create the need for teachers who were able to use both outdoor education and traditional education. Shortly after the first Outward Bound courses were offered, the University of Northern Colorado began an extensive training program to prepare teachers in the use of outdoor activities. Although organized camping had been part of the curriculum at many colleges and universities before the mid-1960s, it was usually associated with the department of recreation. However, the Outward Bound teacher training program in outdoor education became connected with the school of education at Northern Colorado and later at the University of Colorado at Boulder. This somewhat subtle change in academic affiliation helps explain why both outdoor and adventure education can be found in a variety of academic departments.

Because adventure education was a relatively new discipline, it needed to be linked with a broader and more recognized corpus of educational theory, and experiential education became the theoretical base that provided an explanation for why outdoor education seemed to be effective. In 1974, educators from North America who were involved with outdoor education gathered at Appalachian State College. This was the first assembly of educators interested in outdoor education, and it marked the beginning of what would become the AEE (Garvey 1999a).

In the early days of adventure education, it was expected that educators would bring students into the wilderness, but it became increasingly important to find ways to bring outdoor adventure into the classroom. If the experience of outdoor education could be modified to fit within the more traditional school curriculum, it would add great value to the educational system.

Project Adventure helped create the link between adventures that were occurring in the outdoors and adventures that could occur in a school. In 1971, Jerry Pieh, principal of Hamilton-Wenham Regional High School in Massachusetts, received a grant to set up a program that brought public school teachers together with staff from Outward Bound. He named this initiative *Project Adventure* (see chapter 1). In 1974, after a three-year test period, an evaluation of the Project Adventure grant showed it to have been successful in making significant changes in students' self-concepts and locus of control. That year the U.S. Office of Education touted the program as a model to be disseminated to other schools (Priest and Gass 2005).

Today, adventure education takes many forms, from programs for youth at risk to Elderhostel programs for older adults. Clients can select one-day ropes course activities or a semester-long NOLS course. Adventure education is found all over the world, and educators from many cultures are developing new methods and curricula. In the end, all who use camping, outdoor education, or adventure education are united by one simple framework: the belief that people learn best through direct personal experience.

Philosophical Foundations of Adventure Education

In this section, we examine the philosophical foundations of adventure education from three perspectives: the role of adventure education within experiential education; the connection between adventure education and philosophies that are associated with the disciplines of education, psychology, sociology, and leadership; and the effect of philosophy on the practice of adventure education.

Experiential Education

For the purpose of this chapter, we are defining experiential education according to Kraft and Sakofs (1988):

> Experiential education is the process of actively engaging students in an authentic experience that will have benefits and consequences. Students make discoveries and experiment with knowledge themselves instead of hearing or reading about the experiences of others. Students also reflect on their experiences, thus developing new skills, new attitudes, and new theories or ways of thinking.

Thus, experiential education stresses the use of direct experience, discovery learning, and reflection to form new skills, attitudes, or ways of thinking about a particular subject. Likewise, we define adventure education as a variety of educational activities and experiences, usually involving close interaction with the natural environment and a small group setting, that contain elements of real or perceived risk. The outcome, while uncertain, focuses on the intrapersonal and interpersonal development of the individual or group. Rock climbing, mountain climbing, high ropes courses, white-water rafting, wilderness trekking, and caving are examples of activities that are often engaged in under an adventure education rubric.

CAREERS IN ADVENTURE

NAME: Dr. Pete Allison, FRGS

JOB: Lecturer in Outdoor Education, Moray House School of Education, University of Edinburgh (Scotland)

BACKGROUND: PhD in moral philosophy and wilderness expeditions

When I was a teenager I became interested in natural history, in particular ornithology. I explored the local area and really enjoyed being out in nature. I got an opportunity to go to the Arctic on an expedition with the British Schools Exploring Society (BSES). After spending six weeks in Greenland, I developed a passion for camping, skiing, and climbing. I went on more expeditions in the following years to Africa and back to Greenland in between some studying. It seemed obvious that I should do a degree in outdoor education in the community. When an opportunity presented itself to work at Outward Bound in Malaysia, I jumped at it! Later on, two years of work at Bradford Woods (Indiana University) provided an opportunity to explore different forms of practice and to work with a range of different populations.

Returning to the United Kingdom, I spent four years completing a PhD in moral philosophy and wilderness expeditions. Fortunately, this involved going on more expeditions—to Greenland, Kilimanjaro, and the Himalayas. Some were for personal adventures and others for taking young people to explore wilderness for the first time. At Bradford Woods and during my PhD study, I had opportunities to teach both out-of-doors and also in the lecture theatre. This proved to be helpful in developing a portfolio, along with writing journal papers and book chapters, which secured a lecturing position when I completed the thesis. Since then I have been teaching at the University of Edinburgh.

WHAT'S YOUR JOB LIKE? The greatest part of my job is also the greatest challenge: There are lots of parts to it, lots of different roles and responsibilities I have to juggle. There are three main aspects to consider—teaching (outside and in the classroom), research, and administration. Working at a large and prestigious university, there is a responsibility to ensure that our teaching is of the very highest standard and that our writing and research is at the forefront of our fields.

Teaching is one of the most rewarding parts of the work—I spend time with postgraduate students both in the classroom and outside. This means that I have to move from theory and academic content to practical work in both of these contexts. Much of the work in the classroom is, I would argue, more experiential than the work that occurs out of doors. It also means that I need to have the skills for teaching in both environments and be technically competent. In the United Kingdom, technical competence is a career-long path that involves gaining a range of national governing body awards (NGBs). Another requirement of teaching is that I need to keep up with both literature (journals and books) and the news (current policy). Outdoor education is closely linked to educational policy and curriculum developments as well as other government policies such as health promotion.

As well as formal teaching with groups, a big part of my work is supervising MS and PhD students. We have a growing number of MS students and more PhD students in outdoor education than anywhere else in the world! This is a treat because it means we have a strong community of research and critical thinking in a range of areas that are all related to outdoor education. Making sure that students have the support they need—both in academic matters and in logistical support—takes a lot of energy and is a great joy.

Being part of a big university, there is an expectation that we will conduct research and publish journal papers and books. This is a bonus of the job for me since I enjoy writing and most of my research is either qualitative or philosophical in nature. This means I get to keep learning, always thinking about theoretical and philosophical issues both for writing but also to inform practice. This integration challenges and fascinates me! I am also expected to bid for research contracts that bring funds into the university. This means that I get to choose the areas to concentrate on and connect areas of interest with writing and philosophical issues. Perhaps the most appealing aspect of this is that it creates the chance to work with people in different parts of the university and enhances the interdisciplinary nature of research and practice.

The final part of my job involves administration and staff support. Ensuring that the courses we run are of the highest standard from conceptualization and validation to teaching and assessment is crucial. Talking with students and with staff about various situations and dilemmas in order to understand context helps us to interpret regulations appropriately and ensure that a just process is followed.

Finally, looking over the profile thus far, it is clear that it is more than a full-time job! I work hard and I work long hours—both when away with students but also at home, often starting work at 6 a.m. and not finishing until late in the evening. I love the work that I do, I am passionate about it, and I enjoy the range of roles and responsibilities. Most of all I enjoy the autonomy I have and the possibilities for exploring different research interests, going to different conferences, and designing curricula that are relevant and stimulating for students. It is hard work but it is the most rewarding work I have found!

Exposure to these activities and experiences is typically followed by group discussions and a *processing* or *facilitation* of the experience (Meyer and Wengler 1998). The purpose of these processing sessions is to give participants a structured opportunity to reflect on and internalize the adventure experience. Often this internalization focuses on *transferring* what participants experienced during the adventure activity to other parts of their life (Luckner and Nadler 1997).

Thus, by heavily relying on direct experience and then using reflection and facilitation to gain meaning from those activities, adventure education is a subset of the broader field of experiential education. The differences between adventure education and experiential education often lie in the types of activities, use of the natural environment, and deliberate inclusion of apparent or real risk in the experience.

Psychological and Sociological Theories

Numerous philosophies and theories are associated with the fields of education, psychology, and sociology, some of which have some direct connections to adventure education. For example, in the case of education, the philosophy of experimentalism suggests that the world is constantly changing. Moreover, reality is based on experience, and schools exist to facilitate the act of discovery on the part of the students.

In a similar fashion, there are numerous theories related to various aspects of psychology. The theories that are related to the tenets of adventure education, with its connection to direct experience, small group context, appropriate risk taking, problem solving, and dealing with uncertainty, are shown in table 2.1.

Doubtless there are many other theories that could be added to table 2.1 (see, for example, Shaffer 1988). In each case, the psychological theories listed have some connection to the ability of people to develop, learn, and increase their awareness through the input of personal experience, feedback from others, or taking direct action. In considering these components of personal experience, feedback, and action, the connection to adventure education becomes clear.

Within the same context, a number of sociological theories also present connections and continuities with adventure education. The most notable of these are shown in table 2.2.

Central to the link between adventure education and many of the socio-psychological theories listed in table 2.2 is the fact that these theories describe how people behave, learn, use symbols, or assume differing roles within a group context. Many of these dimensions are also present in the adventure

TABLE 2.1

Psychological Theories Related to Adventure Education

Theory	Proponents	Salient points
Behavioralism	Albert Bandura, B.F. Skinner, Edward Thorndike	Only that which can be seen and measured (behavior) is a reliable indicator of individual change.
Cognitive evaluation	E.L. Deci, R.M. Ryan	Perception of personal competence and control over outcomes is a powerful force in motivation.
Functionalism	William James	Behavior is adaptive; focuses on causes of events.
Gestalt process	Kurt Lewin	Relationships among the parts of the whole are critical.
Goal-driven behavior	V.H. Vroom, L. Festinger, M. Csikszentmihalyi	Actual or expected goals serve to guide individual action.
Social learning	Albert Bandura, Julian Rotter	Interaction between individuals and their environment is key.

TABLE 2.2

Sociological Theories Related to Adventure Education

Theory	Proponents	Salient points
Attribution	Fritz Heider, H.H. Kelly	People assign causes for outcomes as internal (i.e., self) or external (i.e., outside of one's influence).
Self-efficacy	Albert Bandura	Participation is a function of how successful people feel they will be at the activity.
Optimal arousal	John Hunt, Michael Ellis	Factors such as novelty, variety, and change are important variables in psychological health.
Cognitive dissonance	Leon Festinger	Focuses on situations when an individual is faced with competing thoughts or beliefs.

education setting. Thus, knowing something about the theories in both tables 2.1 and 2.2 allows us to have a better understanding of what happens during an adventure experience.

Philosophy and the Practice of Adventure Education

As suggested by Ajzen and Fishbein (1980), philosophy and practice intersect primarily at the individual level; that is, our personal philosophy or set of values and beliefs regarding a particular subject often guides our attitudes and behavior toward that subject. For example, do you believe that a person's behavior is primarily determined by the environment and the people they associate with (nurture), or is it determined by some innate combination of genetic makeup (nature)? Adventure educators generally believe that the experiences they offer can have a positive benefit regardless of the genetic predisposition of the participant. Thus, their philosophy generally causes them to believe in the ability to change a person through systematic and structured programs.

In a similar fashion, theories serve to organize our thinking about a particular phenomenon. From a scientific perspective, theories tend to develop from systematic and controlled research studies, whether the approach is qualitative or quantitative (Iso-Ahola 1980). Just as theories help us explain and understand how something happens during an adventure experience, they can also be helpful in categorizing events. Theories that are **idiographic** help explain a particular event in a specific case. Usually, however, theories are **nomothetic** in that they seek to explain a class of situations or events rather than a single instance (Babbie 1998).

Thus, both philosophy and theory can be useful tools in understanding and designing activities in adventure education. While most of us have a philosophy or set of beliefs regarding different aspects of adventure education, understanding what theories might be applicable in adventure education tends to be more sporadic among adventure educators. Both concepts are important, however, because while philosophy can inform us about issues related to values and beliefs, theories can help us understand how and why something happens. To a great extent, theories help us predict outcomes and can ultimately allow us to prescribe a program. That is, having a theoretical understanding of the adventure experience can help us design more effective adventure education experiences for our students.

Outcomes of Adventure Education

In this section we will focus on some of the results of adventure education and look at how adventure education is being used as an educational and developmental experience. We will examine the influence adventure education can have on how we see ourselves and how we interact with others. In the early days of adventure education, practitioners may have had strong intuitive beliefs about the efficacy of these methods, but it is only in recent years that comprehensive scholarship has begun to research the possible impact of adventure education.

What follows in this chapter are examples of positive changes that have been thoroughly researched so that we can feel confident that adventure education is highly effective with each of these client groups. A developing body of research continues to examine the possible effectiveness of adventure activities with an ever-increasing list of clients. You are encouraged to critically examine the efficacy of adventure education and add your reasoned experiences to the developing research on adventure education.

Moral Development

Perhaps one of the most important results that could be claimed by any educational offering is that it helps participants learn how their actions affect others and encourages them to act in a way that supports positive social interactions (Rachels 1999). A useful definition of moral development is "[a] psychological construct that characterizes the process by which people determine that one course of action in a particular situation is morally right and another course of action is wrong" (Rest, Thoma, and Edwards 1997).

Jasper Hunt, a former Outward Bound instructor and professor at Minnesota State University, provided the philosophic framework for understanding the potential value of adventure education and its relationship to ethics (2002). Using Hunt's foundational work, other authors began to view adventure education as a powerful tool in support of moral development (Garvey 1999b).

Experiential education in general and adventure education specifically have been found to have a positive effect on participants' sense of fairness and moral reasoning. For example, Conrad and Hedin's assessment demonstrated that "the combination of significant role-taking experiences and active reflection [are] an effective means of promoting growth in this [moral] aspect of development" (1981, 15). Rest's meta-analysis of 56 educational programs reinforced connections made between advanced cognitive abilities and stages of moral reasoning (1986). Garvey (1991) found improved moral reasoning in 50 college students as a result of a semester-long adventure education program. Change in moral development was found by Pan-

owitsch (1975) as a result of a semester-long course in ethics. More recently, Penn (1990) and DeZeeuw (2002) have documented significant improvement in students' moral development as a result of carefully designed classes and programs in which ethical scenarios are thoroughly discussed, and Giampietro (2001) noted elevated moral reasoning in a group of outdoor education students exposed to a variety of adventure activities such as rappelling.

These results appear to confirm that when participants are given an opportunity to analyze their behavior and the behavior of others within an adventure education setting, positive results occur in their level of moral development. Such improvements in moral reasoning hold great potential for many different client groups. It might be accurately stated that adventure education has the potential to make participants view themselves differently

Working with others in an adventure education setting helps participants to understand why cooperation is necessary for group success.

and select better behavior when interacting with others—behavior that will be more effective in the attainment of personal and group goals. It seems clear that the process of working with others in an adventure education setting helps participants gain insight into why cooperation is necessary for group success.

Personal Growth

One of the most visible and advertised outcomes of adventure education programs is personal growth. This growth has been characterized as changes in constructs such as self-concept, self-esteem, confidence, and personal motivation. These outcomes have typically been measured with a variety of self-report instruments administered before, during, and after an adventure experience.

Numerous theories have been associated with research in outcomes related to personal growth including self-efficacy, attribution theory, change theories, and cognitive dissonance. Regardless of what theoretical position might be taken to explain a specific outcome, the following characteristics are often associated with positive changes within an individual from participation in an adventure experience (adapted from Hopkins and Putnam 1993):

- Potential learning and self-system change must involve an active construction of meaning.
- Past experience can be a useful touchstone in facilitating personal growth through adventure education.
- The learning context (e.g., group dynamics) is often critical in successfully precipitating positive growth and change within a participant.

Thus, although hailed as a primary outcome of adventure education, changes in constructs such as personal growth most commonly occur through a skillfully designed adventure education curriculum with trained and experienced leaders. In other words, personal growth, while usually experienced by participants of adventure education programs, is not an automatic outcome; the programs must be properly designed and executed.

Group Development

In addition to facilitating personal growth and development, adventure education has been found to help make groups more effective. Adventure education is being used with large and small businesses, medical staff, astronauts, naval officers, and sport teams, to name only a few examples in which group performance is improved through the use of adventure activities.

Much has been written about group effectiveness, but Tuckman and Jensen's five-stage theory is still one of the most frequently used frameworks to help explain group development (1977). In this theory, groups are seen as moving through the accomplishment of five tasks on their journey toward group effectiveness.

1. *Forming* is when people first come together and recognize themselves as a group. This is often a time of increased anxiety because individuals are trying to figure out who else is in the group and what expectations are present.

2. *Storming* is the process by which members negotiate their individual expectations in relationship to the group. The storming stage can appear chaotic and tense because individuals are attempting to assert their personality within the context of the group.

3. *Norming* allows the group to agree upon certain rules that will help facilitate group success. During the norming stage, the group attempts to create a culture of acceptable performance for individuals.

4. *Performing* is when the group functions as a unit in the accomplishment of a task. The performance stage allows the group to get things done and provides a window into the relative success of the previous three stages.

5. *Adjourning* is the stage of closure and separation where the group ceases to function as a unit. In some instances groups simply assemble and disband with little regard to formal endings, but most often, group members attempt to find some way of marking and ritualizing the end of the group experience.

The ability of adventure educators to design activities that improve group performance has been remarkable. Because adventure education has the potential for concrete, demonstrable outcomes, these techniques can be highly effective as a window into group process. To cite only one example, in a raft-building exercise, group members are asked to assemble a raft using limited resources. Once constructed, the raft will be used to float participants to a predetermined location on the water. If the group communicates and functions well, the raft will be sound and everyone will stay dry. But

CAREERS IN ADVENTURE

NAME: David Calvin

JOB: Outdoor Program Coordinator, Indiana University (Bloomington, Indiana)

BACKGROUND: Master's degree in recreation with an emphasis in outdoor recreation and 15 years' experience working within collegiate outdoor recreation programs; strong background and teaching experience in a variety of outdoor activities such as white-water canoeing and kayaking, coastal kayaking, rock climbing, ice climbing, backpacking, vertical caving, high angle rescue, mountaineering, and wilderness medical skills; certifications and trainings in ropes facilitation, legal compliance, high angle rope rescue, and swiftwater rescue; certification as emergency medical technician; instructor for a variety of organizations including the WEA, ACA, American Red Cross, and AHA

WHAT'S YOUR JOB LIKE? As Outdoor Program Coordinator, I serve as the liaison between Indiana University (IU) Outdoor Adventures and the Department of Recreation, Park, and Tourism Studies in planning, designing, staffing, and implementing academic electives and administering the grades for over 600 students annually. I'm responsible for the overall leadership development of 50 student trip leaders, teaching industry standards in regards to training, risk management, field manuals, and technical skills, as well as enhancing their decision-making and judgment abilities. Specific responsibilities include serving as the coordinator and administrator of IU Outdoor Adventures, as well as supervising two full-time staff and three graduate assistants and developing course syllabi, written exams, and skills checklists for 36 different elective skills courses.

I also develop and maintain the department budget, conduct the biweekly payroll, oversee the development of a thorough marketing scheme, assist in the planning and development of 100 to 110 adventure trips and skill courses annually, serve as an outdoor leader for a handful of extended trips and weekend courses annually, assist in training and supervising 50 trip leaders and skill course instructors, develop and facilitate semester leadership weekends for trip leaders in training, and manage an effective outdoor equipment rental program. In addition, I revise and update the risk management policy, trip leader manual, and various other training materials and manuals.

On a daily basis, I recruit, hire, train, and supervise program supervisors and IU Outdoor Adventures leadership staff; update syllabi, grade student papers, and create and modify expedition behavior assessment tools; and develop practical skills evaluation forms for academic elective courses.

The most enjoyable aspect of the position is teaching, modeling, and fostering the development of students and their decision-making, judgment, problem-solving, and leadership skills. Financial restrictions and state government's bureaucratic processes can provide a challenge at the most opportune time.

Leadership skills in the backcountry and office setting are vital for departmental success. If participants and groups are challenged and fairly successful, a program will flourish within the outdoor recreation department. Communication skills are the most important, followed closely by safety, technical, and teaching skills.

If you're looking to enter this field, you must be comfortable working with a diverse group of people in a variety of settings. Working with several different groups in an outdoor setting for various lengths of time would be a great start to the outdoor adventure field. Know the group development process and how to identify where a group is within the process; then provide the appropriate style of leadership to maximize group development and success.

if the group is dysfunctional because one person dominates or the process becomes bogged down, the raft may not be able to support the group. After the initial experience, a trained educator can help the group deconstruct the activity and examine what worked well and what might need to be improved in order for the group to become more successful. This raft-building activity can serve as a metaphor for other tasks that the group faces when they return to regular work.

Leadership Development

One of the most commonly sought outcomes from adventure education is **leadership** development. Whether this development is in the form of internal leadership attributes such as motivation, organization, and personal responsibility or external leadership attributes such as leading others, technical skills, and facilitation techniques, leadership training is a significant outcome expected by many adventure education programs.

Numerous studies have been conducted on the construct of leadership. Many of these have focused on questions related to the genesis of effective leadership. For example, is leadership a set of traits that a person is born with? Is it based on the situation? Can it be learned? Much of the research on leadership in adventure education has focused on the identification and development of competencies such as technical skills, facilitation, communication, navigation skills, and so on.

However, Johnson and Johnson (2002) suggest that, whatever the genesis of effective leadership or the competencies required in a specific situation, there are five leadership issues that all effective leaders must grapple with:

1. Challenging the status quo (i.e., making change)
2. Inspiring a mutual vision
3. Empowering members through cooperative teamwork
4. Leading by example
5. Encouraging members to keep developing their personal expertise

It is perhaps in the realm of these five areas that adventure education will achieve its most noteworthy gains in leadership training. That is not to say that specific competencies, such as map and compass skills, are not important; they are, particularly in many adventure situations. The difference is that highly specific technical skills such as navigation or

Web Links

Institute for Outdoor Learning and Education: www.indiana.edu/~outdoor

Conservation and Recreation Education Program: www.indiana.edu/~core

Leave No Trace techniques are less generalizable to nonoutdoor leadership situations. And it is in this area of generalizibility that Johnson and Johnson's five leadership issues gain more importance, both for their intrinsic value and for their value in the field of adventure education.

Thus, the success of leadership training through adventure education is a result of how generalizable the learning is to other leadership situations. The ability of the program to train students in the ability to institute change, inspire a shared vision, empower members, lead by example, and promote member improvement will typically offer more value than simply teaching specific outdoor skills.

Summary

It should be clear by now that philosophy and theory are necessary in order for us to understand why we do what we do in adventure education and why it works. We encourage you as adventure educators to make a commitment to be intentional in your work. As leaders ourselves, we are aware of the powerful potential of adventure education. We have witnessed the evolution of our profession from the days when almost any risk could be justified because people seemed to enjoy themselves to a time when we must carefully examine the potential benefit of any risk, physical or psychological. Gone are the days when educators can simply offer activities with little or no understanding about the intended outcome. Intentionality commits us to choose the most appropriate activity to achieve the intended educational outcome. Carefully consider everything you do as an adventure educator and know why you have chosen one activity over another to accomplish your educational objective. As leaders, we should always be ready to answer questions about why we are asking participants to do what they're doing.

We hope that the history, philosophy, and methods described in this chapter have helped establish a context within which to consider your adventure activities. The field of adventure education is only now beginning to seriously reflect on the most appropriate practices to achieve desired outcomes. Allow your contribution to be one of purpose and intention by understanding the underpinnings of this wonderful profession.

Review Questions

1. Define the following terms: (a) experiential education, (b) adventure education, (c) leadership, (d) philosophy, (e) theory.

2. In what ways do the uses of philosophy and theories differ in the adventure education field?

3. Select one theory discussed in this chapter and describe its development, major tenets, and how it can be used in adventure education. Provide an example of how you might use it as an instructor.

Student Learning Activities

1. Locate one or two past participants of adventure education programs and interview them to determine what outcomes they gained from their experience.

2. Form small groups and discuss your personal philosophies regarding adventure education.

3. Write down the research-based or experiential-based theories you believe are relevant to adventure education. Provide examples of how you saw them actually work.

4. Discuss the difference between intentional learning and random learning and how each is part of adventure education.

5. In groups, describe the experience that has had the most powerful impact on your choice to become an adventure educator.

6. Develop an outline of an adventure education curriculum that emphasizes leadership development. What types of skills, attributes, or abilities would you try to achieve?

CHAPTER 3

Cornerstones of Adventure Education

Jane Panicucci

> " Wonderful ideas are built on other wonderful ideas. In Piaget's terms, you must reach out to the world with your own intellectual tools and grasp it, assimilate it, yourself. All kinds of things are hidden from us—even though they surround us— unless we know how to reach out for them. "
>
> **—Eleanor Duckworth**

Chapter Concepts

✦ Three relevant learning theories presented by Dewey, Duckworth, and Kolb are reviewed.

✦ Understanding the experiential learning cycle and its application to learning theory is important for the adventure practitioner.

✦ Challenge by choice and behavioral contracting are essential components of an effective program.

✦ Leadership development is a critical component of adventure learning.

✦ Service learning can be a powerful addition to an adventure program.

✦ Proper activity selection can be accomplished by using the GRABBSS assessment tool.

Beneath adventure education, or any professional practice for that matter, lies a guiding set of foundational theories and concepts. These cornerstone concepts provide professionals in the field with a basic structure for their programs. An institution or individual practitioner may practice these concepts in different ways, label them differently, and emphasize some more than others, but rooted in the basic nature of their program are common practices that link their work together and form a professional field. Allowing participants to have choices in how they are challenged, incorporating behavioral contracts into an experience, and providing reflection time to support learning are examples of adventure education cornerstones. Each promotes the primary attributes of adventure: risk taking, fun, challenge, and safety.

Learning Theories

Adventure experiences are powerful and offer many opportunities for learning. An experience can be so compelling that learning occurs regardless of the knowledge and skill of the facilitator. However, the more knowledgeable a facilitator is about how and why people learn, the greater the chances are that the experience will support the outcome goals of the participants. Facilitators should craft experiences that incorporate these theoretical concepts.

Facilitators who understand basic learning theory and who can apply that learning theory directly to their work will craft experiences that have strong impact on their participants. Relying solely on the experience rather than incorporating techniques such as allowing students to get at

their own understanding truly limits the power of experiential teaching. The following three learning theories are foundational for anyone's work as an experiential educator.

John Dewey and the Foundations of Experiential Education

John Dewey (1859-1952) is the father of experiential education. His groundbreaking text, *Experience and Education,* was published in 1938 during a time of very traditional education—students sat quietly in rows while the teacher imparted information to them. Dewey's progressive views of the educational experience were met with significant resistance at first, but they have been the steady force that has shaped the field of experience-based learning today.

Dewey's theory, quite simple in nature, is more complex in practice. He believed that all genuine education comes through experience. He advocated placing the learner at the center of the learning experience and the teacher as guide and coach. He noted that this transition from teacher to guide is not easy for many, but it is imperative to creating experiential-based learning. He believed that the human mind is a meaning-making organ relentlessly driven to make sense of its world. Consequently, a learner strives to make a personal connection to the content at hand. Content needs to have relevance and learners must have an opportunity to make their own meaning, something that does not easily occur in a "teach and tell" environment.

Dewey also believed that not all experiences are educative; some are "mis-educative," meaning they

John Dewey advocated placing the learner at the center of the learning experience.

halt or distort the growth of further experience; some "engender callousness"; and some reduce "the possibilities of having richer experience in the future." The traditional classroom may provide experiences, but they are "largely of a wrong kind" (Dewey 1938). Students may thus lose their desire to learn. The most powerful learning experiences are those that engage learners in posing and solving problems, making meaning, producing products, and building understanding. The manner in which students learn is as important as the subject matter they learn; they should be taught in a manner consistent with becoming interactive and dynamic learners.

The field of adventure education, which embraces the use of experience, is enhanced with a solid understanding of Dewey's ideals and philosophies. Whether a program's goals include intellectual development and academic content or the powerful personal learning that often results from adventure experiences, Dewey's theory forms the foundation for the field's teaching practices. Skilled practitioners are constantly looking for ways to connect content to students' everyday lives. They provide opportunities for students to solve their own problems—adventure is about doing, not

about being told. The experiential learning cycle, described later in this chapter, is an excellent tool to ensure that the actual experience that Dewey describes is educative.

Eleanor Duckworth and How People Learn

Eleanor Duckworth, a well-known educational theorist, developed her theories of learning from her work with Jean Piaget as they observed how young children learn. She states that "the having of wonderful ideas is the essence of intellectual development," which is the essence of learning. She goes on to say that "wonderful ideas are built on other wonderful ideas" (Duckworth 1987).

The experiential facilitator, then, is responsible for providing relevant opportunities for students to have their own wonderful ideas. The question is how a leader can support these moments and allow participants the time and space to develop their own thinking. Until participants grasp something in their own way, whether that means learning about themselves or learning a technical skill, they won't fully understand it. Duckworth's simple concept captures this notion that people must acquire ideas or skills in their own way, and we as educators need to craft experiences to allow for these important moments. Ideally, students will gain a better understanding of how they learn.

How we learn is one of the cornerstones of how we live in this world. Quite often, adventure program goals include helping participants learn more about themselves, which is an appropriate outcome for adventure experiences. Self-awareness allows us to access previous knowledge and thus develop more of our own ideas. Whether participants are striving for the acquisition of academic content or personal growth and development, the role of the facilitator in Duckworth's theory is the same:

- To seek and take advantage of all possible learning pathways

- To structure subject matter or experiences in a way that enables learners to access their thoughts about the subject or experience

- To take students' thoughts seriously and help them discover those thoughts in greater breadth and depth

- To give participants an appreciation for their own way of learning

Like Dewey, Duckworth favors experiences that have relevance to the students, that truly engage the students, and that allow the students to connect the experience to previous and future experiences for continued growth and learning. Her theory expands the notion that every learner approaches the attainment of knowledge in different ways. She suggests that teachers focus on allowing students to work through their ways of thinking, not the teacher's way of thinking, and to structure experiences that support how each person learns. She provides a simple example of how two people can see the same thing in different ways:

> What does it really mean, 24 divided by 8?

> Someone answers, "It means you have 24 things, and you distribute them evenly into 8 piles, and you count how many end up in each pile!"

> A second person answers, "NO, that is not what it means. It means that you have 24 things, and you put them into piles of 8 and see how many piles you get!" (paraphrased from Duckworth 1987)

Duckworth presents us with one problem and two different ways to look at it. Let's apply this concept to adventure experiences and imagine watching a group engaged in a problem-solving activity that is usually solved in a particular way. For example, take the pipeline activity in which participants pass objects down a line using short pieces of PVC pipe. Most groups roll the objects from one pipe to another, using an orderly sequence of pipes. As the new group begins to discuss alternative solutions, perhaps tossing the objects gently to each other, or trapping the objects between pipes without breaking any of the stated rules, the instructor might feel compelled to guide the group toward the more common solution. But, this does not allow for the development of the "wonderful ideas" from which learning occurs.

Allowing groups to get at material in their own way is a cornerstone to effective teaching using adventure experiences. Some might wonder whether there is often a correct answer to a problem, but you can see that although there may be one appropriate final solution, there also may be many avenues to get to that point. A prominent provider of adventure services teaches his advanced technical workshops using Duckworth's philosophy. Groups explore rescue scenarios and problem solve to come up with unique solutions to getting someone down from height. The result is the development of increased technical problem-solving skills coupled with the actual skill of performing rescues.

David Kolb and the Experiential Learning Cycle

The most common learning theory that is applied to adventure and experiential education is that of David Kolb. There are four phases in **Kolb's experiential learning cycle:** concrete experience, reflective observation, abstract conceptualization, and active experimentation. Concrete experience and abstract conceptualization focus on how we absorb experience, while reflective observation and active experimentation illustrate how we deal with experience (Kolb 1984). In experiential settings, these phases are often referred to as *experience, what?, so what?,* and *now what?* These basic questions become debriefing guides and help us incorporate all four phases into an experience (see figure 3.1). When crafting and guiding learning experiences for participants, it is important to create opportunities for each phase to occur. This expands the potential of participants to completely engage in the learning process. Following are simple examples of the four phases in action.

- **Concrete experience:** Let's say an instructor asks the group to solve the following problem. The entire group must traverse a 25-yard (23-meter) expanse without touching the ground. Each person has a small foam square that can touch the ground. A variety of rules are dictated, including that if anyone touches the ground, the entire group must return to the beginning, and that the foam squares must always remain in contact with a person or they will be lost. A time frame is given for completing the task. After multiple attempts, the group successfully crosses the expanse.

- **Reflective observation ("What?"):** Upon completion of the activity, rather than moving immediately to the next experience, the group pauses to discuss or reflect on what just occurred. This can take the form of an organized discussion, individual journal writing, or other assorted reflection activities. The intent of the reflection phase is to replay important events from the experience as a way to capture that experience for the next phase of the cycle. In this example, the group sits together and reviews what happened. Statements such as the following may be heard:

> "At the beginning, we were all talking at once until Sarah stopped us."

> "I never heard what the plan was before we started."

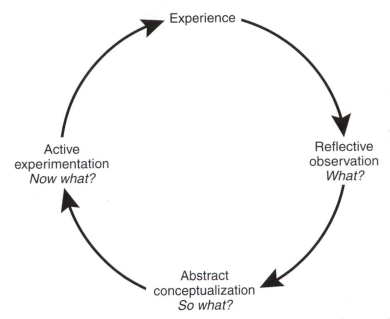

FIGURE 3.1 David Kolb's experiential learning cycle and the common questions often used in debriefing experiences.

From D.A. Kolb, 1984, *Experiential learning: Experience as the source of learning and development* (New Jersey: Prentice-Hall, Inc.).

"Once we got underway, we really worked hard to support each other."

"I want to thank Bob for being honest about touching the ground even though we all had to start over. That felt like the right thing to do."

- **Abstract conceptualization ("So what?"):** The discussion or reflection experience should move from replaying the activity to making generalizations or abstractions from the experience. In this example, some of those generalizations may sound like the following:

"If we designate a leader to help us plan, we can all be heard during our planning time."

"It's important to make sure that everyone knows what's going on before moving forward. But, it is everyone's responsibility to both speak and listen!"

"Using integrity during these exercises makes them more enjoyable even though it may be hard to do."

Participants who take in experience through abstract conceptualization are connecting to the content more during this discussion than during the actual initiative.

- **Active experimentation ("Now what?"):** More important than gleaning learning from specific experiences is being able to apply that learning in other settings or activities. This critical transfer stage can be enhanced if the facilitator gives participants time to apply new skills and ideas to other activities and encourages experimentation in the participants' real lives. Discussions in this phase may sound like the following:

"In the next activity, let's go around in a circle and get a thumbs-up from everyone who says they clearly understand the plan."

"If there is a rule infraction, let's compliment whoever sees it and calls us on it."

"When we're back in school, we should designate who is leading particular activities when the teacher lets us work in small groups. This means that we all need to help the leader and pay attention."

The experiential learning cycle and Kolb's work can be applied to wilderness experiences, classroom experiences, or any other type of learning experience. The cycle can begin at any phase; at times a particular phase may be skipped, emphasized, or minimized due to the circumstances at hand.

In addition to identifying the various ways that people take in and process experiences, Kolb labels four **learning styles:** diverging, assimilating, converging, and accommodating. Each style combines and emphasizes different phases of the learning cycle. (See figure 3.2.) He suggests that everyone uses one of these styles as a primary way of learning.

For example, a person who combines concrete experience and reflective observation has a *diverging learning style*. This learner tends to diverge from conventional solutions, is often imaginative, and is effective at brainstorming and generating many ideas. A person who uses reflective observation and abstract conceptualization has an *assimilating learning style*. This person takes a learning experience and connects it to a larger framework of ideas and develops theories from that experience. There is an analytical component to this style, taking an experience and translating it into concise and logical form. A learner who emphasizes abstract conceptualization and active experimentation prefers the *converging learning style*. This person gathers information to solve problems and tends to be a commonsense thinker. Finally, someone who primarily uses the learning phase of active experimentation and concrete experience uses the *accommodating learning style*. This person is a doer, wanting to put ideas into immediate practice. Hands-on experience is crucial for these learners.

When working with a group of students of any size, it is safe to say that each of these learning styles

is represented by at least one person in that group. When a learning experience follows the experiential learning cycle, everyone's learning style is supported. Note that teachers and facilitators tend to teach using their own primary style. Facilitators with an accommodating style, for example, may need to be very intentional in programming reflection experiences, because such experiences do not naturally support their own learning. Educators should explore their own learning style and understand the impact of their style on their teaching.

Stretch-Zone Experiences

With an understanding of the ideas of Dewey, Duckworth, and Kolb, one might still ask the question, "What is the role of *adventure* in teaching and learning?" Clearly, educative experiences, opportunities for wonderful ideas, and multiple phases within a learning experience are important. But where does adventure come into the picture? Some would argue that it is the proper use of **stretch-zone experiences** that is the catalyst in using adventure education to promote learning.

There are three primary states or zones in which people exist (see figure 3.3). The first is called the *comfort zone*, a place where everything is calm and there is no disequilibrium. The second zone is the *stretch zone*, a place where interest is piqued, our senses are enlivened, and there is some disequilibrium. The third zone is the *panic zone*, a place

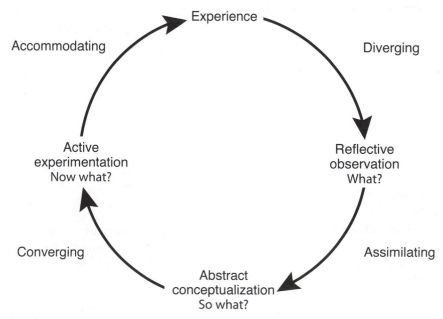

FIGURE 3.2 The four learning styles associated with Kolb's experiential learning cycle.

From D.A. Kolb, 1984, *Experiential learning: Experience as the source of learning and development* (New Jersey: Prentice-Hall, Inc.)

where stress is so high that information cannot be integrated and high adrenaline makes it impossible to settle into a learning environment.

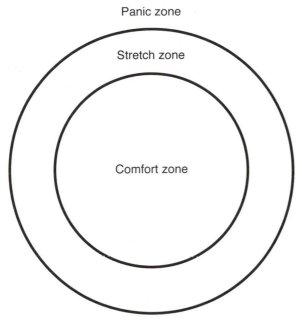

Panic zone

Stretch zone

Comfort zone

FIGURE 3.3   The three zones, or states of mind, where individuals exist.

Experience has shown that learning occurs when people are in their stretch zone. Intellectual development and personal growth do not occur if there is no disequilibrium in a person's current thinking or feeling. However, learning will also shut down if that disequilibrium gets so high that the person enters the panic zone.

Adventure education is known for creating stretch-zone experiences that take on many different forms. For example, consider one particular Outward Bound course for women that took place at sea. Participants used a 30-foot (9-meter) wooden boat with two masts with sails. Long oars were lashed to the middle of the boat to power it when there was no wind; there was no engine on board. Inside were slats running across the boat, beneath which duffel bags overflowing with participants' personal items and tins of food were stored. In the stern of the boat were a tiller and rudder for steering and a small cookstove; in the bow was a yellow bucket for a toilet.

On a beautiful night, the participants sailed in convoy with another Outward Bound boat across Florida Bay to the Everglades, crossing over 30 nautical miles (56 kilometers) of open water. This is a large expanse to traverse with limited navigational

What's Your Zone?

To further explore the three zones, try the following experiential exercise with a small group of friends or alone. If you are doing it alone, target three areas within the room to stand. If you are doing it with others, place two ropes on the floor in the configuration shown in figure 3.3. The small circle should be large enough to accommodate a majority of the people in the group. The circles represent the three zones. Give the group the following scenarios and ask them to move to the zone that each scenario would cause them to be in. After each scenario, observe how members of the group moved in and out of different zones. If you are alone, ask yourself the following questions and move to the designated area in the room. Sample topics include the following:

- Spiders
- Snakes
- Singing a solo in front of 100 people
- Singing in a choir
- Comfort at height
- Confronting a peer
- Solving a mathematical problem
- Cooking dinner for 20 people

You can make the topics more specific depending on who you are with and what you are interested in thinking about. What zone does learning occur in? Does learning occur in the comfort, stretch, or panic zone?

equipment on board (a compass, a chart, and a ruler). The following morning, the students arrived at the destination, a wilderness beach, and they paused for some solo rest and reflection time. But the trip back after a restful time on the beach offered new challenges. One student, in response to a questionnaire asking her to recall vivid memories of her course, wrote the following about her experience:

I can close my eyes and remember our wonderful afternoon on the sand, each with our own thoughts . . . realizing that a storm was coming and hurrying back to the boats, switching the anchor lines (I was in the bow and handled the exchange). I remember the effort to pull us out using the anchor line and the sinking feeling when the anchor pulled off the bottom long before it should have. I can still feel the wind, feel the chill coming. I can even hear the sick sound of the wood breaking in the rudder/tiller assembly. I can remember vividly listening to your voice (the voice of the instructor) giving instructions to "Row, row!" I remember thinking that we were rowing on sand, but then realized that that was fine, as some oars were in the water and we were working as a real team! I can remember my real fear for Beth as I watched her running across the sand to retrieve the anchor and line, and then running back and swimming out to the boat with it after we had rounded that small jut of sand. I

remember the feeling of accomplishment after we got the boat anchored again, and were able to look at the damage and review our options. I remember sitting there and realizing that Alberta, Viking, and I were your best options for sailing, but that Judy, Sally, and Vicky could and would help, and that I felt very protective of Debbie, who I knew would not be able to help. I remember just accepting that fact, and actually feeling sorry for Debbie, knowing that her terror would paralyze her. I can see Judy and her bruises grinning at me while we reefed the main and lashed the second sail to its mast. I remember being cold, wet and tired, but not really feeling it—I actually felt warm. We all knew that we were "safe" with each other, and we were confident of your calculations to get us home so we were all able to do what we could, and as we are all able to brag about our sail. We obviously did things correctly and proved to ourselves and each other that the trust we had been building was well founded!! That we were powerful and capable.

What a common story this is—the typical adventure education scenario. We take an experience, infuse some stress, pull students gently out of their comfort zone, keep them physically safe, and voila! A pathway to learning is created. How does the stretch zone work? It exposes students. Their usual defenses are taken away, and there is an oppor-

The stretch zone exposes students and allows them to experience their inner being.

tunity to experience their inner being—to have wonderful ideas. People rarely take themselves to this place purposefully because it is uncomfortable, so it is a special growth opportunity when they are brought there during a carefully facilitated experience. But facilitators must remember that these dramatic adventure scenarios are not the only types of experiences that promote learning.

Another example of using the stretch zone in an adventure education context involves a student's climbing experience on a 70-foot (21-meter) sheer granite cliff above a freshwater quarry. When asked what aspect of the climb had the greatest impact on her, she replied, "When I was belaying and the instructor told me to put my brake hand back on the rope." Now, instructors frequently have to remind students to do that when they are learning to belay. Yet this student remembered that moment in her course as much as the climb itself. She explained, "At that moment I felt completely exposed. [The instructor] reminded me that I have a wandering attention span, that I have trouble focusing in my job and in my life. That experience gave me an opportunity to stop and take notice."

For this student, the move into her stretch zone was subtle, not dramatic, and it was unique to her. Clearly, opportunities to stretch comfort zones exist in areas beyond the obvious fears aroused in the outdoor settings.

Stretching the comfort zone is at times as simple as playing a game that requires a 17-year-old boy to look silly for awhile. It can be a student poised, with cross-country skis strapped on for the first time, at the top of a schoolyard hill, not a steep mountain pass. It can be that same student taking her hat off at the end of class, seeing her hair destroyed, and deciding that she will go on with her day.

The catalyst for personal growth exists both in the events that are central to a given experience, like learning how to ski, and in ways peripheral to that experience, like dealing with one's appearance in front of one's peers. The stretch zone may vary widely from person to person. Educators must provide stretch-zone experiences that do not become panic situations and that offer students the chance to grasp the moment and grow.

Challenge by Choice

Project Adventure established the simple concept of **challenge by choice** to support the evolution of the field to a more sophisticated approach that focuses on allowing students to choose the level of experience that supports their optimal learning. Rather than coaxing people into taking on difficult tasks (which really only teaches them that they can be talked into doing something), challenge by choice provides participants with the right to choose the level of challenge that best supports their learning goals. This teaches them how to make positive decisions and helps them become lifelong learners.

Challenge by choice is more easily managed in a facility-based setting than in some wilderness settings where the level of challenge is dictated by natural circumstances such as weather and terrain. Yet, even in these settings, students can be coached to manage the intensity of their involvement and work to move from panic zone to stretch zone in order to maintain an educative experience. This thoughtful facilitation by the instructor is a vital skill.

Challenge by choice does *not* give participants the choice to continually opt out of activities because they have chosen not to play. It assumes that participants will learn how to work safely in their stretch zone while avoiding situations that will put them more into their panic zone. It does not allow students to choose to remain in their comfort zone.

Some find it easy to understand challenge by choice in the following way:

- Students have the right to choose when to participate and in what way.
- Students must add value to the experience at all times. Sitting out is rarely an appropriate option.
- Students must respect and value the decisions of their classmates.

Behavioral Contracts

In order for participants to choose to move into their stretch zone, there has to be a feeling of physical and emotional safety within the group and the experience. Behavioral contracts, institutionalized by Project Adventure with its full-value contract, provide a structure for creating behavioral norms that everyone in a group agrees to follow and maintain throughout the life of the group. This norm-setting process establishes an atmosphere of caring, efficacy, and appreciation for each other. Such an atmosphere is critical for students to be able to fully value themselves and others while participating in the group process, all of which leads to a sense of safety within the group.

A full-value contract should match the unique spirit and purpose of the group. It is a shared creation, developed in words or symbols that all group members can understand. All full-value contracts ask the group

- to understand and create safe and respectful behavioral norms under which it will operate,
- to commit to those norms, and
- to accept a shared responsibility for the maintenance of those norms.

There are many ways to develop a full-value contract. It can be as simple as presenting a series of commitments and asking the group to discuss and agree to the commitments or as complex as developing an exercise that supports the group's own creation of their contract. Figure 3.4 shows some

examples of age-appropriate contracts (Panicucci & Hunt, 2003).

Depending on the goals and length of the adventure experience, it is often productive to provide tools for the group to better understand the concepts of the contract as well as to allow the group to develop their own contract. Following are some sample activities that can be used.

Pi Charting

Pi charting (as in the Greek letter π; not to be confused with the traditional pie chart) is a technique that helps participants define the concepts of the full-value contract. The activity begins with a flip chart set up with three columns, resembling the letter π (see figure 3.5).

Many assumptions can be made about words. This system helps the group define these assumptions in greater depth by asking members to reflect on what a word or phrase looks like, sounds like, and feels like. The phrase *Care for self and others* is used as an example in figure 3.5.

The Being

Barry Orms and Buddy Orange, former counselors at the Harbor for Boys and Girls in New York City, introduced the idea of The Being. The idea is to trace a person, selected by the group, onto a large piece of paper to be a symbolic representation of the "body" of the group. The group members then add what is productive for their group on the inside of the shape and what is destructive on the outside of the shape. For example, a group may write "clear communication" inside the body and "putdowns" outside the body.

Tracing a person is not recommended where there are concerns about physical boundaries or bodily safety. In such cases, the group should decide on another symbol to represent themselves.

Primary (Grades K-2)

Be kind.
Be gentle.
Be safe.

Elementary (Grades 3-5)

Play hard.
Play fair.
Play safe.

Middle School (Grades 6-8)

Be here.
Be safe.
Set goals.
Be honest.
Let go and move on.

High School and Adult (Grades 9-12)

Be present.
Pay attention.
Speak your truth.
Be open to outcomes.
Create a safe environment.

FIGURE 3.4 Sample age-appropriate behavioral contracts.

Norm: Speak your truth

Looks like	Sounds like	Feels like
Face-to-face talk	Direct comments	Scary
Honest expressions	"I feel..."	Relief

FIGURE 3.5 Sample pi chart.

CAREERS IN ADVENTURE

NAME: Tom Stuessy
JOB: Professor, Green Mountain College (Poultney, Vermont)

BACKGROUND: BS, Western State College, Gunnison, Colorado; MS Aurora University, Aurora, Illinois; PhD, Indiana University, Bloomington, Indiana

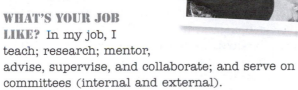

WHAT'S YOUR JOB LIKE? In my job, I teach; research; mentor, advise, supervise, and collaborate; and serve on committees (internal and external).

Being a professor entails many duties. I am consistently seeking new ways to engage students while in the classroom and the field. I am inspired to teach by the amount I am learning while doing it. I enjoy the interaction among the students as they test ideas, respectfully challenge each other, and find solutions.

Each day is met with course preparation. I rarely go into the classroom with the same plan twice. If the theoretical can become applicable through engaging instruction, every student is one step closer to becoming a professional.

In addition to Green Mountain College (GMC) responsibilities, being a professor requires that I stay engaged with the industry. I enjoy committee work because it provides me with an opportunity to communicate with colleagues and professionals outside of GMC on a variety of different topics. To do so, I serve on a board of directors, earn and maintain multiple certifications, publish research, and present at conferences.

The most important skill that any outdoor professional can have is being an effective communicator. My favorite analogy to describe effective communication is that of a good comedian. If everyone in the audience gets the joke at the same time, the comedian effectively communicated with the audience. Without an ability to effectively communicate, I would be a poor instructor and thus a poor outdoor professional. In addition to communication, I must have a solid grasp of my discipline's theories, models, and literature, and I must be an innovative thinker on the subject myself. Further, technical skills are an important dimension of my job. I teach a variety of technical skill courses, including rock and ice climbing, white-water kayaking, canoeing, outdoor living skills, ropes course facilitation, and expedition courses. Being a successful professor takes a commitment to your students, colleagues, institution, and industry.

The Adventure Wave

Every educational adventure experience, lesson, or activity should include the following three components:

- Briefing of the experience (framing or introduction)
- Doing the experience
- Debriefing of the experience (reflection)

Figure 3.6 illustrates a wave, a common metaphor for the ideal components of an experiential lesson or program. The beginning of the wave, shown as "briefing," is the lead-up to the actual event. It is the anticipation and the preparation phase. The crest of the wave, shown as "doing," illustrates the peak of the experience, the climax of the event. When the wave passes, the stillness that follows allows time for reflection. This is captured in "debriefing."

The slang sometimes used for this concept is "Dunk 'em and dry 'em," which suggests that a student needs to be immersed in an experience and then given an opportunity to dry off and reflect on that experience. The wave can be applied to the full experience (whether it's a day or a month), to a specific lesson, and to each individual activity. By considering the wave at each of these levels, the facilitator can be sure of providing participants with a well-balanced program. Participants will have opportunities to reflect on both the activities and the full scope of the program.

Clearly, this wave or adventure flow supports the experiential learning cycle as described earlier. The briefing or framing of the activity has greater emphasis in the adventure flow, however. The briefing is a critical component of setting the stage for a particular experience and can take the form of a simple story to engage the learner in an initiative or can be a thorough briefing of a final, culminating expedition during a wilderness program. Setting the stage helps define expectations, clarify goals for the session, and provide the parameters for participants to operate within.

The peak of the wave correlates with the experience phase of the experiential learning cycle, and the **debriefing** component of the wave encompasses three of Kolb's phases, including reflective observation, abstract generalization, and active experimentation (i.e., what?, so what?, and now what?).

Leadership Development

Leadership development is a hoped-for outcome in nearly all adventure programs. Some organizations rely on the leadership opportunities inherent in many adventure activities as their primary method of developing leadership. Reflections and debriefing the experience center on who the natural leader was, what role others had in the leadership of a particular outcome, and so on. These experiences offer participants astounding insights into their own and others' leadership abilities.

NOLS has taken the notion of leadership development using expeditions and has developed a deliberate curriculum to teach leadership to its participants. The following leadership principles are incorporated into every course. Instructors are given much latitude in how they teach these principles and are coached to make them an integral component of every NOLS experience.

Leadership Types

NOLS designates four leadership roles. The goal is for every member of a team to step into each of the following roles during the expedition:

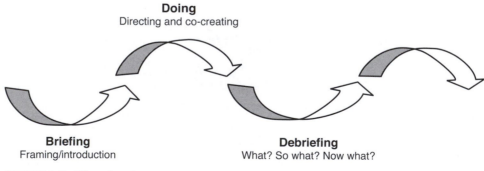

Doing
Directing and co-creating

Briefing
Framing/introduction

Debriefing
What? So what? Now what?

FIGURE 3.6   The adventure wave.

- **Designated leadership.** The designated leader is appointed and takes responsibility for the group and the achievement of group goals. This leader needs to determine the best actions for a group to achieve their goals.
- **Active followership.** Active followership means supporting and following the designated leader. This includes actively participating in group discussions and decision making as well as giving and receiving feedback to and from the designated leader and other group members. The word *active* is important in this concept.
- **Peer leadership.** All members of a group need support in order for a group to achieve its goals. Peer leadership is the act of helping one's peers. This can be done by participating during group tasks, providing one-on-one assistance, and pitching in whenever something needs to be done.
- **Self-leadership.** It is only when individuals care for themselves that they can be helpful to others. Each group member needs to demonstrate personal initiative and character.

Leadership Skills

A variety of skills foster strong leadership regardless of the leadership role someone is practicing. These skills translate into any setting where one is applying a particular leadership role. The seven leadership skills that NOLS identifies are as follows.

- **Expedition behavior.** Teamwork can be the overarching principle of expedition behavior. Teamwork consists of cooperating with others, motivating self and others, and managing diversity within a group.
- **Competence.** Appropriate knowledge and skills must be mastered as well as organizational skills.
- **Communication.** This is a critical leadership skill. Being able to give and receive feedback in appropriate ways, to listen actively, and to clearly speak one's mind in a way that others can hear are all part of effective communication skills.
- **Judgment and decision making.** This skill is the ability to use one's existing level of experience to help make good decisions in a variety of situations. This requires the ability to incorporate multiple decision-making styles and to effectively mobilize the resources present within the group.
- **Tolerance for adversity and uncertainty.** Managing hardship and uncertainty are crucial

components of leadership. Great leaders turn challenging situations into opportunities, use humor to keep things in perspective, and enjoy hard work and challenge.

- **Self-awareness.** Leaders must possess an accurate understanding of their strengths and weaknesses. This enables them to learn from experience and to see how their actions affect others.
- **Vision and action.** An effective leader should be able to imagine the future as well as motivate and guide a group to reach that future. Creativity and execution are managed side by side.

Leadership Style

Each person adopts their own leadership style that may differ from the style of others. There are many tools and inventories that assess styles of leading and being in a group. Common tools are the Myers-Briggs and the DISC profiles. NOLS manages this assessment in an experiential manner in the field where students learn about their natural tendencies and discuss the strengths and liabilities of their natural style. Regardless of the method used, the final step in becoming a great leader is clearly understanding your leadership style and managing that style to its greatest effectiveness.

Leadership Training Through Experience

NOLS expedition-style teaching creates an ideal setting for students to observe, experiment with, and ultimately learn these important leadership skills and attributes. Courses often begin with a strong instructor presence where content is explicitly taught and where instructors demonstrate strong leadership skills themselves. As the course progresses, students provide more input into course goals and into managing daily life in the backcountry. Designated leadership evolves as students are asked to be leaders of the day, and evening discussions center on giving feedback to those leaders as well as to the other group members. Many courses include a final expedition where students plan and execute a short expedition without the assistance of any instructors, practicing all leadership skills and roles. NOLS makes a concerted effort to assist students in understanding how the skills learned in the backcountry apply to their home setting.

Facility-based programs that offer leadership training do not have the wilderness as their classroom, but rather use problem-solving initiatives to teach leadership behaviors. Classroom techniques are integrated with active learning and a strong emphasis is placed on the transfer of skills to the participant's home or work setting.

Service to Others

The notion of serving others as a way to learn more about oneself is present in nearly all adventure education settings. Kurt Hahn, founder of Outward Bound, suggested that the way to influence young people is not to ask them to do or participate, but to let them know that they are needed: "There are three ways of trying to win the young. You can preach at them. That is a hook without a worm. You can say, 'You must volunteer.' That is of the devil. And you can tell them, 'You are needed.' That appeal hardly ever fails" (Miner and Boldt 2002). By intentionally providing opportunities to serve others, more personal insights emerge. At Outward Bound, for example, service starts with being trained and ready to perform rescue duties when called. Additionally, many Outward Bound courses include specific service projects in which students work in the local community. These projects may include painting a town building, visiting a nursing home, or clearing trails in the wilderness area where

the course is operating, to name just a few. Students learn the difference between service and work, and they are given reflection time to glean key lessons they have learned from the experience.

Embedded in almost all adventure programs is the notion of helping others, even when specific service projects are not a component of the program. This can include belaying another person on a climbing wall, supporting someone through a spiderweb, selecting a partner you know is shy for a two-person reflection exercise, or taking additional weight from the back of a fatigued group member. Regardless of the task, the idea of focusing attention on others results in great rewards for all involved parties. Josh Miner, an icon in adventure education, was often heard offering this type of advice to nervous participants on a strenuous hiking course. This is the paraphrased essence of his message:

> The best tactic for you, especially if you are nervous about this experience, is this: Always be the first awake in the morning. Get up and quietly stuff your sleeping bag, store your clothes, and secure your pack. Fire up the stoves and start the hot drinks for the others. As your group mates rise, help them with their tents, offer to organize the group gear. When it is time to clean up camp, be the first to finish breakfast and do

The notion of helping others can include supporting a teammate through a Spiderweb.

the final preparations for departure. When it is time to leave, help others shoulder their packs after you have already shouldered yours. These actions will compel you into an energetic remainder of the day, will busy your nervous mind, and ready your body for action.

The experience of serving others and the powerful results for both the served and the servers are wonderful when translated into daily life. What does service look like when backpacks are replaced with book bags? The transfer phase of the experiential learning cycle is critical, and specific reflection time on what is being learned from service and its application to the real world gives students a clear sense of what they can do to experience those same results back at home.

GRABBSS Assessment Tool

How can a leader integrate leadership development, service learning, stretch-zone experiences, and other cornerstones of adventure education into a training plan? How does a facilitator decide which activities to use and when to use them?

The adventure experience requires spontaneity and flexibility on the part of the facilitator. Facilitators can plan a sequence of events, select campsites in advance, and designate particular challenge course elements for a particular day. However, there are so many dynamic factors in outdoor and adventure settings that the facilitator must continually reassess the appropriateness of a particular activity for a specific group. Facilitators must be able to redesign an activity quickly.

Imagine a hiking course where students are traveling faster than expected. It appears that they will be at their food drop a day early. So far the weather has been crystal clear and the students are in better physical shape than predicted. This is a good time for the instructor to step back and evaluate whether to insert an additional activity into the program. This activity could include a bushwhack route to the drop (if trace regulations are not jeopardized), an added initiative problem, or giving a rescue scenario to the students. How does the facilitator make this decision?

Or, imagine a challenge course and initiatives day with a group of executives. The director of this group indicated that she wanted a fast-paced day including significant physical challenges and assured the program leader that the group was fit and would bring the medical forms when they arrived on site. When the team gathered for the program, it was clear that the director was fit but

that the condition of her team was not nearly as appropriate for a very physical day. How can the facilitator change the plan?

An easy guide is the GRABBSS assessment tool, developed and taught by Project Adventure. Ask the following questions to help select the right activity at the right time.

- **Goals.** How does this activity relate to the goals of the group and the program? Always keep in mind the outcomes you are designing into a program or activity.

- **Readiness.** Is the group ready to do this activity? Are group members emotionally and physically prepared? Do they have the necessary skills to complete the activity? If not, can the activity be altered to meet their level of readiness? Is there something that can help them increase their level of readiness? Does the group agree with their level of readiness?

- **Affect.** What is the feeling, or affect, of the group? Are they excited and energetic, or are they apathetic and low on energy? What is the level of empathy in the group? Are students at a stage where they can emotionally support each other? Selecting a rigorous off-trail hike may fit the physical pace of the group, but emotionally they may not be able to support each other in a productive way through the experience. Remember to go back to the goals of the experience in deciding which route to take.

- **Behavior.** How is the group acting? Are they agreeable or disruptive? How do group members interact with each other? Are they positive or negative? Will their behavior be appropriate for this activity? Will this activity promote further positive or negative behavior? What is needed to support the outcomes of the experience?

- **Body.** Is the group physically ready for this activity? Are they too tired or too hyper? If physical touch is involved, is that OK for this group at this time?

- **Setting.** What is the setting for the lesson or experience? What is the weather? What are the physical conditions of the setting, such as the ground, the water temperature, and so on? Is your space limited? Is the space quiet enough for the reflection you have chosen?

- **Stage.** At what stage of group development is your class? Are they ready for a more difficult activity, or do they need to return to basic norm setting? Do they need additional skills to work better together?

Summary

The cornerstones of adventure education exist because they are integral to any successful program. Well-trained and effective adventure educators are familiar with all of the concepts presented in this chapter. Beyond familiarity, however, leaders need the discipline to apply these concepts to actual events and programs. When facilitating, ask yourself if you are being mindful of the program's suggested outcomes. Consider the learning styles of all participants in the program. Establish a safe learning environment by empowering students rather than coercing them. Always be mindful, and be sure to schedule time for reflection. Finally, continue to be a learner, constantly improving your craft as an experiential facilitator.

Review Questions

1. Discuss two learning theories relevant to experiential education. Cite specific examples of how these theories can be applied to teaching.

2. Why are behavior contracts important? Provide examples of when a behavior contract should be used.

3. Describe the four leadership roles used by NOLS. Which one are you most comfortable with?

4. What is GRABBSS and how is it used?

5. Describe a noneducative adventure experience (either your own or someone else's).

6. Why is it important to reflect on or debrief an experience?

Student Learning Activities

1. Take Kolb's Learning Style Inventory (available at Hay Resources Direct, 800-729-8074 or www. hayresourcesdirect.haygroup.com). Describe the influence that your learning style will have on your facilitation of adventure activities. Determine one or two strategies you can use to ensure that you provide learning experiences that support all the learners in your group.

2. Redesign an adventure activity that you have facilitated or participated in so that it fits into the experiential learning cycle. Did you have to change the activity from its original form?

3. Research inventories on leadership style and find an inventory that you would like to take. How does your natural leadership style affect your ability to be an adventure educator?

4. Describe a significant learning experience that you have had. Were any of the cornerstones of adventure education included in this example? Which ones?

CHAPTER 4

Risk and Safety in Adventure Programming

Charles R. Gregg

> "Without risk, a society may turn passive in the face of the future."
> —Peter L. Bernstein

Chapter Concepts

✦ Risk and safety are opposite sides of the adventure coin.

✦ Risk is a real, and even desirable, element of an adventure program. Safety, literally freedom from risk or harm, is not attainable in an adventure program.

✦ Personal growth and development are enhanced by risk if the risk is reasonably managed.

✦ A responsible adventure program manager will offer only activities that serve the program's mission and that have physical and emotional risks that staff and participants can reasonably manage. The manager will assist participants in determining suitability of the activity, will inform program participants of the activities' risks, and will thoughtfully allocate responsibilities for achieving the goals sought by the program and its participants.

✦ Managers who act reasonably and fairly and meet the standards of the industry may expect to be, but may not always be, protected by the laws applicable to adventure programs.

This chapter will discuss the role of real and perceived risk and safety in adventure programming. I am a lawyer specializing in legal liability in adventure programming, and I will discuss risk and safety from a legal perspective.

Risk is unavoidable and important in adventure programs. A quality program will manage, but will not (and cannot) eliminate, the risks of its activities, and will inform participants of the certainty that the activities are not, strictly speaking, safe. Programs that deal fairly with participants, reasonably meet their expectations, and reasonably manage the risks to which participants are exposed will deliver a quality product and reduce legal liability.

The title of this chapter, Risk and Safety in Adventure Programming, is intended to be provocative and to stimulate your thinking about these two components of adventure programs. **Risk** is exposure to the possibility of some loss, including physical or emotional trauma. Dictionaries generally define **safety** as being free from harm or risk. The terms *risk* and *safety* are mutually exclusive. A conscientious program manager will use the term *safe* sparingly and will not lead a participant to believe that activities of the program are without risk.

A professional who uses the term *safe* generally intends to represent only that the program anticipates no serious injuries. The legal implications of misusing the term *safe* should be obvious. It is a misrepresentation of fact. If a loss is suffered, the misrepresentation can produce disappointment,

anger, and even a lawsuit. Consider this excerpt from a form of waiver I recently reviewed:

> All possible precautions are taken to ensure that the activities are conducted in a safe and responsible manner.

Can all possible precautions ever be taken? Can a program manager ensure anything (except some degree of risk)? What exactly is safe and responsible?

Risk in Adventure Programs

Helen Keller (1880-1968) is reported to have said, "Life is a daring adventure or nothing." It is difficult to conceive of an activity without risk. Risk is present in everything we do. Risk is "a reminder of the variability and mutability and general rumness of things" (Davies 1990). The word *adventure* has its roots in the Latin word *advenire*, which means "to arrive, or to come." The word usually refers to an undertaking involving danger and risk. Adventure is at least movement, physically or mentally going to another place. With movement, there is risk—if nothing else, the risk that you may not like where you *are* as much as where you *were*. Movement is not safe. In the context of an adventure program, change and risk, whether artificially created or inherent in the activity, sharpen the opportunity for learning and growth. Risk is a critical ingredient of learning by doing (experiential education). Safety, strictly defined as the absence of risk, is the enemy of such education.

As a noun, the word *risk* refers to the potential of a condition or event to produce loss. For example, there is a risk of falling from an elevated platform, and there is a risk that a participant might fail to properly belay a climber.

Derivations of the verb *risk* include several words (including the Italian *risicare)* that mean "to venture upon," indicating some intentionality—a conscious decision to expose oneself to the chance of loss or harm in order to achieve a desired result.

How does risk relate to the other components of an activity—its hazards and potential outcomes? Consider a challenge course exercise. **Hazards** of the activity are aspects that might cause harm, including the condition of the course; the competency of staff; the screening, training, and supervision of the participants; the general morale, or emotional state, of the participants; and the environment, including weather and the surrounding premises.

The **risks** of the challenge course activity are those events or circumstances that might be created by the hazards. A supporting cable may break, or a harness may tear. Staff may fail to properly supervise the movement of a participant; an inattentive participant may fail to properly belay another participant.

Favorable outcomes of the risks may include increased self-confidence and personal growth or a more effective corporate team. Unfavorable outcomes may include falls, scrapes, intimate contact with others, and other forms of physical and emotional trauma, including death.

Hazards, risks, and outcomes all represent exposure and often are used interchangeably to describe what can go wrong in a program.

Risk as a Value

Professionals and thoughtful participants will measure the risks and likely outcomes of an adventure when deciding whether to offer the activity or participate in it. Risk and the achievement of goals are independent, and independently valuable, components of an adventure experience. The possibility of failure or other loss adds energy and excitement to the experience and enlarges the potential for learning. In other words, risking loss—physical harm or embarrassment before one's peers—is valuable in itself, regardless of the outcome of the adventure.

Failure as a Value

Failure may be valuable. In a recent visit to a government agency facility, I saw a chart that ranked outcomes of certain training exercises, from an outcome with minor or no problems (the highest ranking) to one with major problems that require rescheduling (the lowest ranking).

In the middle of the five rankings, major objectives are changed and others are accomplished that were not originally planned. This concept is important: Failure creates new opportunities. A diversion from original goals results in new discoveries, new planning, and unexpected outcomes. The agency recognizes that there may be value in failure and in risking failure. Success may be a matter of only luck, not competency. In other words, "invoking luck obscures truth, because it separates an event from its cause" (Bernstein 1996). Failure forces an analysis of policies and procedures that may be ignored by seemingly successful managers. Failure enables the achievement of unanticipated objectives and the rejection of unsuccessful techniques or practices. Failure educates. Dr. Jasper S. Hunt, Jr., in a 1998 essay titled "Ethically Tolerable Accidents," describes the unethical accident as one that is not discussed openly and from which nothing is learned.

Risk is common to both success and failure, and all three are valuable.

Perception of Risk

The literature of adventure programs may include references to perceived risk, that is, the appearance of risk. These references serve a number of purposes, most of them helpful in alerting the participant and others to aspects of an activity. A suggestion, or interpretation, that the risks are *only* perceived—not actual—would be dangerous and misleading. A representation that an aspect of an adventure experience has no actual risk is, well, risky. The issue is not that a person, place, or activity is safe or unsafe. The issue is that none of them are quite as safe as they appear.

Real risks are an unavoidable, even desirable, part of adventure experiences. A risk may be more or less than it is perceived to be, but accidents, claims, and lawsuits arising from adventure programs contradict any notion that their risks are only perceived, not real.

Perception as a Risk

Perception is fundamentally an emotional reaction. The perception of a risk will be determined by the life experiences and present circumstances of the participant. Individual skills, confidence in one's ability to control the apparent risks, and confidence

Risk is an unavoidable, even desirable, part of adventure experiences.

in the staff and other participants all contribute to a person's perception of the overall risks involved in an activity. Each participant will view and react to the experience differently. This reality presents a significant challenge for adventure program staff.

The perception of risk, whether accurate or not, may create stress and anxiety. Such emotions are themselves risks, may be painful to the participant, and may enlarge the overall riskiness of the activity for the participant and others.

In a recent lawsuit involving a scuba-diving accident, *Yace v. Dushano* (2003), a California court found that panic is an inherent risk of scuba diving, one that is an inseparable part of the sport. It simply comes with the territory. Professionals know that heightened anxiety and fear are a very real aspect of certain adventure activities. The activities may even have been designed to produce those emotions in order to create certain learning opportunities.

Well-drawn descriptions of a challenge course activity will refer to such emotions, including fear, heightened anxiety, and other emotional and psychological events. As noted, under certain circumstances these emotions can be harmful and create

more harm. They may arise from only a perception, or misperception, of real risk.

A person who is standing on a pole many feet from the ground and is being belayed by a stranger or by someone competing for her job may have been told there is no real risk, but the fears and anxieties are there. It all is risky—the perception and the reality.

Perception as a Value

Like any other risk, the perception of risk, whether it is justified or not, artificially created or not, and faithfully represented or not, exposes the participant to loss. But it may also be valuable.

Is there value in the failure to perceive a risk? The answer to this depends on the program strategies. Failure to perceive a risk will at least eliminate some of the anxiety normally accompanying the activity, and the participant may better focus on other matters at hand. But that anxiety may be an intentional element of the activity and contribute to some desired result, such as the discovery of the courage to proceed. Failure to perceive a risk may also produce careless behavior and injury.

What of a risk that is represented by an operator to be substantial, but is not? Lying to a participant has doubtful educational value. It certainly will not create the confidence in the operator that is important to a successful adventure experience.

Types of Risk

More and more people, with a greater variety of expectations and physical and emotional issues, armed with an increasing variety of medications, and encouraged by aggressive marketing can now get into risky situations more quickly and with less preparation. Staff members who were once expected only to move a group from one place to another now must contend with significant behavior and other suitability challenges—frequently not disclosed—that might greatly exceed staff training and expectations.

Inherent Risks

The risks of adventure programs vary. Certain risks are such an integral part of an activity that, if they were removed, the nature of the activity and the participant's expectations of it would be significantly modified. Such risks are described as *inherent*. A common example of an inherent risk is a spectator at a baseball game being hit by a foul ball. People who prefer to view the game from close to the field are considered to assume this risk. A number of years ago a lawsuit was brought by a visitor who was struck by a foul ball while using an interior walkway behind a baseball stand. The Supreme Court of Pennsylvania ruled that the person did not assume the risk of being struck by a ball under such circumstances. The problem, rather, was a defect in the stadium design *(Jones v. Three Rivers Management* 1978). Being struck by a ball while walking behind the stands is not an inherent risk of watching a baseball game.

The operator of an adventure program has no duty to protect participants from the inherent risks of an activity and is not legally liable for failing to do so. Service providers do, however, have an obligation not to enlarge those inherent risks. A service provider who enlarges the inherent risks of an activity has a duty to care for persons who may be harmed by that enlargement. Being jostled, and even bruised, is an inherent risk of rafting. Improper distribution of the raft occupants or failure to secure gear on the raft may increase the risks of injury and create a duty to protect those passengers from a danger that is not inherent.

Figure 4.1 shows a progression of loss-causing acts, omissions, or events, ranging from intentionally wrongful acts of the service provider through gross and simple negligence, to inherent risks, to unforeseeable risks and acts of God, to the conduct of the participant. As described in more detail later in this chapter, simple negligence is carelessness—the failure to act as a reasonable person would have acted under the same or similar circumstances. Gross negligence, sometimes referred to as recklessness, is an aggravated form of negligence so severe that a judge or jury is entitled to believe that the actor was indifferent to the prospect of causing harm.

Physical and Emotional Risks

The profession and court rulings applicable to the profession recognize emotional as well as physical risks associated with adventure programming. Of the two, physical risk may be more accurately anticipated and understood by participants and staff, but emotional risk, generated by both the effort and the outcome, may be more significant and more likely to occur.

The two types of risks cannot be uncoupled. Emotional risks may have physical manifestations. Physical risk may produce emotional upset with long-term consequences. A responsible operator will inform participants of both the emotional and physical risks of the activity; and staff should be able to recognize the prospect of physical harm and emotional upset, reasonably manage the risks of both, and deal with an incident involving either.

Risk Management Plan

A **risk management plan** should include an analysis of what the program is doing, why it is doing it, and how it expects to manage the risks of what it is doing.

The program must be satisfied that its activities serve its mission or goals. A program may deviate from activities originally designed to serve its mission, thereby confusing staff and participants and likely enlarging the risks of its activities. This is referred to as *mission creep*.

The program must undertake only those activities whose risks it can reasonably manage. Management staff must be aware of the activities and understand the physical and emotional risks of those activities.

Provider's responsibility			No responsibility	Participant's responsibility		
Intentional acts	Gross negligence	Negligence	Inherent risks, unforeseeable accidents, acts of God, etc.	Negligence	Gross negligence	Intentional acts

FIGURE 4.1   Progression of loss-causing acts.

Staff and participants must be competent to perform the activities and to manage their risks. Finally, the program must accurately inform participants of the activities and risks.

An experienced practitioner in the field will be able to identify the risks of an activity through personal experience and documentation of the experiences of others who conducted the same activities. Attending conferences where such matters are discussed will produce valuable insights that can be used to better understand one's own operations. Actual site reviews of the program by a qualified independent expert will do the same.

Studies, including the 5-, 10-, and 20-year Safety Studies by Project Adventure, tell us a great deal about accidents in programs similar to those of Project Adventure (games, initiative activities, low and high ropes courses, and some expeditionary components including top-rope climbing instruction). The injury rate was dramatically lower for the Project Adventure–type programs (described in the 1996 survey as "remarkably low") when compared with backpacking, skiing, and competitive sports. Serious injuries and deaths in adventure activities are described as "extremely uncommon" (Furlong et al. 1995). Subsequent and current studies support the findings of Project Adventure.

The maintenance of incident and near-miss reports, which are events that produce some loss or that signal the possibility of some future loss, is another important tool for understanding the risks of adventure activities. The program should have a mechanism for regular reporting—at the end of the activity, at the end of the day, at the end of the week—to provide information regarding occurrences that might alert the program to risks and how to better manage them.

For example, several years ago a staff member of a well-known outdoor program reported, at the conclusion of a trip into the mountains, that a certain avalanche-prone area had produced a serious scare and was a "death trap." As one would expect of professionals in the field, the program managers immediately sent experts to the site to assess the conditions. Subsequent routes were modified, and an accident was possibly avoided.

A program history regarding such potentially dangerous events will recognize both the severity and the frequency of what is occurring and what might occur. The reports will concern not only the activities themselves, but personnel, environment, and gear. Considering activities, people, places, and things, the program manager should decide where a potential for loss falls on severity and frequency scales.

Figure 4.2 represents a grid for determining the significance of a risk. The left axis ranks the severity of a loss, whether real or potential. The bottom axis measures the frequency of occurrence. The square has four quadrants. The upper-right quadrant represents high frequency and severity. The lower-left quadrant represents low severity and low frequency. Issues that fall in the lower-left quadrant deserve only limited attention but may predict future problems. People, places, activities, and things that are producing frequent, serious negative consequences fall in the upper-right quadrant and should be abandoned.

What actual occurrences, or near misses, should be recorded? Every program will have a different threshold, recognizing that some matters are too minor to burden the reporting system and personnel with the duty of recording. A case can be made for recording every event that produces a loss (only those interrupting the activity perhaps, but certainly including the withdrawal of the participant from the activity), and near misses that, had there been an accident, would have produced the threshold result.

Managing Physical Risk

Some physical risks are obvious, including to first-time participants in an activity. Court cases hold that even young children may understand the risks of height, water, and fire. A novice climber approaching a rock face or artificial wall will consider the environment and activity and understand the risks

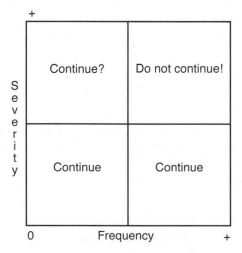

FIGURE 4.2 Grid for determining significance of risk.

of falling or, if suspended by a rope, of swinging into a fixed object or a person. And a participant's life experiences will tell him that a fall can mean broken bones, sprains, bruises, and other trauma. Viewing a stream that the group proposes to cross, a teenager will understand the possibility of a fall that may produce an unpleasant dunking or even drowning in cold, fast-moving water.

However, young people may have difficulty comprehending their deaths or even serious injury. Several years ago, I was involved in an investigation of the drowning of a 15-year-old girl. Her family, reflecting on the voluntariness of her participation and her willingness to engage in an activity (crossing a mountain stream) that, according to her personal journal, she faced with some anxiety, urged that she was too young to anticipate the possibility of dying. They believed she lacked a sense of her own mortality. The program learned from its discussions with the parents and enlarged and clarified its descriptions of risks and outcomes in its literature and its preactivity instructions.

Program managers often are reluctant to refer to serious injury and death in describing the risks and possible outcomes of their activities. While the concern may be primarily one of marketing (why frighten a potential client?), part of the problem is a failure to come to grips with the reality that a person may die during an adventure program. We and the people we purport to serve deserve to know and understand this reality, and we should make decisions to offer the activity or participate in it with that knowledge. We are quick to accept the risk of injury in justifying what we do. The real possibility of death or serious physical or emotional injury forces a more sobering analysis of what we do and why.

Other risks, not obvious but reasonably contemplated by experienced staff, must be explained to participants in preliminary literature and as encountered in the activity itself. This explanation, except in unique circumstances and programs (where nondisclosure may be considered a strategic value), is fair to the participant and smart from a standpoint of legal liability. Participants cannot be considered to have assumed a risk that they did not understand, such as foot entrapment, lightning strikes, an avalanche-prone slope, anxiety associated with heights, and close personal contact with others.

Managing Emotional Risk

Emotional risks may be associated both with the perception of the activity and actually participating in the activity. Such risks might include reliance on others, announcing to one's peers a decision not to participate, and recollections of earlier traumatic life experiences.

As in the case of physical injury, a person causing emotional harm to another may be legally liable for doing so. The person suffering the harm may be entitled to monetary compensation for the injury suffered, though the harm is sometimes difficult to measure. Some state laws may require a physical manifestation of an emotional injury or loss, but courts are retreating from this requirement. A great deal has been learned in recent years about emotional upset, repressed memory, and other psychological or emotional trauma. Experts today can convincingly argue that severe damage has been done even if it has no physical manifestation and is not accompanied by physical trauma.

Adventure experiences of a certain type can bring forth emotional reactions of the most painful kind. Staff members' understanding of the possibility of such emotional trauma may not be matched by appropriate skills for dealing with the resulting upset. It has been said that prudent practitioners should not open doors they cannot close, and certainly practitioners must be trained to recognize the symptoms of a potentially dangerous psychological event and deal with it reasonably or refer the problem to a professional.

Emotional risks are best addressed before an event, although there may be rare circumstances where certain goals are served by not revealing the potential for such upset. In any event, the program manager must create an environment that allows a participant to choose not to participate or that can tolerate a new sequencing of the participant into the intimidating activity.

Physical and Emotional Safety

As we've discussed, total physical and emotional safety is not a realistic goal for an adventure program, or for any educational program, for that matter. But the elimination of serious accidents and the management and reduction of other accidents are reasonable aspirations.

Using the term *safety* to mean the reasonable management of risks, what are the safety concerns regarding the participant, the instructor, the group, the equipment, and the surrounding environment? Reasonable management of such risks includes at least the following:

- An early and continuing exchange of information with participants so that they can make an informed decision regarding enrollment and participation

- An effective risk management plan (consider what might happen, how to reduce the chances of it happening, and what to do when it happens)

- Strong administrative support (regarding morale, food, staff salaries, logistics, and other such matters)

- Effective selection and supervision of staff and participants

- Suitable, well-maintained gear as well as training for staff and participants in the use of that gear

- Understanding the environment and its risks

- Continual assessment and reassessment of practices and policies

The participant, staff, group, equipment, and surrounding environment each contributes to the activity, and each presents unique hazards and solutions. Combined, they present a challenging mix of risk and opportunity. A risk management plan for an adventure will address at least these components of the experience and consider their interaction and compatibility with each other.

For example, competencies of participants and of staff and the condition and suitability of equipment must match the environmental hazards and risks that can be reasonably foreseen. Participants must submit to their role as members of a cohesive group and be prepared to follow instructions from what presumably is a competent staff. Participants and staff must understand and perform their responsibilities for managing the risks of the venture. All persons, both staff and participants, must be familiar with the equipment and trained in its use and must be similarly educated concerning environmental issues.

A significant concern in adventure programming is the appropriate allocation of responsibility for determining whether a participant is suitable for a certain activity or program. Suitability may be determined by, among other things, an evaluation of skills, physical and mental health, and expectations. Some programs would prefer to shift the entire responsibility for determining suitability to participants, but doing so assumes that the participants know more than they realistically can about the true nature of the activities, equipment, and environment. If 100 pieces of information would answer all the questions about a participant's suitability, what share of those 100 pieces is known to the participant? What share is known to the program? When I ask this question of audiences, the consensus generally is that 65 to 70 percent is known by the program and 30 to 35 percent is known by the participant or the participant's family or physician. It is generally recognized that the program knows more, or can learn more, than the participant.

It is not often recognized that some aspects of what will happen in the field or during the activity cannot have been known or reasonably foreseen and thus surprise both the participant and the program. A fair allocation of who knows what might be 60 percent for the program, 30 percent for the participant, and 10 percent for the unknown.

Risk, whether physical or emotional, can be aggravated by a participant's prior condition. It is important that both the program and the participants understand and discuss preexisting physical or emotional conditions that, when affected by the anticipated activity, might cause the participants to be a risk to themselves or others.

A potential participant should be told the nature and degree of physical exertion likely to be required in the activity. Good programs suggest a conditioning routine to better prepare participants for what they will experience in the field.

Disabilities are a concern only to the extent that they prevent a participant from performing the fundamental aspects of an activity. Most programs are required by law to accommodate persons with disabilities, provided the cost of doing so is not unreasonable and the accommodation does not alter the basic nature of the activity or create safety problems.

Suitability, risk management, and realization of the goals of an adventure are best achieved by establishing a partnership between participants and the program and its staff at the earliest stages of their relationship. Skillful and honest marketing, including descriptions of the goals of the program and the nature of its activities and risks, will instill trust and confidence at the outset, causing participants to feel that they are an important part of a shared enterprise. Through the selection or orientation phase and the activity itself, a partnering approach to achieving tasks will mold a relationship that will improve the prospects for safety and carry the individual, the group, and the organization through disappointments and more serious losses. Safety is compromised by

CAREERS IN ADVENTURE

NAME: Bob Ryan

JOB: Risk Management Director, Project Adventure (Beverly, Massachusetts)

BACKGROUND: BS in biology, Middlebury College, Middlebury, Vermont

I grew up in upstate New York and southern Ontario. Right after college, I took a NOLS mountaineering course. My first job was in a public high school that was starting an outdoor experiential program that included physical education based on the Project Adventure model. This job included building a challenge course, running groups, and leading extended outdoor trips year round. After that I worked at Outward Bound as an instructor and course director. I also spent a year working on a sail-training vessel in Europe. For the past 23 years I have worked at Project Adventure, where I currently serve as the risk management director and as a member of the senior management team.

WHAT'S YOUR JOB LIKE? One of our important goals is to minimize the occurrence of accidents and injuries to Project Adventure program participants and employees. We also strive to provide products and services that help our clients develop quality programs. A key strategy is to integrate risk management into our day-to-day operations at many different levels. If we succeed, we don't create a tangible product so much as an absence of something negative (e.g., accidents, injuries, lawsuits). On a daily basis, this translates into a wide variety of job responsibilities. I work closely with our safety and risk management committee to establish policies and procedures. I work with our legal consultants on issues such as contracts, waivers, and liability. I spend part of my time working with client programs on issues related to safety.

I also serve as an internal resource for other Project Adventure staff. Ensuring that staff members are properly trained is one of our most important risk management strategies, and consequently I work with other staff to develop training and credentialing programs that help ensure that practitioners have the necessary skills and competencies. Another part of my job involves broader issues related to the challenge course field. I have been involved with the ACCT for many years and currently serve on its board of directors.

relationships of mistrust, misunderstanding, or conflict.

The physical and emotional safety, then, of the participants (and of the staff) depends very much on relationships. The philosophical or spiritual side of participants may respond well to the notion that this partnership extends to the environment itself. So, instead of attacking a mountain stream or a rock wall as an adversary to be conquered, that aspect of the environment is embraced as a partner in pursuing personal and program goals.

Inherent risks exist in group conduct, instruction, moving about in certain environments, and, to a lesser degree, in the condition and use of equipment and other gear. Accidents will occur as an expected and even necessary part of maintaining the nature and quality of the experience. More specifically, active participants in recreation may cause harm in the ordinary pursuit of the activity. We should be reluctant to reduce a participant's enthusiasm for

the activity, or change its basic nature, by holding a person responsible for what, in another context, might be considered simple carelessness. Chances must be taken. If we were to eliminate the possibility of injuries in tackling a football player, sliding into home plate, falling off a horse, or losing a belay, we would have to change those activities so considerably that they would lose their appeal and purpose.

When existing skill limits and judgments are challenged, injuries may result. The opportunity for learning and growth is sufficiently important that instructors and participants in these activities should be allowed some freedom to make mistakes, even unintentionally harm each other, so that learning and educational goals might be achieved.

Managing the risks of an activity that brings together people of various talents, expectations, and dispositions; gear of uncertain origins and condition; and an environment that itself presents hazards is a challenging theater of education. The blend of risks is an exciting medium in which to learn and grow.

Legal Concerns

Adventure programming is a relatively young industry and the law developing around it is sparse. But certain trends are apparent, perhaps the most important of which is the development of the doctrine of primary assumption of risks.

Primary Assumption of Risks

The doctrine of **primary assumption of risks** applies to injuries or losses arising from aspects of a sport or other recreational activity that might be dangerous but are such a part of the activity that to eliminate the risk would discourage vigorous participation. The doctrine teaches that carelessness, or negligence, associated with participation and instruction in active recreation may be forgiven for the sake of maintaining the unique character of the game or the learning experience. Simple carelessness, or negligence, in this context is considered an inherent risk of the activity and in most states is considered assumed by the participant even if that particular participant is not aware of the risk. A coparticipant or instructor is not allowed to be reckless or to otherwise enlarge the risks ordinarily associated with the activity, but the law recognizes that these experiences are not safe, even if other participants and instructors are behaving as required by law.

© Jumpfoto

The physical and emotional safety of participants and staff depends on relationships.

The nature of instruction is such that participants usually are stretching themselves beyond existing skills and abilities. The law forgives accidents that result from this stretching, recognizing that, without taking chances, students will never move to the next level. Negligence, then, in an instructional context, may be forgiven or even expected as long as the instructor has properly sequenced the student into the training exercise that causes the harm. Losses will be suffered along the road to achieving instructional goals, and instructors should not be penalized for losses arising from simple carelessness.

In activities involving active sports or recreational pursuits, courts also may forgive the simple carelessness of a participant who causes harm to another participant. The logic of this forgiveness is that it would be very difficult if not impossible to draw the line between a careless act and one that is the result of exuberant participation in the activity; further, to hold a person accountable for such acts would discourage active participation and reduce the exhilaration, pleasure, and other benefits of participation.

Gear, equipment, hardware, and structures are not infallible and can malfunction or break without warning and in spite of reasonable maintenance and inspection before use. Courts do not ordinarily consider malfunctioning or defective gear or a defective structure as an inherent part of an adventure activity. On the other hand a program is not responsible for every injury that is caused by a piece of gear, and in certain circumstances the program and an injured participant may have recourse against a builder, manufacturer, or seller (or renter) of that structure or product.

The concept of inherent risks and the forgiveness of injuries produced by them—including acts or omissions of instructors and participants—may not yet be available to newer adventure activities, including challenge courses. In 2002, a California appellate court found that only after more than 50 years of hockey had the community understanding of the game and its environment matured to a point where the court could consider the inherent risks of observing the game *(Nemarnik v. Los Angeles Kings* 2002). In a 2003 lawsuit involving a collision of jet skiers, the court found that there was not enough information about this new water activity to identify its inherent risks.

Does the community at large know enough about challenge course activities to understand their inherent risks? Much is still being learned about the real and perceived risks; the attitudes of participants, instructors, and counselors; the possible

failure of certain physical properties of the course itself; and the extension of the use of challenge courses into therapy, team building, and purely recreational applications. It is not clear that the defense that an injury was caused by an inherent risk will be as available to a facilitator or a participant on a challenge course as in older and better understood adventure activities. In a recent case in Ohio, however, a court of appeals ruled that the loss of a belay supporting a person descending an indoor climbing wall was an inherent risk of wall climbing, and found that the injured climber could not sue for this act of apparent carelessness *(Holbrook v. McCraken* 2004). The court ruled that falling was an inherent risk of such climbing and the possibility was understood by the climber and accepted by him. The loss of the belay, according to the court, was an ordinary and usual risk of climbing.

As noted, the adventure experience brings together many elements, such as a structure, hardware and other gear, individual participants, the group, the instructional staff, administrative support, and the environment itself. The cause of an accident may be the conduct of the facilitator, guide, or instructor; the site operator; the staff or other participants; a defect in the construction of a facility; the condition and adequacy of gear, tools, or other implements; or the environment or condition of the premises at which the event takes place. An incident provides a veritable feast for aggressive attorneys looking for fault, liability, and compensation for an injured person. The careful operator must understand and coordinate the components of the activity and enlist the help of participants in managing their separate and collective risks.

Minors

Another trend, although slow in development, is the allowance of parents and guardians to sign preinjury waivers and releases (discussed later in the chapter) on behalf of minor children (usually under 18 years of age). Courts allow parents and guardians to sign for children most frequently in community-based, volunteer-led recreation activities, but the law is expanding to other recreation, including commercial programs. Thus far, only a few states have recognized this right of adults to surrender children's rights to sue in the event of injury, but there is movement. For example, Colorado and Alaska have recently passed laws allowing such waivers.

Without the protection of a binding release of a minor's claim, a program should take care to describe the activities and risks in sufficient detail to allow it to argue that the minor understood the risks and assumed them and should be fully or partially responsible for an injury arising from those risks.

Negligence

Negligence is the failure to act as a reasonable person would have acted under the same or similar circumstances. If it is the conduct of a professional that is being judged, the applicable standard would be the conduct of a reasonable professional conducting a similar activity.

The elements that must be shown to support liability for negligence are the following:

- A duty (to act reasonably)
- A failure to meet that duty
- An injury or loss (including emotional or physical trauma and loss of property)
- A causal connection between the breach of the duty and the loss that occurred (that is, the loss would not have occurred but for the breach of duty)

A claim of negligence will fail if any one of these elements is missing.

A duty arises from a relationship, a reasonable expectation that care will be taken with respect to another person, and the reasonable foreseeability of harm if care is not taken.

As we have seen, in some adventure activities the duty may be reduced for instructors and coparticipants in active sports. Similarly, a service provider or operator has no duty to manage or protect a participant from the inherent risks of an activity.

Duty may be enlarged in certain custodial situations (a children's camp, for example). Duty may be eliminated or modified by an expressed assumption by a participant of the risks of an activity and by a waiver or release of a claim that may arise from the activity.

A court may find that a participant impliedly assumed a known risk by choosing to participate in spite of that risk.

These basic negligence concepts apply to adventure programs, but, as noted, the nature of the duty and the defenses to a claim may vary.

Releases

Releases, or waivers, are a means by which a program and usually its owners and staff are forgiven in advance for acts or omissions, including negligence, that might cause harm. The participant agrees that the released parties will not be liable for the loss, which may be physical or emotional and may include death. Releases work! If clearly written and signed voluntarily, courts of all but a few states will enforce releases, including for negligence. Although, for ethical or other reasons important to its culture, a program may choose not to seek a release for injuries caused by its misconduct, the protection generally is available, and it may even be required by a program's insurance carrier. Releases are rarely allowed for reckless or intentionally wrong conduct. Minors are not allowed to make legal agreements and therefore a minor's signature on a release has little or no legal effect. As noted previously, only a few states allow a parent or guardian to sign a release on behalf of a minor.

Agreements of release are often part of a larger document that describes the anticipated activities and their risks and requires the acknowledgment and expressed assumption of those risks. The description of activities and risks is important. Participants deserve to know what to expect from their activities, and the law will only enforce an assumption or release of risks that are known or reasonably should have been known to the participant. This larger document may include other protective language, including an agreement of the participant (or parent of a minor participant) to indemnify, or protect, the organization from claims.

A release should be carefully designed to meet the specific needs of the organization that is seeking its protection. Do not presume that a release used by another organization will work for you. Usually it will not. The release, whether or not it is part of the larger document just described, must be clear regarding who is releasing whom and for what. A very simple release provision might read as follows:

> I (the participant) hereby release and promise not to sue (the organization), its owners, directors, employees, and volunteers with respect to any claim I might have, including a claim of negligence, arising from my enrollment or participation in an activity of (the organization).

For a release that will provide the protection you seek, you must consult with an attorney who understands your organization and the laws of the state where it operates.

Summary

As discussed in this chapter, the primary concern for an adventure program is not legal liability, but the development and maintenance of a quality program—one that reasonably manages the risks to participants and achieves the goals of the program and the participants.

A quality program, generally, will avoid liability. But, more important, it will contribute significantly to the training and development of its clients and students in an environment of energy and excitement, confronting risks that are real and well managed by a collaborative effort of staff and participants.

Review Questions

1. What are your best arguments for and against staff carelessness being an inherent risk of an adventure activity?

2. Describe the principal issues involved in developing or assessing a risk management plan.

3. Who should bear the larger responsibility for determining the suitability of a participant for a program, the participant or the program? In the information exchange, who should tell whom about what?

4. Should parents be allowed to waive the rights of their children to sue for injuries they subsequently suffer? Why or why not?

5. Is a program that seeks to be released for its negligence contributing positively to the adventure experience? Explain.

Student Learning Activities

1. Select an adventure activity with which you are familiar. Describe the nature of the activity as if you were informing a new participant of the activity's hazards, risks, and losses that might be caused by those risks.

2. A parent asks you, the program manager, to justify your requirement that you be released in advance for negligently harming the parent's child. What is your explanation?

3. Describe a process for collecting, evaluating, and retaining information about injuries or other incidents that may be pertinent to effective management of the risks of your program.

Individual Outcomes of Participating in Adventure

Jim Stiehl and Melissa Parker

❝ What motivates the adventurer? It has never been an easy question to answer in anything less than a ramble, since, like describing the beautiful scent of a flower, describing the "why" of adventure must always fall short. It is all in the experiencing. ❞

—Will Steger

© Getty Images

Chapter Concepts

◆ Present-day benefits of adventure are best understood in their historical context.

◆ Following the merger of the camping and education movements, specific adventure education outcomes began to be delineated.

◆ Adventure education can accomplish many outcomes in several domains, including positive identity, social skills, physical and thinking skills, and positive values and spirituality.

◆ Attempting to achieve too many outcomes, especially if any contradict or compete with others, may dilute program effectiveness.

◆ Achieving desired outcomes requires a deliberate alignment of philosophy, goals, instruction, and assessment.

◆ In today's educational climate, many people are skeptical of claimed benefits unless those benefits have been empirically validated.

The time is late July. A five-day, 65-mile (105-kilometer) river trip is slated for 11 adults and 2 children: a mother and her 23-year-old daughter on the river for the first time without Dad; a couple who run about 10 rivers every summer; another couple who are raft guides and their 7-year-old; a third couple who have not taken a backcountry trip together in years; a woman recently divorced after 30 years of marriage; and a former NOLS instructor and her 13-year-old child, neither with any river experience. Each participant knows someone else in the group, but no one knows everyone.

Embarking with five rafts, two duckies (an inflatable cross between a kayak and a raft), one canoe, and a kayak, the group begins their travels down a remote southwestern river. In a high-walled canyon carved through wilderness, the group navigates a river that is flowing at 900 cubic feet per second (26 cubic meters per second) with an 8-foot (2.5-meter) drop each mile. Rapids, though not extreme, are challenging and frequent. After the first night, however, circumstances change dramatically. Following violent thunderstorms, flash floods pour down the canyon sides. The river quickly becomes deep red, and the flow increases to 2,600 cubic feet per second (74 cubic meters per second). What are the benefits of adventure for the participants in this scenario? Later in this chapter we will explore the answers.

In 1974, Maurice Gibbons compared a young aborigine's readiness for adulthood with that of city children. The young aborigine must survive a severe but appropriate six-month trial in a forbidding wilderness. He must demonstrate that he can be a contributor to the tribe. By contrast, youngsters in our society often face "written examinations that test skills very far removed from the actual experience he will have in real life" (1974). In a similar vein, a college president in a newspaper cartoon belittles graduating students as having grown up in front of screens, saturated in popular culture, mesmerized by a world of fantasy, where entertainment is a national obsession and even "reality" is staged. The tone of the Gibbons article and the cartoon is reminiscent of renowned scholar James Coleman's earlier indictment of Western education, that too many of today's young people grow up information rich but experience poor. Quite the opposite, adventure programs are experience rich, using real-world experiences to achieve learning goals. But what are those goals?

Excitement, personal growth, achievement of goals, learning to trust and respect others—these and countless other desired outcomes have been associated with participation in adventure experiences. Not surprisingly, lists of adventure outcomes and the importance attached to each outcome vary considerably. This is due at least in part to the fact that discussions have not always used the adventure construct in similar ways. We believe that adventure education should be defined in the context of other constructs, such as adventure-based recreation, therapeutic adventure, and outdoor education. By drawing boundaries among such constructs, adventure programmers can be more specific about intended program goals.

In this chapter we begin by briefly describing the underpinnings of present-day outcomes of adventure programs. The benefits to participants are then grouped into several categories. These categories can assist in determining program intentions, verifying whether those results are achieved, and designing instructional activities that will engage participants in attaining the benefits. We conclude with some questions that might help determine the extent to which you are being mindful of adventure benefits and outcomes.

Foundational Adventure Outcomes

Several people have received credit for advancing our thinking about the role of adventure situations in promoting educational goals (see Hunt 1999). Plato and Aristotle, for instance, agreed that young people could acquire and strengthen virtues (e.g., wisdom, bravery, temperance, and justice) by engaging in adventurous experiences that demanded those virtues. William James, a 19th-century philosopher and psychologist, argued that nature-based adventure could bring out many of the virtues taught through war, such as fidelity, conscience, inventiveness, discipline, and tenacity. In the mid-20th century, Kurt Hahn, embracing principles of the ancient Greek tradition, featured adventure education in his celebrated Outward Bound program. Adventure experiences were used to promote qualities such as spiritual tenacity, personal growth, service to others, and physical preparedness.

It is worth noting that a goal common to Plato, Aristotle, James, and Hahn is the teaching of virtue, and that each of their perspectives was somehow linked to the notion of war. Plato emphasized virtues in his descriptions of the best way to raise children to become responsible adults and, if necessary, warriors. Aristotle reinforced this position in his firm contention that virtues are acquired by forming good habits; that is, by living the virtues (e.g., becoming brave by doing brave acts). William James applauded risk taking in war as a means to teach human virtues, but he detested war. Thus, he did not advocate learning virtues through war, but rather through what he described as moral equivalents of war.

Kurt Hahn advocated military virtues such as facing dangers, dealing with unexpected difficulties, enduring hardships, and developing a fighting spirit. Unlike his predecessors, however, he also encouraged qualities that were not necessarily tied to war, such as service to others and respect for the environment. Regardless of the specific virtues championed by these forebears, all discussed adventure as a means, not an end in itself. As stressed by Jasper Hunt, adventure was viewed as the "mere means to a much loftier end—human virtue" (1999).

Thus far, we have drawn attention to the implications of adventure education for living and learning virtues. But as Hunt contends, adventure education "has applicability far beyond the teaching of moral virtues" (1999). True knowing, for example, cannot be equated with passive reception of knowledge, unquestioned acceptance of authority, and the absence of risk. Rather, it is more complex and requires ingredients fundamental to adventure such as taking risks and facing uncertainty. At the heart of work by Henry David Thoreau and John Dewey is the conviction that genuine learning derives from thinking, inquiring, and questioning in situations connected to one's own experience. This questioning is linked to risk: What might happen if I question my current understanding? What might it cost me to change my viewpoint? Looking good? Being right?

Since adventure education involves questioning and risk taking, Hunt (1999) concludes, "If adventure is an effective means for learning virtue, then . . . it is a good means for learning other things as well. As adventure education shows its effectiveness in the moral education realm, it gains additional justification for branching out into other educational areas."

Let's survey some traditional outcomes of adventure experiences. Though certainly not exhaustive, the list provides a sense of commonality as well as diversity in trying to identify and categorize the multiple benefits of adventure.

Traditional Adventure Outcomes

The earliest adventure outcomes were derived from outdoor education in the context of general education. More specific outcomes were not clearly articulated until L.B. Sharpe began experimenting with education in camp settings in the 1920s. As the field matured, more sophisticated organizations emerged that worked to gain support for outdoor education in public schools. A pioneer in these efforts, Julian W. Smith, contributed in 1955 to the Outdoor Education Project, a cooperative enterprise between the American Association for Health, Physical Education, Recreation and Dance (AAHPERD) and educational programs throughout the nation (Smith et al. 1972). The purpose of the project was to expand and enrich educational programs in public schools, colleges, and universities through outdoor education.

The first specific adventure education outcomes were articulated in the context of camping.

Smith and colleagues (1972) viewed outdoor education as "an approach to teaching, and a setting and process whereby learning is facilitated." Supporting earlier notions of means rather than an end, Smith and colleagues remarked, "Since outdoor education has no identifiable content of its own, it has no goals other than those of general education." A task force of AAHPERD's Council on Outdoor Education and Camping submitted a number of educational goals that could be achieved through outdoor education. The list of eight goals follows (see Smith et al. 1972):

- To develop the full potential of the individual

- To develop knowledge, skills, attitudes, and appreciation for the constructive and creative use of leisure time

- To promote the development of social relations and individual responsibility

- To promote the development of civic responsibility

- To promote the development of aesthetic interests and appreciations

- To help people become more self-reliant and secure

- To provide opportunities for people to strengthen their self-concept

- To develop awareness, appreciation, understanding, and respect for our relationship and stewardship responsibility to the natural environment

Later, Paul Darst and George Armstrong (1980) were convinced that the "addition of outdoor adventure activities to recreation programs and physical education curriculums should prove to be a most significant development in this century." This was a time of considerable growth in adventure activities, which provide participants with a degree of excitement, risk, and challenge absent in many traditional sport and recreation activities. Aspiring to include outdoor adventure activities in schools and recreation programs, Darst and Armstrong identified numerous benefits. They reasoned that the benefits could be attributed to three motives—personal, economic, and social-psychological (see table 5.1).

Yet another set of benefits is offered by Alan Ewert (1989), who has been prominent in helping to give us a better understanding of outdoor adventure. He views the adventure experience as "a highly personal experience entirely understandable only to the individual." Emphasizing two commonalities ("uncertainty of outcome and elements of risk and danger"), he separates the benefits and expectations of participation in outdoor adventure into four categories: psychological, sociological, educational, and physical (see table 5.2).

TABLE 5.1

Darst and Armstrong's Benefits of Outdoor Adventure

Personal	Economic	Social-psychological
New experience—adds a kick to participants' lives, allows them to experience something they haven't tried before.	Minimal financial investment— provides interesting and pleasant activities at a reasonable cost.	Socializing—provides a chance to meet others who have similar interests.
High-risk experience—facing perceived danger may help participants overcome fears, gain self-confidence, and enhance their ability to cope.		Unity—promotes cohesiveness and doing things together without the distractions of everyday life (e.g., television, telephone, social responsibilities).
Escape—offers release from the tensions and complexities of modern life.		Cooperation and trust—promotes better relationships through cooperation, appreciation of others, compassion, and respect.
Success—allows participants to achieve a highly personal sense of accomplishment.		Nature and the outdoors— promotes aesthetic appreciation for nature and concern for vanishing wild places.
Knowledge—participants learn more about themselves and the environment.		
Physical fitness—physical activity can help burn calories and increase strength, stamina, and flexibility.		

TABLE 5.2

Ewert's Benefits of Outdoor Adventure

Psychological	Benefits on a personal (versus group) basis: Self-concept (enhanced or strengthened view of oneself), self-efficacy (self-confidence), self-actualization (well-being, or improved self-expression and feelings of psychological health)
Sociological	Compassion, cooperation, respect for others, communication
Educational	Improved academic abilities, awareness of nature and the environment, problem solving, outdoor skills, value clarification
Physical	Strength, coordination, balance, cardiovascular endurance

In his introductory chapter to *Adventure Programming*, David Webb (1999) refers to the "great diversity" of organizations, products, services, and delivery of outdoor adventure today. Webb asserts that, despite this diversity, the goals and benefits of all outdoor adventure can be associated with three developmental objectives: recreation, skill, and character. See table 5.3 for examples of Webb's objectives.

Much of the early literature about the outcomes of adventure derives from insights from various champions of adventure. Despite the consistency of these perspectives, it is no longer acceptable to claim benefits without attempting to validate such claims. Thus, in the last decade there has been a rise in objective empirical studies designed to assess participant perceptions of various outcomes (e.g., Holman et al. 2004). Nevertheless, categories of adventure outcomes continue to vary according to authors' and researchers' findings and intentions (e.g., program development, enhanced academic understanding, marketing and advertising), definitions used (e.g., adventure education, outdoor education, outdoor adventure pursuits, experiential education, adventure therapy), and discipline (e.g., recreation versus education).

Acknowledging this diversity, Simon Priest (1999) suggests four distinct categories of adventure programming that are based on the program's primary focus: recreational (changing how people feel), educational (changing how people think), developmental (changing how people behave),

and therapeutic (changing how people misbehave). Jude Hirsch (1999) elaborates on the primary goals for each of these categories:

- Recreation: fun, laughter, challenge, excitement, initiative, and so on
- Education: change in sense of identity or self-concept
- Development: learning associated with a generic theme such as cooperation, communication, or trust
- Psychotherapy: learning about interpersonal processes that apply to relationships with significant others

Priest (1999) asserts that "one adventure program can deliver all four types of programming," and Hirsch (1999) concurs that "we are all doing adventure education; therefore, there will be universals." However, classifying programs into such categories does not seem to provide programming directives that address the needs of the individual or outcomes that apply to the whole person using adventure as a means rather than an end in itself. While programs may be designed for different purposes, the individual outcomes or benefits should transcend program type to meet the needs of the individual.

Although outcomes across categories sometimes overlap, they also often contain concepts that are vague in terms of actual learning or outcome gains. In the next section, we offer categories that encom-

TABLE 5.3

Webb's Goals and Benefits of Outdoor Adventure

Recreational	Skill	Character
Enjoyment	Goal setting	Independence
Relaxation	Decision making	Interdependence
Entertainment	Problem solving	Self-efficacy
Excitement	Responsibility	Willingness to take risks
Catharsis	Physical development	Tolerance
Self-expression	Nature awareness	Respect
	Communication	Trust
	Leadership	Compassion

Adapted from S. Priest, 1999, Introduction: Experientia. In *Adventure programming*, edited by J.C. Miles and S. Priest (State College, PA: Venture), xiii-xiv.

pass both educational and recreational goals and that provide tangible definitions of outcomes that are designed for and taught through adventure.

Tangible Outcomes of Adventure

For the purposes of this chapter we suggest that there are distinctions between adventure and outdoor programs that reside in their primary purpose, the setting in which they are conducted, and the risk involved. Outdoor programs focus on the development of technical skill in the natural setting and thus involve actual risk. On the other hand, adventure programs focus on personal and group development in developed areas and concentrate on perceived risk. While adventure and outdoor could be two ends of a continuum with much overlap in the middle, the distinctions become important when determining goals and benefits of programs.

Our interest in original and current proponents of adventure led us repeatedly to the American Camp Association (ACA). Founded in 1910, the ACA represents all segments of the camp profession and is dedicated to enriching the lives of children and adults through camp experiences. A recently published ACA document provides a starting point for defining and categorizing adventure outcomes (2005b). The document summarizes a large

research study of camper outcomes. Results from the study provide evidence that camp is a positive force in youth development. Moreover, many of the aspects of positive growth mentioned in this study correspond with outcomes cited in previous literature. The following domains used in the ACA study can assist in identifying specific goals for adventure programmers.

Positive Identity

If we address the possible goals or benefits of adventure education in terms of benefits to the participant, the notion of positive identity has remained primary through the decades. While *positive identity* is a bit of a nebulous term, it generally includes various aspects of character development such as self-esteem, determination, dependability, ambition, and independence. Increases in self-esteem lead to feelings of worth, competence, confidence, and optimism. Independence fosters stepping out of one's comfort zone into unfamiliar territory that produces anxiety and fear as well as exhilaration, initiative, and calculated risk taking.

Social Skills

The acquisition of social skills extends beyond the individual benefits of positive identity by focusing on participants' interactions with each

Adventure provides occasions for being together and feeling connected to something outside ourselves.

CAREERS IN ADVENTURE

NAME: Heidi Shingleton

JOB: Senior Wilderness Instructor, New Horizons for Young Women (Springfield, Maine)

BACKGROUND: BS in social work, Colorado State University; MS in sport pedagogy, University of Northern Colorado

WHAT'S YOUR JOB LIKE? I lead eight-day therapeutic wilderness expeditions throughout the state of Maine. Mode of transportation depends on the season (backpacking, canoeing, snowshoeing, and dog sledding). I am responsible for the supervision of three coinstructors and six adolescent girls.

New Horizons for Young Women is a therapeutic wilderness program that lasts six to nine weeks. The focus of the program is emotional growth, requiring me to run groups and facilitate personal enlightenment aligned with the girls' treatment plans. The backwoods of Maine is used as the vehicle that promotes change. Each day is unique, posing its individual challenges and splendor.

One minute I may discover a moose enjoying its afternoon snack, the next I might have to reduce a girl's injured shoulder. I spend the majority of my life living out of my tent and in the company of adolescents, many of whom have been kicked out of school, some of whom have been raped, and all of whom have undergone numerous psychological diagnoses. The dynamics of my job require me to rely on a multitude of skills: communication, navigation, outdoor technical competence, wilderness medicine, crisis response, and written documentation.

I am fortunate to have a job that allows me to enjoy the natural world while facilitating personal discovery. I am amazed by the girls' resiliency and I am empowered by their ability to reset their lives and forge ahead. My advice to others wanting to enter this field is to jump in with both feet, expect to be exhausted, and always remember to listen to your intuition.

other. The social dimension of adventure can be highly significant. For example, challenges in an adventure setting can facilitate group bonding and cooperation. Working as a team, people can learn to resolve disagreements, appreciate differences, develop new friendships, and generally get along with others. Adventure experiences also can offer opportunities to demonstrate leadership and to accept responsibilities unavailable in other settings. Finally, adventure provides occasions for being together, having a sense of community, enjoying the company of like-minded people, and feeling connected to something larger than oneself.

Physical and Thinking Skills

In their 1929 classic book, *Camping and Character,* Dimock and Hendry list skills in camping activities such as canoeing, swimming, riding, and sailing accompanied by the associated knowledge as the first and second objectives of the summer camp experience. Few would argue this potential benefit of adventure education. Physical benefits can be classified as the psychomotor and technical skills required for participation in activities that entail moving across land or water by natural means. The physiological gains of exercise constitute another aspect of physical benefits.

Depending on the setting, adventure education can provide the venue for the acquisition of a vast array of physical and thinking skills that are usually associated with living outdoors. Thinking skills include knowledge of safety measures and the need to follow them as well as knowledge of skills and the environment in which they take place (Ford and Blanchard 1985). Higher-order thinking skills such as planning and solving problems are an often sought-after benefit. Additionally, most adventure programs tap into their setting to provide environmental awareness as a cognitive outcome.

Positive Values and Spirituality

As mentioned earlier, acquiring and strengthening virtues was an overriding concern for early proponents of adventure experiences. The need for virtuous conduct is just as important now as it was then (some would argue more so). Successful participation in today's complex society demands making appropriate decisions and accepting the consequences of one's choices. Insights gained from constructive adventure experiences can help instill positive values and principles such as selflessness and compassion, keeping commitments and fulfilling obligations, self-discipline, and honesty, to name

a few. These values and principles are important in that they can assist in "achieving some harmony between principles of self-interest and altruism. It suggests that not only can we explore, develop, and appreciate our own unique potential, but that we can use our emerging abilities to benefit others and the environment in which we all live. Consequently, by becoming responsible we can reaffirm our own worth, our sense of belonging, and our awareness of place" (Parker and Stiehl 2005).

Certainly for many, outdoor adventure experiences involve a spiritual component. Spirituality, although often associated with religion, can be painted with a much broader stroke. When adventure programs are conducted in the outdoors, contact with the natural environment can add a spiritually moving dimension; "either because of the beautiful natural setting, the opportunities for bonding with others, or meaningful religious practices, young people have an opportunity to connect to the earth, to each other, and perhaps to a higher power" (ACA 2005a).

We believe in a humble orientation to the environment—that the outdoor world does not exist for the hedonistic pursuits of a privileged few, that loud people who speak before listening, who use more than their share of the air to announce their identity, are like destructive initials on a tree trunk tarred with a brush of unsustainable and repugnant attitudes. The natural world rejuvenates the soul and reminds us of our place in this awe-inspiring world. It is where we come closest to appreciating our connectedness with the rest of creation.

Achieving Benefits

It is abundantly clear that adventure education has a vast potential for achieving a multitude of goals, educational and otherwise. The uniqueness of the environment and the activities provide a venue not only for learning new skills and acquiring relevant knowledge, but also for promoting calculated risk taking, camaraderie with others, and reverence for the natural world. The larger question, however, may be this: Is adventure education reaching its potential? In 1918, Bobbitt stated,

> The controlling purposes of education have not been sufficiently particularized. We have aimed at a vague culture, an ill-defined discipline, indefinite moral character building, an unparticularized social efficiency, or nothing more than an escape from a life of work. Often there are no controlling purposes; the momentum of the educational machine keeps it running. So long as objectives are but vague guesses,

or not even that, there can be no demand for anything but vague guesses as to means and procedures. But the era of contentment with large undefined purposes is rapidly passing. (41-42)

While Bobbitt was speaking of traditional education in kindergarten through 12th grade, it would not be unreasonable to substitute adventure education for education in his admonition.

All too often adventure education has relied on its novelty as an attractor while neglecting to design learning environments in which deliberate goal acquisition is the chief aim. If adventure programs are to mean something, they must first

- be built on a solid philosophy that reflects the values and beliefs of the program designers,

- state important goals,

- include a way of measuring those goals, and

- incorporate instructional practices that allow participants to demonstrate achievement of the goals (Tannehill and Lund 2005).

Good content that is poorly delivered or good intentions with weak or inappropriate content are unlikely to produce favorable results.

Stating a Philosophy

The philosophy of any adventure program provides the foundational beliefs that undergird all subsequent decisions of a program. The philosophy emanates from the beliefs and values of the program designers, the participants the program serves, and the setting of the program. In adventure programming, a philosophy might range from providing participants with the physical skills necessary for being more active in the outdoor environment to simply offering a venue for fun and escape. Adventure programs, whether recreational or educational, should contain a clear philosophy that leads to discernible learning or benefits, even if those benefits are an escape from ordinary life.

Determining Goals, Assessments, and Instructional Strategies

Once a philosophy has been articulated, the following three questions can guide what educational experts have referred to as **backward design** (Wiggins and McTighe 1998), an **outcomes approach** (Spady and Marshall 1991), and **design-down curricular process** (Lambert 2003).

1. What do we want our participants to know and be able to do as a result of being in our program? In educational terms, this is a curricular question of what is to be taught. By answering it, adventure programmers and educators identify what's important and the deliberate, intended outcomes of their programs. Wiggins and

Adventure programs should result in discernible learning.

Stiehl and Parker

McTighe (1998) define this information as "enduring understandings" because it represents what we want participants to gain from our programs.

2. How do we know when participants have been successful? The answer to this question allows programmers and educators to know when they have achieved the desired outcomes. Traditionally, adventure educators have used subjective observation to answer this question, if they answer it at all. To guide future programming and assist in participant achievement of desired benefits, systematic and objective means of documenting the achievement of benefits must be identified.

3. How can we get participants to achieve desired outcomes in the most challenging and engaging ways possible? Adventure activities are alluring for most participants. Over two decades ago, Young and Parker (1987) cautioned that this attraction could lead to a laxness in instruction resulting in haphazard acquisition of the desired outcomes. If adventure education is to reach its potential, learning experiences (instruction) must be designed to intentionally and purposefully lead participants toward the desired goals and benefits.

An example from a college-level basic hiking class may help clarify these points. One of the class goals is for students to acquire a greater appreciation and knowledge of the natural world around them—to really see what is out there. This includes curricular aspects of flora, fauna, and geological features. The use of written journals accompanied by teacher questioning and an out-of-class partner hike reported through a written and pictorial portfolio were determined to be meaningful and reasonable ways to determine if participants have, in fact, gained this information (assessment). Several instructional activities can then be designed to help students achieve the goal.

- In an effort to guide novice students' initial journal entries, questions are given at the beginning of every hike that focus on the environment. Questions include such things as identifying a unique rock formation, signs of past human habitation, and five new flowers.
- Another strategy is to acquire a deck of cards with the suits changed to birds, flowers, trees, and animals and provide each participant with five cards. They then look for those things throughout the day.

- The instructor identifies flowers and birds along the trail while helping students learn key identification points.
- Knowing that beginning students most often walk looking at the back of the person in front of them, students can travel a designated section of trail in groups of three, increasing their ability to see.
- Candid camera is an instructional activity that asks students to walk in pairs, one person behind the other. The lead person is unsighted and guided by the sighted partner from behind through hands on the shoulders. When the sighted partner says "Click," the unsighted partner quickly opens and shuts her eyes and reports to the sighted partner what she sees.
- Finally, after acquiring requisite skills and knowledge, participants walk solo for a while.

Because many of these activities require cooperating with a small group or partner, they might also have social benefits—especially if the groups are designed so that participants work with people they do not know.

Lambert (1999) uses the metaphor of a three-legged stool to emphasize the importance of each aspect of program development. If all three legs of the stool—**curriculum, assessment,** and **instruction**—are weighted equally, the stool is solid. If one or two legs are removed or weighted unequally, stability is compromised.

Customizing Outcomes

One of the unique aspects of adventure education and programming is its ability to be used to achieve multiple goals, yet it is precisely this uniqueness that can become its Achilles heel. While in the quest to accomplish everything, nothing may be accomplished. Research on benefits from adventure programs supports this notion. For example, in terms of positive identity the results are equivocal; several studies report positive gains in self-esteem constructs (Carson and Gillis 1994; Hattie et. al 1997), some report mixed results (Hazelworth and Wilson 1990; Kaly and Heesacker 2003), and still others report no effect (Danziger 1982; Jernstedt and Johnson 1983; McBride 1984; O'Connell 2002; Pann 2000). The possible benefits of adventure programs cannot be argued, but the reality of those effects is varied.

CAREERS IN ADVENTURE

NAME: Tim O'Connell

JOB: Associate Professor, Department of Recreation and Leisure Studies, Brock University (St. Catharines, Ontario)

BACKGROUND: BSE in recreation education, SUNY-Cortland; MEd in outdoor education and outdoor recreation, University of Minnesota; PhD in recreation resource management, New York University

WHAT'S YOUR JOB LIKE? My job responsibilities include teaching undergraduate and graduate classes in outdoor leadership, skills, and programming; conducting research on topics such as how a sense of community develops during wilderness trips; delivering semester-long skills-based courses in rock climbing, backpacking, canoeing, and other outdoor pursuits; and coediting the *Journal of Experiential Education.*

Being a university professor is a great job! After working for Wilderness Inquiry, an organization that provides integrated wilderness trips for people with and without disabilities, I accepted a university job. As a professor, I continue to be able to blend earlier work experiences with my personal and professional interests. It is exciting to support students in realizing their potential as outdoor and adventure professionals. While many people think that university professors have a cushy job with time off during the summer, it is actually quite the opposite. My summers are filled with many undertakings such as conducting research, writing, teaching in various programs around North America, volunteering to lead sea-kayaking symposia, preparing new course materials, developing grant proposals, and trying to keep my technical skills sharp. Thus, one of my biggest challenges is to balance the many demands of being a university professor with spending necessary field time with students as they experience outdoor recreation and adventure education firsthand. My advice for anyone who is thinking about becoming a university professor? Prior to pursuing graduate work, spend substantial time in the outdoor and adventure education field. Those experiences and skills will enhance your credibility and will make your job much easier.

As previously indicated, adherence to the guidelines of curriculum planners can better ensure the achievement of benefits. However, Jensen and Young (1981) and Stiehl and Parker (2005) take the achievement of benefits a step further. Even adventure programs with a clear philosophy are affected by time, clientele, location, expertise, and a host of idiosyncratic differences. Thus, it is unlikely that one program can be all things to all people. In the desire to have participants achieve all potential benefits, a program may not achieve any.

A useful delineation according to primary and secondary goals (Jensen and Young 1981) may help adventure programmers and educators focus on certain goals and benefits. Their contention is that programs may have primary goals or benefits and others are secondary or concomitant. For example, an outdoor adventure program that is part of a school physical education program might have as its foremost benefits the acquisition of outdoor skills such as orienteering, hiking, and so on for safe participation in outdoor activities. Therefore, physical and thinking goals would be primary. However, while students are learning those skills, they may well acquire social benefits through working with others, and they may develop a positive identity as they gain competence in a new activity. On the other hand, an adventure program that is part of a summer camp with articulated spiritual and social aspects would likely program experiences that use the outdoors as a medium to primarily gain increased spiritual awareness and social competence and secondarily teach necessary skills. Programs would thus be well served by articulating their philosophy to delineate primary and secondary goals and design activities to meet those goals.

Author Tom Robbins (1976) may have summed it up best: "If you believe in peace, act peacefully; if you believe in love, act lovingly; if you believe in every which way, then act every which way, that's perfectly valid—but don't go out trying to sell your beliefs to the System. You end up contradicting what you profess you believe in, and you set a bum example." Adventure education has many potential benefits. However, attempting to achieve too many benefits, especially if any contradict or compete with others, poses a risk of diluting program effectiveness.

Here are some questions that might help you determine the degree to which you are directing efforts toward the benefits and outcomes of adventure in your program:

1. Do you have clearly developed, publicly stated outcomes that underscore the benefits of adventure?

2. Do your outcomes align with the values and beliefs of your sponsors, advocates, and participants?

3. Are your outcomes appropriate for your participants' needs, interests, and abilities; your resources; and your staff knowledge and skills?

4. Do your activities and policies support your stated outcomes?

5. Do you have functional assessments for your stated outcomes?

6. Is there ongoing evaluation of the extent to which outcomes are being achieved?

Summary

Benefits to adventure participants can be grouped in four categories: positive identity, social skills, physical and thinking skills, and positive values and spirituality. Establishing a program philosophy and then deliberately deciding the intended results of the program, identifying how it will be known if those results are achieved, and designing specific instructional activities to engage participants in the attainment of the benefits all enhance the acquisition of these benefits. In the effort to avoid trying to do too much, program planners may want to establish primary and secondary goals.

How did the participants on the river trip in the opening scenario benefit from their adventure? For the 23-year-old daughter, it was a physical challenge because she had never rowed the river by herself. She was testing her technical skill. For the recently divorced woman, it provided feelings of increased self-worth and optimism as she ventured out on her own. For the couple that had not had the opportunity to take a trip together for a while, it provided a bonding experience and a chance to rediscover the things they enjoyed doing together. For the 13-year-old and the paddlers who took 10 or more trips a year, it was social—visiting, talking, making new friends. For the raft guides, it allowed appreciation of one of the most incredible natural resources in the southwestern United States. The medium of the river provided an adventure that allowed each participant to enjoy his own rewards. Furthermore, continuous fluctuations in river flow provided ongoing challenges, which served to bring this diverse group closer together.

Review Questions

1. How did Plato, Aristotle, William James, and Kurt Hahn each affect our understanding about the role of adventure in promoting education goals?

2. What did Henry David Thoreau and John Dewey contribute to our thinking about adventure education?

3. What are the historical roots of today's use of adventure and outdoors for promoting educational goals?

4. Compare and contrast Julian Smith's list of outdoor and adventure goals with those of his successors.

5. List and provide several examples for each of the four adventure outcome domains suggested by the ACA.

6. Select one of the ACA adventure outcome domains and discuss reasons for its justification as an independent domain.

7. Comment on the statement, Adventure education tends to be attractive, and yet also has been neglectful.

8. What are some key ingredients of a successful adventure education program? Elaborate on one of these ingredients.

Student Learning Activities

1. Present a time line of historical events and views that lead to present-day concepts of adventure education goals and benefits.

2. Based on readings, observations, and personal experience, develop a list of adventure education benefits and compare them with those discussed in the chapter.

3. Identify several principal benefits of adventure education and design ways to assess or verify whether participants realize those benefits.

4. Describe some adventure activities and how their design plays a role in accomplishing explicit adventure education goals.

5. Design an overview of a proposed adventure education program, including (or perhaps debating) purported benefits.

PART II

Defining Skills and Competencies for Adventure Practitioners

CHAPTER 6

Responsibilities of Adventure Education Leaders

Denise Mitten and Kent Clement

" Leadership and learning are indispensable to each other. "

—**John F. Kennedy**

© Getty Images

Chapter Concepts

✦ Leadership is a relationship between leaders and their groups. Leaders build caring relationships with participants while maintaining professional boundaries; authenticity and relational skills are vital.

✦ There are four types of skill competencies an adventure leader should possess: technical and activity skills, teaching and modeling skills, group process skills, and decision-making and judgment skills.

✦ Leaders have a great deal of responsibility in several different areas, including keeping participants safe, providing instruction, modeling positive behavior, and leading to ensure that group goals are met. This responsibility should not be taken lightly.

✦ There are many types of adventure activities and each has different goals that require the leader to lead in different ways. To be an effective leader, every decision should be designed to help the group members reach their personal and collective goals.

✦ Because of the inherent risk in adventure activities, leaders need to be skilled in decision making and judgment.

Leadership in adventure education is a dynamic process that can be thought of as the actions necessary to lead a group successfully through an adventure activity. Adventure leadership is so much more than simply climbing with good-natured clients or leading dangerous wilderness excursions like you see in the movies. Such activities might be part of the experience, but developing a vast array of technical and personal skills is far more important and needs to precede leadership activities.

In this chapter we discuss the skills leaders need. After introducing the concept that leadership is about relationships and that people learn about leadership more through the ways leaders treat them than from the activities they do, we describe the three aspects of the leader's job—providing responsible, effective, and psychological leadership. To skillfully perform these three functions, leaders need to gain competency in four major areas: technical and activity skills, teaching and modeling skills, group process skills, and judgment and decision-making skills. After we describe and discuss these four areas, we'll talk about specific skills needed by the responsible leader.

Leadership as a Relationship

Leadership is a relationship, not a persona to put on for a trip or program. Leaders build caring relationships with participants while maintaining professional boundaries; authenticity and relational skills are vital. Priest and Gass (2005) define leadership in

adventure programming as a process of influence. We influence group members to learn activity skills, judgment skills, and life skills through our relationship with them.

In the long run, leadership in adventure education is about the relationships one forms rather than task completion or accomplishments. We do not focus on task completion or accomplishments alone because we are looking for sustainability in both a personal and a global sense. We could say that we are here to climb a mountain and any way we do it as long as we come back alive is fine. However, in adventure programming we use experiential education to purposefully help students learn life skills, including cooperation, self-efficacy, and other skills that help them become successful community contributors.

A phenomenon called **parallel process** happens: If leaders treat their participants with care and respect, the participants will be more likely to treat other participants with care and respect. If you are teaching your participants to be leaders, they will likely replicate what you have modeled to them though your actions. The concept is to do unto others as you want them to do unto others. It is the *process* that is the goal, rather than the accomplishment. If participants can go out and re-create this process, then we have met our goal of adding to the sustainability of society with positive influences on the participants' families, communities, and the environment. Most people learn skills more easily when they perceive their leader to be a warm and caring person (Clarke 1984).

Defining Leadership Jobs

Within this concept of leadership as a relationship, the leader has three main functions: to be a **responsible leader,** an **effective leader,** and a **psychological leader.** These three functions of leadership are all essential to the welfare of groups (Berne 1963; Clarke 1984). Each function is equally important and leaders need to be able to perform all three jobs competently. Sometimes group members will help with the effective and psychological leadership jobs; however, the adventure leader is always the responsible leader (see figure 6.1).

The responsible leader is the person who, if anything goes wrong, is called into account by higher authority. The responsible leader has the last word on safety and is constantly mindful of safety considerations. These responsibilities include details such as checking knots and belay systems, making sure the life jackets are packed and worn, making sure everyone knows the plan for the day, and vigilantly maintaining a steady emotional state. The responsible leader is the person who has the ultimate responsibility for maintaining the goal of the trip or program. The leader is constantly monitoring the group members and thinking about the group's process.

The effective leader makes sure things get done and also may be the one who does those things. The effective leader gives direction and the direction is most likely followed. This includes taking leadership in problem solving, getting the canoes loaded, starting dinner, and teaching participants to kayak. On a ropes course, among other things, the effective leadership job includes setting up the course, teaching spotting and belaying, and facilitating activities. Effective leaders use an appropriate leadership style, whether it involves directing the group members or delegating tasks.

Psychological leadership includes creating group morale, encouraging and supporting group members, tending to emotional needs of self and group members, and other relationship considerations. For example, when a participant begins to climb at a climbing wall, the leader might ask, "How do you like to be supported while you climb? Would you like us to be verbal with our encouragement and tell you about holds we notice? Would you like us to be quietly attentive and add our ideas when asked?" Another example of psychological leadership is when, after a particularly strenuous day on a wilderness trip, a leader suggests watching the sunset as a group. This can have a calming effect, and quietly sharing a beautiful moment in nature can have a positive influence on relationships (assuming there are not too many mosquitoes and black flies and too few head nets!).

While the responsible leadership job is not shared, by the end of a program or trip, the participants might be performing a great deal of the day-to-day effective and psychological leadership functions. If so, this frees the leaders to do deeper work. For example, leaders can work one on one to teach more skills. The responsible leader has the job of creating the atmosphere and direction for this shared leadership to occur. At the same time, leaders monitor how group members perform as effective and psychological leaders. Both the effective and psychological leadership functions can also negatively influence group members. For example, a participant can set a tone of complaining or scapegoat another group member. The responsible leader needs to step in to help model positive psychological leadership.

Sharing effective and psychological leadership can come about organically or can be delegated. For example, after the facilitator explains an activity, a participant might jump in and suggest a plan for moving forward. Or, on a wilderness trip a participant might say, "How about if I work on setting up tents. Anyone want to help?" These are examples of participants organically (without being told) sharing the effective leadership job. An example of a participant sharing the psychological leadership job might be when one says to a group member starting to climb, "How do you want support from us? We're here for you and want to honor what you think works best for you."

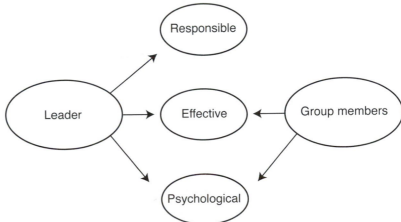

FIGURE 6.1 Group members can share effective and psychological leadership with the adventure leader, but responsible leadership is reserved for the adventure leader.

When participants organically share effective and psychological leadership, acknowledging and encouraging this behavior validates and reinforces both the process and the individual's behavior in the eyes of other group members. For example, you might say, "Sally, I'm delighted that you are thinking about the jobs we need to do to set up camp tonight. While a few other people help Sally with the tents, could Isabelle and Jason help me with dinner?" Later in the program or trip, when it has become a group norm for participants to share the effective and psychological leadership jobs, the responsible leader will need to spend less time reinforcing directives given by participants.

The more that effective and psychological leadership are done positively and spontaneously by participants (without delegation), the better. However, if these jobs are being done by only a few participants, especially at the beginning of a trip, leaders may delegate jobs to group members. Some participants have the notion that there is only so much room for leadership (i.e., "If Joe is taking care of things, then I should hang back"). Likewise, some program and trip leaders look for the emergent leader, assuming that one or two leaders will emerge from within the group. However, the more the effective and psychological leadership jobs are shared, the more the program and the competencies and accomplishments can be shared by all group members. It can be thought of as drafting in a bicycle club or breaking snowshoe or ski trails. Each person takes a turn at the lead so that the work of leadership is shared and everyone shares in the trip's success.

Defining Skill Areas Necessary for Leaders

In order to safely lead a group through an adventure activity and create an appropriate atmosphere conducive to positive relationships, a wide array of skills is required. To use the three functions of leadership effectively, four major skill areas are required:

- Activity and technical skills
- Teaching and modeling skills
- Group process skills
- Judgment and decision-making skills

Each of these areas is essential to quality leadership. Leaders of adventure activities often begin by building their technical and activity skills. Once they're technically competent, they can apprentice with more experienced leaders and learn teaching and modeling skills or learn how to integrate the skills they already have. With more time, practice, and expertise, leaders can perform and teach activities while using group process skills. Over time and through experience leaders gain solid judgment and decision-making skills in adventure education environments (see figure 6.2). Finally, competent leaders need to have technical and activity skills that they can teach while modeling positive expedition behavior, monitoring the group members and helping them develop a cohesive group, and making decisions in challenging and diverse environments.

The responsible leadership function requires mastery in all four of these areas. As an assistant leader, for example, a person may be competent in technical and activity skills and still be working on other skill areas. The assistant leader may be helpful to the responsible leader in the effective leadership function but not yet have the skills to lead a trip alone. The following discussion gives examples of skills in each area; however, the skills required for the exact adventure you will lead may not be listed.

Activity and Technical Skills

Traveling in the wilderness, facilitating a group on the high elements of a ropes course, teaching rock climbing, and leading sea kayaking all require specialized skills. There is no substitute for the ability of outdoor adventure leaders to travel safely in a variety of technical terrains, have sufficient paddling skills to stay upright in a rapid, or complete a rescue on a ropes course with ease. The diverse adventure environments require specialized skills in rope handling, belaying, knots, paddling, and rescue.

Activity and technical skills are interrelated. Leaders need to have mastered the activity for the program they are leading. For example, on a kayaking trip the leader has to have mastered the activity

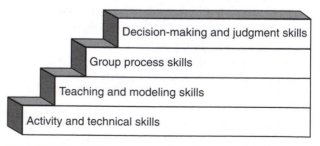

FIGURE 6.2 Skills necessary for adventure leaders.

CAREERS IN ADVENTURE

NAME: Claire Wyatt

JOB: Outdoor Instructor and Program Coordinator, Whenua Iti Trust Outdoor Pursuits Centre (Nelson, New Zealand)

BACKGROUND: Diploma in teaching; BS in chemistry, Canterbury University, New Zealand; master's in counseling, Massey University, New Zealand; New Zealand Outdoor Instructors Association qualifications in alpine, rock climbing, bushcraft, and kayaking

My first experiences in some of the outdoor pursuits were hideous . . . a terrifying backward descent of a 1.5-meter drop in a kayak . . . two excruciating days of blisters, rain, and an external-framed pack that had only shoulder straps (at the age of 12) . . . a day of feeling completely inadequate while rock climbing on friction climbs with studly rock jocks. I'm not sure what kept me coming back for more.

WHAT'S YOUR JOB LIKE? I design outdoor instruction programs, facilitating groups and managing the educational standards and design quality of all programs at the center.

There is something so delightful about a blank page, the start of a program and all the possibilities of activities and experiences that might lead a group to become a supportive community and stimulate thought and learning about being part of a team. I enjoy possibilities, so I find it hard to settle on the nuts and bolts of a program. And then the process begins: the weaving together of progressions, activities, and challenges that will stretch both the individuals and the team. Whenever I meet a new group, I feel nervous (10 years of experience prepares me for only half of the work). The most important part of the job is to know and like the people who come to the center. Only then will I have permission to walk beside them, paddle beside them, climb beside them, and laugh and cry beside them.

Our changeable weather is a challenge, and yet it brings the most spectacular adventurous moments: braving a sudden hailstorm as we descend Mount Tongariro, sharing rain-soaked smiles as we joke along the trail, putting our heads into a 2-meter swell that appears out of nowhere in order to reach the safety of the campsite.

The hardest part is looking at myself and realizing that in a moment of not thinking, I damaged a relationship when my frustration turned me into a dogmatic dictator. The best moments are a conversation with a young woman watching a sunset, the wry smile of admission as a young person faces his or her behavior, and the proud stories that are told to parents as young people return home.

of kayaking; the same goes for rock climbing and other kinds of activities. Additionally, leaders need to have mastered technical skills for a wide variety of activities and situations, such as reading the weather, using a global positioning system (GPS), and tying knots. Finally, leaders need to have the physical skills and stamina to complete the activity. A day program may take a different level of stamina and physical strength than a 30-day trip, just as a mountaineering trip might take a different level of stamina than a hiking trip using a base camp. Leaders need to be realistic about their physical abilities and understand that they need the strength not only to care for themselves but also for group members.

You cannot cram to develop proficiency in technical skills. For some, learning such skills comes easily, and for others it does not. But with practice, a reasonably fit person can acquire a competent grasp of virtually any technical skill needed in adventure settings. Specialized instruction is essential to learn the safety aspects of the skill areas in which you need to become proficient. Individual practice is essential to help make newly acquired skills your own. When you do an activity regularly, you begin to learn the nuances of it. When you do not have to devote all your attention to just moving around safely in a new environment, your senses have time to become attuned to environmental changes—ripples in the water that warn of a submerged rock or that subtle feeling of urgency when the barometer drops at the approach of a storm.

Very experienced people have been hurt or killed on technical terrain by momentary lapses of attention—errors in judgment that result from fatigue or other distractions that take attention away from the immediate tasks at hand. The more a simple skill like knot tying can become ingrained into your subconscious or in the realm of muscle memory, the safer you will be when you become momentarily distracted by cold or fatigue. The only way to do that is to perform the activity multiple times. If you can, practice your skills in many different geographical areas and work with many different people. You will learn different techniques from different people. Professional leaders come with a variety of experiences and outlooks on safety, technique, and other concerns, so be flexible and open to learning new methods.

Ensuring Safety

Leaders have the ultimate responsibility to maintain safety for participants and themselves. This responsibility is often referred to as *risk management*

or *safety management*. Leaders have the responsibility to foresee, understand, and assess potential risks for themselves and participants in each of the five personal domains (physical, emotional, social, behavioral, and spiritual). Participants need to know that they can depend on leaders in case of an emergency and for reliable information about safety and risk. This promotes a feeling of security, makes it easier for people to learn new skills, and enables people to handle routine activities comfortably and safely.

Leaders usually function as the chief medical resource for the group. Appropriate first aid and medical training is critical, and advanced training in first aid and wilderness medicine has become standard practice for adventure leaders. Many programs require Wilderness First Responder (WFR) certification, an 80-hour training program. Leaders need well-prepared safety briefings for environmental considerations as well as program considerations. More considerations regarding safety are discussed in chapter 4, Risk and Safety in Adventure Programming.

Judging Climate

Climate affects almost everything you do in the outdoors. A qualified outdoor leader understands weather (large-scale and local weather patterns, how to use clouds and wind in weather prediction, how to interpret a barometer) and how it affects travel plans and the comfort of group members. For example, let's say you are leading a group through the high elements and you hear thunder. Should you initiate emergency evacuation right away? Should you wait until you see a flash of lightning? How many seconds between the flash of lightning and the clap of thunder relate to how many miles? Education about weather is gained through experience, reading, making your own predictions and seeing if they are accurate, and working and learning from more experienced outdoor leaders. Currently, a useful Web resource about weather education is www.weather.com/education.

Planning Food

Surveys have shown that the number one fear participants have about an isolated wilderness trip is the fear of being hungry (Ewert 1986). Mutinies have occurred on wilderness courses as a result of food shortages or the fear of food shortages. Generally, leaders have several choices of ration planning, but they usually fall into two major categories: meal-by-meal planning and bulk-ration planning. Meal-by-meal planning is exactly what it sounds like. A leader plans for how many meals the group needs times how many people need to be fed and then collects the proper ingredients for the meal. Bulk rationing involves buying bulk items such as pasta, flour, hash brown potatoes, and the like and storing them in bins. The participants then place the desired amount in plastic bags based on preference and duration of the trip. The amount of food to be packed is determined by the caloric needs of the group members.

Using Technology

The outdoors is a place where most people go to get away from technology, but technology is part of outdoor experiences—for example, using GPS, researching trips on the Internet, and acquiring permits. There are a number of Web sites that allow you to access the National Park Service and USDA Forest Service permitting procedures, complete with forms, deadlines, compartment maps, and pretty much everything you need to plan your trip. Equipment, maps, books, and even hard-to-find items like a replacement cap for your water bottle can be located and purchased on the Internet. Finally, some programs are experimenting with wireless technology powered by batteries and solar chargers in the form of palm-sized computers that can be carried in waterproof bags so that assignments can be written in the field and turned in to the instructor and tests can be sent to students'

GPS Resources

A useful Web site for background information about GPS is www.colorado.edu/geography/gcraft/notes/gps/gps.html. Popular GPS providers include Garmin (www.garmin.com), Magellan (www.magellangps.com), and Lowrance (www.lowrance.com).

computers and then back to the instructor and graded, all without using paper. Look for this area to advance quickly in the future.

Performing Administration

Technical skills also include administrative skills, such as budgeting, marketing, handling money, acquiring land use permits, developing itineraries, completing incident report forms and trip and participant evaluations, and complying with the Americans with Disabilities Act (ADA). (For complete information on ADA compliance, see www.usdoj.gov/crt/ada/adahom1.htm.)

For most governmental organizations that manage public land and water resources, if you receive compensation for leading a group or an individual in your care, you will be required to get a permit. If you lead trips for no compensation, you

Effective leadership gets dinner under way along the shores of Lake Michigan.

may still need a permit but of a different type, one that is much easier to obtain. Conducting adventure experiences and getting paid for your services without obtaining a permit is termed **rogue outfitting.** It is unethical and unprofessional and carries a hefty fine if you are caught, plus you may lose any opportunity to get legal permits in the future.

Teaching and Modeling Skills

The ability to teach technical information and skills as well as plan educational activities that have measurable and desired outcomes is especially challenging in adventure education. A curriculum should help group members develop in four areas:

- **Skills,** such as collaboration, teamwork, and effective communication
- **Behaviors** (values and attitudes), such as helping the group members accomplish tasks, being a supportive group member, and expressing concerns in a way that works for other group members
- **Critical thinking and problem solving,** including being able to apply, analyze, and synthesize information in order to solve problems and make sound judgments
- **Content,** such as what are the parts of a paddle, what is the flora and fauna of an area, and how to read water

Planning Programs

Thorough planning of your program is essential to teaching well. Programming an adventure activity is like setting the table for a great meal. If the seating arrangement is correct, there is good conversation, and the food is well prepared, then everyone feels satisfied. Thinking about the goals of your adventure experience helps you to program who, what, where, when, and many other important aspects of good planning. Be concrete in planning your objectives to meet the program outcomes promised to the participants.

In every lesson plan, leaders should define what outcomes are expected in each of the four areas—who, what, where, and when. Learning about the philosophy and methodology of experiential education will help aspiring adventure leaders understand what kind of teaching and learning to expect. Leaders have a responsibility to keep communication simple and direct and to provide opportunities for their own and participants' reflections. Excellent planning means that you understand and incorporate the current best practices used in your activity and set or follow the best current standards of other programs of similar size and type.

Although adventure leaders need detailed lesson plans, they also need to be flexible in their execution of the plans. For example, weather, group attitude, or other factors may influence the timing or appropriateness of a certain lesson. Often information is conveyed in sound bites throughout the trip. By the end of the trip, participants have a great deal of information that they have received as it became relevant and in manageable chunks both in terms of content and attention span. Teaching in adventure leadership is often informal and repetitive. For example, a small group of people may be up early and as the leader you may teach them about baking and make some cinnamon rolls. Other participants may learn this skill from you or the participants later during the trip.

Teaching Technical Skills

The ability to teach technical skills is gained through practice and observing people who teach well. While leaders of adventure activities have the benefit of their participants actually doing the activity—not merely listening to a lecture—it is still challenging to teach necessary skills. For example, knots and navigation are considered by many professional outdoor leaders to be among the most difficult skills to convey to others. They both require the ability to picture three-dimensional spaces in our minds, and they require leaders to describe complicated movements using words. Leaders need a great deal of practice with a variety of learners. Additional information about teaching methodology is found in chapter 11.

Creating a Positive Learning Environment

Leaders have the responsibility to create positive and healthy learning environments. A positive learning environment is one that is nonthreatening and is conducive to helping participants learn the skills, knowledge, and behavior management that they need to accomplish their program. It is the leaders' responsibility to have clear behavioral objectives in mind, divide learning into orderly steps, and be willing to acknowledge what they do not know. A learning environment that is nonthreatening helps maximize participants' learning potential. Current research shows that when people feel scared or threatened, learning ceases. When learning is pleasurable, the frontal lobe is activated. The brain remembers the pleasure and wants to learn more in order to replicate the pleasure (Zull 2002). Ideally, leaders can motivate participants to feel engaged, excited, and involved. Leaders can help set the stage for participants to experience flow (a state where participants are relaxed, alert, and focused on the present without self-consciousness) as they learn and engage in adventure activities. In flow, participants experience intrinsic motivation, a perception of mastery and control, and very little or no stress (Csikszentmihalyi 1993). After flow experiences participants experience stronger self-efficacy and self-affirmation.

Specifically, leaders create a climate for their program where

- people get support for achievement,
- it is safe for people to practice even when they are uncomfortable,
- it is safe for people to feel or be awkward, and
- it is safe for people to try out a new behavior before they choose to keep or discard it (Clarke 1984).

Risk, Challenge, and Challenge by Choice

In her book on learner-centered teaching, Maryellen Weimer (2002) says over and over again that at the heart of engagement is choice and control. In order for people to internalize an experience, they have to choose it and acknowledge that it was a personal choice (Mitten 1985). It is the leader's responsibility to maintain an atmosphere of choice.

Participants' choices need to be informed choices, rather than "I'll do it because you say I should." A participant might say, "I want to do this but I'm not sure I have the skill." Leaders can certainly give opinions, but then they should let participants think over the options and make their own choices.

At the same time, teaching in adventure education involves risk and challenges for participants and leaders alike. There can be a fine line between powerful learning and destructive and emotionally scarring situations. The best course of action is to not go too far and, as Paul Petzoldt (1983) said, err on the side of prudence. If you are not a licensed psychotherapist, do not attempt to get inside someone's head, especially in the field. People can have significant issues that the wilderness can begin to bring out, and if you delve into those issues, you are likely to get in over your head and possibly cause harm to participants.

That said, given the proper encouragement, the trail, weather, group dynamics, and whatever else happens can stimulate life-changing experiences. As the leader, you are a significant part of this, and it is your responsibility to understand the kinds of risks participants take in the five personal domains (physical, emotional, social, behavioral, and spiritual) and be able to judge participants' needs as they take risks in these domains.

It is not unusual for participants to feel coerced into participating in programs by their spouses, who want them to learn skills but don't want to teach

A nonthreatening, positive environment maximizes learning potential.

© Getty Images

them; by their employers; or by therapists or family members who want them to heal emotionally or to behave differently. Unless participants make free choices to participate, they may struggle the entire time with feelings that keep them from being fully present in the group. Even if participants do not come on the trip through their own choice, leaders can help participants feel a sense of control and choice during the program.

Leaders have a lot of power in defining choice. It is not a real choice to say, "Today we are climbing, tomorrow taking a day hike, the next day learning knots, and you can do it or not." Choosing not to do something is not really choosing. A way to offer genuine choice in a program is to have a flexible schedule where activities are done more than one time. There isn't one day only to portage a canoe or learn knots. On a trip, a coguiding system gives the option of subdividing groups. This encourages individual choices and immediately gives the group members more flexibility. Some members might start moving early to catch the sunrise. It is the leader's responsibility within safety boundaries and trip goals to be accepting of participant decisions.

How does choice relate to encouragement or support from the leader? There is a thin line between pushing and encouraging. It is not useful to foster an attitude of pushing through one's feelings or physical discomfort to get to a better place. Having this attitude as a norm takes away choice. It reinforces people not listening to their bodies and minds. As an example, for survivors, the meaning of sexual abuse is to be pushed physically and emotionally, against one's will, beyond what the person can manage. An attitude of pushing through can reinforce trauma and cause unnecessary stress. In an assessment of a program for survivors of violence, Webb (1993) says that "for some clients, it may be therapeutically appropriate for them to take a firm stand in saying 'no' to an activity." This personal decision making leads to empowerment and allows people to better take responsibility for their actions. By respecting individual differences, leaders encourage clients to take responsibility for their own health, safety, and well-being. A go-for-it attitude is different from a "pushing" attitude; it is compatible with participants having a choice because participants need to feel that the leaders and the group members are supportive of them and want them to succeed.

Teaching Through Modeling

An additional aspect of teaching in adventure education is modeling or teaching by example. Acting like a leader includes understanding how much participants look to the leader for direction, being able to engage in positive expeditionary behavior and healthy relationships, and in general being a stellar model of the behavior that you would like participants and other leaders to have. As mentioned previously, participants will practice parallel process, so act the way you would like your group members to act. If a leader makes a risky jump over slick rocks in a stream, you can be sure that the participants will follow suit. Group members take a great deal of behavioral cues from the leader. For example, erratic behavior or lots of emotional ups and downs can create insecurity and fear for the group members, so it is best to present an attitude of calm steadiness.

An aspect of choice that could be modeled and discussed more with participants is choice of attitude. We may not have a choice about the mosquitoes joining us for dinner, but we do have a choice about our attitude concerning the situation. As leaders, we can model appropriate choice of attitude and encourage participants to see the choice as well as their control in that aspect of their behavior.

Keeping the group members safe while expanding their ability to learn skills and manage risk requires leaders to have high ethical standards. According to Hunt (2002), ethical issues for leaders can arise in many categories, such as lying or deceiving, misuse of power, environmental concerns, paternalism, secrecy, student rights, and sexual misconduct. Leaders of adventure education programs should constantly examine their behavior and work to have high ethical standards and consistently appropriate behavior. This includes examining one's motivation to be an adventure leader. Hunt (2002) points out that some outdoor leaders are in the field primarily because they want to take free expeditions. Outdoor leaders need to enjoy teaching and relating to participants and be intrinsically motivated to aspire to be ethical professionals.

Group Process Skills

As our world becomes more global and as we need more than ever to be able to live and work with other people and build communities, we need the skills to do so. Adventure education can help group members to have a positive experience and then replicate this experience with other groups. In order for leaders to use adventure programming successfully, they need a deep understanding of group process and dynamics and the skills to teach and model how to successfully work with people. Leaders as role models and mentors need to examine and develop their relationship-building skills where necessary.

The Power of an Adventure Education Leader

Issues of power and control are especially relevant to adventure educators. We are in positions of power and influence that are unique in many ways to this profession. Many participants come to adventure programs with increased feelings of insecurity because of the newness of both place and activity. Group members participate in activities perceived as dangerous and the activities often take place in isolated areas. This accentuates the power difference that already exists between leaders and participants. Unlike visiting other professionals such as doctors, lawyers, or therapists, adventure participants are unable to just walk away, especially on trips. If the leaders understand their own manifestation of core ethical values such as respect, responsibility, fairness, caring, trustworthiness, self-control, and the like, this power can be used to effectively teach or model positive behavior. On the other hand, this power can unintentionally reinforce negative values and behavior when used incorrectly.

Understanding Group Dynamics

It is critical that leaders understand group development and have the skills to influence it positively. In adventure programming, many leaders have been taught a sequential-stage model of group development and use this to guide their expectations and intervention. We encourage leaders to look at a variety of models and use one that fits their values and beliefs.

As leaders, our own beliefs about group development can influence the way our groups develop. To take an example from child development, consider the effect of renaming the so-called terrible twos to a more positive name, the terrific twos. A two-year-old practices saying no and tests limits, but this is not necessarily a bad thing. After all, saying no and understanding limits is certainly a skill you want children to have when they are teenagers. When put to the test as a parent, people find that a positive concept of this developmental stage influences them as parents to be more patient, accepting, and excited when they see their children saying no and testing limits. Parents who expect the terrific twos experience less conflict and fewer tantrums than parents who expect the terrible twos. Our expectations of others influence our behavior and their outcomes.

Many adventure education leaders use Tuckman's (1965) forming, storming, norming, performing, and adjourning model. This model is addressed further in chapter 2. The purpose of our discussion here is to encourage adventure leaders to apply critical thinking to models and other leadership techniques taught to us, including this particular model. For example, in the storming phase of this model, there is an expectation that participants will experience conflict with one another and that power positions within the group will be worked out, among other things. But both the word *storming* and the leader's expectation that there will be conflict during this stage can transfer the leader's expectations to participants. Some use a model with a similar stage, called *sorting,* and instead of expecting the group members to work out power issues, it is expected that the group members will sort out operating procedures and responsibilities (Mitten 1999). For example, members might ask, how will we make decisions as a group? What time will we get up in the mornings? What tasks need to be done and who will do what? Other group development models to consider include Robert Terry's leadership tasks in which the leader influences the group members to follow six ethical principles in order: 1) dwelling (acknowledging one's own history and values), 2) freedom, 3) justice, 4) participation, 5) love, and 6) responsibility (Lehman 1991) as well as Pamela Kerr and Mike Gass' (1987) model using preaffiliation, power and control, intimacy, differentiation, and separation as the stages.

In our experience, if leaders set a tone for inclusivity and collaborative leadership (modeled by having coleaders and sharing effective and psychological leadership functions), there may be few or no power and authority issues leading to reactionary conflict. If power has not been misused, then most members find power accessible when they feel ready to embrace it. The leaders include others in the leadership by sharing decision making and encouraging participants to help with effective and psychological leadership jobs. Leaders also need to be patient during this sorting stage and realize that each person will be on a different timetable in sorting out their expectations and in understanding how they can contribute to the group. Of course, there can and may be conflict in every stage. The leader sets the tone for working with the origins of conflict—unclear communication, role ambiguity, and values difference—and resolving the conflicts accordingly.

An experiential activity during an adventure education trip can help participants learn how to sort out expectations, jobs, and other group operations.

Leaders have many opportunities to influence attitudinal norms on programs or trips. Subtle or not-so-subtle comments help set the tone of the experience and can encourage and discourage certain norms. For example, at the beginning of a trip, participants often feel nervous, awkward, anxious, excited, and expectant. If the leader is excited, eager to embark on the journey, and at the same time calm and confident, the participants will probably relax and feel assured that the leader will be able to help make the trip safe and successful. Establishing certain norms is conducive to healthy relationships and helps people feel included and safe. These norms include the following: It's OK to ask for help; everyone is welcome; and anyone can speak up when tired or hungry. Leaders can promote norms that help people feel safe. For example, people may learn to watch out for each other or make sure that everyone gets served the first helping of a meal before people have seconds. Leaders can discourage norms that tend to alienate people such as sarcastic teasing; ethnic, racial, or homophobic jokes; and pushing limits.

Monitoring Group Process

Leaders need to be able to understand, follow, and interpret group process. **Group process** is what is going on in a group, who is saying what, what stage the group members are in, and the like.

Our goals and assumptions influence our interpretation of participants' behaviors and our subsequent actions. When working with groups, it is useful for leaders to check if we are making assumptions about participants' behavior or their character and if these assumptions are based on biases. Our assumptions directly affect the experiences of the participants. For example, if a leader sees a person being quiet during the planning phase of a group activity, the leader may assume that the participant is disinterested, interested but needing information, too shy to speak, or holding back to give others an opportunity to speak, to name just a few possibilities. Any of these assumptions can be correct or wrong. Leaders need to be cognizant that these are assumptions, and assumptions need to be examined before one reaches a conclusion.

Mitten's (2003) research on ethical frameworks that leaders use in decision making indicates that if a leader blames a participant for the participant's condition, then the leader is less likely to help that participant. For example, if a participant doesn't have the skills for an activity and the leader sees that lack as the participant's fault, then the leader is less likely to help her acquire the skills. If the leader thinks the participant didn't hear directions because he was goofing around, then the leader is less likely to make sure the participant has the information. Leaders need to practice the skill of examining their assumptions.

Creating Healthy Group Cohesion

Leaders' understanding and ability to engage in healthy relationships is integral to positive **group cohesion,** or a group's commitment to a common set of values and a shared idea of goals. Over time a group will form a group identity or persona as a function of the ways that personal, environmental, and task variables mix. Adventure educators care about group dynamics and people's abilities to form long-term relationships; therefore, they pay attention to how cohesion is developed and have the skills to assess and influence this development.

Adventure educators often work to foster high group cohesion. However, there are both positive and negative aspects to group cohesion. Interestingly, in terms of task completion, both cohesive and noncohesive groups complete tasks at a similar level. Potential positive outcomes of high group cohesion include the following:

- Group members feel satisfied and want to remain affiliated even when they have a choice to leave the group.
- Group members are less likely to feel lonely or isolated.
- Group members' individual mental and physical health is positively influenced because of the buffer against stress that can come with being part of a group.
- Group members feel affirmed and try new skills.

The list is actually longer for potential negative consequences of highly cohesive groups, and lead-

ers need the skills to avoid these negative consequences. Potential negative consequences include the following:

- Groupthink, or a cycle of poor decision making, results from stifling opposition from within, resulting in members being exposed to limited and asymmetric information that supports the group's decisions (Janis 1982).
- Scapegoating and other hostile and aggressive actions are more common toward nonconformists or deviants.
- Individuals may not speak up or leave the group when the group goals are harmful to them.
- Individual identity is stifled or restricted.
- Groups are less productive because of the internal pressure to conform to potential norms that are not consistent with goal completion.

In an adventure program, a relaxed, supportive atmosphere, punctuated by frequent, unrestrained laughter and appropriate humor, indicates healthy connections and positive cohesion. Humor is typified by laughing with rather than at other group members. Individuals accept themselves and other group members and there is an absence of a pattern of group crises. When stressful situations do come up—a challenging low-elements problem or having to bivouac unexpectedly when a storm prevents the group from returning to camp as planned—the group members cope with the situation with good cheer and resourcefulness. Members work together to solve the problem, and there is an absence of blaming as well as an absence of saying "if only we had."

Decision-Making and Judgment Skills

In carrying out the functions and responsibilities of leadership, one needs to know when and how to make effective and safe decisions. Adventure activities by their nature involve risk. A leader's primary responsibility is to understand and predict risk in order to make decisions that ensure the safety of group members and themselves. To do this effectively, leaders need solid judgment and decision-making capabilities.

Leaders use judgment in choosing their leadership style, their decision-making method, their role in the decision-making process, and in making the actual decisions. Additionally, leaders continually teach participants about judgment and decision making by modeling their own judgment, decision-making, and leadership-style choices.

Decision Making

The role of the leader in the decision-making process, including the leadership style chosen, depends on the kind of decision, the level of decision-making skills and experience the participants have, the specific environment, and the goals of the program. For example, on most days, the dinner menu can be decided by participants. Deciding if thunder and lightning create a risk for the participants is the leader's decision. It is quite clear who ought to have the responsibility for certain decisions, but for other decisions the line of responsibility is harder to determine.

In general, decision making that allows for maximum participation increases people's sense of inclusion in the process as well as a sense of choice and ownership about the situation. For example, involving participants in the decision about the pace of a trip can help ensure that it will be a comfortable pace for everyone. The leader must choose the combination of leadership style and decision-making method that maximizes participant involvement while not compromising safety.

Part of the judgment and decision-making process includes knowing what leadership style best fits the situation. Leading with authenticity and caring or using the ethic of care allows leaders to use different leadership styles, such as democratic, authoritarian, collaborative, consensus, feminist, and laissez-faire styles, as situations dictate the need. A leader might tell group members what to do in an emergency situation, using an authoritarian style. When we use an authoritarian style of leadership during an emergency situation, we do so because we care about the safety of the participants. Because of the relationship building we have done during the experience, the participants usually know that we care about and respect them and that a certain style of leadership is called for in the current situation. A leader might let the group members decide what peak to climb, using a democratic style. The leader might decide to cook for the group or clean up their dishes because they had a particularly difficult day, using a servant leadership style. Or, a leader might decide to do nothing at all, using the power of the experience to teach a lesson.

Leaders use their judgment when choosing the decision-making method as well as when making decisions. Leaders who can be transparent about their decisions and the circumstances that have influenced their judgment can help participants gain decision-making and judgment skills.

Judgment

To successfully navigate their responsibilities, leaders are constantly receiving and processing information and make many judgments each day. Judgment is at the top of the list of an outdoor leader's most necessary competencies. To make good judgments, a leader must have abilities in several areas. Researchers have published several lists of behavioral traps, and a compilation follows. Many of them will probably sound familiar to you since they are often witnessed in everyday life, as well as on outdoor expeditions (Cross and Guyer 1980). They are:

- **Time differential traps:** Benefits in the present outweigh long-term consequences, for example ignoring social problems within the group which may lead to group noncohesion versus dealing with the problem when it occurs.

- **Investment trap:** Investment of time, money, effort, or other resources lead people to make choices they would not otherwise make. For example, the time and effort put into the approach of a peak influences the decision to go forward in the face of uncertain weather or to climb past the turnaround time set by group leaders. The turnaround time is set to counteract the investment trap when the party is more removed from the moment and good judgment prevails. You can set limits for virtually any situation.

- **Ignorance trap:** Information that could prevent an unwanted situation is not known or understood or foreseen at the time a decision is made. For example, there could be a dangerous rock just ready to release 500 feet over your head that you just plain do not know about until it comes down. Anticipation and prior planning can do a lot to prevent the situations arising from ignorance traps by, for example, not traveling under cliffs where there could be potential loose rocks.

- **Variable needs trap:** This trap is similar to the investment trap except that it changes over time like an addiction. For example, an adrenaline addict may take more and more chances in order to keep from feeling the symptoms of withdrawal or boredom.

Mitten and Clement

- **Egocentricity trap:** The pursuit of individual self-interest results in adverse consequences for the collective. For outdoor leaders, this trap may also be viewed as the antithesis of the well-known criterion of good leadership, selflessness. Leaders would seem selfish if they wanted to proceed with an activity without due regard for the needs or desires of the rest of the group.

Behavioral traps can be harmful because they give permission to act in a destructive manner, but they also can be beneficial by trapping people into positive behavior like doing sit-ups or running even though there are other things you would rather be doing because of the investment you've already put into your routine.

Second, leaders need enough experience in the field and knowledge of various environmental conditions and activities to be able to make informed decisions. Without the proper knowledge about an activity or the environment in which the activity takes place, leaders may make poor judgments not because of lack of ability or ignoble intentions but simply because they did not have adequate knowledge. Leaders must do their research into climate, terrain (which includes geology and map study), and natural history and seek local knowledge where possible. With this information, leaders can make informed decisions on the likely weather they will encounter, the terrain and the likely traveling conditions they will encounter, and the animals and plants they will likely encounter.

In addition, local people are usually more than happy to share their information, especially if you present yourself as someone who will take care of the area and treat it with respect. This said, be aware of *sandbagging*, when local people give advice on rock climbing, hiking, or boating routes that will take you to areas that may be too difficult to negotiate. Sandbagging occurs when locals feel their areas are being encroached upon by out-of-towners and they want to retaliate by giving misinformation.

Finally, leaders need to practice making decisions first during the learning process by watching other leaders and assessing decisions made by other leaders and then as an assistant under the tutelage of a more experienced leader. A leader in training can shadow an experienced leader on a ropes course or other adventure activity; shadowing involves watching the leader closely, taking notes on the experience, and responding to reflective questions about the leader's leadership. The leader in training learns from watching without having leadership duties.

Another training method is the leader of the day (LOD) format, where the instructors of an activity give the responsibility of route selection, camping location, and other daily decisions to a participant or a team of participants for a day. The leaders are there to intervene if the LOD makes a decision that may lead to trouble, although leaders should not intervene too early in the process because some great advances in leadership training are made if there is some struggle. There is usually a debriefing period at the end of the day to give feedback to

Experience and knowledge will help you make good decisions.

the LOD. Additionally, decision journals wherein participants write about their decisions or analyze others' decisions can be very effective. Note that even experienced leaders make mistakes, and following the steps just described will not guarantee that a person will always make good decisions. Additionally, an appropriate decision still may result in an accident or misadventure. To compensate for the occasional poor decision or unexpected circumstance, a leader should have several options for different courses of action.

Judgment training can be found at many outdoor schools, including National Outdoor Leadership School (NOLS), Outdoor Leadership Training Seminars (OLTS), Outward Bound, Passages Northwest, and the Wilderness Education Association (WEA), and we strongly suggest you get the appropriate instruction and training before engaging in professional leadership.

Decision Making in Different Types of Activities

The type of trip or experience that leaders create for group members can vary greatly in adventure education. Trips can range from short excursions to several months in length, and experiences can even be one activity lasting 20 minutes. Trips vary widely in purpose, and the way a person leads and makes decisions is directly tied to the purpose.

Take, for instance, two different trips, both lasting one month. One trip is to climb Denali (Mount McKinley) in Denali National Park. The other is to teach leadership and facilitation skills and includes a peak climb as part of the overall curriculum. Both trips have the same skill requirements and both trips cost the same. One day a student tells you that his knee is hurting and you determine that he cannot fully participate in the activity. Your next move depends on the purpose and goals of the trip, combined with safety considerations.

For the Denali climbing trip, you likely would say "Sorry Fred, you'll have to stay in camp today and miss the summit." Fred, of course, might take issue with your decision, but your obligation is to keep him safe and continue with the goal of the trip, which is to climb the mountain. On the other hand, on the outdoor education trip where the main purpose is to develop leadership and facilitation skills, you might say to the group members, "OK, Fred's knee is hurting today—what should we do about it?" Through a consensus-building process, the group members might decide to distribute the weight Fred is carrying between the able group members, forego the summit, and hike the rest of the day slowly to camp. Similar circumstances are handled differently depending on the purpose of your outing.

For technical or activity-based trips with a single purpose or focus, such as a technical experience like climbing a peak or a cultural experience like photographing flora and fauna, decision making tends to be less ambiguous. This type of leadership is fairly straightforward in that you have clear goals—always consider safety, complete your route or itinerary if it's safe to do so, make sure your clients' physical and emotional needs are met, and complete other duties (such as teaching natural history, for example) as assigned. If a person cannot make the route and there are others who can continue the trip and desire to do so, you are obligated, unless other arrangements had been made, to leave that person in camp with the proper safety measures in place or, if possible, evacuate.

Adventure experiences that are more instructional in nature can be challenging because usually you are both the instructor and the group leader, and occasionally there is a conflict between what is best for instruction and what group members see as the trip's goal or purpose. Sometimes it is hard to determine how far to let experiential learning go before stepping in and giving more information. We don't want to step in too soon or too late. For example, your group, led by a student team, is heading into an area you know to be full of cliffs that are just under the height of your map's contour interval so that they do not show up on the map. You know it now will take twice as long to complete the hike, and you had lessons planned for the afternoon on how to interpret the fine points of contour lines. You have to decide whether the lessons learned from your students struggling to negotiate the terrain are more important than the lesson you have planned. Factors to consider include the following:

- Time—Is there enough time left in the course to cover the remaining material?
- Skill—Is your group well functioning and skilled enough to succeed in their endeavor?
- Energy—What is the energy level of your group members? Are there folks who are at the edge of their physical tolerance?
- Safety—Is the terrain too difficult to be traveled through safely?

- Learning—What do you want to teach the group members? If you let them flounder in a potentially unsafe area, what are they learning and what will they replicate when they leave your trip?

If you decide to let nature teach your lesson, then watch for safety considerations and let nature work its magic. You will get questions such as "Is this route OK?" or "Should we go to the right or to the left here?" You should answer directly and simply say something like, "I think it is safe for you as a group to make this decision. Work with all the information you see in the landforms and with all the information on your maps to make your decision. I will stop you if you are entering a situation where safety is compromised." If the lesson is valuable and not dangerous, stay the course since it may turn out to be a powerful learning experience.

Therapeutic experiences require additional specialized leadership because of the needs of the clientele. The right environment and activity level can enhance therapeutic programming greatly, and the wrong activity level and environment can render therapeutic programming almost useless or even harmful.

These categories are not exhaustive and can overlap. Adventure education leaders have a great deal of responsibility regardless of whether they are paid or volunteer. One common message we hear from former students in college outdoor education programs is that in their first paid position they were expected to run a ropes course, a climbing wall, or an adventure trip without a great deal of help on specific details. You will be expected to be prepared to lead in many different types of adventure experiences.

Defining Leadership Responsibilities

In adventure activities, although the specific purposes of the trips can vary, an overarching purpose is to provide a space where people can grow, develop, and learn healthy relationship skills. To accomplish this, leaders have certain responsibilities. There may be activity skills to teach, such as spotting techniques, knot tying, tent or tarp pitching, stove use, and cooking. At the same time, leaders are assessing group members' emotional states

© Photodisc

Leaders know when it's appropriate to let nature do the teaching.

CAREERS IN ADVENTURE

NAME: Marian Marbury

JOB: President, Adventures in Good Company, Inc. (Baltimore, Maryland)

BACKGROUND: BS in health sciences from Johns Hopkins University; MS and ScD in Epidemiology from Harvard School of Public Health; guided for Woodswomen 1988 to 1999, Pacific Crest Outward Bound 1993 to 1994, and Wilderness Inquiry 1995 (As you can imagine, my degrees have not been useful other than making WFR courses easier and helping to develop excellent analytical skills.)

WHAT'S YOUR JOB LIKE? I guide 8 to 10 trips a year, develop new trip itineraries, hire and train new guides, work with marketing and public relations, do accounting, and supervise all other aspects, including logistics and administration.

One of the things I love the most about my job is that each day is usually different. For example, some days I'll focus on marketing, while other days I'll work on logistics and making sure guides have all the information and equipment they need for a trip. I spend about three months a year guiding trips, which is my first love. Owning the company allows me to guide as much as I want and also have a stable home life. The small size of the company is both the biggest challenge and a great pleasure. The challenge is that there is always more to do than can be done, and there are always too many balls in the air. The pleasure is the personal relationships I develop with the women who travel with us, my guides, and the other companies we work with.

Essential skills for both guiding and running a small company include excellent organizational and analytical skills, skill at managing interpersonal conflicts, technical skills in several different areas, and a large amount of personal experience in the outdoors. But equally important as skills are character traits. These include patience, flexibility, an ability to evaluate your performance without being overly self-critical, a good sense of what is important, a genuine interest in hearing the stories of other people, and the ability to laugh. And especially important for any small business owner, you need a passion for what you do.

and needs and watching weather systems. In this section we will talk about five major areas in which the responsible leader must be competent.

Leading the Group

Leaders have the responsibility to be aware of the different leadership techniques and styles available to them. Leaders should know and understand leadership theory, as well as critically examine biases they may have about leadership. Specifically, leaders should understand the basic leadership styles, including authoritative, collaborative, consensus, democratic, feminist, and laissez-faire styles. Leaders need to assess the strengths, weaknesses, and appropriate situational uses of each and how group members typically react in different situations. Leaders should understand how to use appreciative inquiry and critical-thinking skills in their leadership. Armed with this information, leaders will be less likely to be surprised by novel situations.

In leading a group of people, an important skill for leaders is to be flexible in their approach. For example, while we believe that adventure educators should model and strive for collaborative leadership as much as possible, there are times when other leadership styles are necessary. In situations of high risk or in an emergency, authoritative or autocratic leadership often is appropriate, and when it is late in the day and everyone is tired and hungry, consensus probably would not be the best kind of leadership or decision-making method to use in deciding what to have for dinner.

Leading Toward Goals

Leaders are responsible for motivating and influencing the group members to accomplish both program goals and individual goals. This means ensuring that everyone understands the program goals and helping participants to clarify their individual goals. This clarification is a process and most likely cannot be fully completed at the beginning of a program. As the program unfolds, participants can more clearly see the possibilities and limitations and better determine their goals.

At the same time, leaders have a responsibility to maintain a certain amount of detachment from the outcome for each individual and for the group. In other words, leaders should not have preset agendas for participants' growth. Leading toward the goal in this context means monitoring and selectively intervening or not intervening to help reinforce positive progression of group development. It also means bringing group members back to the task without making task completion or completion in a specific manner the only measure of success. In fact, on a low element the idea is for leaders to use activities as tools rather than for the activity to be an end in itself.

Knowing the Area

Leaders have the responsibility to be well acquainted with the area in which they are leading. Leaders need to know the environmental and cultural aspects of an area, emergency facilities available, fastest and safest emergency exit routes, locations of water, and other information germane to that particular program or area. Successful leaders project a genuine feeling of comfort and ease in a variety of environments, whether on a ropes course or outdoors.

To gain knowledge of the facility or the area usually requires that the leader actually travel in the area before the trip—perhaps as an assistant leader or as a personal traveler. If a leader has traveled, say, in the Boundary Waters Canoe Area Wilderness (BWCAW) several times and feels comfortable in the area, it may work for her to lead a group on a different route but still in the BWCAW. In the case of a challenge course, even if a leader has done the wall activity before, if he is doing the activity at a different facility it is important to check out the wall at that facility.

There is an exception to the leader having traveled in an area before taking a group of people there. If a trip is billed as an exploratory trip with the leaders having the skills to safely complete the trip, then the leader may not have traveled in that specific area. This sort of exploratory trip is a special kind of adventure that, for some people, is the learning edge they seek.

Conveying Information About the Natural Environment

Many adventure programs take place out of doors and leaders have the responsibility to know about the natural environment, including common weather systems, flora, fauna, and geology. Wherever or whatever the activity, leaders have the responsibility to know how to convey natural and cultural history information of these environments and prevent environmental damage. For example, you should practice Leave No Trace techniques for the area.

Some adventure programs have been criticized for using the environment but not protecting or appreciating it. Appreciating natural beauty and the environment includes appreciating biodiversity, using state-of-the-art low trace traveling and camping techniques, discouraging conquering or adversarial attitudes and language, and working with the challenges that inevitably come up when traveling in the outdoors with good cheer and resourcefulness. Using the outdoors as a testing ground is inconsistent with fostering respectful and comfortable connections with nature.

Leaders also have the responsibility to convey cultural information to participants. If a leader is traveling in the Four Corners region of the southwestern United States, being able to impart knowledge about the peoples who lived there before Europeans came to the United States is important. If a group of people are canoeing on the Muskegon River, knowing the human history of the river connects them to a world larger than themselves. Leaders have the responsibility to act ethically and with sensitivity to both the human community and the biosphere and help participants to understand, thrive in, and enhance our world community and environment.

Modeling Positive Behavior

Participants watch their leaders. They take cues from their leaders, and leaders have the responsibility of continuously modeling positive expedition behavior whether they are facilitating a 10-minute adventure education activity or traveling on a six-week trip with clients. According to Jean Clarke (1984), people make lasting opinions about a program based on their first 3 minutes of contact with the leader. People feel an affinity with leaders who tend to like and trust rather than fear other people and who have the ability to establish warm relationships.

"Leaders are always the big kids" is a saying we use in leadership training. What does that mean? Leaders need to remain steady, mature, ethical, and available. Leaders avoid being defensive and entering into useless power plays. Especially on trips, leaders take up the slack. This means that if everyone is too exhausted to check the canoes when a wind comes up, the leader does it. If everyone is too tired to realize they need to drink water, the leader reminds them and helps make it happen.

Another aspect of being the "big kid" is not to compare groups or talk about other participants. Common questions include "Are we the fastest group to complete this task?" and "Are we as good as other groups?" It may be hard to dodge these questions, but it is definitely in the participants' best interests not to compare them or their group with others. The process is what the current participants learn. In this situation, they learn that if the leader talks about others, then he'll talk about them. As leaders, we have a responsibility to model not talking about others.

Being excellent does not mean being perfect. Leaders should strive for excellence and should do an excellent job in completing their duties. As human beings we will never be perfect, even though we may be very, very good. If we strive for perfection in ourselves, we will unrealistically expect perfection in others. This expectation leads to disappointment, frustration, and poor relationship potential. It doesn't allow us to see that there are many ways to complete tasks. Knowing the difference between being excellent and being perfect is an important responsibility.

Summary

Leadership of adventure activities is a complicated task requiring skills in a variety of disciplines and competency in responsible, effective, and psychological leadership functions. Adventure leaders must achieve a high degree of proficiency in four major areas: activity and technical skills, teaching and modeling skills, group process skills, and decision-making and judgment skills. Each of these areas is essential to quality leadership, and one is not necessarily more important than the others.

In this chapter, we have covered the main points concerning the responsibilities and skills that competent adventure leaders need. However, no amount of reading can replace the experience and nuances of the leadership skills gained by getting out there and doing the job of a leader. Even being the second in command has a different feel than being the person in charge, so find opportunities to lead whenever and wherever you can.

Review Questions

1. In the responsible leader position, describe your role in making decisions regarding safety of the group members as you determine whether or not to paddle in a moderate wind in a coastal region.

2. Describe a specific process an outdoor leader might use to gain technical skills involving technology, such as GPS use.

3. List four or five reasons why the power differences already present between leader and participant are accentuated in adventure settings. Describe how you could actively mitigate this difference for at least two of the reasons you gave.

4. Describe what it means to be mindful of the goal and process but not focused on the outcome. Provide a concrete example from your life experiences.

5. Describe how a leader modeling healthy relationships is likely to contribute to healthy group cohesion. Then describe the similarities between modeling healthy relationships with people and modeling a healthy relationship with the environment.

Student Learning Activities

1. Know how far to go to make your lesson powerful. As mentioned, leaders walk a fine line when it comes to knowing when an experience ceases being good education and becomes dangerous either in a physical, emotional, or spiritual sense. How do you know when you are about to go too far? Here is a group activity to help you think about these issues. (a) Working alone, think about past situations you have been in where people in your life have gone too far to make a point or crossed a boundary during an activity that resulted in an injury or a near-miss. (b) Again think about past situations where people in your life have not gone far enough to make a point or fell short of the mark during an activity that resulted in a missed opportunity for growth. (c) Write down at least one situation in each area that you can share with your class. (d) Finally, get back together as a large group (maybe 15 to 20 maximum) or a small group of 3 or 4 and share your situations and then look for commonalities and differences between your situations. What conclusions can you draw from this exercise about making lessons powerful without going too far?

2. Talk about a time when you replicated a process that you experienced (parallel process). Perform a skit or role play three very different ways you, as a leader, could demonstrate caring, respect, and nurturing.

3. Think back to adventure activities in which you have participated. Remember times when you were being an effective or psychological leader or when you saw others being an effective or psychological leader.

4. Create a résumé that addresses the four major skill areas that leaders need: proficiency in activity and technical skills, ability to teach well and use interpersonal skills, ability to model appropriate behavior and healthy relationship skills, and solid experience and judgment skills. Be sure to include a section that lists the trips in which you have participated, their duration, the activity, and your role.

5. Think of four different times when you or someone else made a comment that helped set the tone for a program. Write down several attitudes or norms that you would like group members to have during your program. Then write down several comments that you could intentionally make at the beginning of a program to set a tone for these attitudes.

CHAPTER 7

Facilitating the Adventure Process

Michael A. Gass and Cheryl A. Stevens

> " A leader is best when people barely know he exists, not so good when people obey and acclaim him, worse when they despise him. . . . But of a good leader who talks little when his work is done, his aim fulfilled, they will say, "We did it ourselves. "
>
> —Lao Tzu

Chapter Concepts

- To date, eight generations of adventure facilitation have evolved. Beginning and intermediate adventure facilitators most commonly use two of these generations: debriefing and direct frontloading.

- The adventure leader's facilitation style should be driven by the primary goal of the adventure program and the clients' needs, such as age, maturity, prior experience, education, and level of motivation. Facilitation style is also chosen based on the situation, client readiness and abilities, and facilitator skills and experience. However, in order to maximize client outcomes, the clients' needs must be the primary consideration in choosing facilitation and reflection strategies.

- The 10 facilitation guidelines should be followed in all adventure programs. Tips and techniques to keep your facilitation client centered are covered on page 116.

- There are two main ways to facilitate reflection. The first includes debriefing and discussions (e.g., funneling, frontloading, or empowering the clients to self-facilitate), and the second includes alternative reflections and nonverbal methods (e.g., art, drama, photography, or journaling).

- During debriefings and discussions, follow discussion dos and don'ts to ensure that verbal discussions are as beneficial as possible. The funneling process helps facilitators guide clients through the cognitive process of reflecting.

- By teaching clients to apply funneling techniques themselves, they can use these techniques to self-facilitate, and they can continue learning from the adventure experience long after it is over.

- Use of alternative reflection methods, such as journaling, drama, or photography, can help groups learn more about the diverse talents of their team members and help participants who are reluctant to speak to be seen in a new light by their team. When you use alternative methods, you have a variety of options for different levels of ability and maturity.

- Evaluation and follow-up are often overlooked but are critical for ensuring the transfer of client outcomes back to everyday environments. Action planning can provide the clients with a tool to use back home. When the opportunity presents itself, adventure facilitators can schedule follow-up sessions or additional programs to assist the clients with learning transfer.

The word *facilitate* means to make easier, smooth the progress of, and assist in guiding a group toward achieving their goal. The process of **facilitation** covers everything the adventure program leader does before, during, and after the adventure experience to enhance the client's reflection, integration, and continuation of lasting change (Priest, Gass, and Gillis 2000). The facilitator's ultimate goal can be best expressed in Lao Tzu's narrative on leadership as stated at the opening of this chapter: If you are a good facilitator, your clients will accomplish their tasks and objectives themselves.

Many important facilitation skills have already been covered in chapters 3, 5, and 6. For example, you have learned about cornerstones of adventure programming (e.g., challenge by choice, full-value contract, and the experiential learning cycle), skills for adventure activities (e.g., flexible leadership, assessing groups, and group process), and goal setting (e.g., goals for participants and leaders and appropriate sequencing).

The purpose of this chapter is to present different models of facilitation that may provide structures for you to use in your facilitation process. To date, eight generations of facilitation have been identified. All eight generations will be introduced, and the techniques and tools appropriate for use by beginning and intermediate facilitators will be covered in depth. As you learn how to facilitate, you will also learn how to maintain a student-centered focus in your adventure programs so that when your clients are finished they will feel as though they did it themselves.

Eight Generations of Facilitation

Adventure facilitation has evolved over the years, with earlier styles often fostering the growth of the more recent ones (Bacon 1987; Doughty 1991; Itin 1995; Itin and Bandoroff 2001; Priest and Gass 2005; Priest, Gass, and Fitzpatrick 1999). The eight generations of facilitation are categorized in order of evolutionary development as follows:

1. Letting the experience speak for itself—learning by doing
2. Speaking on behalf of the experience—learning by telling
3. Debriefing the experience—learning through reflection
4. Directly frontloading the experience—direction with reflection
5. Isomorphically framing the experience—reinforcement with reflection
6. Indirectly frontloading the experience—indirect reinforcement in reflection
7. Flagging the experience—unconscious reinforcement in reflection
8. Empowering clients to self-facilitate—coaching and reflection

The first three generations are used after an activity to bring about change, while the next four generations are used by the facilitator before, during, and after the adventure program to bring about change. Self-facilitation, the last generation, is similar but is used by the clients themselves.

Over time, two major philosophical shifts have occurred in the way adventure leaders facilitate. The three earliest generations of facilitation are all similar in that they are used *after* an activity. The first shift occurred when facilitators began consciously applying techniques *before, during, and after* the adventure program. This grouping includes the next four generations, frontloading through flagging. In these styles the experience itself is used as a medium for change through application of the various facilitation methods. The second philosophical shift is to client self-facilitation. In this most recent style, the experience is still the medium for change, but it has the added feature of having the clients, rather than the facilitator, taking on greater responsibility regarding reflection.

1. Letting the Experience Speak for Itself

The first generation of facilitation can be found in recreational adventure programs where clients are simply left to glean their own personal insights from the experience without any formal guidance from the facilitator (Doughty 1991). When adventure programs are properly sequenced and well-designed, adventure activities often lead clients to their own insights and personal discoveries. Participants will learn by doing. Clients in these types of programs often gain new skills, but they are less likely to gain personal insights, enhance relationships, or resolve life issues because they may not reflect on their adventure experiences in meaningful ways. When you use this first generation of facilitation, you refrain from adding insights during or after the activities, and if you make any comments at all, they probably refer to how much fun the experience was and encourage the group to move on to new levels in the activity.

2. Speaking on Behalf of the Experience

This second generation of facilitation evolved in response to a perception that clients would benefit from assistance in understanding what their adventure experiences could mean to them. The facilitator, in the role of an expert, interprets the experience for the clients by informing them of what they learned, giving direct feedback, and telling them how they can apply their new knowledge in future situations. When you use the second generation of facilitation, at the completion of the activity you provide the group with feedback about their behaviors. For example, you tell them what they did well, where they could improve, what they learned from the experience, and how they could apply this knowledge in the future. Also, you might describe for them which behaviors are functional and which behaviors are detracting from the group's success.

While this approach can be appropriate for new or dysfunctional groups, role-playing, and simulations (where there is a need to give clients accurate information and feedback), it is less appropriate in other situations because it tends to invalidate the clients' roles in processing their experiences. When you use learning by telling, you risk invalidating and alienating the participants, disconnecting yourself from them, and limiting your ability to facilitate further learning opportunities with that group. Therefore, when you use this facilitation strategy, make sure you are trained and experienced enough to know the correct information to tell the clients.

3. Debriefing the Experience

The third generation of facilitation, learning through reflection, evolved to resolve the potential problem of client disconnection that results from telling. When using debriefing, the facilitator guides client learning in a supportive role to help the group discover their own learning through goal setting, questions and answers, and guided reflection after each adventure activity and the total experience. The most typical debriefing when using this style of facilitation is guided verbal group discussion where the facilitator asks open-ended questions and encourages clients to respond. Nonverbal reflection methods such as poetry, art, drama, and music are also appropriate. A group discussion in learning by reflection often includes questions modeled after the following: What happened? What impact did this have? How did that make you feel? What did you learn from this? What parts of this activity were similar to other areas in your life (or school or workplace)? Given this information, what can you do differently in the future?

4. Directly Frontloading the Experience

The fourth generation of facilitation creates a way for clients to learn throughout the adventure experience rather than learning just during reflection at the end of each activity. **Frontloading** refers to specifically highlighting the learning that is to take place before, or in front of, each adventure activity. When frontloading, the facilitator engages the clients in a **briefing** discussion during which the following points are discussed:

- **Revisit:** What behaviors or performances were promised and learned from the last activity?
- **Objectives:** What are the aims of the activity and what can be learned or gained from it?
- **Motivations:** Why might experiencing this activity be important and how does it relate to everyday life?

Most beginning adventure facilitators first learn to guide client reflection by using verbal debriefing, asking open-ended questions and encouraging clients to respond.

- **Function:** What behaviors will help bring about success and how can the group optimize these behaviors?
- **Dysfunction:** What behaviors will keep the group from success and how can the group overcome or avoid these barriers?

In frontloading, before the activity begins, the facilitator focuses the participants on distinct learning outcomes that they have codetermined as valuable so the participants can be thinking about these outcomes during the activity. Since the frontloaded briefing has already covered many of the topics that are usually covered in debriefing, the facilitator can focus postactivity discussion on changes the participants wish to make in order to achieve their goals, using information from the frontloading discussion that has already taken place.

5. Isomorphically Framing the Experience

A fifth generation of facilitation, which has origins in the work of Milton Erickson, involves facilitators using metaphoric connections in the adventure experience to enhance clients' abilities to apply learning to their lives. Facilitators need a good understanding of client needs and history in order to use metaphors in this manner. Well-chosen parallel metaphoric structures can add depth to the learning experience and encourage clients to make strong connections between the experience and everyday life. For example, if you decide to use the word *relationship* to describe a canoe, you could be creating an isomorphic (i.e., same-structure connection) between the physical skills of tandem paddling to the dynamics of living with a partner. If you frame the activity in this manner, you create a mirror image of how the adventure experience may match the change desired in daily living between the two people in this relationship.

For framing to be effective, isomorphs need to be directly related to client needs and program goals. In order for this to occur, isomorphs must be based on the proper assessment of client needs. Isomorphic framing can fail when facilitators bring their own favorite frame or interpretation to the adventure experience and the frame makes sense in the facilitator's reality but not the client's. When frames are based on a sound understanding of client issues, are well matched, and are cocreated by the client and facilitator, they can be very successful. The transfer of learning also tends to be effective since the dynamics and processes of the two experiences will be similar. As with frontloading, debriefing afterward tends to reinforce

learning rather than lead to a discovery of the learning itself. Debriefing in this facilitation style becomes reinforcement in reflection because the clients will discuss the close similarities between the frame and their experience and see the obvious connections for themselves. For example, clients think, "If a strategy works here, I can see how it will work in my life as well."

6. Indirectly Frontloading the Experience

The sixth generation of facilitation involves using facilitator-created, indirect frontloading to indirectly address clients' issues. Indirect frontloading can take several paradoxical forms, such as double binding (e.g., win–win frames), symptom prescription, symptom displacement, illusion of alternatives, and proactive reframing (Waltzlawick 1978). This method is primarily used in therapeutic programs and should be used only when the facilitator has advanced training. Effective facilitators use this style only in very specific therapeutic situations: when it is in the clients' best interests and when the goal is to address continual problematic issues.

To ethically use indirect frontloading, you must be skilled at understanding client needs and have training appropriate to program goals (e.g., therapeutic or organizational development) to ensure that you are doing good rather than harm. An example of when indirect frontloading could help is when the more a client tries to eliminate an unwanted issue, the more it occurs, or the more a client tries to attain the result, the more elusive that result becomes. When used appropriately, indirect approaches can work in the clients' best interests because direct confrontation approaches produce such a high degree of resistance that it is difficult for the clients to obtain their learning objectives.

7. Flagging the Experience

The seventh generation of facilitation, flagging the experience, was described by Itin (1995) and Itin and Bandoroff (2001). The facilitator uses hypnotic language to flag the experience, which purposefully absorbs the clients in the natural trance state that often develops when they are dealing with adventure risk activities. As clients become absorbed in the adventure activities, the hypnotic language helps them use the adventure process to access untapped resources of the unconscious mind. Itin states, "Clients are 'more open to learning at a conscious and unconscious level'" because the facilitator can speak directly to the client's unconscious and encourage healthy actions (1995, p. 70). This allows the facilitator to support a healthy change by making it easier for clients to create the change they themselves desire.

Ethical application of this method includes involving the client in goal setting, supporting healthy change, and accurately assessing needs. In addition, facilitators must be trained in the use of hypnotic language. When facilitating in this style, you will tailor activities to each person's needs, and the therapeutic or developmental goal must be formed in partnership with the client or at minimum must be an agreed-upon goal formed by the treatment team in charge of the client's program.

8. Empowering Clients to Self-Facilitate

The eighth generation builds primarily on the first, third, and fourth generations. Client **self-facilitation** involves more mature learners as facilitators in their own experiences. Self-facilitation is necessarily limited to motivated, mature, and capable clients (Priest et al. 1999). When using this approach, the facilitator teaches the group how to use reflection techniques such as debriefing, frontloading, and funneling. The facilitator then assumes the role of coach and assists the clients while they apply these techniques for themselves. In this way, the facilitator and clients work together to cultivate learning from the adventure experiences.

Self-facilitation retains the advantage of making the experience itself a medium for learning (as in the fourth through seventh generations), and returns to having the clients guide their own reflection (as in the first generation), but it has the added bonus of guidance and coaching from the facilitator, who ensures that structured reflection occurs. This facilitation method has two distinct advantages: clients can use their new facilitation skills to foster continued growth after returning home, and clients can focus on what is most relevant to them, which minimizes the need for the facilitator to make assumptions about what clients need while maximizing client responsibility for their own learning.

Selecting a Facilitation Model

Each type of adventure program has different primary goals, and thus certain styles of facilitation tend to be more appropriate or more commonly used with certain types of programs. The primary goal of the program you work for, as well as your skills and comfort level, should determine the facilitation styles you choose.

With self-facilitation, clients can focus on what is most relevant to them.

- In *recreational adventure programs,* when having fun, learning new skills, and being entertained is the purpose, the first and second generations of facilitation tend to be the most appropriate.

- In *educational adventure programs,* when learning is expected, such as understanding new concepts, enriching knowledge of prior concepts, and generating new awareness, the third and eighth generations are the most commonly used methods.

- In *developmental adventure programs,* when improving functional behaviors and training clients in new and different behaviors is the purpose, the third, fourth, fifth, and eighth generations appear to be the best fit.

- In *therapeutic adventure programs,* when changes in metaprocesses—behaviors, cognitions, and unconscious processes that impede or support therapeutic change—is the purpose, the fifth, sixth, and seventh generations are commonly used.

Note that although developmental and therapeutic programs are both directed at changing behaviors, the nature of the clientele is typically different (Itin and Bandoroff 2001). Facilitators who work with therapeutic adventure programs require advanced facilitation skills and often have additional training in psychotherapy. Developmental programs, on the other hand, are typically aimed at corporate clients and youth groups, so while an accurate understanding of clients' needs is important, therapeutic training may not be necessary when the facilitator stays clear of therapeutic goals.

Developing a Client-Centered Facilitation Style

Much like situational leadership, where leaders match their style to the groups' readiness and abilities (Blanchard and Hersey 1996), the adventure facilitator should choose a facilitation style based on the situation, clients' readiness and abilities, and facilitators' skills and experience level. For adventure programs to obtain the best outcomes, clients' needs must be the focus for guiding reflection on adventure experiences. The need for **client-centered reflection** on experience is deeply embedded with experiential education paradigms, and the principles of the AEE leave little doubt as to the client's role in reflection, stating that

"throughout the experiential learning process, the *learner* [italics added] is actively engaged in posing questions, investigating, experimenting, being curious, solving problems, assuming responsibility, being creative, and constructing meaning" (Association for Experiential Education [AEE] 2004b). However, there can be inconsistencies between what adventure education claims to value (client-centered learning) and how adventure education is delivered in practice (facilitator-centered learning) (Estes 2004).

The eight generations of facilitation can be traced through an evolution from a client-centered approach (first generation), to a more facilitator-centered approach (second generation), to a shared approach (third and fourth generations), to a continuum of increasingly therapeutic approaches (fifth, sixth, and seventh generations), and finally to a synthesis and more client-centered approach (eighth generation). The earliest generation, letting the experience speak for itself, tends to be client-centered. When using this technique, the facilitator exerts little, if any, intentional influence over what clients learn from reflection on experiences. However, the facilitator's selection of experiences and direction of client focus during the experience will influence what clients reflect on, even though the clients' reflection is not guided by the facilitator. Therefore, when using the first generation, the facilitator needs to take the program's goals and clients' needs into account when selecting and conducting adventure experiences.

The second generation, speaking on behalf of the experience, is less client centered by nature, but it is appropriate in some situations. When using this style, the facilitator tells the clients what they learned or gives direct feedback about what they need to learn, thus choosing the content of the guided reflection. This generation works best when clients are less mature and have a high need for direct information and feedback. To the degree the facilitator is knowledgeable about what clients need to know, this style may be most appropriate. To avoid a major pitfall of learning by telling—alienating clients—don't make assumptions about what clients need when you lack information or appropriate training and experience to assess those needs.

The third and fourth generations (debriefing and direct frontloading) take the middle ground between the first two generations. In the third and fourth generations, potential exists for sharing client and facilitator roles during reflection. Facilitators influence how client centered the debriefing is through their choices for reflection and their communication strategies. Tips and techniques for maintaining student-centered third and fourth generation facilitation are covered later in this chapter.

The fifth through eighth generations are considered more advanced facilitation styles appropriate for facilitators with more experience, maturity, and training. The fifth through seventh generations have origins in therapeutic practice, with increasing emphasis on knowledge of therapeutic technique required when the facilitator uses the higher levels. These generations can be very client centered when the facilitator is skilled enough to hear clients' stories and work with them to develop healthier approaches to life's challenges.

These later generations also have the potential to be misused by facilitators who are not skilled or experienced enough to tune into clients' stories and instead place their own frames and interpretations on clients, thus risking a mismatch between frame choice and clients' needs. The eighth generation provides the experienced facilitator with strategies for involving more mature clients directly in the learning process throughout the adventure experience. This can result in very client-centered reflection and extend the potential for continued growth beyond the adventure experience because the clients have learned to guide their own reflection processes.

While the most experienced facilitators have matured over time and are able to conduct client-centered programs, it is often more difficult for younger facilitators with less training and life experience (Estes 2004). This may be due to the combined effects of information overload (new facilitators get a heavy load of information and rules) as well as to a Westernized educational background, which teaches that facilitators are supposed to be in-charge authorities (Estes 2004). The third and fourth generations tend to work best for facilitators early in their training because these generations are easier to learn and manage. As facilitators gain experience, training, and maturity, they often find the later generations useful in helping clients meet their goals through adventure programming. Experiential learning, including adventure programming, calls for a different facilitator–student relationship than traditional authority-based classroom teaching. Fortunately, by being aware that client-centered learning is important, beginning or intermediate facilitators can apply techniques to keep programs as client centered as possible.

Facilitation and Discussion Techniques

This section covers tools and techniques you will find useful for facilitating using the first through fourth generations as well as the eighth generation. Advanced facilitation techniques for the fifth through seventh generations will not be used until the facilitator has more experience and training, so these styles will not be covered further in this book.

Facilitation Guidelines

There are 10 guidelines that are derived from the collective wisdom of experienced adventure program facilitators and can start you on the right path. Understanding fundamental factors including group position, time, single speaking, nonviolence, participation, responsibility, and other ethical issues will help you develop and refine your skills as a facilitator (taken from Priest and Gass 2005).

- **Group position** is a critical factor for effective communication, especially in outdoor settings where clients are easily distracted away from verbal communication. Group members need to be in a physical configuration that allows them to see and hear the things that are most relevant to the facilitation process, such as eye contact, facial expressions, and body language. You must gently but firmly direct your group to arrange themselves in the appropriate configuration for the task. For example, position the group in a circle where everyone can see each other. Make the circle large enough to include everyone, but don't make it too large; they will need to see and hear each other. Do not allow participants to sit out of the circle or behind each other. Try to be in the shade so no one is blinded by sunlight, but when required, you should be the one facing into the sun. Other physical configurations, such as amphitheater-style seating, half circles with two or more rows, or one circle within another, may make sense depending on what clients need to see and hear.

- **Time** is critical. You must schedule sufficient time to allow clients to reflect on experiences within the context of the overall program time. This is often a challenge since the length of time for clients to complete adventure activities is unpredictable. Plan ahead and make certain there is time for closure, even if a final event has to be stopped before completion. Do not plan to hold clients past the

Direct your group to arrange themselves in the appropriate configuration for the task.

scheduled completion time for a program unless you have their agreement ahead of time that this is acceptable. Reflection that takes place after a scheduled end time is necessarily rushed and lacks focus, so avoid falling into this habit. Match the length of reflection time to the maturity, needs, and abilities of your clients. Except when working with young children or people who are intellectually challenged, expect to spend equal amounts of time doing and discussing. Keep in mind, however, some people may not be able to sit for this long, so breaking up reflection time with activities and creative reflection exercises is beneficial.

- **Single speaking** is one way group members show respect for each other. Having one person speak at a time ensures an opportunity for each person to be heard and for every group member to hear what is being said. Many facilitators pass around a talking stick (or other object) as a symbol that only the person holding the stick should be talking.

- **Nonviolence** is a must; violence is never acceptable in any form, whether physical or emotional.

You must confront verbal put-downs immediately and redirect clients to more positive commentary as you remind them of the full-value contract.

- Clients have the **right to pass on participation** in activities or discussions (challenge by choice). In this way, they select their own path for getting involved. When a person chooses to pass, carefully consider how much gentle encouragement you or other clients provide. Take care to avoid coercive and manipulative strategies designed to make clients feel guilty for acting on their right to pass.

- Let clients know that they possess ultimate **responsibility** for their own behavior. When a client states, "So-and-so made me do it," redirect the client to a focus on personal responsibility.

- Place clients in situations where they can reasonably offer **personal commitment** to the entire facilitation process. Their basic needs for warmth, shelter, rest, and fuel (food and water) need to be reasonably met so that they can focus on the facilitation process. In outdoor settings, these basic needs are often compromised due to

CAREERS IN ADVENTURE

NAME: Sarah Fox

JOB: Assistant Director for Trips, Venture Program, University of North Carolina at Charlotte (Charlotte, North Carolina)

BACKGROUND: MS in recreation administration, East Carolina University

WHAT'S YOUR JOB LIKE? I manage the trip program and the student leaders program, which includes trip planning, staffing, logistics, and training staff to lead trips. I supervise the performance of logistics staff as well as other student leaders, supporting them in all aspects of their training. I also serve as a head instructor for team-building programs and outdoor wilderness trips, and I teach academic classes in the kinesiology department.

The best part of my job is the day-to-day interaction with students. It is important for me to be available as a resource person and to have a positive impact on the college experience of those I come in contact with. Because I am responsible for running the trip program, it is essential to have solid wilderness-trip leadership skills. My background of working with several university outdoor programs and with Outward Bound wilderness programs has prepared me well for my role with Venture. Not only must I have the physical ability to lead and teach a variety of outdoor adventure activities, I must have a working knowledge of outdoor equipment, usable course areas, and risk management. Since many of my job responsibilities require planning and foresight, organization has been the key to maintaining a successful program.

The biggest challenge has probably been managing my time so that I don't get burned out. There is a lot of freedom to bring new ideas into the program, but never enough time to incorporate all of them. Collaborating with colleagues at other universities has been a beneficial strategy for program development. There are great things happening in the world of experiential education, and it is not always necessary to reinvent the wheel; sometimes you just need to expand upon it.

inclement weather or exhaustion, and it is the facilitator's responsibility to recognize the problem and take whatever corrective action is necessary before resuming the activity.

- Ensuring **role clarity** in the group process is important. Proactively establishing your role as a facilitator and clients' roles as participants avoids confusion, such as clients asking, "Why didn't you let us know an hour ago we were going in the wrong direction?" If you are clear from the start about what you and they are there to do and not do, the tone of your program will be much more positive. When clarifying roles, it is helpful to distinguish between process and product orientation. Inform clients that reflection will focus on group dynamics rather than task outcomes. Also, you can explain the concepts of transfer and metaphor. Prompt clients to search for their own metaphors during the program.

- Promise **confidentiality** only when it can be maintained and with an understanding of its limitations. For example, you are mandated by law to report certain situations, including potential or known abuse. Often a client will state, "I want to tell you something, but you have to promise not to tell anyone." Wise facilitators will tell such clients that they will try to maintain confidentiality, but also inform them that if it involves abuse or neglect, they will be legally obligated to report it. Make certain that clients understand whether information can be shared outside the group.

- Many other **ethical issues** exist beyond confidentiality. Giving prior consideration as to how you will handle ethical concerns is critical to your preparation. Issues include, but are not limited to, conflicts of interest, sexual issues, value differences, client rights, environmental concerns, and individual versus group needs. In addition, remember that it is always unethical to facilitate beyond your training and abilities. For example, if a client discloses a psychiatric concern, don't open that conversation unless you are qualified in psychiatry; instead, refer the person to an appropriate professional. Also, don't allow groups with nontherapeutic goals to proceed down a path of analyzing the psychology of team members. You also have an ethical obligation to find out as much as you can about your clients in advance so you can assess their needs accurately and inform them about what your program can and cannot do for them. Do not attempt to facilitate using the fifth, sixth, and seventh generations if you lack training and a complete and accurate needs assessment.

Planning for Reflection and Debriefing

Planning for facilitating clients' reflection on adventure experiences starts with a thorough and correct understanding of their needs. The time and effort that you put into needs assessment will vary depending on client and program goals and program length. In recreational programs, where fun and excitement are the goal, the needs assessment should focus on clients' physical abilities so that you can plan the appropriate level of adventure challenge. For educational programs, you will want to learn about the clients' educational objectives and outcomes they hope for, in addition to learning about clients' physical abilities. When conducting developmental programs, the needs assessment becomes even more complex. Interview the person in charge of contracting for the developmental program about the goals and outcomes for the program.

Facilitators also need to find out from each participant how individual needs and goals match up with the overall developmental goals in order to arrive at the best fit for program design. One way to accomplish this is meeting with clients before the day of the experience. Shared discussion about program and individual goals and desired outcomes is a big help in planning appropriate challenges and reflection activities. If you are working in a therapeutic program, you will have access to objective, clinical client needs assessments, which you will use in planning and implementing an appropriate therapeutic program.

Once the needs assessment is complete, you will be able to choose activities and plan ideas for reflection. If you are using postactivity discussion, bring a list of open-ended questions that follow the hierarchy of the funneling process to help facilitate discussion (funneling is discussed later in this chapter; see pages 112-114). Also, consider bringing readings and materials for alternative reflection methods like paper, markers, props, or music. If several facilitators are working with one larger group that will be divided into smaller groups (e.g., 48 participants from a school are divided into four groups of 12 clients), make sure all facilitators are equally familiar with client needs, program ideas, and the reflection plan.

Of course, the best-laid plans will never exactly fit reality. Make sure you are prepared to take notes about what you observe during the activities so you can use this information during reflection. Many facilitators carry a small notebook or note cards with a pencil to keep ongoing notes about observations and ideas for reflection as the group proceeds through the adventure program.

Discussions and Debriefing

Verbal discussions are the most common form of reflection in North American adventure programs. Many programs facilitate quality reflection using the third and fourth generations. The following details will equip you with the basic knowledge needed to implement these techniques. These same techniques can be taught to clients who are mature and capable enough for guided self-facilitation. Before you continue reading, carefully review the discussion dos and don'ts in figure 7.1 for an overview of what you should and should not do.

Funneling

One time-honored method of facilitating verbal reflection is the **funneling** approach. Leaders can

Discussion Dos and Don'ts

Several dos and don'ts apply to the when and where of facilitating discussions.

Do

+ Take discussions seriously and schedule plenty of time for them. But if energy levels fall, end the discussion early.
+ Discuss often and immediately after each experience. If this is not possible, have a brief discussion afterward and save a lengthy discussion for later.
+ With most populations, spend as much time on the discussion as was spent doing the activity. If on a multiday experience, hold periodic discussions throughout each day.
+ Discuss in the activity location unless noise from running water or blowing wind interferes with hearing. The location permits clients to more readily visualize what took place and where and how it happened.
+ Pick a special place, such as a rock by a lake or the darkness of a forest, or a regular time, such as campfires or meals, for holding discussions during residential programs. This way, clients will know to concentrate on discussing at the chosen time or place.
+ Encourage clients to ask their own questions that fit the theme. This permits self-discovery, freeing you from some of the responsibility for client learning.
+ Remain alert for client metaphors and incorporate them into the discussion using client language. For example, if a client says, "I feel like a volcano," you might ask, "What kinds of eruptions have you experienced lately?"

Don't

+ Lead clients by suggesting words or finishing their sentences. Ask questions instead of offering answers.
+ Compare clients with other groups that have gone before or judge their actions as good or bad.
+ Give false feedback. Instead, avoid giving insincere praise or unwarranted criticism.
+ Assume you know what is best for clients, forcing them to change.
+ Accept only one answer as correct, since this creates a situation reminiscent of the reward and punishment mentality of institutionalized schooling. If you accept only one answer, soon you will receive only one, because clients will fear being wrong.

FIGURE 7.1 Discussion dos and don'ts.

Reprinted, by permission, from S. Priest and M.A. Gass, 2005, *Effective leadership in adventure programming*, 2nd ed. (Champaign, IL: Human Kinetics), 200.

use this process or teach it to a mature client group and coach them on applying it themselves (i.e., eighth generation). In funneling, you guide the group through a series of stages that mimic the way people make cognitive connections between what happened to them and what it means. The six steps in the debriefing funnel are an expanded version of the three questions from Gestalt therapy: What? So what? Now what? (Borton 1970).

Figure 7.2 illustrates the six filters, or types of questions that distill clients' learning changes through the process of question and answer. In a sense, you pour the experience into the broad end of the funnel, and through the filters (i.e., series of sequenced questions) you distill the essence of learning changes through client reflection and answers. The last question narrows clients' concentration toward the outcome—desired changes. The six filters are review, recall and remember, affect and effect, summation, application, and commitment.

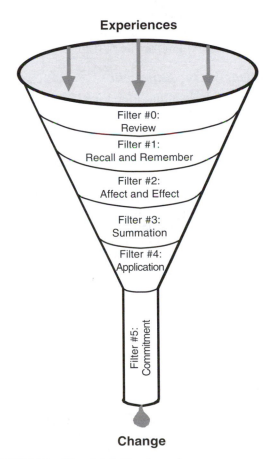

FIGURE 7.2 The debriefing funnel.

Reprinted, by permission, from S. Priest and M.A. Gass, 2005, *Effective leadership in adventure programming*, 2nd ed. (Champaign, IL: Human Kinetics), 203.

Before you begin the funneling process, you must have a thorough understanding of clients' needs. If you don't, you can easily misdirect them and may even do harm, no matter how good your intentions are. Use the notes you took during the adventure experiences to make the best choices you can about topics to debrief.

If the topic of concern is obvious from the outcome of the clients' most recent experience, then filter 0 may not be necessary. However, when you are going to use funneling to focus the clients on a topic that has not been under recent discussion, start at filter 0 to help them reconnect with the relevance of the topic. When the topic at hand is recent, start with filter 1.

Filter 0, review, refocuses the clients on the subject of interest, which you previously selected based on client needs, program objectives, and information that was evident during the activity. In this stage, you ask the group to describe a certain aspect of the experience in order to refresh their memories and get agreement on what happened. You might say, "Let's talk about conflict resolution. Can you review how your team resolved conflicts during the previous activity? On a 5-point scale, hold up the number of fingers that indicates how effective you were at resolving conflicts, with 5 being excellent." Once the group is focused on this topic, you can move to the next level.

Filter 1, recall and remember, has clients identify an incident that took place during the experience and that relates to the topic. If you brought up the topic, the group now needs to gain ownership of the topic by recalling it for themselves. If the group is reluctant to move forward by recalling the topic and describing it for themselves, you may want to switch to another topic until you learn more advanced strategies for addressing group denial. Sample questions include "Do you remember an example of excellent (or poor) conflict resolution by your team?" and "Can you recall a particular time when your team's ability to resolve conflicts was good (or bad)?"

Filter 2, affect and effect, addresses emotions and causes. Once the clients have owned the issue (filter 1), you can ask questions to assess the influence of the event on each person. At this level, you will ask each person questions such as "How did you feel?" and "How was the group influenced by the event?" At this point, the group will note positive and negative effects of behaviors, sharing feelings and noting concerns. You might ask, "What affect (emotion) did you experience? How did this make you feel? How did this emotion affect the group?

What influence did it have on the group's ability to complete the task?" Once again, you must have group buy-in and acceptance before moving to the next stage. If you are driving this process, you are telling people what they did, felt, and learned. This is not reflection because the participants must organize the meaning from the experience themselves in order to have ownership of the outcome and the need for change.

The summation question (filter 3) highlights new learning. Here you will ask clients to summarize what they have learned about the issue, asking questions such as "How does the moral of this story go? What did you learn from all of this? Can you sum up what you have gained from our discussions (reflections)?" So far they have acknowledged what happened, what impact it had, and how they are ready to discuss what they can learn from all of this. When several clients' summaries of what they have learned mirror program objectives, you can move on to the next step.

Once clients have articulated new learning, you ask them to apply it to real-life situations, thereby facilitating transfer of learning from the adventure setting back to everyday life. The application question (filter 4) helps clients establish these links. Help them to make connections in the forms of metaphors and analogies between the adventure experience and real life, asking such questions as, "Do you see a connection between this learning and your life back at school? Can you apply this to your job? Do you see any parallels with your family?" Once clients can articulate and agree on this connection, you are ready to move to the next level.

Filter 5, commitment, urges the clients to look toward change. Ask clients to explain the usefulness of what they learned and how they might apply this lesson in their everyday lives. Sample questions to guide this process include, "What will you do differently next time? Begin with the words, 'I will. . . .' How can you commit to change? Who will help support you in upholding this pledge?" These agreements can be verbal or written. You may want to suggest that clients set up some kind of system to periodically check in with each other and discuss the progress they are making on their commitments.

The following tips will help you use funneling to guide verbal discussions:

- Before using funneling, you must have a complete and accurate needs assessment. One option is to teach the clients how to use funneling and coach them on doing it them-

selves. They probably know their needs better than you do, so this can help make certain the funneling is client centered if the group is motivated and mature enough to do it.

- As you proceed through the filters, ensure you have client buy-in each step of the way. If they don't own what happened, they will be limited in their ability to learn from it. You are best served by switching to a new topic unless you are trained to confront people who appear to be in denial.

- The six-stage process is a lot to remember, so you will probably want to write out a list of potential questions to ask. You will probably change many of the questions based on clients' experiences, but having sample written questions at the starting point has two advantages. First, you can share ideas for facilitation among facilitators of a larger group that has been broken into smaller groups. Second, it gives you a starting point to work from when making revisions to meet the relevance of the moment—your facilitation will be much better if you are modifying plans rather than preparing them for the first time.

Frontloading the Experience

Recall that frontloading is the fourth generation of facilitation, a method in which learning is discussed in advance of the experience rather than after the experience. The type of frontloading appropriate for beginning and intermediate facilitators is called *direct frontloading*, where one or more of the following five functions are addressed: revisiting, objectives, motivation, function, and dysfunction. However, after frontloading, the excitement of adventure activities often carries clients away from thinking about learning as they become driven toward task completion. Intense focus on task completion often distracts clients from the changes they are there to accomplish. A *revisiting question* posed just before the new activity, such as "What were the commitments the group made before the last activity?", can refocus clients on the process and their commitment to do things differently the next time around.

The four other types of frontloading questions can be asked in combination or alone. *Objective questions* ask clients about the purpose of the activity and what they hope to learn through the experience. *Motivation questions* ask why the experience might be important and how learning relates to clients' everyday lives. *Function questions* ask clients to

CAREERS IN ADVENTURE

NAME: Tom Burkiewicz

JOB: Assistant Director of Adventure Programs, East Carolina University Campus Recreation and Wellness (Greenville, North Carolina)

BACKGROUND: MEd in recreation management, University of Georgia; 23 years of adventure program leadership and instruction experience at the college level; WFR certification since 1993; certification in high angle rescue; achieved first descents in open canoe in the Karakoram Range of Pakistan

I have 30-plus years' experience as a whitewater paddler in canoeing, kayaking, and rafting. I started climbing and caving in the early 1970s, have been a challenge course facilitation leader since 1983, and have been a trainer since 1992. I have also led expeditions to Costa Rica and Pakistan. Taken together, I have paddled, hiked, and climbed in 5 countries and 23 states. I have been the director of the adventure program at East Carolina University (ECU) since 2001. Before working at colleges I was with Outward Bound as both field and administrative staff.

WHAT'S YOUR JOB LIKE? As director of the ECU adventure program, I am responsible for the budget, risk management, marketing, enrollment, report writing, and other administrative duties; teaching and leading staff training sessions in field skills and leadership development; supervising the coordinator who directly manages the ECU Adventure Program Center (APC); managing trip enrollment, the climbing wall, and equipment rental; directing our marketing efforts and Web site; and supervising daily operation of the APC by student staff. I also lead trips and challenge courses as needed and coordinate long-range planning and program development.

This job requires attention to detail in arranging challenge course programs; documenting program activity; planning trips, summer camps, and challenge course details; writing reports; analyzing data; and overseeing marketing efforts. My biggest challenges are balancing the adventure activities with the administrative duties and managing long-range planning with short-term needs. Contact with students and developing their leadership skills is the best part of the job. Paperwork in the form of documentation, reports, and consistent program standards is sometimes tedious but necessary. The director of this program has to have solid experience in the activity areas we provide for our clients. The director needs to be able to communicate clearly with student staff, professional peers, and university administration. Integrity and adherence to ethical and program standards is essential for developing solid student leaders. Finally, the director must be creative and adaptable, able to work alone and as part of a team.

Those who wish to enter this field should understand their motivation in terms of what they want to gain from experiential education and what they can offer their clients. Take the time to both acquire a range of skill experiences and master at least one. Take every leadership and adventure opportunity before becoming an administrative programmer, and never give up those kinds of experiences.

describe specific behaviors that will ensure success and positive group dynamics. *Dysfunction questions* ask the clients to describe which behaviors are blocking their success and think about how the group can avoid or remove those barriers.

You may have noticed that frontloading questions follow a sequence similar to funneling. The main difference is that frontloading takes place before the activity and funneling is used to discuss the activity after its conclusion.

Frontloading can occur before or after clients receive orientation information about time schedule, meals, facilities, and so on. Don't cover too many topics in the frontloading; five to nine thoughts at once are all the short-term memory can handle. Because the logistical briefing (safety rules, activity guidelines) often contains six items or so, the leader or clients should choose just two or three more key points for guiding their learning. Sample frontloading and funneling questions are covered by topic area in figure 7.3.

Empowering Clients to Self-Facilitate

Facilitation refers to process-oriented skills used by group members to enhance a team's capabilities and efficiency for reaching objectives. Greenaway (1993) proposed that a future generation of facilitation should involve learners as facilitators of their own experiences. A study conducted by Priest and Lesperance (1994) paralleled those beliefs by training select corporate groups to self-facilitate. Not surprisingly, they discovered that groups who self-facilitated showed the greatest learning gain and retention when they were able to apply the techniques to the workplace.

Only groups with adequate maturity, motivation, and ability can use this technique. Corporate groups and mature student groups attending the adventure program in intact teams are good candidates. When using this approach, the facilitator teaches the group how to use reflection techniques such as debriefing, frontloading, and funneling and then coaches the clients while they apply these techniques themselves. In this way, clients assist the process of learning from their adventure experiences. Recall from our earlier discussion that this technique has two distinct advantages: Clients can use their new facilitation skills to foster continued growth after returning home, and they can focus on what is most relevant to them, thus minimizing the need for the facilitator to make assumptions about what clients need while maximizing client responsibility for their own learning.

Although the most familiar form of reflection is postactivity debriefing and you need to be prepared to conduct these discussions, there are alternative methods to consider as well. Beginning- and intermediate-level facilitators should be able to use any of the following methods, which will help keep reflection sessions client centered (Estes 2004):

- Rely less on the standard practice of talk circles and more on alternative techniques to facilitate reflection, like journaling, art work such as collages, or poetry.

- Have a client choose a reading or story to introduce a day or activity or to begin post-activity reflection.

- Let the clients decide what they need to learn. For example, allow clients to set their own individual and group goals.

- Allow clients to cocreate metaphors—after the activity briefing, ask "What do you do in everyday life that this experience might be similar to?"

- Teach clients about funneling and frontloading. Allow clients to frontload and debrief their own experiences by discussing what they need to work on as individuals and as a group. You serve as a coach and cheerleader. Encourage them to hold each other accountable. At the end of the program, let them decide how well they did, and then let them set their goals for the next activity.

- Listen, listen, listen. Don't be too eager to share your stories, metaphors, frames, and thoughts about what you think clients learned.

- Have clients paraphrase their own statements to avoid misinterpretation. At a minimum, get their agreement that you restated their thoughts correctly.

- Encourage clients to talk to each other and not just to you. By avoiding eye contact with the speaker, you will encourage the speaker to look at others.

- Avoid judging students' comments as right or wrong. Native Americans use a universal sound, such as "uh," to signify that they heard what was said but are not judging it. The leader could use this technique by having the group decide on their own sound or phrase, such as "I hear you."

Sample Questions for Funneling and Frontloading

Knapp (1990) identified a series of questions associated with common adventure program topics that may prove useful for formulating funnels or frontloads. These topics include communication, feelings, prejudice, listening, leadership, followership, decision making, cooperation, diversity, trust, and closure. Use these questions as models for developing your own funnels and frontloads, making them your own so you can ask them in a natural manner tailored to specific client needs. Remember that you can't cover every topic in one discussion. Instead, pick one topic that may lead to another and stop discussion before clients become tired or restless.

Communication

1. Can anyone give an example of when you thought you communicated effectively?
2. How did you know that what you communicated was understood?
3. Who didn't understand someone's attempt to communicate?
4. What went wrong in the communication attempt?
5. What could the communicator do differently next time to give a clearer message?
6. What could the message receiver do differently next time to understand the message?
7. How many different ways were used by the group to communicate messages?
8. Which ways were the most effective? Why?
9. Did you learn something about communication that will be helpful later? If so, what?

Feelings

1. Can you name a feeling you had at any point in completing the activity?
2. Where in your body did you feel it most?
3. What personal beliefs were responsible for generating that feeling?
4. What was the main thought behind the feeling?
5. Is that feeling a common one in your life?
6. Did you express that feeling to others? If not, what did you do with the feeling?
7. Do you usually express feelings or suppress them?
8. Would you like to feel differently in a similar situation?
9. If so, how would you like to feel?
10. What beliefs would you need to have in order to feel differently in a similar situation?
11. Could you believe them?
12. How do you feel about the conflict that may result from expressing certain feelings?
13. How do you imagine others felt toward you at various times during the activity?
14. Were these feelings expressed?
15. What types of feelings are easiest to express? Most difficult?
16. Do you find it difficult to be aware of certain feelings at times? If so, which ones?
17. Are some feelings not appropriate to express to the group at times? If so, which ones?
18. What feelings were expressed nonverbally in the group?
19. Did expressing appropriate feelings help or hinder completing the initiative?

(continued)

FIGURE 7.3 Sample frontloading and funneling questions.

Reprinted, by permission, from S. Priest and M.A. Gass, 2005, *Effective leadership in adventure programming*, 2nd ed. (Champaign, IL: Human Kinetics), 208-211.

Evaluating Others

1. Is it difficult for you to avoid judging others? Explain.
2. Can you think of examples when you judged others in the group today?
3. When you didn't judge others?
4. What were some advantages you gained by not judging others?
5. What were some advantages others gained when you didn't judge them?
6. How did judging and not judging others affect the completion of the activity?
7. Were some behaviors of others easy not to judge and other behaviors difficult?
8. Would deferring judgment be of some value in other situations? Explain.
9. Can you think of any disadvantages of not judging others in this situation?

Listening

1. Who made suggestions for completing the activity?
2. Were all of these suggestions heard? Explain.
3. Which suggestions were acted on?
4. Why were the other suggestions ignored?
5. How did it feel to be heard when you made a suggestion?
6. What interfered with your ability to listen to others?
7. How can you overcome this interference?
8. Did you prevent yourself from listening well? How?
9. Did you listen in the same way today as you generally do?
10. If not, what was different about today?

Leadership

1. Who assumed leadership roles during the activity?
2. What were the behaviors that showed leadership?
3. Can everyone agree that these behaviors are traits of leaders?
4. How did the group respond to these leadership behaviors?
5. Who followed the leader even if you weren't sure that the idea would work? Why?
6. Did the leadership role shift to other people during the activity?
7. Who thought they were taking the leadership role? How did you do it?
8. Was it difficult to assume a leadership role with this group?
9. Why didn't some of you take a leadership role with this group?
10. Is it easier to take leadership in other situations or with other group members? Explain.
11. Did anyone try to lead the group, but felt you were unsuccessful?
12. What were some possible reasons for this? How did it feel to be disregarded?

Followership

1. Who assumed a follower role at times throughout the activity? How did it feel?
2. How did it feel to follow different leaders?
3. Do you consider yourself a good follower?
4. Was this an important role in the group today? Explain.

FIGURE 7.3 *(continued)*

Reprinted, by permission, from S. Priest and M.A. Gass, 2005, *Effective leadership in adventure programming*, 2nd ed. (Champaign, IL: Human Kinetics), 208-211.

5. How does refusal to follow affect the leadership role?

6. What are the traits of a good follower?

7. How can you improve your ability to follow in the future?

Decision Making

1. How were group decisions made during the activity?

2. Were you satisfied with the ways decisions were made? Explain.

3. Did the group arrive at any decisions through group consensus?

4. Were decisions made by one or several individuals?

5. Did everyone in the group express an opinion when given a choice? If not, why not?

6. What is the best way for this group to make decisions? Explain.

7. Do you respond in similar ways in other groups?

8. What did you like about how the group made decisions? What didn't you like?

Cooperation

1. Can you think of specific examples of group cooperation? Explain.

2. How did it feel to cooperate?

3. Do you cooperate in most things you do?

4. How did you learn to cooperate?

5. What are the rewards of cooperating?

6. Are there any problems associated with cooperation?

7. How did cooperative behavior lead to successfully completing the activity?

8. How can you cooperate in other areas of your life?

9. Did you think anyone was blocking the group's efforts to cooperate? Explain.

Diversity

1. How are you different from some of the others in the group?

2. How do these differences in people in a group keep a group from reaching certain objectives?

3. When do differences in people in a group keep a group from reaching certain objectives?

4. What would this group be like if there were very few differences in people?

5. How would you feel if this were so?

6. In what cases did being different help or hinder group members from reaching objectives?

7. How are you like some of the others in the group?

8. Were these common traits helpful to the other group's approach to the task? Explain.

9. Did these common traits hinder the group's approach to the task? Explain.

10. Do you think you have other things in common with some of the group members?

11. How did this setting help you discover how you are similar to others?

Trust

1. Can you give examples of when you trusted someone in the group? Explain.

2. Is it easier to trust some people and not others? Explain.

3. Can you think of examples when trusting someone would not have been a good idea?

4. How do you increase your level of trust for someone?

(continued)

FIGURE 7.3 *(continued)*

Reprinted, by permission, from S. Priest and M.A. Gass, 2005, *Effective leadership in adventure programming*, 2nd ed. (Champaign, IL: Human Kinetics), 208-211.

5. On a scale of 1 to 10, rate how much trust you have in the group as a whole.

6. Can you explain your rating?

7. How does the amount of fear you feel affect your trust of others?

8. What did you do today that deserves the trust of others?

Closure

1. What did you learn about yourself?

2. What did you learn about others?

3. How do you feel about yourself and others?

4. What new questions do you have about yourself and others?

5. What did you do today of which you are particularly proud?

6. What skill are you working to improve?

7. Was your behavior today typical of the way you usually act in groups? Explain.

8. How can you use what you learned in other life situations?

9. What beliefs about yourself and others were reinforced today?

10. Would you do anything differently if you were starting the activity again with this group?

11. What would you like to say to the group members?

FIGURE 7.3 *(continued)*

Reprinted, by permission, from S. Priest and M.A. Gass, 2005, *Effective leadership in adventure programming*, 2nd ed. (Champaign, IL: Human Kinetics), 208-211.

Alternative and Nonverbal Methods of Reflection

Alternative reflection methods include art, drama, music, dance, poetry, writing, storytelling, photography, presentations, client-selected readings, and even repeating the same activity. Alternative reflection methods have several advantages over verbal discussion and are worthy of serious consideration. For one, not all clients are good at expressing their feelings through words. This may be due to differences in learning styles, languages, or cognitive maturity. Second, alternative reflection techniques have the advantage of being more client centered because it is the clients who create their nonverbal connections and present these reflections to portray what they learned or felt. Third, using alternative reflection takes pressure off you as a facilitator to come up with the questions that best fit with clients' needs and experiences. As the facilitator, you set the stage for reflection by posing the activity, and the clients run with it.

It is important to choose alternative methods carefully so they fit the age, maturity level, and culture of the clients. Further, be aware that these methods can become routine if used too frequently, so use them in moderation and make sure you have a variety of options so you can alternate methods frequently.

Realistic art is the most difficult to create and is usually the least useful. Consider forms such as cartooning, making collages from magazines,

---

Two books can assist you as you expand your knowledge of alternative reflection options. *Playback: A Guide to Reviewing Activities* (Greenaway 1993) covers instructions for many creative options, including cartoons, human sculptures, self-images, stories, performing, and many more. *Reflective Learning: Theory and Practice* (Sugerman et al. 2000) has thorough instructions for both pre- and postexperience activities with many creative options such as journals, finishing the story, and using art materials.

graphing, painting, sculpting, or mapping. Collages can be created that interpret and illustrate clients' experiences. A graph could illustrate how energy levels change over time and reflect on morale and motivation. A group can paint a mural to share the lessons from their experience with others. Sculpting clay can be used to create shapes that illustrate emotions.

Drama can empower clients to act out what happened during the experience, what should have happened but didn't, and what they expect will happen next time. Dramatics ideas include fantasy skits, modeling group members as if they were clay, or reenacting the activity. Drama can be silent or spoken.

Other options include music, dance, poetry, writing, storytelling, and client-selected readings. Clients can sing songs, play instruments, or create rhythms. Expressive dance or creative movement can be done with or without music. Poetry in the form of cinquains, couplets, haiku, or limericks can be created from an instructor-provided model. Writing can be analytical, like a newspaper article, or creative, in the form of journaling or short stories. Fantasy storytelling, in which people make up a story as they go, by leaders and clients can illustrate metaphors that encourage clients to make new connections. Client-selected readings such as quotes, fantasies, legends, short stories, parables, or fables can illustrate and elaborate a lesson they learned.

Photography, slides, or videos can be useful in facilitating reflection. As the group reviews images, you can pause for discussion, or if the group is mature enough, let them run the presentation and discussion themselves. Images can be turned into permanent displays for other groups to view and may include captions and other written comments.

Presentations are more formal. Clients may prepare a report about trip outcomes to share with others, give presentations to incoming clients, or interact with the general public and other potential clients. In doing so, they review their own experiences and see the benefits through the eyes of an outsider. In order to communicate their thoughts, they must process their experience and find ways to verbalize their personal, life-changing experiences in ways others can understand.

Another option is to ask clients to repeat the same activity for a second time without any debriefing or frontloading. This can create an immediate space for reflection on what they can improve from the first experience. They may focus more on improving product or process, which will provide additional insights. One twist on this reflection experience is to repeat the activity but ask clients to change roles. They may act differently when moved into a different viewpoint and may become more open to other group members' positions.

Evaluation and Follow-Up

One of the primary criticisms of adventure programs is that learning tends to be short-lived. Clients often end the program with good ideas for things they want to do differently back in their home environment, but it is difficult to measure whether these gains have any lasting impact. Most clients come to adventure programs as a one-time experience, but there are a few things you can do to help clients transfer their learning.

Creating an Action Plan

Many adventure programs end with a summary activity where clients commit to what they intend to do differently back home based on what they have learned. One thing you can do is ask for a verbal or written plan of action for the changes clients are committing to. An **action plan** has three parts:

- A task to be accomplished
- Resources and support people to help with the task
- Dates for checkpoints and evidence showing that the task was completed

This action-planning format can easily be presented in a simple handout with columns for clients to fill in during and after the program. Clients leave with a written plan of what they intend to do, by when, and whose help and what resources they might enlist. This plan can help with follow-through in the clients' home environment. Figure 7.4 illustrates a simple model for an action plan.

Following Up

In some programs, you will have an opportunity to schedule visits or other follow-up programs with your clients. When this is the case, you can keep records of their action plans, reassess needs, and design follow-up programs to focus on continued development. You may be invited to attend meetings at the clients' home base to help them review their commitments and progress. To the extent that you can document client commitments, follow-through, and transfer of learning, you will

Participant name: _____

Position: _____

Date: _____

These are the main things I learned from this experience: _____

_____

_____

_____

✦ About the team: _____

_____

_____

_____

✦ About myself: _____

_____

_____

_____

Based on what I learned, this is what I plan to do:

	Goals	Resources I need	Time frame
For the team:	_____	_____	_____
	_____	_____	_____
	_____	_____	_____
	_____	_____	_____
For myself:	_____	_____	_____
	_____	_____	_____
	_____	_____	_____

FIGURE 7.4   Sample action plan.

strengthen the reputation of your program as one that facilitates lasting change.

Summary

If you are a beginning facilitator, try not to be overwhelmed by all the information contained in this chapter. You should start practicing your facilitation skills using debriefing, direct frontloading, and several alternative reflection techniques. As you gain experience, periodically revisit this information because some things will become clearer as you develop a context in which to understand the information. Above all, make sure your choice of facilitation style is driven by the primary goal of the adventure program and the client's needs and goals. The ten facilitation guidelines, discussion dos and don'ts, and sample discussion questions for funneling and frontloading are great things to review as you learn to be an adventure facilitator. Also, don't forget that there are good alternatives to guided discussion, such as journaling, drama, art, and photography. Last but not least, remember how important evaluation and follow-up are for ensuring that clients are transferring what they learn back to their everyday environments. Schedule time for action planning or other follow-up sessions when it fits with your program's goals.

Review Questions

1. Explain the rationales for choosing appropriate facilitation styles, taking into account program goals, client characteristics, and the facilitator's abilities.

2. Explain why it is important to keep your facilitation style as client centered as possible. Summarize the techniques you would be likely to use in the type of adventure program you work for or would like to work for.

3. Describe the main considerations that an adventure facilitator should take into account when using verbal reflection and debriefing.

4. Describe how you could use follow-up and evaluation to further your clients' goals following an adventure program.

Student Learning Activities

1. When the class is learning how to conduct ground-level initiative activities, each member takes a turn debriefing the experience using the "what, so what, now what" model described in the section on debriefing the experience (third generation). Following the debriefing, have the student leader critique herself as to how well she followed the cognitive hierarchy of what, so what, and now what.

2. Following a student-led debriefing, the student self-critiques how well he followed facilitation guidelines and the discussion dos and don'ts. The teacher and class should give feedback on what was done well and what areas needed improvement.

3. Design and implement facilitation strategies and reflection plans for adventure program scenarios presented to you by your class instructor.

4. Consider a common client need for improvement such as listening skills, conflict resolution, or decision making. Write sample questions for the six stages of funneling and share them with the class.

5. In a group, interview a potential client such as a team manager or classroom teacher in order to assess the needs of the client's team. After the interview, prepare the following items: (1) clients' needs, (2) goals, (3) selection and sequence of activities, and (4) suggestions for how to best process the activities, including what types of facilitation would work best and questions or activities that might be used to facilitate client-centered reflection.

6. Prepare instructions for five alternative methods of reflection. Then use one of your methods during a practice initiative with the class.

7. After your instructor leads the class as a model of client self-facilitation by teaching funneling, apply it yourself during an adventure experience.

Major portions of this chapter were taken and adapted, with permission, from the book *Effective Leadership in Adventure Programming*, written by Simon Priest and Mike Gass and published by Human Kinetics in 2005.

PART III

Planning and Implementing Adventure Experiences

CHAPTER 8

Portable Adventure Activities

Lisa Faulkingham Hunt

I tried to teach my child with books.
  She gave me only puzzled looks.
I tried to teach my child with words.
  They passed her over, quite unheard.
Despairingly I turned aside.
  "How can I teach this child," I cried?
Into my hand she put the key:
  "Come," she said, "and play with me."

Anonymous

Chapter Concepts

✦ Although there are many valid and valuable ways to classify adventure activities, most can be classified as icebreakers, cooperative activities, initiatives, and trust activities.

✦ Adventure activities are appropriate for many different participants and are increasingly used in such diverse organizations as schools, businesses, hospitals, camps, after-school programs, violence and substance abuse prevention programs, and therapeutic programs.

✦ The adventure leader can use or adapt pre-existing games in the public domain, or create games.

✦ Effective leadership, including careful briefing, attention to safety, and a spirit of fun, is vital to bringing an activity to life.

Play is a powerful medium in which to learn. Adventure games, initiatives, and activities can enhance the experience of many groups, from a team of automobile engineers to second graders at recess to young adults in a therapeutic hospital. Adventure activities are designed to create growth in participants and are composed of the following elements:

• Significance: They contain meaning and relevance to the participants.

• Challenge: They involve new experiences that encourage creative thinking.

• Support: They emphasize teamwork to develop trust and healthy risk taking.

• Satisfaction: They build on successes to create greater successes.

• Fun: They capitalize on the inherent joy of learning.

Adventure activities and games add value to programs of all kinds, all around the world. A simple Internet search will reveal that the word *game* is popularly conceived of in the context of video and computer games, which are solitary and competitive in nature. Adventure games are different, almost the opposite of this modern definition—they bring people together, fostering a sense of community, a spirit of fun, and inclusiveness. Effective adventure activities will leave a group saying, "That was fun. What are we going to do next?"

In this chapter we will explore basic definitions, components, and illustrations of adventure activities. Additionally, strategies for creating activities are discussed. The chapter will conclude by discussing the broad applications of adventure games and activities, including illustrations of activities in action and consideration of factors that influence the outcomes of activities. Opportunities for reflection will be given throughout.

Types of Adventure Activities

Adventure activities take many forms. Facility-based adventure programming refers to adventure activities that occur indoors or in a sport field, not in the wilderness. Facility-based programming takes advantage of **portable adventure activities** that use unique props and equipment. Portable adventure activities are opportunities for people to interact, learn, solve problems, and laugh together via facilitated activities that are not based on the outdoors. The outdoors naturally provides opportunities for participants to be challenged and to learn together, but meals must be prepared, living through all kinds of weather is necessary, and many programs that want to use adventure experiences are constrained by the time and space required for an outdoor adventure. Facility-based portable adventure activities mirror the need for cooperative problem solving found in outdoor adventure; however, the problems are contrived. Over the course of the past 25 years, the power of such experiential learning has been brought into the places where people work and live rather than bringing people to the outdoors.

There are many valuable ways to classify adventure activities. Icebreakers, cooperative activities, initiatives, and trust activities are four categories into which most of these activities comfortably fit, and they are typically performed in this order.

Icebreakers are activities that are designed to do just that—break the ice. Sometimes called *convening activities,* icebreakers set a positive tone and make participants feel comfortable. Most programs begin with an icebreaker. Cooperative activities can be high-energy experiences that engage a group in laughter and movement. **Initiatives** are activities that require the initiative of the group to solve a problem. Initiatives usually follow cooperative activities, which are then typically followed by trust exercises. **Trust activities** help not only to establish trust, but also to gauge the level of trust that exists in a group. At this point in a program, the low and high challenge courses are often introduced (see chapters 9 and 10 for more detailed information about low and high challenge courses). Let's explore each of the four categories in greater depth.

Icebreakers

Also called *convening activities, energizers,* or *acquaintance activities,* the objective of icebreakers is to provide opportunities for group members to get to know and begin to feel comfortable with one another by engaging in activities that are fun, uncomplicated, and brief.

Fun is a major component of icebreakers, giving a newly formed group the opportunity to interact in a nonthreatening way. Nobody is put on the spot during icebreakers. A quality icebreaker allows success to come easily and can be accomplished with minimal frustration or decision making.

Successful icebreakers need to be led by facilitators who are willing to model the behavior that they want from the participants, typically energy and laughter. The facilitator participates in the activity, keeping the briefing simple and light.

Icebreakers are often carried out in the convening stages of a group experience and in reconvening stages after that; therefore the group may not yet know the concept of challenge by choice (for more on challenge by choice, see chapter 3). Quality icebreakers, therefore, have challenge by choice naturally built in. Consider the activity Gotcha (see page 130). There is no tallying up of who grabbed and who escaped; the rules are simple; and, quite often, the facilitator is ready to move on to the next activity while the participants are extending their palms and index fingers for yet another round.

Origin of Adventure Activities

The basic concept of playing together for the sheer joy of it is timeless and cross-cultural. The New Games Foundation is largely credited with the creation and dissemination of cooperative games. Cooperative games are elemental adventure activities.

The New Games Foundation began when Stewart Brand and George Leonard brought their unique interests together, hoping to create change through noncompetitive play. "How we play together may turn out to be more important than we imagine, for it signifies nothing less than our way of being in the world," Leonard wrote (Fluegelman and Tembeck 1976).

Brand and Leonard shared their ideas with others, gathering energy and support that culminated with the New Games tournament in October of 1973. Their goal was to create an "opportunity for the community to relate to the natural environment in a new and creative way" (Fluegelman and Tembeck 1976). The event was attended by at least 6,000 people. The second New Games tournament took place in 1974, getting notice from national news outlets. Conferences, regional meetings, and increased demand from schools that were looking for alternatives to traditional sport programs were signs of the foundation's success. As people learned more about cooperative games, their popularity grew. *The New Games Book* (1976) and *More New Games* (1981) were written by the foundation and continue to provide the basis for adventure activities today.

Simultaneously, Project Adventure began to use cooperative learning and games to bring physical and academic education together. Its foundation was (and still is) experiential adventure learning. In a suburban high school, Project Adventure brought fun into the classroom—intentional fun, that is. Not only were the games cooperative, but they were tied to the curriculum and cooperative learning. One of Project Adventure's core competencies is developing games and activities that are linked to desired learning outcomes. The organization's numerous publications are evidence of such.

The New Games Foundation and Project Adventure create and disseminate a vast number of adventure activities; however, there is no single source for all of the icebreakers, cooperative games, initiatives, and trust activities out there. They often come from a combination of creative people, willing participants, and leaders who are agreeable to modifying and sharing their ideas.

Icebreakers *Gotcha*

The facilitator invites all of the participants into a circle and then gives the following instructions: "Please identify your right hand and slide it in front of the neighbor to your right, with your palm flat and facing up. The circle may have to shift a bit to get everyone into the proper configuration. Next, take your left pointer finger and aim it toward the sky. Good. Now, using the sound effect of your choice, place that left pointer finger into the extended palm of the neighbor to your left. When you hear the magic word, 'Gotcha!', grab your neighbor's finger with your right hand while escaping your neighbor's grasp with your left. Ready, set, gotcha! All right! Let's go again."

Cooperative Activities

Cooperative activities, sometimes called *cooperative games,* require the whole group to participate in a fun activity. A step beyond icebreakers, these activities help the group form by asking them to work together. The activities often introduce concepts of the full-value contract, even if the group has not yet developed one. The debriefing or reflection of a cooperative activity often brings up issues about caring for self and others and being safe. They set the stage for the more intense work of the initiative.

In creation activities, the solution requires building something or finding an answer to a stated problem.

Cooperative Activities
Everybody's It!

The facilitator gathers the group into a huddle and explains, "We're going to play a simple tag game. In this game of tag, everybody will be it! When you're tagged on the shoulder, crouch down in that spot for a rest—you've been frozen. While you're frozen, you may put your palm up, and anyone who is not yet frozen may touch your palm, serving as the 'anti-freeze,' and you may rejoin the game. Let's play for five minutes and see how we do."

A successful cooperative activity is designed so that all group members can participate equally or at least all can have important roles. The facilitator should ensure that the activity is safe and fun for all participants. This includes reminding participants about safety concerns. Because these activities can sometimes bring up feelings, such as joy or frustration, a facilitator may choose to observe rather than participate and should provide an opportunity to reflect on the activity. However, cooperative activities are typically designed to give participants the experience of having fun and being successful as a team.

Initiatives

Also called *problem-solving activities* and *team-building activities,* there are at least three categories of initiatives:

- **Transport activities** involve moving an object or many objects from one point to another or in a particular pattern.
- **Creation activities** require building something or finding an answer to a stated problem.
- **Retrieval activities** involve recovering an object or manipulating it in a specific way.

Many low elements are also considered to be initiatives. For more information on low-element initiatives, see chapter 9.

Initiatives are problem-solving activities that take the initiative of group members to solve. The objective is to provide an opportunity for group members to communicate, cooperate, and compromise with each other to solve a problem. Participants typically use a process of trial and error as they work together. Physical activity and verbal

CAREERS IN ADVENTURE

NAME: Vincent Canziani, LMSW

JOB: Camp Director, the Children's Aid Society (Chappaqua, New York)

BACKGROUND: BA in philosophy; MSW in group work; employed as a teacher, manager, budget director, dean of students, administrative supervisor, and camp director

WHAT'S YOUR JOB LIKE? As the director of Wagon Road Camp, my job covers several aspects. I manage the day-to-day business operations of the camp: billing, sales, and paying the bills. I make strategic plans for the camp's development over a 10-year period. I manage the maintenance and upgrading of the camp facility from the buildings to the landscaping to the forest. I participate in capital projects and manage contractors. I plan and implement the budget. Finally, I directly manage the summer day camp, the respite program for developmentally delayed children, the adventure program, and the visiting group program.

Adventure ropes course programming has played an important role in my development as a leader. In all my work, in every position from line worker to supervisor to director to administrative leader, the most important skills have always been effective communication, patience in the face of obstacles, and openness to new information. Adventure programming was the place where I learned, tested, and developed these three skills. I have been in many meetings where these attributes were poorly represented. The result is always the same: misunderstanding, frustration, and poor decision making. In meetings where these attributes were in great supply, the converse was true: clarity of understanding, energy, well-reasoned decisions, and satisfaction that included a strong sense of fun. Although there were other experiences and influences that solidified my skills as a leader, it was the experiences in adventure programming that created my standards for what good communication, successful problem solving, and openness to new information look like, sound like, and feel like.

In my work as an adventure facilitator, I have observed, guided, and supported many people as they formed relationships, challenged themselves, confronted each other's behavior, forgave each other, learned to ask for help, and committed to being present for each other. I have seen this group process over and over so many times that I have learned what to expect and how to be helpful. It is this confidence in my understanding of human nature that I bring to all the work I do. I am the leader in my program, but I am also a servant to the needs of my staff and the group process that is required for any staff to be a peak-performing team. That is what being a facilitator is.

So every time you set up a sequence of games and lay out the ground rules as you invite a group of people to work together, you have entered into a powerful learning opportunity. It could be for you what it has been for me, the keystone in a career of helping, facilitating, and leading.

communication are usually involved in solving the problem. Sometimes participants become frustrated. Often, facilitators will present an initiative that is intentionally frustrating in order to further develop the group. Success in these activities usually depends on the individual members of a group being able to learn how to support and encourage each other's efforts.

Initiatives tend to help participants learn the value of thinking and planning ahead rather than reacting in an impulsive and random manner. They require participants to communicate and cooperate with their group verbally and physically. Initiatives help participants develop skills in assessing problems, formulating solutions, and working effectively with the strengths and weaknesses of group members. Because they require teamwork, initiatives also promote the development of social and leadership skills.

Initiatives have the greatest impact when they are selected with a thorough knowledge of the group's goals and abilities. A facilitator may change the parameters of an activity, which will influence its outcome and the group's level of frustration. More or less time can be given for a task, or a play space can be made smaller or larger. Transport activities can involve multiple objects, or a creation activity may have the added component of blindfolds or certain group members may not be permitted to speak.

The way an activity is briefed also has significant influence. For example, in the Warp Speed activity that is described in the following paragraphs, the successful group will realize that they are allowed to change places in the circle, standing next to the person they are to receive the frog from and throw the frog to and thus greatly improving their time. That discovery is an essential part of the activity. If the briefing had included a list of rules, such as "The group is allowed to reconfigure itself," it would have changed the problem-solving nature of the activity—participants would not have been able to discover the solution, it would have been provided to them.

Good facilitation of initiatives requires a thorough understanding of the assets as well as the developmental stage of your group. For example, a challenging initiative given to a group with limited ability could easily lead to frustration the group can't surmount, whereas a simple initiative given to a highly functioning group may lead to boredom. Initiatives that have multiple solutions, that are enjoyable, and that provide a unique experience are a key ingredient for learning.

Initiatives *Warp Speed*

The facilitator invites the group into a circle; introduces a soft, tossable object (a beanbag frog); and says, "To begin this problem-solving activity, we need to first create a pattern of tossing that begins with me, includes everyone catching and tossing the frog once, and ends again with me. Let's establish our pattern." The facilitator begins by tossing the frog across the circle, explaining that it's ideal not to toss to one's neighbors, but rather in a crisscross fashion. Once the pattern has been established, the facilitator begins the pattern again, explaining, "This will give us our base time. Our goal in subsequent rounds is to improve our base time. The guidelines that we need to follow are that we always need to catch and toss in the established order, and the group must designate a timekeeper and communicate with the timekeeper. We are competing against our base time. Warp Speed is so fast, it's almost impossible to time it. Can we achieve warp speed?"

Trust Activities

Trust activities both gauge the level of trust within a group and build group trust. In these activities, group members support each other and cooperate to ensure each other's safety.

A trust activity involves real or perceived emotional or physical risk; for example, in the Trust Run activity unsighted participants travel toward their group, and in trust falls, participants fall backward from a platform into the arms of the group (do not try this activity without training). Introductory trust activities can begin to build trust in a group, and more advanced trust activities can test and further develop the level of trust that the group has as a whole and how participants feel toward one another. The concept of trust can mean different things to different groups and can also vary among activities. The climber on the edge of the Trust Fall platform may wonder, "Will they really catch me?", whereas the student about to attempt the Trust Run may be wondering, "Do I trust this group not to laugh at me as I run across the gym blindfolded?"

Often trust activities involve the loss of sight because participants are offered blindfolds to increase their reliance on each other. Most facilitators would agree that any activity that uses blindfolds or closed eyes would classify as a trust activity.

The climber on the edge of the Trust Fall platform wonders, "Will they really catch me?"

Trust Activities *Trust Run*

The facilitator is ready to increase the level of challenge—and improve the level of trust—with an advanced group. Gathering the group together in a large open space, the facilitator explains, "You will have the opportunity to travel toward trust by moving across this open space, without eyesight, toward the rest of the group, who will be waiting to let you know that you have reached the other side. We will call them spotters. Most of you will be standing along a line at one end of the space, with your hands up. A few will be positioned on the sides. I will be standing with the person at risk, at the other end of the space, to offer a blindfold and to go over the procedure. The person at risk may choose to walk, run, skip—it's up to you, as long as you travel with your bumpers up (in other words, with your hands out in front of you) and communicate with the spotters."

Many trust activities are experienced during a sequence, which is typically taught as a lead-up to low challenge course activities. In a trust sequence, participants perform a variety of exercises that involve partners and groups taking care of each other's physical safety. It may begin with one person standing in front of a spotter and leaning back into the arms of that spotter. For more on the trust sequence and spotting activities, see chapter 9.

Applications of Adventure Activities

Icebreakers, cooperative games, initiatives, and trust activities have broad applications. Adventure activities are appropriate for many different participants and are increasingly used in such diverse organizations such as schools, businesses, hospitals, camps, after-school programs, violence and substance abuse prevention programs, and therapeutic programs. Schools are implementing adventure units in their physical education programs; corporations are holding monthly sessions with adventure consultants to develop strategic plans; and therapeutic hospitals are reducing behavioral problems in clients through adventure-based counseling and challenge course experiences. Let's consider several examples of how adventure activities can be used in these diverse settings.

Schools

An eighth-grade health and wellness class is doing a unit on nutrition. The semester began with some icebreakers and the creation of a full-value contract (see chapter 3) to help students feel that the class is a safe place to talk about health and wellness.

On this particular day, the lesson objectives are for the students to understand the components of the USDA Food Guide Pyramid. Rather than lecturing on the topic, the teacher uses masking tape to outline the shape of a large pyramid on the floor and labels each section with the proper food group: grains; vegetables; fruits; milk and dairy; meat, beans, fish, and nuts; and fats and oils. Next, the teacher tapes a card with a type of food to the back of each student. "Your challenge," announces the teacher, "is to find out what the card on your back labels you by asking yes or no questions of your peers. When you have discovered your identity, place yourself where you think you belong in the food pyramid."

As students place themselves where they think that they should be, the group discusses some tricky questions (e.g., "Is corn chowder a dairy product? A vegetable?"). Students also talk about how many servings they should have from that food group. A collective debriefing reiterating what a balanced diet looks like closes the lesson. Learning about the food pyramid has turned into an adventure initiative that helps students engage with the material in a new and exciting way (activity developed from Kilty 2006).

Therapeutic Settings

A group of inner-city youth is participating in an after-school program that explores diversity. They will be doing many projects over the course of their time together, and the facilitator wants to help the group, in its convening stages, understand issues of trust and the concept of making assumptions.

After introductory meetings that include some icebreakers, adventure games, and the creation of a full-value contract, the facilitator designs a session around Saboteur, an initiative activity. The facilitator sets up the activity beforehand by gathering two identical decks of playing cards and small pieces of paper with *Xs* written on them, enough for one per participant. The pieces of paper are folded in half and put into a hat, and cards of one deck are laid out in an intricate pattern in a place that is not visible from the main meeting area—in a side room, or behind a screen.

The facilitator briefs the group, saying, "Our challenge today will be to work together on a project, just as we will be doing throughout the school year. Today you will use this deck of cards to replicate the pattern of cards laid out in the other room. The name of the game is *Saboteur*—as you are trying to replicate the pattern, you will also be attempting to figure out who is trying to help the process and who is trying to sabotage the process.

"Please pull a slip of paper from this hat, without showing it to anyone. If you draw an *X*, you are trying to help the process. If you draw an *O*, you are trying to sabotage the process. Once everyone has drawn, you will leave the room, one at a time, to look at the pattern of cards. When you return, you may instruct the group as to how to set up the replica deck, but you may not touch the cards until after the next person has taken a turn. At any time, any one of you may accuse someone of being a saboteur. If this nomination is seconded by someone else in the group, the accused must be a silent member of the group."

Play begins and accusations start. For example, it's Joe's turn to leave the room to look at the card pattern. He's concentrating on not forgetting the pattern, so as he returns to the group, he avoids eye contact. This is his way of keeping focus. This lack of eye contact is perceived by Henry to indicate that Joe is trying to sabotage the process. Henry accuses him, with Shelly giving the second, and Joe is, in effect, out of the game. After participants reveal that they were not saboteurs, but rather helpers, emotions become heightened and defenses go up. Joe wants to know why he was accused, and so on. There are no real saboteurs in the game, because the facilitator did not write an *O* on any of the slips of paper.

Following the activity, there is an intense debriefing covering the objectives of the session—looking at issues of trust and the concept of assumptions and what happens when we judge people just by our perceptions of their behavior. In the debriefing, the students connect the experience to memories of how they have been treated by others as well as to ideas of how their group will work together. Through the activity, they develop insights into building trust and moving past their assumptions. The facilitator helps them transfer these insights to future activities—the "so what" of the experiential learning cycle (see chapter 3). The debriefing ends with the facilitator inviting the group to revisit their full-value contract and asking if they need to add anything to it.

Corporate Settings

A team of 12 executives from a large manufacturer of photocopy machines has hired a consultant to help them look at how to make a product that is consistent with their values of maintaining or increasing production speed, providing the consumer with good value, providing the consumer with a quality product, and minimizing product waste. The consultant has selected Mass Pass, an adventure initiative, and has set it up in advance by creating a 5-by-10-foot (1.5-by-3-meter) rectangle using a rope for the boundary markers and placing two buckets on opposing corners of the rectangle.

One of the buckets is full of various tossable objects such as fleece balls and beanbag animals. The consultant briefs the clients, saying, "As a leadership team in your company, you are charged with creating a production system that is as efficient as it can possibly be. Efficiency balances the components of speed, value, quality, and waste. Your challenge is to juggle these things as you create photocopy machines of the highest quality possible. In bucket A, there are several dozen objects that represent components of the machines. Every fifth object that lands in the other bucket, B, will represent a

CAREERS IN ADVENTURE

NAME: Mark Collard

JOB: Adventure educator and facilitator, self-employed (Melbourne, Australia)

BACKGROUND: BBus in Accounting, Monash University, Australia; MBA, Clarkson University, New York

I was senior trainer and director of Project Adventure Australia for 10 years, which involved duties such as answering telephones, meeting with clients, writing proposals, coordinating office and training staff, and delivering approximately 120 days of programming a year.

Since 1999, I have been contracted on an independent basis to deliver many Train the Trainer workshops and team development programs for groups throughout the United States, Australia, Taiwan, and Japan. In 2005, Project Adventure published my book, *No Props: Great Games With No Equipment,* which is now sold worldwide.

I also pursue an active career as an actor and voiceover artist, which is inspiring my passion to host my own TV show one day.

WHAT'S YOUR JOB LIKE? I design and deliver a variety of adventure education programs (three to four weeks a year), mostly team development and Train the Trainer workshops for older youths and adults.

In the past, managing the business of Project Adventure in Australia, I would do everything from answering the phone to running programs. Today, the work comes to me. I write up the proposal and then design and deliver the program. Although it's a lot less stable than a regular job, being an independent practitioner allows me to devote more time and energy to each program I deliver, which I believe results in a better outcome for my clients.

You gotta love working with people, and I mean with people, not just at them. They are not just clients, or another program, or whatever other label you wish to give them—they are living, breathing, feeling entities. People are not machines, so you must treat all of your participants with deep respect. This is the first step toward building a trusting relationship with them. You will make mistakes, but not because you took your eyes off the road.

Thankfully, I have a deep passion for working with people, inspiring and empowering them to bigger things than they think they are capable of. As an actor, as with my work as an adventure educator and facilitator, I rely on certain skills to help me create these experiences: listening, as much for what my group is saying as for what they are not saying; humor, which allows me to invite people to play, trust, and learn (humor is one of the most useful social lubricants I know); sequencing, or the skill of using the right activity at the right time so that I can prepare my group for their success; and finally, being at choice—always creating an atmosphere where people can make appropriate and safe decisions to be how they want to be.

market-ready machine. You will have five production rounds of 90 seconds each to become as efficient as possible while making as many machines as possible." Then the consultant gives the rules:

- All objects must be inside the bucket at the beginning of every round.

- Time for each round starts when the first object is removed from the bucket.

- All sides of the rectangle must be occupied by at least one participant, representing the company's shared leadership.

- Once participants have chosen a side, they may not switch sides within a round, representing the importance of expertise and longevity in an established role.

- Each participant must touch the object after it leaves the first bucket and before it lands in the other bucket, representing the team nature of manufacturing.

- Objects may not be passed to anyone to the immediate right or left; in other words, the object must skip at least one person when it is passed.

- Whenever an object is being passed from one side of the rectangle to another, it must cross over the inside of the boundary area (i.e., it cannot be passed around the corner outside the perimeter of the rectangle).

- Any time an object is dropped, it becomes waste and must return to the resource container (bucket A) to be recycled.

- If an object is dropped inside the boundary markers, it may not be retrieved and is lost for the duration of that round.

The executive team attempts the activity and at the end of round 2 has established a pattern of tossing and catching that meets the rules. Rather than looking at other patterns of production, they decide to keep doing what they are doing, only faster. Round 3 becomes so fast that participants begin to drop objects and make mistakes, representing the reality of waste and the difficult balance between speed and quality. This leaves the group with a very real question: How do we balance speed, value, quality, and waste? By the final round, the group has worked out a system that uses the same tossing and catching pattern as established in the first rounds but involves better communication about the timing of tossing the objects. The consultant guides them through a reflection exercise that helps to solidify the powerful lessons they have learned

from the exercise, such as the importance of balancing speed with quality and taking the time to communicate before executing a plan.

Strategies for Finding and Creating Adventure Activities

There are numerous adventure activity guides and curriculum guides that can provide you with ready-to-use activities. The New Games books mentioned earlier in this chapter are out of print but can be found at some online bookstores. Many newer books of cooperative games exist, such as Terry Orlick's *Cooperative Games and Sports, Second Edition* (Human Kinetics, 2006). Both the AEE (www.aee.org) and Project Adventure (www.pa.org) offer excellent activity books.

The majority of popular adventure activities are in the public domain and do not have names of their creators associated with them. Facilitators put their mark on any given activity by changing the rules or modifying the objectives slightly—either intentionally (to fit group goals or assets) or by forgetting a piece of the briefing. Sometimes a new piece of equipment will spark a fresh idea, sometimes creativity is required when a week of bad weather keeps an outdoor program indoors, and sometimes an unusual client request serves as inspiration. When adapting and creating activities, keep these guidelines in mind:

- It is easier to create within the framework of an idea than it is to create from scratch. Adapting an existing game is easier than creating something totally new.

- Making one change at a time allows the practitioner to evaluate the impact of that change, good or bad.

- Try many ideas. Some will be fun, some won't; those that are fun and exciting will stick around.

- The more facilitators experiment with the process of creation and understand the components of games, the better the games become at the end of the creative process.

These guidelines have been adapted from an article by Steve Butler, *ZipLines Magazine*, 2000.

For learning to happen through adventure, activities must be intentional. It is critical that activities be appropriate to both the constituency and the goals of your group. For example, you wouldn't design the same activities for a group of first grad-

Adventure activities are a lot more than fun, although fun is a major theme.

ers that you would for adolescents; obviously there are major developmental differences between the two groups. Further, you wouldn't design the same program for adolescents trying to develop leadership skills that you would for adolescents trying to remain sober.

A good facilitator will use activities in sequence. For example, it is important not to jump right into trust activities when the group has just met or when there is unresolved conflict from yesterday's initiative. When preparing the adventure session, it is vital to know where your group is. For example, are they cruising along and ready for an activity that provides challenge, or are they having difficulty and are in need of an activity that ensures triumph? You can use your group's performance on previous activities to assess their readiness for future activities. Other things to consider when creating an adventure experience include the following:

- Are my activities appropriate to the fitness level and physical abilities of my group?
- Are the group's behaviors telling me they need to blow off some steam, take a break from intense activity and laugh, and so on?

- Are my activities appropriate to the setting—inside or outside, urban or rural, challenge course or no challenge course?

The sample adventure lesson plan on page 138, designed for middle school physical education students, exemplifies proper planning. Group goals, age development (readiness, group affect, group physical ability, group behavior), and program setting are all accounted for.

Conducting Adventure Activities

Facilitating adventure activities requires much more than reciting a set of rules. Without careful briefing, good equipment, boundary and time-frame selection, attention to safety, and a spirit of fun, the activity will remain a simple list of instructions and not become a learning opportunity. Effective leadership is vital to bringing an activity to life.

Careful Briefing

The way that an activity is briefed should be viewed as a step in the planning process. There is no right or wrong way to brief an activity, but there are some basic guidelines for planning your briefings.

- Allow time for questions (especially for initiatives).
- Provide written instructions.
- Be aware of your choice of language. "Everyone must tag their partner" has the same meaning as "You will have the opportunity to chase your partner," but the wording can help decrease anxiety. Use language that reinforces the commitment to challenge by choice.
- For initiatives that involve creative thinking, explain in advance what is and is not permitted within the scope of the rules so that a group's creative thinking is not shut down in the midst of the activity.

Good Equipment

Many adventure activities require no equipment whatsoever. For those that do, select equipment (often called *props*) that is unique and will help set the tone of the adventure experience. In Warp Speed (page 132), the facilitator used a beanbag frog instead of a tennis ball. Why? Most participants do not look at a beanbag frog and make assumptions about their ability to throw it and catch it, as they would a tennis ball, and they are likely to handle

Lesson 1

This is an introductory lesson where students learn names as well as some fun facts about each other.

ACTIVITIES

- ✦ Hustle Bustle
- ✦ Categories

MATERIALS

None needed.

Activity 1: Hustle Bustle

LESSON OBJECTIVES

Students will be able to do the following:

- ✦ Recognize each person by name
- ✦ Experience a sense of community

ESTIMATED TIME

5 minutes

SETUP

Ask the class to stand in a circle.

FRAMING

Say to students, "This game will help us to learn each other's names."

PROCEDURE

1. Ask everyone in the circle to say their name.
2. Ask the group to repeat the circle of names, this time saying them as quickly as possible. Each name must be said completely.
3. Time this first round. The time begins when the first person speaks and ends when the last person is done.
4. Complete multiple rounds going in the same direction. The fastest time in this direction is team A's time.
5. Establish team B's time by repeating the exercise in the opposite direction.
6. Have team A and team B compete by going in both directions at the same time!

DISCUSSION

Ask students the following:

- ✦ Did you align yourself with team A or team B? Why?
- ✦ Was there any real difference between team A and team B?
- ✦ How can competition and cooperation exist at the same time?

SAFETY CHECK

No special safety procedures are required for this activity.

TIPS AND COMMENTS

This activity can provide a good opportunity to discuss healthy competition.

Activity 2: Categories

LESSON OBJECTIVES

Students will learn about the following:

- ✦ General space
- ✦ Personal space

ESTIMATED TIME

15 minutes

SETUP

No setup is necessary.

FRAMING

Say to students, "We have many things in common and many things that are different. This activity will give us a chance to discover some of these things."

PROCEDURE

1. Say to students, "I am going to ask a series of questions. When you know your answer, find other people who answer the question in the same way that you do and stand with them. If no one shares your answer, stand alone."
2. After thinking about each question (see sample questions under Tips and Comments), students should find others who have common responses and stand together in groups.

DISCUSSION

Ask students the following:

- ✦ What did you learn about your classmates?
- ✦ Did you have things in common you thought you wouldn't? Like what?
- ✦ Was anyone alone in a group? How did that feel? (Don't ask these questions if you've already observed that no one was alone.)

SAFETY CHECK

Make sure students walk when moving among the groups.

TIPS AND COMMENTS

Create questions that are both fun and meaningful, and have students talk about their answers when they are in their small groups. Here are some sample questions:

- ✦ What is your favorite pizza topping?
- ✦ What is your favorite color?
- ✦ How many siblings are in your family, including yourself?
- ✦ How many pets do you have?
- ✦ What do you like most about going to school?
- ✦ What do you like most about physical education?

the frog more gently than the ball. Introduce only the props that are necessary for any given game and keep the rest in a bag or out of sight. A pile of fun-looking toys can be distracting. Keep equipment clean and in good shape. Introduce new props to keep a group engaged.

Boundary and Time-Frame Selection

The size of the play area and the duration of the activities and activity sessions have a significant influence on adventure activities. Consider the following guidelines:

- The boundaries for active games and for initiatives should fit the goals of the session. For example, Everybody's It (page 130) is played in a small rectangular area so that a group can explore issues of safety and personal space. If played in a wide-open gymnasium, it can be a great fitness activity.
- Many initiatives, such as Mass Pass (described in the previous corporate example), involve multiple rounds. Be clear with participants as to how many rounds will be allowed. For example, you might say, "You will have three rounds or 30 minutes to complete this activity, whichever comes first."
- End adventure games at a time when participants are fully engaged; don't wait for the activity to get boring or for behavior to deteriorate.

Safety

It is important to consider the safety aspects of each activity and to address the concerns that each one presents.

- When briefing activities, point out hazards in the play area that may cause harm, such as dips in terrain. If grass is wet and slippery, be especially wary of running games.
- Be aware of medical and physical concerns in your group that may cause a particular activity to be inappropriate. Shoulder injuries, sprained ankles, and back problems are common and can be exacerbated given the nature of some activities.
- Challenge by choice is more than a cornerstone of program quality; it's also a vital tool in keeping people safe. Make sure that participants understand their choices.

- Do participants have the skills to perform the activity? Follow the guidelines for sequencing to increase the chances of a safe experience for all.
- Maintain an emotionally safe environment.

Fun

The energy and spirit of a group is largely influenced by that of the facilitator. Participate when it is possible and safe to do so, and model what you desire from the group. Use fun metaphors and fantasy when briefing an activity. Point out rule infractions in a way that keeps the spirit positive.

Summary

Adventure facilitators have a wealth of fun, engaging, and challenging activities available to them. Exploring them all, although really fun, is not as important as knowing how to properly sequence and run them. However, don't bore your group by repeating the same 10 activities over and over. As with any profession, you need to enhance your knowledge with application. So put what you've read here into practice—get coaching and feedback whenever you can. The more you work with groups, the more effective you will be at helping participants achieve learning objectives through adventure.

Review Questions

1. Think of a time when you experienced an activity like the ones we've discussed in this chapter. Was it a good experience? What made it positive? If not, what was missing?
2. Can an activity fit into more than one category? What would move a particular activity from one category to another?
3. What factors might influence the outcome of a particular activity?
4. What are some things you would think about in planning an adventure program?
5. If an activity is failing to engage your group and you thoroughly planned ahead so this wouldn't happen, would you stick with it or switch to another activity? Can you explain why your choice makes sense?
6. Why do you think the activity sequence is important?

7. Can you imagine ever using the activities explained in this chapter out of sequence? If so, with what kind of group and what kind of goal?

Student Learning Activity

Select one of the subsequent scenarios and do the following:

+ Identify the goals of the session.
+ Describe what activity types would be appropriate to use with the group.
+ Create an activity that would help to meet the goals of the session or else modify an activity that you already know.
+ Explain why the activity helps to meet the goals of the session.

The football coach at the local high school has come to you and your coworker for help. He knows that you can use adventure methods to help his team. There have been several incidences of stealing in the locker room. There are bad feelings among the team members, and trust and communication have broken down. He wants you to take two full practices with the varsity team, about two hours each session. There are two of you to do this work. You have portable adventure equipment available to you.

You are working at a summer camp. As a cabin counselor for 13-year-old girls, you are asked to do 90 minutes of adventure activities with the girls in your cabin during the first day of camp to help the girls feel comfortable. Some girls know each other from last year, and four of them are new to the camp. You have portable adventure equipment available to you.

CHAPTER 9

Low-Element Challenge Courses

Alison Rheingold

"" I see low elements as a central means for fundamental change. More change occurs on low elements, in many instances, than other types of experiential learning activities. Personal growth and group development occur simultaneously. Groups can become very cohesive as a result of the processes evoked, a shift often occurs at this point in programming. Low elements can also be a positive test of group dynamics for established groups. People often come to a challenge course with some amount of fear that can be reduced or eliminated on low elements because they are not as physical or as threatening as high elements. They do present a combination of the physical and cognitive challenges. ""

—Cindy Walker

Chapter Concepts

+ Low challenge course elements are used in a variety of settings and locations, including indoors in gymnasiums and outdoors in woods, fields, and parking lots.

+ In an adventure setting, low elements are used for two primary purposes: team development and personal challenge.

+ Low elements are used with a variety of populations, including schools, therapeutic agencies, camps, the military, and corporations.

+ To deliver quality programs on low elements, instructors need to develop facilitation skills that include the ability to assess a group and process the experience.

+ Awareness and understanding of safety and risk management are critical characteristics of quality programming on low challenge course elements.

Low challenge course elements are one method that adventure educators use to create powerful learning opportunities for individuals and groups. The purpose of this chapter is to provide you with a basic understanding of what low challenge course elements are, how they are used, and what professional opportunities they offer.

A low challenge course element is any apparatus intentionally designed and used in adventure learning that requires participants to be off the ground—anywhere from 1 inch (2 centimeters) to approximately 12 feet (4 meters). **Low elements** are constructed activities that do not occur on the ground and do not require being attached to a belay system. Other terms often interchanged with low challenge course elements include *initiative course, ropes course,* and *teams course.*

Although not always the case, low elements typically involve teamwork: For an activity to be successful, participants must work together by physically, mentally, and emotionally supporting each other. For instance, all group members could be on the element at the same time trying to accomplish a task. Or, one person could be on an element attempting a personal challenge while the rest of the group members are responsible for safety by spotting or managing the apparatus. In this vein, low challenge course elements fit into a continuum of adventure activities that range from games and problem-solving initiatives (see chapter 8) to high challenge course elements (see chapter 10). While low elements are often confused with obstacle courses—which are typically designed to provide personal physical challenges without the support of group members—the focus of this

chapter will be courses designed for adventure and educational purposes.

From Obstacle Course to Challenge Course

What is the difference between an obstacle course and a low-element challenge course? The heart of the difference rests in the evolution of purposefully installed equipment used by experiential educators. This progression started with the use of apparatus as facilitated physical challenge components of an educational experience. The institutional use of this equipment in an educational setting, coupled with the **intentional design** of elements for a physical and social purpose, has led to the present-day use of the low challenge course.

Evolution of the Low Challenge Course

Kurt Hahn, founder of Outward Bound, began using the obstacle course as a means to develop the individual and group in the late 1930s and early 1940s. His early use of these courses was comparable to military use of similar equipment, focusing primarily on individual accomplishments, both physical and mental, with an emphasis on self-confidence. At the first Outward Bound school, Hahn used apparatus to teach survival skills to British seamen. The events were meant to simulate real-life obstacles, such as getting back on a boat after going overboard (Priest and Gass 2005).

When Outward Bound came to the United States in 1962, low elements evolved into equipment used to physically and mentally train participants for wilderness trips. These courses included "a set of initiative tests and the aerial ropes course" and were used to promote "group cohesion and esprit" (Miner and Boldt 1981). Early elements included the Wall and the Beam,* which still are staples of many programs at Outward Bound and beyond.

In the late 1960s and early 1970s, low challenge course elements began to be installed in contexts other than training for wilderness expeditions. Seen as valuable learning tools unto themselves, low elements became a way to bring wilderness-based learning outcomes to facility settings. One of the first courses of this type was built by Project Adventure at Hamilton-Wenham Regional High School in Hamilton, Massachusetts. Project Adventure, whose founders wanted to bring the learning outcomes of Outward Bound to a nonwilderness setting, used ropes courses as one of their tools. The low course was used in conjunction with a high course for the purpose of bringing adventure experiences to the 50-minute class period (Rohnke 1989). (See chapter 1 for more details.)

Early courses were constructed of rope and wood and attached primarily to trees. The design of these early elements was often based on the natural environment and incorporated its existing physical features, such as creeks, gullies, and swamps. A classic example is the Sneaker Pit, located at Hamilton-Wenham Regional High School. This element involved the Tension Traverse—walking on a cable rope over a muddy, swampy area with the aid of a hand line. If you stepped off the element, you fell into the mud, and you usually left your sneakers where you landed because they were stuck in the bottom of the swamp (Schoel 2005).

Low Elements Since the 1970s

Throughout the 1970s and early 1980s, ropes courses were installed by vendors and built by facilitators of these experiences, many of whom evolved into installation vendors. Project Adventure built several hundred courses during this time, primarily in schools. Many of the installations at schools received federal funding to replicate the positive results seen at Hamilton-Wenham Regional High School.

During the 1980s, low challenge courses began to be used by a wide range of institutions, including therapeutic agencies, corporations, and summer camps. As more people and organizations became interested, additional vendors entered the business of designing and installing low and high ropes courses. (See chapter 1 for more information on the **Association for Challenge Course Technology [ACCT]** and the growth of challenge course vendors.)

Challenge course popularity continued to grow into the 1990s. Around this time the adventure field shifted terminology away from **ropes course** to **challenge course** in an attempt to use words that were more accurate and descriptive. Old courses had been built out of rope, but new courses were built using cable.

Current trends in the challenge course field include an ever-expanding use of low elements, an ever-growing number of professional vendor members of ACCT, and a move toward standards and certification for both facilitators and installers of challenge courses. The future looks bright for challenge courses. Because of the innovations in programming and creativity in design, more and more institutions and organizations are seeing the benefits of using challenge courses in their programs.

Settings and Types of Low Elements

Over the last 40 years, the types of elements and low-element courses have evolved as a result of innovations in use, design, and construction. The different types of elements and courses include indoor and outdoor courses, portable elements, single elements, circuit courses, individual and team elements, and universally accessible elements. When deciding on the type of course and elements, organizational leaders take into consideration many logistical and programmatic factors; if they didn't, it would be difficult to design a course that fits their needs. Consider these questions before installing a low challenge course:

---

*While some names of low elements are fairly standard in the field, practitioners and vendors often use different names to describe the same or similar events or apparatus. For the purpose of this chapter, we will use names that were standardized through their original use. For example, the Mohawk Walk, which was named in the 1970s by a group with whom Karl Rohnke was working (Rohnke et al. 2003), is also called Team Traverse, Cable Walk, and Swamp Crossing.

- What space is available? Do you have indoor space, outdoor space, or storage space? If you build outdoors, do you want to build on trees or poles?

- If you want to build on trees, what is the health of the trees?

- What is the year-round weather like? In what seasons would you be able to hold programs? When would you typically want to use your low elements?

- What is your budget? What are your funding sources?

- How many staff members will use the course? What is their level of experience in using low elements? How will they be trained?

- Who are the people you are serving? What types of needs do they have?

- Why do you want to use a low-elements course as part of your programming? What are your desired outcomes? What do you hope participants will learn?

- What size groups will you work with?

- What is a typical time frame? How long will groups be on the course?

No matter the type or setting, low challenge course elements or courses should be designed and installed by a level 3 or level 4 professional vendor member of the ACCT. These vendors follow an established set of standards that help ensure both quality construction and applicability to program design.

Settings

One of the preeminent characteristics of low elements is the diversity of settings in which they can be installed and used. The two types of physical settings are indoor and outdoor. Both have been used since the early 1970s (Rohnke et al. 2003), and both provide unique opportunities for adventure programming. Whether installed indoors or out, you should have your site inspected by a qualified person who can tell you whether your physical structures can support the elements you want to install.

Although most people think of low elements as solely outdoor equipment, they can also be installed indoors in gymnasiums, classrooms, multipurpose rooms, hallways, cafeterias, indoor sport facilities, and any other arenas in which there is the proper space. Many people around the world choose to use low elements indoors for both logistical and programming reasons. There are both advantages and disadvantages to installing low elements indoors. Advantages include potentially lower cost (no need to install poles or posts or drill through trees), convenience of location (less time to get a group to the course), and also the fact that weather does not affect programming or the wear and tear of the equipment. The disadvantages of using indoor elements are that participants remain indoors, you need proper storage for the equipment, fewer types of elements are available, and open spaces such as gymnasiums do not provide privacy if multiple groups are using the course.

Although indoor courses can be convenient, outdoor courses provide greater possibilities in terms of materials, types of elements, and locations. Outdoor low elements can be built in a wide range of venues, including parking lots, wooded areas, open fields, and other spaces. The location of outdoor courses depends on a number of factors, including available space, type and health of trees, overall budget, proximity to facilities, and desired program outcomes. Outdoor low elements can be installed on trees, telephone poles, or metal or wood posts.

Installed and Portable Low Elements

Adding to the versatility of low elements is the fact that both installed and portable elements are available. For outdoor courses, post and pole material may be telephone poles, wood (4 by 4 inches, or 10 by 10 centimeters), or metal structures. Indoors, elements are often secured to overhead beams or other appropriate ceiling structures. Finally, some low elements are installed semipermanently. These elements, known as put-up–takedowns, are fixed to permanent anchors but can be partially dismantled. Some programs prefer having the option of taking down installed elements so they can ensure that the course is used only under the supervision of trained staff.

Although most low elements are permanently installed, some low elements are portable. Portable elements are any apparatus that can be set up and moved without great effort. The benefits of portable elements are that they can be used in multiple locations (whether within a building or from site to site), they can be transported easily, and they typically cost less than installed elements. The disadvantages of portable elements are that they require adequate storage area and that there are a limited number of them. Examples of portable low elements include Islands, the Meuse, Trolleys, and the All-Aboard Platform. Finally, often there is a perception that portable elements can easily be made by volunteers or someone with basic carpentry skills. While this is sometimes true, care should be taken when having someone who is not a challenge course professional build apparatus for educational or institutional use.

Purposes of Low Elements

As previously mentioned, low elements are used for two main purposes: individual outcomes and team-oriented outcomes. While both typically require a group to physically and emotionally sup-port each other, the first type focuses on individuals or dyads attempting a challenge on the apparatus while other participants remain on the ground in the role of spotters and encouragers. Examples of elements typically used for this purpose include the Wild Woosey, Triangle Tension Traverse, and Swinging Log. On these elements, participants challenge themselves to complete a task at the level that meets their physical and emotional needs. These types of elements are often used as a precursor to high elements, since they follow a similar format: one or two people accepting a challenge with the rest of the group on the ground, responsible for safety and support.

Islands

Islands is an example of a portable low element that is typically used as a problem-solving initiative. Islands can also be permanently installed.

MATERIALS

+ 3 portable platforms set 8 feet (244 centimeters) apart; typically two large platforms (3 feet by 3 feet, or 91 centimeters by 91 centimeters) and one smaller platform (1.5 feet by 1.5 feet, or 46 centimeters by 46 centimeters)
+ 2 boards, 4 feet (122 centimeters) and 6 feet (183 centimeters) in length

SETUP

Make sure that the boards do not reach between the islands by themselves. If the islands are not fixed, make sure that they are properly positioned and secure. The platforms should be a foot (30 centimeters) or so off the ground.

FRAMING EXAMPLE

Say to students, "There is a major epidemic on its way. You will be stranded in this school for the rest of your life if you do not get to the final platform without touching the ground. For any of you ever to leave the school, *all* of you must get to that final platform." Be sure to explain all safety considerations.

PROCEDURE

1. The group starts either on or behind the first island. Once they are standing on the island, they may not touch the ground again until they have traveled to the final platform.
2. If any participant touches the ground, the entire group must go back to the beginning.

3. If a board touches the ground, choose an appropriate penalty for the level of your group. Often this consists of sending one person of the group's choice back to the start. However, you may decide to send more people back if you like.

SAMPLE DISCUSSION TOPICS

+ In pairs, discuss the various roles that group members took on during the activity and which roles each of you played.
+ In pairs, list three examples of how your group took risks during the activity.
+ In pairs, discuss one strategy that your group used to be successful and one thing you could have done differently.

SAFETY

+ Participants may not jump from platform to platform.
+ Warn spotters to be aware of the movement of the boards, which can swing sideways.
+ Spotters may be needed for participants on the platforms. Assess the group and use spotters as needed.
+ Do not allow participants to hold a board in their hands while somebody steps on it.
+ Make sure the person who is traversing steps on and off the board in line with the board so that it does not move sideways.
+ Do not allow participants to jump off the end of the board.
+ Make sure there is always enough counterweight on the board before a participant steps on it.

Adapted from Panicucci et al., *Adventure Curriculum for Physical Education – Middle School.*

Triangle Tension Traverse

The Triangle Tension Traverse is an example of a traversing low element that is typically used as an individual or paired event.

MATERIALS

Triangle Tension Traverse low element, installed on trees, poles, or metal beams, or portable version to be used indoors. Typically consists of 3-foot (91-centimeter) cables set up in the shape of a triangle, with two hand lines.

SETUP

Check that the element is properly set up, including hand lines. Make sure that the ground is free of obstructions. Gather the group around the element.

FRAMING EXAMPLE

Say to students, "Here is a chance for you and your partner to give feedback to each other on your ability to lead and to follow. The task is for both people to get around the triangle of cables, moving in opposite directions and crossing in the middle of the back cable."

PROCEDURE

1. Ask students to partner up.
2. Use a ground demonstration to show how the element works.
3. Explain that, within each partnership, one person will be the leader and the other will be the follower. Roles will change at the halfway point of the activity.
4. When participants cross, they switch roles.

5. The leader is the person who directs the activity, keeps spotters attentive, and gives support to the follower on the cable.

SAMPLE DISCUSSION TOPICS

+ In pairs, give feedback on what was effective about how your partner led and followed.
+ Talk with each other about real-life examples of when you have led or followed.
+ Individually, reflect on the feedback that you were just given.

SAFETY CHECK

+ Each participant on a foot cable should have at least two spotters. Additional spotters are commonly used and should be added if necessary.
+ The most effective position for spotting is a half-step back from the participant, toward the starting point.
+ Tell spotters that if a fall occurs, the hand line will cause the participant to fall back toward the starting point.
+ If a fall occurs, spotters need to move in toward the participant and not back away.
+ Spotters need to help keep the hand line free from snagging.
+ Instruct participants to step off the cable and let go of the rope if a fall is imminent.
+ Do not allow participants to jump off the cable in an attempt to regain balance.

Adapted from Panicucci et al., *Adventure Curriculum for Physical Education – High School.*

Low elements can also be used as problem-solving initiatives. These elements typically require groups to work together to traverse an area; solve a problem; or go up, over, or through a piece of equipment. The intention is for participants to use a combination of physical, cognitive, and social and emotional skills to attempt the task. These low initiatives include Trolleys, Spiderweb, Mohawk Walk, the Wall, and Nitro Crossing. See the Islands activity for an example of this type of low element (page 145), as well as the photo of the Wall (page 156).

Design Styles of Low-Element Courses

Over the years, two main styles of design have evolved for low-element course layout. One design

style consists of low elements that are separated from each other and require a group or an individual to return to the ground before attempting the next event. A second type of course is called a *circuit course*. While not as common, these kinds of courses offer participants the chance to attempt several elements in succession without returning to the ground between each event. Each of these course styles may offer both individual- and team-oriented elements.

Classification of Individual Elements

Another helpful way to classify low elements is by the physical requirement or type of action a group will take when engaging in the activity. When you combine the setting (indoor and outdoor) and type

CAREERS IN ADVENTURE

NAME: Kathy McGuigan

JOB: High school and middle school physical education instructor, Cairo American College (Cairo)

BACKGROUND: MS, California State University, Sacramento; teaching credential and BA in physical education, Westmont College, Santa Barbara, California

My first involvement with Project Adventure occurred when my husband wrote a pilot program to bring Project Adventure to the Grass Valley School District, where we worked in California. A course was built at our middle school consisting of over 80 elements from ground to 110 feet (34 meters) high. I was trained there and began using the course with my seventh- and eighth-grade physical education students, but the sheer size of my classes made the efforts challenging at best. While working on my thesis, I used the activities in the curriculum with home school and summer school students in grades kindergarten through 8 with excellent results.

WHAT'S YOUR JOB LIKE? In 1993, we went to Egypt, where I teach high school and middle school physical education in a private American school in Cairo. I proposed the idea of adding Project Adventure activities to our physical education curriculum there. The department and administration were totally supportive and we were able to fund, build, and furnish all the equipment for the full spectrum of Project Adventure activities over a three-year period. Currently, we use Project Adventure games and initiatives in all our classes on a regular basis to build teamwork, to encourage movement (to elevate heart rates), to improve self-confidence, and for the joy of play. Within the physical education curriculum, each grade has one or

two units of climbing a year. We use trust-building and risk-taking activities along with the technical instruction of climbing and belaying. I also use Project Adventure activities and games to develop teamwork and trust with our high school teams, and I have facilitated team-building sessions with groups of students and teachers of all grade levels.

Currently I teach team sports in grades 7, 9, 11, and 12. I also coach varsity boys' volleyball, junior varsity boys' basketball, and varsity girls' softball. Our students are from 45 countries and are children of Egyptian nationals, diplomats, military personnel, oil company executives, and people in private industry. Our school teams travel to Europe and the Persian Gulf for sport tournaments, and they travel outside and within Egypt extensively for school trips. Cairo American College is a fantastic place to work because we have small classes with motivated students and supportive parents, we have incredible facilities and equipment, and we have well-trained, high-energy professionals in our physical education department.

As a professional, I have been teaching since 1978 and coaching since I was in high school. I have done many camps and coaching clinics, and I have also given many workshops on the use of Project Adventure in physical education. I have presented to professionals at the European Council of International Schools (ECIS); educators from the western United States at the PEACH conference in San Luis Obispo, California; and with my colleagues in Cairo. I have attended Project Adventure workshops in Beverly, Massachusetts; Malibu, California; Salt Lake City; and Cairo.

(continued)

(continued)

I love working with kids; time with them is the best part of my day, every day. Because we are a K through 12 school, it is fantastic to be able to watch students progress in class and on teams from middle school through high school and on to college and adulthood. To see them grow and develop as people and to have them return and share the experiences of their lives and reminiscences of their time here in school is an awesome, rewarding experience.

I would highly recommend teaching as a profession, because for me the most important thing one can do is to contribute to the development of children. However, teaching physical education is a physically demanding profession and takes a great deal of flexibility, creativity, and humor. In addition, oftentimes only problems are noticed and the positive goes unnoticed or unrewarded. Dealing with parents, administrators, and colleagues as well as budgets, scheduling, and assessment are challenging at times. However, if you want to get rich in the heart rather than the pocket; don't mind working under the radar; and want the rewards seen on the faces of students after they experience an improved effort, a skill mastered, the pure enjoyment of play, and the camaraderie of wearing your school's colors, this is just the job for you.

(group and individual challenge), the full range of choices can be seen. Although not every element fits into these categories, the following four encompass most elements: swinging, traversing, lifting or catching, and initiative. Swinging elements are simply those that require a back-and-forth motion either on a rope or other apparatus. Examples include Nitro Crossing, Swinging Tires, and Seagull Swing. Traversing elements require a group or an individual to travel from point A to point B. Examples include Low Traverse Wall, Wild Woosey, and Mohawk Walk.

Lifting and catching elements typically require a higher participant skill level and require people to lift each other off the ground and through or over the apparatus. Examples of lifting elements include Spiderweb, Port Hole, the Beam, and the Wall. Catching elements, such as the Trust Fall, Hickory Jump, and the Trust Dive, require both a fall and a catch. Finally, as mentioned earlier, elements can also be classified as initiatives. Initiative elements can be traversing, lifting, or swinging or not involve any of these physical characteristics. Examples include Whale Watch, Trolleys, Islands, and Swinging Tires.

Many elements fall in more than one category depending on how they are used. For example, Swinging Tires can be both an individual challenge and a group initiative. It is both a swinging and a traversing element. The purpose of classifying elements is not to dictate their ultimate use, but to help practitioners organize the available adventure tools.

Universal and Accessible Low Elements

Low elements are designed to be used by people with different types of abilities and disabilities. Termed *universal* or *accessible,* these courses and elements are designed to offer educational opportunities to people who have physical, developmental, intellectual, emotional, or behavioral challenges. The ADA mandates creating inclusive programs, and many organizations have taken this mandate as an opportunity to reach out to a more diverse population (Rogers 2000).

Several organizations have written standards to help raise awareness of the need for accessible challenge courses. The ACCT states in its installation standards, "Location of elements and activities must include but are not limited to consideration of the following: terrain, presence of existing structures, erosion potential, accessibility, overhead utilities, etc." (Association for Challenge Course Technology [ACCT] 2004). The **Association for Experiential Education (AEE)** states, "Programs should proactively identify the essential elements of their activities and the conditions that may limit accessibility. Participation in the normal activities of a program and associated group work should be fostered and barriers should be removed or accommodations provided to permit full participation in accordance with the letter and spirit of the law. Note that 'available' means that persons have both access and opportunity" (Association for Experiential Education [AEE] 2004a).

Depending on how an organization chooses to develop its program, either a universal or an accessible approach may be chosen. The difference between these two is that a **universal approach** creates a holistic program from the get-go—designing the entire course to be inclusive of people with many different needs. Taking an **accessible approach,** making a course accessible, is more of a physical emphasis, thinking about how to retrofit standard element designs to accommodate people with disabilities. The first is a programmatic view; the second is a physical view (Rogers 2000).

Examples of accessible low elements include Whale Watch, Universal Person Sender (an accessible version of Nitro Crossing), and Universal Islands. While some of these elements are constructed differently to accommodate wheelchairs, a course that is truly accessible meets a much wider range of needs—how the elements are facilitated is as important as how they are constructed. As Rogers states, "Whatever value individuals have to contribute to the process; whether it be physical, cognitive or social, a universal course should provide the context for their expression" (2000).

Level of Difficulty

The level of difficulty for each element is based on the skills required of the spotters, the participants, and the facilitator. Practitioners should consider all three factors when choosing whether to have a group use a specific low element. More information on facilitator choice and group assessment will be covered later in the chapter. Table 9.1 classifies the difficulty of elements as beginning, intermediate, or advanced. This is not meant to be an exhaustive list of all low challenge course elements in existence, but a sampling of activity types.

As previously mentioned, one of the main characteristics of an experience on a low challenge course is the lack of belay and the reliance on group members to keep participants safe while they are on the apparatus. This type of safety is called **spotting** (ACCT 2004; Ryan 2005). Depending on the element, a person's spotting skill can be classified as beginner, intermediate, or advanced.

Proper spotting requires participants to learn specific body movements and techniques and then apply those skills in the context of actual elements. When teaching participants how to spot, you should

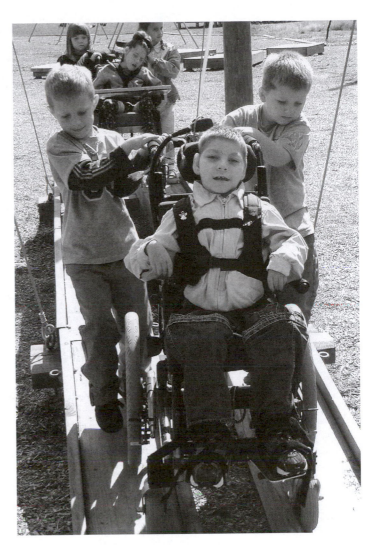

Students at C.E. Lawrence Elementary School on a custom-designed universal element known as the Lawrence Labyrinth.

cover the following basic information, as defined by Ryan (2005):

The spotter moves with the participant, positioning him or herself to be ready for a fall; the goal of spotting is to prevent injury, not necessarily to prevent a fall; basic spotting should be taught using a planned sequence; participants on low elements should be taught to prevent unnecessary falls by stepping off an element when a fall is imminent; less experienced participants will generally need a higher degree of spotting; less mature spotters will need a higher degree of supervision.

Ryan goes on to define the physical requirements of spotting: Spotters should assume an athletic stance, with knees bent and one foot forward. To be in the ready position, spotters should have their hands raised with the palms facing the participant.

TABLE 9.1

Low Element Level of Difficulty

Beginning	Intermediate	Advanced
All Aboard	Bosun's Chairs	Fidget Ladder
The Maze	Crisscross	Hickory Jump
TP Shuffle	Tension Traverse	Trust Fall
Trolleys	Seagull Swing	Trust Dive
Islands	Swinging Log	The Wall
The Meuse	Swinging Tires	The Beam
Whale Watch	Wild Woosey	
Mohawk Walk*	Mohawk Walk*	
Low Traverse Wall	Porthole	
Multiswing (i.e., Nitro Crossing, Prouty's Landing, Disc Jockeys)	Spiderweb	
	Vertical Pole and Tire	
	Team Triangle	
	Multiswing (Do I Go?)	
	Geocrossing/the Cube	

*Many elements, such as Mohawk Walk, can cross into different levels of difficulty, depending on construction and the facilitator's instructions.

Adapted from Project Adventure's *Adventure in Low Elements* training manual.

Also, spotters should be ready to move with the participant on the element, whether this is left, right, up, or down.

Facilitation of Low Elements

By combining intentional construction with program design, low elements can be a powerful tool for learning. The greatest low element is nothing without the intentional design of the person who is guiding a group through the element. As shown in this section, a facilitator should consider several factors when planning low-element experiences.

To effectively and safely lead groups through the low challenge course experience, facilitators should start by getting proper training. Training should cover operating procedures, managing a group while they are on the element, inspecting the element on an ongoing basis, deciding what tasks to give the group, and **framing** and debriefing.

Assessment and Sequencing

When planning an experience for a group, a facilitator should start by assessing the purpose of the experience. Ask questions such as, What do I hope the group will learn? What do they want to learn? What do my curriculum objectives state? Second, a facilitator should take into account both the physical and emotional needs of the group. Questions to ask include, What is the group physically ready for? How well are they working together?

The acronym GRABBSS (see chapter 3) is an effective way to organize your assessment into seven categories: goals, readiness, affect, behavior, body, setting, and stage of group development (Schoel, Prouty, and Radcliffe 1988; Schoel and Maizell 2002). By listing your thoughts on the GRABBSS topics, you can better plan a group's experience on a low challenge course.

One of the most important aspects of assessment and facilitation is assisting a group in their readiness.

By creating an intentional sequence of activities and fostering a spirit of challenge by choice before bringing a group to the low elements, a facilitator has a better chance of creating safe and powerful learning experiences. Consider a progression that will build participant skills in a way that is right for them, meets the overall goals of the program, and fits your time frame. To ready a group for the Spiderweb, a facilitator might teach basic spotting skills and have them practice these skills using Trust Leans, Wind in the Willow, and Levitation. All of these activities will prepare participants to lift each other, be lifted, and develop basic communication skills.

Running the Element

Within an established sequence of activities, a practitioner has a final layer of choice: how to actually run the element. Always working within the minimum safety guidelines for the element, a facilitator decides how to frame the activity, what the guidelines are for the task, how much time to allow, what other props or equipment to use, and how to debrief or process the experience.

Framing or briefing an activity is how a facilitator initially engages a group in the task. A facilitator

has three basic choices when framing an activity: telling a story, using a metaphor, or just giving the group the basics. A story involves crafting a fictional tale that will invoke the imagination of a group and will communicate the components of the task. A metaphor makes a direct connection to the group or applies to real-life experiences outside of the group. Finally, giving the group the basics is a straightforward way of telling the group what you are asking them to attempt. However you frame an element, you should include multiple ways of engaging in the activity to honor participants' chosen level of challenge. Consider the following examples of how a facilitator could frame the Spiderweb.

1. Story: "Your group has been hiking on the Appalachian Trail for several weeks. You have braved the woods, cooked over a fire, and slept under the stars, and you're ready for a hot shower! As you approach the trailhead, you see your van around the corner; you're almost to civilization! Suddenly you stop in your tracks. You are faced with a magnificent spiderweb that spans all the way across the trail. Going around the web is not an option, for the rivers are too high! Upon closer look, you see a plaque that describes the web. It says, 'Welcome, one and all to the home of Matilda

The Spiderweb gives students the chance to be physically and emotionally responsible for each other.

the Spider, the oldest and largest spider on the Appalachian Trail. Stewardship of the trail calls for keeping this historic web intact. You are invited to cross through if you are willing to commit to the following guidelines: You must be very gentle with the web. Do not touch any part of the web as you go through the holes. If someone touches the web, the group must be completely silent for one minute to allow Matilda to resume her nap.' Do you think that you can pass through without disturbing Matilda?"

2. Metaphor: "You have worked together as a class for the entire year. This web represents all of the things you have accomplished together. Take a moment and think of one thing that you are particularly proud of, either for yourself or on behalf of the group. Now, look at the Web of Accomplishments and decide which hole you would like to be passed through. Before you go through or are passed through the web, point out the hole that you have selected and share the accomplishment that you have in your mind. The rest of the class will take care of your words and you at the same time by ensuring that you are safe."

3. The Basics: "Before you is a classic activity called the Spiderweb. There are many openings in the web, some high and some low, some larger than others. Your challenge as a group is to end up on the opposite side of the web. The only way to get to the other side is to go through the openings in the web. There are a few rules: Each hole may only be crossed through once and after that, it is closed; if anyone touches the web, the last three people who have crossed through the web must come back; the group may select one hole that will be open for a total of four crosses, and you must select that hole before starting the activity; proper spotting and communication needs to be in place; and finally, the Spiderweb will close up in 30 minutes. Good luck!"

Other factors that affect a group's experience on a low element include time, physical setup, use of goal setting or consequences, number of participants, impairments, and accessories. *Time* refers to the actual amount of time the facilitator gives a group to complete a task. Giving a time frame can often be a positive way to motivate a group to complete a task. For example, saying, "You have 20 minutes to see how many people you can get into correct position on the TP Shuffle," can keep a group moving. It also may be a real-life need: "This class period is 45 minutes, so you have 5 minutes

for planning, 30 minutes to complete the task, and 10 minutes to process the experience." A potential downside of using time as a parameter is that some groups may feel rushed and therefore actually accomplish less than they would have without the time constraint.

As a facilitator, you often have choices about how you set up an element and the resources you provide to a group. For example, the Wall can include a rope to assist the group in getting members up and over. Do you choose to give this resource to the group, or do you ask them to attempt to go over the wall without the rope? Go back to your original goals and assessment to help determine the best course of action.

During the actual activity you may also choose to give the group a goal or ask the group to create one. On the Whale Watch, for example, you might say, "You must start again after the board has touched the ground five times," or "How many touches do you think you can do it in?" Giving a group a goal to work toward, similar to a time parameter, can help keep them on task and focused. If they have created the goal themselves, it can increase individual engagement and overall responsibility for the success of the group.

Finally, you may choose to give the group or certain group members an impairment, such as keeping their eyes closed, not using an arm, or not speaking. While this is common practice in the field, care should be taken when "handicapping" participants. Always ask yourself, "Why am I creating this rule? How will it increase their learning? How might it actually convey incorrect information about people with disabilities?" Alternative ways of creating varying levels of challenge include asking participants to ask their group questions instead of giving answers, allowing each person to speak twice during the planning session, or designating certain roles for each person (one person is the timekeeper, one is the safety manager, one is the resource manager, and so on).

When planning a learning experience on the low elements, a facilitator should also guide the group through an intentional processing of the experience. By taking time to plan how they will facilitate reflection, instructors will help groups glean meaning from their time on the elements (Ryan 2005). Consider the amount of time it will take, the topic and questions, and the method you will use. Without processing, a low element can become just a sequence of events instead of an opportunity for learning.

Innovative Uses of Low Elements

In an attempt to offer innovative experiences to participants, adventure educators are always thinking of new ways to use low elements. Consider the following examples. How do these examples change a participant's experience? How would the learning outcomes change?

1. Popcorn meets the Whale Watch (see page 157)—Imagine a problem-solving activity where the goal is to get a group to bounce Wiffle balls into a bucket as quickly as possible. Now imagine doing the same activity, Popcorn, on the Whale Watch. The group is trying to manage several tasks at once—both keeping the Whale Watch board balanced and bouncing balls into a bucket.

2. Object Retrieval meets TP Shuffle—In this merger of activities, the group first tries to balance on two parallel, horizontal telephone poles that are 10 feet apart. The group then attempts to transfer a bucket of balls using ropes from point A to point B. The group must manage physical and mental problem solving on a variety of levels.

3. Collective progress on the Wild Woosey—A typical use of the Wild Woosey involves two people working together to see how far they can traverse two cables in the shape of a V while the rest of the group physically supports the pair. Usually one pair's success has little to do with another's. In an attempt to make the Wild Woosey more of a group problem-solving experience, the facilitator asks the group to set a goal for the total number of feet or meters that the group can traverse. Each time a pair makes an attempt, their footage is added to the collective total.

4. Point system on the Wall (see page 156)—Because of the height and physical nature of the wall used in this activity, often participants are reluctant to actually go up and over the wall. Instead of making it an all-or-nothing proposition, consider developing a point system so that all roles add value to the success of the group. Spotting once would earn the group a point. Actually lifting a person would earn another point. Being on top of the platform and assisting someone up and over the wall would earn another point. If a person makes an attempt and makes it halfway, a point is earned. If they get to the platform they earn 2 points. Ask the group to set a goal for the number of points they think they can earn during their time at the Wall.

Safety Concerns

Facilitators of low-element experiences should have a basic understanding of safety concerns associated with low elements. With proper training, a facilitator should know how to set up and run an element and how to avoid accidents. A good place to start is with the **standard operating procedures** (SOPs) (Ryan 2005) for the elements. SOPs, which are developed by internationally recognized experts in the adventure field, refer to the minimum requirements to safely run an element no matter where the element is installed.

Once an element is installed, the team who manages the course should develop **local operating procedures** (LOPs). These LOPs take into account any unusual terrain, oddities in design, and programmatic concerns. LOPs should always be within the boundaries of the SOPs, taking the parameters of the SOP and making them more conservative.

When facilitating an element, it is essential to follow the LOPs. For more information, see chapter 10 on high challenge course elements.

To effectively run low elements, a facilitator should have information on accident types and rates associated with low elements. In Project Adventure's *20-Year Safety Study* (Furlong et al. 1995), the two low elements with the highest number of accidents were the Trust Fall and the Wall. In both cases, there is potential both for the climber and the spotter to get injured. In general, if used properly, low elements provide limited opportunities for people to injure themselves. Compared with high elements, there are more injuries, but compared with warm-up games and activities, there are far fewer (Ryan 2005).

Before using a low element, it is the facilitator's responsibility to visually check the element, both for proper setup and for any unusual events that have occurred since it was last used. A visual check

CAREERS IN ADVENTURE

NAME: Angel Martinez

JOB: Director of Adventure Programs, Crossroads for Kids (Duxbury, Massachusetts)

BACKGROUND: My experience in the outdoors began by participating in an Outward Bound semester course in 1993 for South Bronx High School students in New York. I also attended a six-week literacy wilderness course at the North Carolina Outward Bound School (NCOBS). I quickly started working for the New York City Outward Bound Center (NYCOBC) at the age of 16, running a mentoring program in the South Bronx. I became an assistant instructor for the NYCOBC and worked until I was 21. During that time I attended an instructor course at the Pacific Crest Outward Bound School (PCOBS), now called Outward Bound Wilderness. At the age of 21, I became an intern at the Thompson Island Outward Bound Education Center (TIOBEC). I went from being an intern to an assistant instructor to a lead instructor and finally a course director. I run an outdoor program for Crossroads for Kids. This program was featured on The Learning Channel (TLC) on a special airing in September 2006.

WHAT'S YOUR JOB LIKE? My current responsibilities consist of directing two three-week sessions of outdoor wilderness programs.

One session is dedicated to the surviving children of 9/11 victims. The other session is provided to 11/99 union members as part of their union benefits. In addition, I maintain all high and low challenge course elements and equipment. I also provide staff training in these areas.

As a director, I am responsible for writing policies and procedures and maintaining all logistical gear. I am also responsible for budgets, grant writing, course curriculum, staff hiring, training, course preparation and debriefing, food ordering, Web site management, student recruitment, and program development. I train the staff in the following areas: hiking, biking, canoeing, rock climbing, rappelling, fur trader canoes, and high and low ropes courses and initiatives. Focus areas are diversity, urban youths, conflict resolution, reality therapy, and managing young people in a wilderness setting.

The key to success is finding committed people who share the common goal of reaching our young people. By setting a good example of supportive relationships and drive, our students are surrounded by a culture that fosters positive change.

should include an inspection of the ground area, the area above the element, and the element itself (Ryan 2005). Examples of potential hazards include weather-related damage, poison ivy, wasps, vandalism, missing equipment, splintering or cracked wood, cable fray, debris on the ground, and overhanging dead branches.

Using Low Elements With Varied Populations

Low elements are used in a wide range of venues with an even wider range of purposes. A few of the venues in which low-element courses can be found include schools, therapeutic agencies, recreation agencies, camps, corporations, and the military. In this section we will explore the range of uses, highlighting several examples.

Schools

Tens of thousands of schools throughout the world use challenge courses as part of their curriculum. Low-element courses are often just one part of a challenge course and are found in elementary, middle, and high schools; in urban, rural, and suburban schools; and in public, charter, and independent schools.

At Seabrook Middle School in Seabrook, New Hampshire, low elements are used in a number of ways. First, the 11-element course is used as part of the physical education curriculum. By rotating through four main curriculum topics (lifetime activities, fitness, target games and net games, and adventure), students have the chance to experience the low elements. The purpose of using low elements in physical education classes at Seabrook Middle School is to provide physical challenges while building self-esteem, teamwork, communication, and problem-solving skills.

The low elements are also part of an alternative program for students with behavioral issues. The students in this self-contained classroom are guided through the elements as part of a larger program to help students become more accountable for their actions, learn to work with others, and make connections back to the classroom and to their lives.

The low elements at Seabrook include examples of beginning, intermediate, and advanced elements

Students from Seabrook Middle School work together to reorder themselves while staying balanced on the TP Shuffle.

and are installed on trees, are portable, or are stand-alone elements at the edge of the woods. The elements of the course are Islands, TP Shuffle, Whale Watch, Multiswing, Spiderweb, Mohawk Walk, Wild Woosey, Swinging Tires, Bosun's Chairs, Trust Fall, and the Wall.

Cindy Shoer, adventure educator at Seabrook, is intentional about her use of the lows. She keeps the framing and debriefing simple, weaving one idea through the students' experiences. One example is her use of the TP Shuffle. One of the first elements that students experience, it involves arranging students on a horizontal telephone pole that sits on the ground. Cindy starts by splitting the class into two groups and asking each group to come up with a country and a product from that country. She then arranges the groups on the element and explains that they are here today to negotiate a peace treaty. They need to work together to arrive at a peaceful solution to conflict (exemplified by how they change places on the log) and offer each other gifts from their country (their products). Afterward, Cindy asks students to make connections between how the students worked together and situations in their lives that require teamwork.

Military Settings

As previously mentioned, challenge courses are in part derived from the obstacle courses used in militaries. While obstacle courses are still widely used, challenge courses have also become mainstays in some parts of the U.S. military. Examples of where low elements are used in the military include the National Guard, Police and Fire Training, Coast Guard, and Air Force.

At the Coast Guard Academy in Connecticut, Chief Warrant Officer Guy Cashman uses low elements in a number of ways. He uses the lows during a course for chief warrant officers, as part of officer candidate training, with Coast Guard units, and occasionally with cadets. The course at the Coast Guard Academy consists of four low elements and several high elements, all built outdoors. Many of the elements are used specifically to teach team building (relying on others) and to analyze leadership skills. The Mohawk Walk and the Wall are used specifically to illustrate leadership and followership.

After attempting an element, participants process the experience by discussing the role that they took during the activity. Guy asks questions to investigate why people assumed different roles

and the importance of the roles that were taken. He uses questions such as "Why is following just as important as leading?" and "How did positional power play a role in this element?" He also helps participants make connections between the activity and importance of physical and emotional support. Time is taken to make connections between the activity and the real-world setting of their work in the Coast Guard.

Working with an older demographic group has been particularly powerful for Guy and the participants. The low elements offer a place for people who are not as physically fit as they used to be, people who often are not very active because they have desk jobs in the guard. Giving these people an opportunity to challenge themselves in ways that are right for them has provided opportunities for

Adult participants from the U.S. Coast Guard on the classic low element known as the Wall.

what Guy calls moral courage—making the right decision and doing the right thing.

Therapeutic Settings

Low elements provide powerful opportunities for participants to work on counseling or therapeutic goals. Participants can become more aware of their behavior, work on social and behavioral skills, and set goals for the future, all within a group environment.

For over 10 years, the Capital Area Intermediate Unit (CAIU) in Harrisburg, Pennsylvania, has used low elements as a tool to work with students with psychiatric disorders and those who are emotionally disturbed. Capital Area Adventures, a department within the larger agency, runs programs for students in grades kindergarten through 12 that are part of public schools throughout the area around Harrisburg. The program does in-school adventure programming, including team-building and trust-building activities. After students have progressed through a sequence of skill-building lessons, they travel to the main site to experience the low and high elements.

Tracy Keene, a social worker in the program, highlights the Whale Watch as one of the most powerful low elements of the program. She often uses the Whale Watch to build a metaphor about the ups and downs of life. As students try to balance the large platform, she helps them make connections between how they are working on the low element and how they are able to balance things that change in their lives. She makes the comparison between changes in real life and how adding one new person to the Whale Watch can throw participants off unless they are able to make the necessary adjustments and communicate them to the team.

Tracy remembers one group of high school students who had an exceptionally powerful experience on the Whale Watch. Because of the metaphor she built around finding balance and dealing with change, students were able to share things from their lives. One student spoke of what it was like when his mother died. Another student made a connection between the Whale Watch and what it was like to be a foster child and move around often, and the changes associated with each move. Being in a safe learning environment with the intentional framing of the Whale Watch allowed participants to share in a way they had not previously been able to do. The group ended the experience with a few main themes: We can balance our lives. We can support each other. We need each other to find balance.

Another powerful element in the therapeutic environment of the CAIU is the Wild Woosey, also called the Relationship Traverse. Bob Fleming, retired psychologist and former coordinator of the program, used the Wild Woosey as a way for students to talk about the changes in relationships that people naturally see over time. On the element, two students progress on foot cables, leaning on each other for support and balance as the cables spread farther and farther apart. The only way to make progress on the Wild Woosey is to rely on another person. The physical act of relying on another person forms the basis of the metaphor. After being on the element, students are asked to look at their own relationships and to make connections between the element and real life.

Corporate Settings

Finally, low elements can be used to work on matters that are relevant to the work environment, such as communication, trust, accountability, performance, leadership, behavioral styles, collaboration, and honesty. With the combination of a thorough needs assessment and proper framing and debriefing, low elements are powerful tools for change in the corporate setting. Instead of highlighting a specific program, in this section we will look at examples of how two elements can be used as tools in a corporate context.

The first example is a corporate use of the Whale Watch. The outcomes for the group are to learn how to prioritize tasks, build skills around gaining consensus, and lead and follow in the workplace. Given the four following tasks that can be completed in any order, the group must give the facilitator a goal for the number of touches that will occur within their given 30-minute time frame: Everyone must get on the element, two groups must change sides, the group must do a 360-degree rotation on the element, and the group must exit the element. Afterward, the group is guided through a debriefing that focuses on the outcomes. Potential questions include the following: What strategies did you use to make decisions? Was your decision making effective? Was everyone on board with the decisions that were made? How did your decision making mirror what happens in your workplace? Who took on leadership roles? Were there times when it was important to follow? How did the group prioritize the given tasks? What can you learn from this element that applies to your workplace?

A second example of a corporate use of a low element is the Team Triangle, which can help coworkers make connections between executing strategy and assuring that strategy is linked to organizational goals. The element is comprised of three cables that are connected in a triangle to three trees or poles. The cables are purposely not tightened so that they drape slightly. In the middle of the triangle is a platform positioned so participants cannot touch any of the trees. For this use of the Team Triangle, all group members start in the middle on the platform. While relying on the support of the group members, each person must touch three trees. The trees represent reaching organizational goals, and how each person gets to the trees represents the strategies the organization uses to achieve those goals. Each person must touch all three trees because each person is responsible for helping the company reach the goals. After a group has completed the task, several types of debriefing questions can be asked: How do you support each other in the workplace? Does everyone clearly understand how their role in the organization relates to the strategic objectives?

As these two corporate examples show, low elements can be tools for change within work organizations. By providing a vehicle through which participants can look at the work they do as well as how they relate to their coworkers, facilitators can create meaningful learning experiences for corporate groups.

Summary

In this chapter we have discussed the many types of low elements and low-element courses, facilitation of such courses, and differing applications and uses. When designed, installed, and maintained properly and when programs are intentionally planned, low elements can be an important means for individuals to learn in the context of a group. The powerful combination of physical, mental, and emotional involvement that they require as well as their general accessibility sets low challenge course elements apart from other types of learning experiences.

Review Questions

1. What is the difference between a ropes course and a challenge course? Do you think it is important to create and use consistent language across

the adventure education industry? Why or why not?

2. What are the two types of physical settings in which low elements are used? Why would an organization choose one setting over another?

3. Describe the different ways to classify low challenge course elements. What are the practical reasons for classifying low elements?

4. What is the difference between an accessible and a universal challenge course?

5. Look at the sidebars that describe Islands and the Triangle Tension Traverse (pages 145 and 146). In each example, how are the discussion questions connected to the framing of the group's experience?

6. Write a definition of *spotting*. What are the components of good spotting? How can spotting be a learning opportunity that is as important as actually being on a low element?

7. Why is it important for a facilitator to take time to guide participants in a reflection of their experience on a low element? Give an example of a question you might ask after a group completes the Mohawk Walk.

8. Compare and contrast Capital Area Adventure's use of the Whale Watch with that of the corporate example. To conduct a more in-depth look at these two uses of the Whale Watch, consider what follow-up questions you would ask for each use.

Student Learning Activities

1. On the ACCT Web site (www.acctinfo.org), go to the section on challenge course service providers and click on several different professional vendor members. Find low elements on each vendor's Web site and compare the similarities and differences between the types of elements, how they are designed, and how the vendor describes their use. If low elements were mentioned in this chapter that you are not familiar with, see if you can find them on a vendor's Web site to gain more information.

2. Do you have experience in adventure facilitation? Do you hope to get a job that uses adventure-based skills? Go to the Project Adventure Web site (www.pa.org) and click on their information on credentialing and practitioner certification. See if you can quantify the experi-

ence you have had. What level of certification would be right for you? What practical experience would you need before you would be eligible to take the tests at the different levels?

3. Many innovative schools and organizations around the world use low elements. Using the Internet or other means, find an example of a therapeutic agency, a residential camp, a private school, and an after-school program that uses low elements. Find at least one that is outside of the United States. How do these programs use low elements? How do their uses differ?

4. Do a literature search for research that shows the effectiveness of low elements as a tool for learning. What do you notice about the types of programs that have been researched? Where do you see a need for more research?

High-Element Challenge Courses

Christopher J. Damboise

" The ropes course is the Swiss Army knife of outdoor education. "

—Mike Stratton

Chapter Concepts

◆ The modern challenge course has its roots in early 20th-century European physical education and military physical conditioning.

◆ High-element challenge courses are installed in a variety of locations, settings, and mediums.

◆ Program goals, objectives, and design play a significant role in the choice of high elements, course layouts, and operating systems.

◆ Appropriate facilitation and operational skills are important to ensure effective and safe programs.

◆ Understanding and operational implementation of strategies to manage risk are critical characteristics of quality challenge course programs.

◆ High-element challenge courses are used in a variety of settings and with a variety of participant populations, including those in educational, therapeutic, recreation, corporate, law enforcement and military, and edutainment areas.

High elements can be team oriented, but they are often individual or small group challenges commonly installed 20 to 50 feet (6 to 15 meters) above the ground, requiring the use of climbing equipment and a **belay** system for safety. Participants often find the high elements the most memorable part of their challenge course experience because of the anxiety and exhilaration they feel during these activities. Whether they're traversing the Cat Walk beam or diving for a trapeze from the Pamper Pole, participants go far beyond their recognized limits. They often come away with a clearer understanding of their capabilities and a greater willingness to tackle challenges in their lives.

Peak experiences such as these are the cornerstone of perceived risk, a tenet of adventure programming. If not applied properly and managed safely, high elements can be merely a diversion or even have a detrimental effect on all that has been accomplished previously in the adventure sequence. When participants forget, ignore, or overlook the skills and awareness they have gained in their experiences on the low elements and other activities, the high elements can become a sideshow, much like the popular television show *Fear Factor* or an amusement park ride. The support systems and trust that the group members have developed during their previous experiences will be critical to their continued growth and exploration while using the high challenge course elements.

In this chapter, we will give an overview of high challenge course elements in the context of a larger adventure program. We will start with a brief historical perspective and then review the diversity of high challenge course systems, including settings, installation mediums, elements, course layouts and designs, and universal design. This will provide a foundation to survey the facilitation and operation of high-element challenge courses, including the following: assessment, sequencing, facilitation, challenge course technical information, and basic risk management. The concluding section will explore several programming uses of the high challenge course.

Origins of the Modern Challenge Course

It's difficult to pinpoint where the first challenge course was built. Individuals and organizations have used similar activities for a hundred years or more. The modern challenge course is an amalgam of philosophy and ideas from the likes of George Hébert and Kurt Hahn. These first courses were typically constructed for training military personnel, improving physical fitness, and increasing personal confidence. When these methodologies moved across the Atlantic Ocean to North America, permutations and adaptations started taking root. Colorado Outward Bound was the first educational organization to install a challenge course in the United States, in 1961. Project Adventure popularized the use of challenge courses in public schools starting in the early 1970s. Many adaptations, models, and new uses for the high challenge course have flourished in the ensuing years.

George Hébert

One of the first recognized advocates of modern adventure activities was George Hébert (1875-1957). As a naval officer, he traveled throughout the world before World War I and was influenced by the physical development and skills of indigenous peoples. When Hébert returned to France to work in physical education, he defined his own principles of physical education and began to create apparatus and exercises to teach his natural method, as he called it. He rejected competition and performance because he felt they diverted physical education from both its physiological ends and its fostering of sound moral values. Hébert once stated, "The final goal of physical education is to make strong beings. In the purely physical sense, the Natural Method promotes the qualities of organic resistance, muscularity and speed. . ." (Urban Freeflow 2006).

Hébert's methods expanded and became the standard for French military physical conditioning. The training sessions usually consisted of exercises in an outdoor environment. The course was often a kilometer in duration and a "natural method" session involved walking, running, jumping, progressing quadrupedally, climbing, walking on unstable surfaces, lifting and carrying an object, throwing, fighting, and swimming. This course could be natural, an undetermined route through the countryside, or a designed environment (Urban Freeflow 2006). It could be said that he was among the earliest proponents of the par course or obstacle course of physical training. Around 1949, Hébert's tenets and designs, often referred to as hébertisme, made their first incursion into North America. Two Canadian army officers who had served in France during World War II brought back some ideas and designed a course for Camp Ecole Trois-Saumons in Quebec (Wagstaff 2003).

Kurt Hahn and Outward Bound

After World War I ended, Kurt Hahn helped open a number of schools in the United Kingdom. His mission was to foster balance in the mental and physical growth of students, and he developed an educational plan that included increasing levels of physical challenge. Next, Outward Bound grew out of Hahn's school activities. Physical conditioning on apparatus, seamanship training, and working among the rigging of ships was embedded in the program (North Carolina Outward Bound 2006).

The first primitive ropes courses grew out of these humble ship-rigging beginnings.

Educators from the United States witnessed the use of ropes courses as part of the daily curriculum at Outward Bound schools in England. In 1961, Ernest Tapley designed the first U.S. Outward Bound ropes course in Marble, Colorado. He had just returned from England, where he experienced a ropes course, and he borrowed from his experiences with military training in the design of the elements. Outward Bound instructors were often the first to build ropes courses, during the late 1960s to early 1970s. Wagstaff found that "Mike Stratton, former Colorado Outward Bound instructor, constructed a few elements for the Carroll School near Walden Pond in Massachusetts . . .[and] Karl Rohnke, North Carolina Outward Bound instructor, created a challenge course for Southern Illinois University" (2003).

Modern History

Today there are thousands of challenge courses around the world, with the majority installed in

Zip wire use in the 1970s. Note the use of the hand-held lanyard.

the United States. Some estimates put this number as high as 12,000 in the United States. This explosion in the popularity of using challenge courses to achieve educational and other aims did not go unnoticed. A large number of vendors who build challenge courses and train others in their use have sprung up all over the United States and are expanding internationally. Project Adventure popularized the use of challenge courses in schools, therapeutic agencies, and other educational settings. Many of the current challenge course designs and elements are the direct result of Project Adventure's early influence.

This rapid expansion in technology, installation methods, and operating systems has created a need for unification and standards. In 1988, the North Carolina Outward Bound School hosted the first official gathering of ropes course builders and professionals. In 1993, this initial group of visionaries formed the Association for Challenge Course Technology (ACCT) to support the industry and develop standards of practice.

Today, challenge courses can be found in a variety of programs, which has led to an amazing diversification of high-element products and systems. The original ropes courses were constructed in trees with whatever kind of rope could be attained cheaply. Now the choices of element challenges, settings, and construction media boggle the mind.

Types of High Challenge Courses and Elements

The high challenge course has many variables in its design and organization. Challenge courses can be installed in many different settings, and there are many kinds of support structures and individual elements to choose from. This section explores these options.

Settings

Currently, there are three possible settings that challenge course activities can be conducted in. Historically, the natural outdoor environment was the first choice; however, with advances in technology and the need for year-round programming, the use of indoor facilities has flourished. A few challenge courses are also now available in a portable format.

Outdoor Environments

The outdoors is the primary setting for most challenge courses, which reflects the roots of ropes course development. Hahn and Hébert were advocates of the authentic, natural experience. Outdoor environments lend themselves well to groups of people engaged in team-oriented activities. They offer a myriad of design opportunities that can take advantage of the local terrain. Open space offers exciting possibilities for interesting designs among trees, utility poles, or other created structures (e.g., climbing towers).

Indoor Facilities

An indoor facility can provide year-round programming during the hot or cold seasons and during inclement weather. Many programs in colder climates go indoors to avoid the snow and cold, whereas an increasing number of programs in warmer climates choose the indoor option to avoid the heat and humidity of the summer months. Programs may choose to install an indoor course if the outdoor options are limited or to augment an existing outdoor course. These elements can be built high in the ceiling beams so they do not interfere with the other shared uses of the indoor space, or they can be installed so that the elements can be removed or conveniently raised out of the way using simple haul systems.

Portable Structures

A recent innovation that has expanded the possibilities of programming location involves the design of portable structures. For many people, their first climbing experience occurred on a portable climbing wall at the local fair or at a corporate party. These hydraulic-powered climbing walls are fitted to a steel trailer and are raised into place once the trailer is stabilized at the site. Similarly, small steel-framed challenge courses are now being manufactured that can be hauled by trucks for short-term events.

Installation Mediums

Trees, utility poles, steel frames, and existing building structures currently provide the backbone of modern challenge courses. Each installation medium offers certain advantages and limitations in their design and use. Currently, utility poles are the most commonly used.

Trees

Some practitioners and challenge course installers feel that trees provide a superior medium for challenge courses. Advantages include the following:

- The elements are hidden and participants appreciate being in a natural setting.

- Trees provide protection from weather extremes. They diminish sun exposure, rainfall, and wind.
- Trees have proven over time to adapt well to the techniques used in challenge course construction. A tree course can last many years with ongoing maintenance of the elements and surrounding environment.

Disadvantages may include the following:

- Trees may rot, become infected or infested, or die.
- They have higher maintenance costs due to overgrowth of hardware.
- They have hazards, including widow makers (overhanging dead branches), uneven ground due to roots, and so on.

Utility Poles

If appropriate trees are not available or you choose not to use them and you wish to run groups in the outdoors, a utility-pole course would be the best choice. Some of the main advantages of elements built on utility poles include the following:

- Poles offer freedom to design a variety of element configurations that best suit program and site needs. They offer the ability to fully customize the design and layout.
- Utility-pole courses generally last longer than tree courses since they do not depend on tree health. Poles do not grow around the bolts, cables, and other hardware, which can mitigate maintenance costs.
- Lower maintenance costs over the life of the elements make pole courses a better long-term investment, even though the initial cost is higher.

Challenges of utility-pole course fabrication include the following:

- Dealing with rocky soil, exposed ledge, or loose soil often leads to greater cost.
- High water tables can be problematic if the underground portions of the poles rot due to long-term or seasonal wetting.
- Poles take several months to settle and the guy anchors to solidify. Belay cables and guy wires can become loose, requiring the installers to retighten them.
- Heavy equipment used to set utility poles can negatively affect the surrounding environment (trees, existing lawns, and athletic fields).

Mixed Media: Trees and Utility Poles

Mixed courses of trees and poles can be a way of having the best of both worlds: the aesthetics of trees and the longevity and customization of a pole course. Many people feel that low elements constructed in trees and high elements installed in utility poles that are in a wooded setting are the ideal format. The flexibility of the design offered by utility poles coupled with the weather-mitigating properties of a natural tree site is resourceful and ideal.

Steel Exterior Frames

Steel is the newest medium and the one with the shortest track record. Increasingly, challenge courses are being built with this rigid framework. Benefits include the following:

- Steel courses are less expensive in the long run than wood courses due to lower maintenance costs.
- They can be moved as site plans or program needs change. Many frames unbolt from their independent footings and can be relocated.
- There are no concerns about woodpecker damage or insect infestation.
- Materials don't dry out and crack.
- Steel courses minimize participant contact with chemical pole treatments.

Some disadvantages of steel include the following:

- There is an increased, if not exorbitant, initial cost.
- They have little aesthetic value; some would even say they're ugly.
- There are relatively few professional fabricators to choose from.
- They are extremely hot to the touch in hot, sunny environments unless shade canopies are incorporated in the design.

Existing Facilities and Buildings

Many existing structures may be suitable for the installation of a challenge course. High-element courses have been built in structures as diverse as barns with posts and beams and municipal buildings with poured concrete beams from the 1940s. Other potentially suitable structural constructions include quarried rock, steel beams of many types, traditional wood frame construction, glued laminated timber beams, and so on. All of these options will require a sound engineering plan to ensure that the design loads of the intended challenge course will be adequately carried by the beam structure and provide a margin of safety.

Types of High Elements

A myriad of individual elements are produced by reputable vendors. Element selection comes down to matching the program goals with curriculum guidelines and participant population. The main high-element categories include traversing, nontraversing, and individual high-impact elements and climbing towers and structures. The descriptions that follow will give you an idea of their diversity.

Traversing Elements

Traversing elements are intended for participants to move from one end of the element to the other, traversing its full horizontal length. The participant is safeguarded by a belay while climbing to height and traversing the element. Some elements require the coordinated effort of two climbers to successfully navigate the challenge. These elements could be a simple cable or log walk or some combination of ropes, cables, and platforms. Element examples include The Burma Bridge and Wilder Woosey.

The Burma Bridge is a three-line bridge installed between two trees or utility poles with a foot cable and two hand ropes, one on either side of the climber at waist height. The task is to walk across the foot cable using the two hand ropes for support. A traversing belay cable provides security.

The Wilder Woosey is a belayed version of the popular low element known as Wild Woosey. Two foot cables at the same height are located close to each other and gradually diverge over a 30-foot (9-meter) or more span, forming an isosceles triangle. Two climbers work together to traverse the two diverging cables.

Nontraversing Elements

Nontraversing elements are designed for ascending straight up to height and involve vertical obstacles. These elements most often employ a **dynamic belay** for safety. The participant climbs straight up the element directly under the belay anchor point. Some of these elements are designed for one person and others require two or more people. The Centipede and Dangle Duo are representative high elements of this type.

The Centipede is a unique single-climber element. The participant climbs a series of timbers hung vertically that are 8 feet (2.5 meters) long and 4 inches by 4 inches (10 centimeters by 10 centimeters) wide and deep. There are a variety of handholds and footholds on the way up, such as climbing holds, staples, and simple notches in the timber. The timbers wiggle from side to side as one climbs.

An enormous high-element challenge course, which uses shade canopies, installed in South Korea. More than 120 utility poles were used in this design.

Wilder Woosey element in use.

The Dangle Duo consists of a horizontal series of timbers that are 4 inches by 4 inches (10 centimeters by 10 centimeters), which looks like a giant ladder. This element is from 20 feet (6 meters) for a shorter indoor course up to 60 to 70 feet (18 to 21 meters) tall for a high outdoor course. The spaces between these rungs often increase as one climbs higher. This element is most often done as a team of two who support one another as they climb vertically.

Individual High-Impact Elements

Individual high-impact elements are typically used one element at a time. A group may focus entirely on one element, especially because some of these elements require multiple people engaged in a variety of roles in order to conduct the activity safely. Examples of these kinds of elements include the Flying Squirrel and Zip Wire.

The Flying Squirrel is a unique activity that is the epitome of a universally designed high element. This activity is typically done by groups of 12 to 15 participants. A suitable belay safe pulley is attached to a stationary overhead anchor and a static rope runs through the pulley. The participant is connected to one end of the static line while being pulled to height by the rest of the group at the other end. The participant can be lifted from a stationary position into the air or can run or walk a small distance to create a dynamic swinging motion as she ascends. The group can easily lift people with limited mobility to height.

The Zip Wire has a platform that is constructed high in trees or poles. An overhead belay cable runs from above the platform across an open area to a distant anchorage on a pole or tree. A typical length for a zip wire is 200 to 300 feet (61-91 meters). The participant climbs to the platform while on a ground belay. Once on the platform, he is clipped into the Zip Wire belay lanyard that is connected to the two-wheel zip pulley. The ground belay is then disconnected and the participant is free to leave the platform and ride down the cable.

Climbing Towers and Structures

Climbing towers are dramatic structures that offer thrilling opportunities for participants. They are usually the visual focal point of a challenge course and can act as a beginning and an end for traversing elements connected to the tower. Climbing faces can be designed to challenge anyone from the novice climber to the expert. Many vendors offer tower options that range from budget-conscious two-pole

High-Element Challenge Courses

climbing surfaces to multiple-pole tower structures with inclined surfaces allowing for overhangs, roofs, and slabs. Climbing towers are also engineered out of modular steel that can be configured in a variety of shapes for maximum flexibility.

Course Layout and Design

Ryan (2005) highlights several factors to consider when planning a challenge course layout and deciding on an operating system or belay type.

- **Programming time:** How much time does the average group have to conduct challenge course activities? Will a circuit-style course or stand-alone elements provide the higher quality experience?

- **Transferring belays:** Some course styles require more **belay transfers** than others and many require them to happen at height. Poor execution of belay transfers has been implicated in some accidents. Belay transfers directly affect the number of facilitators required to run a course and the number of participants the course can handle and has implications for the depth and level of training needed for program facilitators.

- **Rescue training:** The likelihood of needing to rescue someone off a course with a dynamic belay is remote. This is not the case for course designs with **static belay.** For programs that install and operate static-belayed elements, rescue training for all staff is of paramount importance.

- **Ratios of supervision and staff to participants:** The desire to build a static-belayed **circuit course** is often based on the presumption that fewer trained staff can manage a larger number of participants. This reasoning is inadequate and often leads to unsafe situations. When belay transfers are happening at height, the need for constant and careful staff supervision is critical. Operating a circuit-style course often means more staff and more investment in technical staff training.

- **Program goals:** The intentional alignment of program activities with the program's educational goals and other desired outcomes is a characteristic of a quality program. Course design, belay styles, and element choices all play an important role in this alignment.

Stand-Alone Element Courses

Courses with stand-alone elements are most commonly designed to make use of dynamic belays. Based on the Project Adventure model, events like the Dangle Duo, Burma Bridge, and Pamper Pole are set up as stand-alone events to be completed before the group moves on to the next element in the sequence designed by the facilitator. This allows maximum focus on the element at hand and provides a clear beginning and ending of an activity in a time frame short enough to accommodate most schools' scheduling. Similarly, this design provides for a focused briefing and debriefing of each element.

Linear Courses

Linear courses work well for programs with high volume that need to keep people moving. They also usually require a lengthier programming period depending on the number of linked elements. This style doesn't work as well in terms of the time to debrief group and individual experiences, since long periods of time may pass before the group is together again on the ground. Outward Bound programs typically use this type of course layout. Quite often, Outward Bound groups have half a day or more to experience a challenge course.

Most elements in this design are traversing. Participants are usually belayed to height, begin at one end of the course, and work their way through a series of elements. They generally exit the course via a Zip Wire or Giant Swing or are simply lowered by a dynamic belay. The method of securing the climbers as they move through this kind of course can be either a dynamic belay or static belay with transfers from one belay to another occurring at height. Linear courses can be fairly staff intensive because of the need to monitor each belay transfer that occurs. Poorly designed linear courses can become bottlenecks because one slower participant can block movement along the continuous string of elements.

Hub and Spoke Courses

Participants typically enter via a dynamic belay up the hub access pole and then move along the spokes (traversing elements) from there, sometimes returning to the hub platform before embarking upon the next element. The method of securing the climbers as they move through this kind of course is usually static with transfers from one belay to another occurring at height. This arrangement allows for more efficient staff supervision of belay transfers since one facilitator situated on a key platform may be able to watch more than one belay transfer at a time. Dynamic ground belays are less common due to the concentrated nature of the elements and lack of room on the ground for multiple belay teams. Like linear courses, hub and spoke courses may work well for programs that need to have a lot of participants in the air at one time. The hub and spoke arrangement in theory prevents the bottleneck scenario of the linear course.

Universal and Accessible Designs

Universal and accessible programs actively engage and challenge all participants. **Accessible design** is the elimination of physical barriers or the construction of barrier-free environments. Often this boils down to access to the challenge course site as well as access to the elements at height.

Universal design moves beyond the idea of accessible design. It is a framework for the design of places, things, and information to be usable by the widest range of people operating in the widest range of situations without special or separate design. In a universally designed program, it is not evident that modifications have been made for a specific user or group.

On a practical level, barriers to the development of universal programs created by social norms are much greater than the physical impediments. Therefore, a thoughtful approach should be directed more toward the exploration of diversity and inclusion rather than toward the creation of an accessible physical environment. Practitioners should seek out training and consultation from organizations that provide programming to users of differing abilities and that create universal environments. Participants with different abilities are also a rich resource to tap into when designing and constructing universal programs. A facilitator should be knowledgeable of current preferred terminology, capable of adapting activities for people with differing abilities, and have understanding of specific health concerns. Finally, practitioners should take care to research the laws and statutes in their region and country regarding the requirements for accessible and universal design.

Adapted from Statement of Philosophy in Universal Challenge workshop manual, Project Adventure, Inc.

Ryan (2005) summarizes the concept of quality challenge course design by stating,

> Course designs have continued to evolve over the years. Circuit courses are still popular with many organizations and some programs have courses with both circuit and stand-alone elements. There is nothing inherently better or worse about circuit versus stand-alone elements or statically versus dynamically belayed courses. The "best" course design for any program is simply the course that accommodates the

program time, participant profiles, and educational goals of the program. This may sound obvious, but it is important that new programs carefully outline their goals before installing a challenge course. Building a course before designing a program can lead to a situation where the challenge course design does not meet the programming needs. Working with a reputable challenge course vendor is an important step in ensuring that the challenge course design is aligned with the program goals and desired outcomes.

Facilitation and Operation of High Elements

Developing facilitation skills and operational competence is important to ensure quality programming on high challenge course elements. Group assessment, activity sequencing, and specific knowledge of technical equipment and technical skills are paramount to safe experiences. A broad understanding of current risk management concerns is also required.

Assessment

Assessment of a group in anticipation of their experience on a high challenge course is done before the participants arrive, while planning a session or lesson, and during the program itself. Your analysis of where individual participants and the group are, both physically and emotionally, prior to the high challenge course will provide key insights. Use the GRABBSS assessment tool as a model (see chapter 3) and ask yourself questions: What happened during the trust fall or low elements? How did participants feel about these previous experiences? Is the group attending to each other's emotional and physical safety? How comfortable are you with managing the group? What is your intuition telling you? These and many other questions will lead you to a better understanding of how to structure the high-elements portion of your program.

Sequencing

When planning an hour, a half or full day, or even a weeklong adventure experience, it is crucial to carefully consider the sequence of activities. You should think critically about how the high elements are going to add value to the experience. Once you have done a thorough GRABBSS assessment (see page 47), you should also consider the following topics.

- **Types of high elements:** What types of high elements would be best to start with? To end with? What types of individual elements, partner elements, group elements, and high-impact elements might be best?

- **Daily program organization:** What general structure do you want for the day? Consider time limits; break periods; time frames for briefing, activities, and debriefing; and proportion of other activities (warm-up games, initiatives, problem-solving exercises, low elements) to high elements.

- **Overall program sequence:** Do the activity choices build logically onto each other? For example, low elements typically precede high elements. An appropriate trust sequence is vital to prepare participants emotionally for the demanding nature of high elements.

- **Kinesthetic and skill progression:** Do the high activities build on one another in terms of participant skill progression? Have participants had an opportunity to warm up and feel what it's like to balance and swing on cables and ropes? Did participants get to experience wearing chest harnesses on the Flying Squirrel before diving for the trapeze bar on the Pamper Plank?

- **Group development:** Do you have a picture in your mind of the group's development from the beginning, middle, and end of the planned sequence? Pick high elements that will facilitate achievement of those outcomes.

- **Deliberate briefing:** Did you deliberately brief the element for a specific outcome? Most high elements can be adapted for a wide range of uses and outcomes.

- **Back-up plan:** What is your contingency plan if a particular high element doesn't seem to fit and starts to fizzle out in regard to the group's progress and goals? Be prepared to rearrange your planned sequence to keep the group moving along.

- **Powerful culminating event:** Does your sequence end with a provocative and engaging event? Many times high elements for large groups work well here, such as Quadrophenia, Giant Swing, and Zip Wire.

This list was adapted from *Adventure Programming Training Manual*, Project Adventure, Inc., Beverly, Massachusetts, 2002.

Facilitator Skill Areas

Learning all the technical aspects to safely run and manage the high elements of a challenge course is a lengthy process. Training workshops and hands-on experience under the tutelage of experienced practitioners are important. The goal of presenting this information is to give you an appreciation for the scope and depth of material that a new facilitator should focus on obtaining and mastering. These lists are merely informative and certainly are not exhaustive.

Safety

As a challenge course facilitator, you should be able to

- perform a general site and surface area assessment (e.g., pavement, wet grass, gravel, sticks, uneven ground);

- recognize movement (e.g., belay paths, other user groups, vehicle traffic, horseplay);

- perform group, individual, and personal GRABBSS assessments (e.g., physical fitness and psychological readiness for participation);

- locate first aid kits, emergency protocols, and communication tools (e.g., walkie-talkies, cell phones, runners);

- secure the challenge course (e.g., disable high elements, lock ladders, tie retrieval or haul cords high and out of the way); and

- prepare the climbers (e.g., no dangling jewelry, no objects in pockets, appropriate attire such as long pants and shirts, warm-ups, stretching).

As a challenge course facilitator, you should have

- awareness of obstacles and other hazards (e.g., exposed rocks, hanging tree limbs, wasp and bee nests, equipment dropped from above),

- access to weather information (e.g., heat, cold, sun, shade, lightning, rain) and its effects on participants,

- awareness of props that limit senses (e.g., blindfolds), and

- knowledge of potential injuries on high elements (e.g., cardiac events, scrapes, cuts and bruises, joint strains and sprains from over-stretching, rope burns from improper belaying).

Technical Equipment

As a challenge course facilitator, you need to know about equipment selection and use for the particular course and operating system you are using, including the following.

- Helmets: Styles; how to fit and secure them properly

- Harnesses: Seat, chest, full body, tied, or improvised types; proper fit; correct buckle closure for different styles

- **Carabiners:** Styles and appropriate uses of each; how to secure or lock them

- Belay devices: Apertures; autolocking; attachment and appropriate use

- Ropes: Dynamic versus static; strengths and uses; rope logs

- Fall-protection lanyards: Attachment to harness; appropriate clip-in or anchor points

- Pulleys and shear-reduction devices: Styles; appropriate belay set-ups; attachments

- Rescue kit: Contents; availability at all times on challenge course

- Challenge course structural components: Differences among belay cables, element cables, and guy cables; belay strength components; anchor points for self-belayed climbing; installation techniques and operating systems of the facility; recognition of damaged or unusable elements

Familiarizing yourself with the various kinds of challenge course equipment can be fun and engaging. A number of different options for gaining this critical knowledge are available. Written resources like *The Guide for Challenge Course Operations* by Bob Ryan (2005) and the ACCT's *Challenge Course Standards* (2004) are excellent. Likewise, professional training with a reputable vendor and mentorship under an experienced practitioner are ideal situations to gain knowledge of this equipment. The ACCT Web site (www.acctinfo.org) has a list of reputable training organizations.

Technical Skills

The breadth of skills that a well-trained facilitator must have command of can seem daunting (see the list that follows). However, with a reasonable training path, mentorship, and **certification** of skill retention by a reputable credentialing organization, you can be reasonably assured of being a well-qualified leader.

- Knot tying: Must be able to identify and tie knots; tie appropriate knots for clipping into

and tying in directly to a harness; tie rescue knots; and improvise seat and chest harnesses

- Setup procedures for high elements: Must know when to use dynamic or static rope, how to set up pulleys and shear-reduction devices, what are appropriate belay cable and anchor clip-in points, and how to set up and use haul lines and access cords

- Belaying and belay systems: Must have personal belay mastery of a variety of belay methods and devices (autolocking, body, aperture); ability to belay traversing and nontraversing elements; creating ground belay anchors and backup belay systems; knowledge of differences between dynamic and static belay systems and their setup; communication signals for both dynamic and static belaying; ability to manage participant belays and roles (primary and backup belayer, anchor person, rope tender, ladder spotter); and knowledge of belay escapes and transfers

- **Self-belayed climbing:** Must have knowledge of leading-edge climbing methods, anchor points, and belay gear retrieval; ability to manage belay system transfers at height; and ability to use fall-protection lanyards

- Belay transfers at height: Must be able to transfer from dynamic belay to static belay, dynamic to dynamic, and static to static plus use communication signals; must have knowledge of common errors and areas for double unclipping

- Descending techniques: Must have knowledge of lowering procedures, including partner lowers and self-lowers, rappelling methods, suitable backups, and self-belayed downclimbing

- Movement and climbing: Must feel comfortable at height and have knowledge of movement techniques, including ascending, traversing, and descending

- Rescues: Must have knowledge of prevention procedure and methods, standard and improvised techniques to create emergency lowering systems, access alternatives, first aid, cut-away rescues, and evacuation of physically injured or psychologically immobile participants

- Logging equipment and rope use: Must understand equipment care, inspection and visual

Belay gear setup and belay gear retrieval.

identification of wear and tear, regular and systematic logging of use time and patterns, and knowledge of equipment replacement

- Operation standards: Must have knowledge of high-element standard operating procedures (SOPs) and site-specific local operating procedures (LOPs), element selection, and ACCT standards

- Inspections: Must be able to make sure the course meets appropriate installation and inspection standards

You should strongly consider seeking out creditable organizations when it comes to certification, internships, and places of employment. Organizations that have a long history in the challenge course field and are known for their excellence in education would be preferable to new programs. College programs like Plymouth State University and Aurora University have excellent degree programs in the field and opportunities for hands-on experience. Likewise, Project Adventure has an excellent internship program and a well-established practitioner certification path.

Risk Management

The systematic application of management policies and procedures to the tasks of identifying, analyzing, evaluating, treating, mitigating, and monitoring risk are critical to a program's success. Risk management is not just a one-time start-up process or the development of a how-to manual. It should pervade everything your program does; it is a way of being. Innumerable topics could be addressed within the broad theme of risk management, which exists within the broader context of good program management. A few subjects have been explored here to give a small sampling of the potential issues involved in running a program that uses a high-element challenge course.

Perceived Risk Versus Actual Risk

For many people, the idea of climbing to height on a utility pole, standing on top of it, and then diving out to catch a trapeze bar brings visions of daredevil behavior. The popular misconception is that these activities are extremely risky. To understand the reality, we need to look at the perceived risk versus the actual risk in two lights. First, we should compare the risk in a broad context as it relates to comparable activities. Second, we should compare the relative risk of high elements with other components of an adventure program.

According to the Project Adventure 20-Year Safety Study, the overall accidental injury rate for adventure programs is remarkably low (see table 10.1). Participation in a Project Adventure challenge course is about as risky as work in the fields of real estate, insurance, or finance (Furlong et al. 1995).

Additionally, when we compare perceived risk versus injury frequency and severity of common challenge course activities, another story emerges. Many people believe that the level of injury frequency and severity increases as you move from warm-up games and initiatives to low elements to high elements. The reality is different. The potential severity of injury corresponds to the participant's perception of risk, and the actual frequency of injury is inversely proportional (see table 10.2).

Operating Procedures

Every program should have a written set of policies and procedures that serve as guidelines for how to conduct a challenge course experience for the participant populations. Standard operating procedures (SOPs) are the broad set of procedures that are generally accepted as best practice for the given context. Local operating procedures (LOPs) are more narrowly defined and specific to a particular challenge course site.

Addressing LOPs, Ryan (2005) states, "The best way to establish individual program goals is to develop a written LOP manual. The process of developing the LOP manual provides an opportunity to address the uniqueness of your program and create a document that blends best practice recommendations with local needs."

LOP manuals commonly contain information and procedures that address some or all of the following topics. It is important to clearly define which procedures are facilitator requirements or policies and which are simply suggestions or guidelines. This list is by no means comprehensive or prescriptive.

- Facilitator roles and qualifications
- Facilitator-to-participant ratios
- Challenge course inspection and maintenance log

TABLE 10.1

Challenge Course Injury Rate Comparisons

Activity type	Activity	Injury rate (per million hours of program exposure)
Program activity	Project Adventure challenge course activities	4.3
	Backpacking	192
	Sailboarding	220
	Downhill skiing	724
	Competitive orienteering	840
	Basketball	2,650
	Soccer	4,500
Occupational activity	Amusement and recreational services	19
	Educational services	8
	Finance, insurance, and real estate	4.5

Adapted from Furlong et al. *20-Year Safety Study*, Hamilton, MA: Project Adventure, Inc., 1995.

TABLE 10.2

Perceived Risk Versus Injury Frequency and Severity

	General perception of risk	Actual frequency of injury	Actual potential severity of injury
Warm-up games* and activities	Low	Moderate*	Low
Low challenge course elements	Moderate	Low	Low to moderate
High challenge course elements	High	Very low	Moderate to high

*Warm-up games actually have low frequency of injury compared with sports and other activities. However, when compared with other challenge course activities (e.g., low or high elements), games have the highest frequency of injury.

Taken from *Adventure Program Management Training Manual*, Project Adventure, Inc., Beverly, Massachusetts, 2005.

- Emergency action plan (EAP)
- Weather policies
- Opening and closing the high challenge course
- Maps of the site
- Forms (e.g., medical, release of liability, inventories)
- High-element descriptions and operations for the elements specific to the site

Challenge Course Inspections

Challenge courses are typically constructed with components that are far stronger than any loads they will ever have to endure under normal conditions. However, they do not last forever—they continually face the enemies of friction, abrasion, corrosion, vibration, weather, expansion, contraction, erosion, rot, and misuse. For these reasons, the challenge course industry has established a norm for levels of inspection.

ACCT standards state, "The organization has its challenge course(s) inspected by a qualified challenge course professional annually or more often if needed based on significant changes in environmental conditions" (ACCT 2004). Unfortunately, most problems that occur with the challenge course happen on the other 364 days of the year when the professional inspector is not there. This demands a thorough seasonal inspection by the challenge course's internal staff. The frequency of this type of inspection depends on the design of the course, the local environmental conditions, the volume of use, and the expertise of the staff.

A program-day inspection is important. This quick visual walkthrough and check of element setup can identify any recent changes since the last time programming was conducted. This daily check should include not only the element itself but also the attendant belay and climber equipment.

Emergency Action Plans

An **emergency action plan (EAP)** should be in place to address the steps to take if an emergency occurs. Although extremely important, emergency procedures should never be considered a substitute for program design features that will reduce the need for emergency response. EAPs should be site specific and should address the different kinds of possible emergencies. The following are key components of an emergency action plan, according to Ryan (2005):

- Assessing the situation and providing an initial response (rescue and first aid)
- Managing the remaining participant group
- Contacting emergency medical services or transporting participants to medical facilities
- Filing an incident report
- Notifying other staff, informing family members, and informing the media
- Critical incident debriefing

Challenge Course Standards

Many organizations set standards in the broad field of adventure programming. A standard is established by an authority, custom, or general consent to serve as a model or measure of quality. It is commonly used to describe widely accepted practices. There are many standards that affect the management and use of a high challenge course.

CAREERS IN ADVENTURE

NAME: Jessica Ingram

JOB: Challenge Course Inspection Coordinator, Project Adventure (Beverly, Massachusetts)

BACKGROUND: BA in architectural studies with a minor in studio art, Hobart and William Smith Colleges, Geneva, New York

I had my first challenge course experience as a student on an Outward Bound course in Maine. I remember it vividly. I even drew the pole diagram layout in my journal—which I still have, of course.

WHAT'S YOUR JOB LIKE? My job includes administrating all challenge course inspections for Project Adventure (I personally inspect 70 client courses a year); managing a database of 1,500 client site inspections; and developing training and certification plans for all inspectors, both full-time and contract.

Being a course inspector allows me to see a wide variety of courses and their uses. Each client has a slightly different approach to using the tool, and likewise many builders have their own ideas of how to build the ideal course for each location. I have moments when I hate what I'm doing—it's January in Massachusetts, I can't feel my toes, and I'm outside walking around in 2 feet (61 centimeters) of snow, shoveling off elements so I can inspect them. I have moments when I'm scared to death because something just settled on my harness and I dropped a few centimeters. I have moments when getting around a course at height feels like the most physically challenging thing I have ever done.

But I also have moments when I am sitting in my harness, 35 feet (11 meters) in the air under a canopy of pine trees, perfectly dry while it is raining everywhere else, wondering why I would want to go back down to the ground. There are times when I climb to the top of a pole and realize that I'm only a few feet from the ocean, but I had no idea of this from the ground. These are the times that I love my job, enjoying the views that nobody knows are there. Is it scary? Sometimes. Would I trade it for another job? Not if I can help it!

A few of the standard-setting organizations that may have an influence on challenge courses include the ACCT, the AEE, and Project Adventure. Other organizations that may have rules, laws, and standards that apply to a program could include local, county, and state governments and boards. They may have specific regulations that you need to be aware of.

Uses of High-Element Challenge Courses

High elements are used in a broad range of settings within an equally broad range of purposes or missions. This section will explore the diverse uses of high-element challenge courses and provide institutional examples of each. Examples of program uses and settings include schools, therapeutic use, recreation, corporate use, law enforcement training, military training, and edutainment.

Schools

Thousands of schools across the United States have challenge courses. Based on choices in program sequencing and maturity of students, many high-element challenge courses are used in high school and college programs, although more and more middle schools are using scaled-down high challenge course elements.

An exemplary private school using high elements within the academic curriculum is Meadowbrook School, a coeducational independent day school in Weston, Massachusetts. According to David Canfield, the director of the adventure program, teamwork is the focus during sixth grade as students learn and improve skills including communication, decision making, collaborative planning, and leadership. Activities require groups of students to plan and work cooperatively to accomplish tasks ranging from physical challenges to planning and operating games for younger students. Students are assigned to climbing teams that rotate through high elements that require teamwork to accomplish. In seventh grade, human relationships are emphasized as students are challenged to build an inclusive atmosphere characterized by trust, mutual support, and appreciation of others. Activities challenge students to practice creating and maintaining inclusive environments in situations ranging from trust falls to membership on belay teams. The main emphasis during climbing is on the belay teams, which are responsible for the physical and emotional safety of fellow students as they climb.

Personal growth and understanding drive the final year of the program as students set personal goals. After a refresher course in the belay skills learned in seventh grade, high ropes activities occur in three domains: (1) belaying the sixth-grade students during their climbing as a leadership activity, (2) personal challenge elements including a Portable Pamper Pole and a long Overhanging Roof Climb, and (3) revisiting previous elements in new ways (e.g., blindfolded).

Therapeutic Settings

Schoel, Prouty, and Radcliffe (1988) write, "Recreational therapists, social workers, and counselors are using adventure activities with small, growth-oriented counseling groups. These activities are part of the overall treatment plan for groups confronting a whole series of behavioral and psychological difficulties, such as drug abuse and depression. . . . Ropes course experiences . . . encourage trust, risk and empathy."

A variety of programs use high elements as a segment of their curriculum or therapy. Learning-disabled students are fully engaged when learning to use a new belay method to safeguard one another on the climbing wall in their gym. A person who uses a wheelchair for mobility pulls herself to height using a counterweight hoist system in order to gain access to the Zip Wire while her friends and other group members shout words of encouragement. A scared, resistant, and potentially suicidal psychiatric patient allows his belay team to lower him to the ground after successfully traversing the high Multivine. This work has had a profound impact on the use of challenge courses.

Recreation Settings

The recreational uses of high challenge courses seem limitless. Many youth organizations including the YMCA, the YWCA, Boys and Girls Clubs, summer camps, and city recreation centers have embraced the use of the challenge course for not only recreation, but experiences of educational growth.

The Hayden Recreation Centre, a privately endowed nonprofit corporation, provides a wide range of recreational, athletic, and social activities for the young people of Lexington, Massachusetts. Hayden maintains two indoor high challenge courses. One course is located in a small multipurpose gym. The newest course is installed high in the beams of their state-of-the-art ice arena. This new course is designed to take advantage of off-season programming opportunities when the ice is not in use and is not formed. The course simply hauls up out of the way during the winter season when skating lessons and hockey leagues dominate the schedule. Hayden uses these challenge courses for after-school programming, adult climbing instruction, and the summer Hayden Adventure Camp.

Corporate Settings

During the 1980s, some providers of challenge course services began to offer adventure education and experiential education programs to corporations as a means to motivate employees and increase productivity. Smolowe et al. (1999) proclaim, ". . . the corporate audience, with its pressing schedules and exacting demands, has produced the adventure field's swiftest evolution in design and delivery. In rapid succession, the original singular focus on wilderness programming shifted first to fixed-site ropes courses, then to a facilities-based mix of indoor and outdoor initiatives and on to the current emphasis on portable adventure experiences that can be delivered anytime, anywhere: work sites, office buildings and conference centers."

As this sector of programming grew in North America, it took off internationally as well. Asian companies were quick to embrace these concepts and in some cases have asked for some of the most ambitious challenge course projects to date. Netports, a South Korean–based hospitality market provider, installed an enormous challenge course at one of its vacation resorts in 2001. One of the primary goals was to accommodate corporate training for a complete workforce from any manufacturing facility at one time. This necessitated the installation of approximately 120 utility poles to create an interlocking layout of triangular clusters of high elements that can absorb up to 300 participants at a time. The idea was to allow each participant the same experience so that common goals and workplace values would be formed.

Law Enforcement and Military Settings

Military units and law enforcement have historically used high-element challenge course technology in the format of an obstacle course. Training recruits to gain individual confidence and build team interdependence were often the primary objective. Skills train-

ing in climbing and rappelling were other reasons for using these structures. Lately, many military and law enforcement organizations have found their missions modified to include civilian use and educational goals.

The Norfolk County Sheriff's Office in Braintree, Massachusetts, built a challenge course and received training in its use to work with a variety of youth groups. One example is an enrichment program for an at-risk alternative learning class from Stoughton Middle School. They work with students who are having trouble academically, providing an alternative learning environment. The high challenge course is often cited as one of the activities in which the students first perceive their ability to excel. Another example is the office's Youth Leadership Academy that seeks to promote leadership skills in disenfranchised youths. This summer program brings in a diverse group of kids for one week and

Canopy tour zip wire in St. Lucia.

leads them through a team development and leadership program using field games and initiatives and low-element activities, culminating in two days of high-element adventures that includes use of the large climbing tower installed on campus.

Edutainment

Forest canopy zip-line tours are now offered as entertaining educational experiences, or **edutainment.** They originated in Central and South America due to the need of biologists and botanists to study the flora and fauna of the rainforests without harming the environment. This program style has started to migrate into North America, with some of the first installed in Alaska and the Pacific Northwest. Basically, they are a series of zip wires that traverse a forest canopy. A person could start such an aerial hike by climbing up to a large platform and clipping into the first zip wire. The ride across this element would lead to perhaps another large platform and another zip wire. This may go on for a number of interlinked transfers. Along the way, most often an accompanying guide relates educational details about the flora and fauna of the ecosystem. This kind of activity may provide sustainable development and ecologically conscious tourism in many forest areas in developing countries.

Summary

This chapter has surveyed the high-element challenge course. We have discussed the history of high elements, the types of high challenge courses and elements, the facilitation and operation of these courses and elements, and the common programming uses. A properly designed and maintained course in conjunction with trained facilitators and an appropriate curriculum can be an asset to any adventure program. High-element challenge courses are an excellent tool to provide opportunities for individuals and groups to learn in meaningful and direct ways.

Review Questions

1. What organization has had the biggest historical influence on the development of the high challenge course and why? What individual has had the biggest influence and why?

2. Make a list of needs assessment questions you would ask of a program that wanted to develop and install a high course. What are the primary considerations when designing a high challenge course?

3. Installation mediums include trees, utility poles, mixed trees and poles, steel frames, and existing building structures. Which of these mediums will support the majority of the high-element challenge courses of the future and why?

4. In a short paragraph, discuss the safety and injury rate of high-element challenge courses.

5. Compare and rate on a continuum the most valuable uses of high-element challenge courses from among the following: education, therapy, recreation, corporate use, military and law enforcement training, and edutainment.

Student Learning Activities

1. Create an assessment tool that can be used to verify the technical skills needed to safely conduct high-element challenge course experiences. List all the relevant skills, and provide a framework for assessment (i.e., what is acceptable and unacceptable) and a grading or scoring system.

2. Do an online search of current challenge course installation providers. Pick one provider that interests you and contact one of the lead installers. Conduct an informal interview of this person focusing on their personal and company philosophy on challenge course design and layout. Now compare this information with what is provided on the company's Web site.

Does it match? What points are they getting across well? Which areas need further development?

3. As a group, visit a local challenge course. Break up into partners and take the class period to accomplish the following tasks:

- Draw a plan view of the challenge course layout. Show locations of each tree or support pole, element name and configuration, and the length and height of each element.

- Indicate what type of belay (static, dynamic, self-belayed, etc.) is used for each element.

- Indicate which operating system and course layout are used.

- Indicate which elements are universal in nature. What percentage of the course is universal?

- Find out how old the course is and who manufactured it. Later, look up the manufacturer on the Web and see if this is a typical or atypical installation for them.

- Ask the course owner and document the following: annual maintenance and inspection costs, original course cots, any elements not in compliance with standards, any elements that are underutilized by the staff, and the staff's favorite elements.

- Talk to the owner or challenge course manager and try to discern how the course design and layout affects, restricts, or complements their day-to-day programming.

- Find out the program's goals and objectives (their mission statements may be helpful here). Summarize how you perceive their course layout, design, and element selection supporting their stated goals and objectives.

4. Each student should research the Practitioner Certification scheme of an ACCT Professional Vendor Member.

- Create a matrix to show levels of certification available and prerequisites like number of training days, kinds of training, and days of program experience required.

- As a class, create a larger matrix showing each ACCT vendor's requirement and levels in comparison with all others.

- Have a discussion about which certification scheme provides for the best verification of individual challenge course facilitator skills.

CHAPTER 11

Teaching and Leading Outdoor Adventure Pursuits

Mark Wagstaff,
Aram Attarian,
and Jack K. Drury

" After my first couple of climbs, I got into teaching of climbing. I wanted to teach all I knew if they were interested in learning. It was actually a learning trip which brought on companionship and fun and interest far beyond just climbing up the mountain. "

—**Paul Petzoldt**

Chapter Concepts

- Professional outdoor leadership is defined and described through a core competency approach.
- The current status of outdoor leadership is analyzed by looking at the discipline's history.
- Critical skills such as trip leading, trip planning, orienting, and monitoring groups on an extended expedition is highlighted.
- Teaching, a critical skill, is discussed at length in this chapter using the SPEC approach to teaching and learning.
- Specific methods of instruction conducive to effective teaching and learning during an extended trip, such as teachable moments and the grasshopper method, are covered.
- Common outdoor pursuits are introduced and briefly described.

The theory and practice of adventure programming would not be complete without an in-depth discussion of outdoor pursuits. Navigating a class IV rapid, scaling a 200-foot (61-meter) rock face, descending into a 150-foot (46-meter) vertical cave, or expeditioning in remote wilderness conjures visions of challenging outdoor adventures. This chapter addresses adventure programming in the context of outdoor pursuits. Professional adventure programmers typically plan and lead activities such as kayaking, white-water rafting, rock climbing, caving, mountaineering, and mountain biking. To lead these activities, adventure programmers must exercise the competencies embraced by professional outdoor leaders. In this chapter, the terms *adventure programmer* and *outdoor leader* are interchangeable. A discussion of outdoor leadership and associated competencies will set the stage for a deeper understanding of adventure programming as related to outdoor pursuits. Important skills such as planning trips and leading extended experiences are among the programming components to be mastered.

One of the primary competencies discussed in the second portion of this chapter deals with the ability to teach. Participants in outdoor pursuits must receive quality instruction to maximize safety and enjoyment. The numerous benefits inherent in adventure programming are actualized through proper instruction; therefore, outdoor leaders must be good teachers. An effective outdoor instructor goes about teaching in a systematic way. This chapter will introduce the adventure programmer to the **SPEC method** of instruction. SPEC involves creating a student-centered, problem-solving, experiential, and collaborative learning environment. In particular, the SPEC method will be outlined as a unique teaching tool to maximize learning. Also, the teaching portion of this chapter covers the grasshopper method and teachable moments, two more methods conducive to learning on extended trips.

The chapter concludes with a comprehensive section that transitions from teaching methods to an overview of common outdoor adventure activities. It is beyond the scope of this text to provide all the necessary knowledge and skills associated with outdoor adventure pursuits. Therefore, common activities are divided into three main sections: (1) land-based activities, (2) water-based activities, and (3) ice- and snow-based activities. This last section includes basic information designed to inform the reader about the vast variety of adventure pursuits by highlighting the principal technical, safety, and environmental skills for each activity.

Outdoor Leadership

In order to be an effective adventure programmer, the aspiring professional must embrace the practice of outdoor leadership. **Outdoor leadership** is defined as the practice of leading individuals and groups into natural settings via various modes of transportation: backpacking, biking, canoeing, caving, sailing, kayaking, and rock climbing, to name a few. Three primary goals further define the practice of outdoor leadership:

- Outdoor leaders aim to ensure the safety of people engaging in outdoor experiences.
- Outdoor leaders aim to ensure the protection and preservation of the natural environments into which people venture for outdoor experiences.
- Outdoor leaders aim to enhance the quality of outdoor experiences for their participants (Martin et al. 2006).

In order to expand upon the meaning and purpose of outdoor leadership, it is critical to review fundamental outdoor leader competencies. These competencies form the knowledge and skill base for aspiring outdoor leaders. Therefore, the ensuing discussion will focus on common outdoor leadership competencies followed by a general discussion of outdoor leadership history and the current status of the profession.

Outdoor Leader Competencies

The ability to exercise fundamental outdoor leadership competencies dictates leadership effectiveness. Over the years, the literature on outdoor leadership has provided the profession with rich descriptions of basic competencies (Buell 1983; Green 1981; Martin et al. 2006; McAvoy 1978; Priest 1984; Swiderski 1981). Little variation exists among the dialogues that have evolved within the past 26 years. The following represents a current view of eight core competencies that characterize an effective outdoor leader as described by Martin et al. (2006).

Foundational Knowledge

This competency encompasses four components. *Sense of purpose* refers to the general philosophy on which the practice of outdoor leadership is based. Why do we do what we do in the field of outdoor leadership? What value does the practice of outdoor leadership hold for society? What are you as an outdoor leader trying to accomplish through your work? These questions help us develop a sense of purpose as outdoor leaders and an understanding of the purpose of outdoor leadership.

Sense of heritage refers to the history of the profession. In understanding who we are as a profession, we need to understand our origins. Good outdoor leaders know the roots of the profession, have a sense of future trends in the field, and feel a sense of place within the outdoor leadership tradition.

Breadth of the profession refers to the various ways in which outdoor leadership is practiced. Outdoor leadership is practiced in several contexts, from traditional wilderness programs to public schools. Good outdoor leaders are aware of the different professional contexts that constitute the profession and of the different organizational contexts in which outdoor leadership is practiced.

The final component of the foundational knowledge competency is *understanding leadership*. One of the primary goals of outdoor leadership is to serve as a source of transformation in people's lives. This can be accomplished only through effective leadership. Consequently, competency in the theory and practice of leadership is essential to outdoor leadership.

Self-Awareness and Professional Conduct

This competency consists of four areas. First, *acting mindfully* means that good outdoor leaders are always mindful in their actions. They are intentional in all of their actions, and they always act with regard to the ultimate goals of a group experience. At times, this means being attentive to the needs of group members. At other times, it means being attentive to tasks that must be accomplished. Nonetheless, every leader action involves mindfulness and specific intent.

Knowing one's abilities and limitations is an important aspect of self-awareness. Without a clear sense of one's abilities and limitations, an outdoor leader can hardly begin to define appropriate levels of challenge for participants. Without a clear sense of one's abilities and limitations, an outdoor leader may set the bar too high, thus jeopardizing the emotional and physical safety of the participants. In such cases, the leader may become a danger to the group. At the very least, a leader such as this diminishes the quality of an experience.

The third aspect involves *knowing how we influence others*. In what ways do you typically influence a group? What effect does your personality typically have on others within a group? Without a clear sense of the impact you have within a group, you can hardly begin to consciously fashion experiences for the group that are psychologically rewarding. On the contrary, you might come across as a social oaf serving only to hinder group development.

Finally, *personal and professional ethics* involves the concept of principled behavior. Leaders without moral scruples ultimately serve as negative influences within groups. Having a strong sense of personal and professional ethics is essential to effective leadership. The leader who bends or breaks rules or allows others to bend or break rules undermines the quality and value of an experience.

Outdoor leaders must understand their own limitations before defining appropriate challenges for participants.

Decision Making and Judgment

This competency includes three important areas. *Decision making as a conscious process* is the first. Many of the decisions in our lives are snap decisions that we make without much conscious thought. This approach to decision making is acceptable when the decisions are simple and the consequences are not great. In situations where decisions are complex, uncertainty is high, and the difference in consequences may mean the difference between life and death, this approach is unacceptable. Good decision making is a conscious process that involves weighing options as well as the consequences of each option in choosing a course of action.

Understanding the *role of judgment in decision making* is critical. Judgment becomes part of the decision-making process when the consequences of a particular decision or course of action are unclear or unknown and you as a leader must make a best guess about a course of action. Judgment is defined as an estimation of the likely consequences of such a decision. Effective judgment relies on past experi-ence and knowledge as a basis for estimating likely consequences.

Finally, *awareness of available resources in decision making* is essential to effective decision making. This includes conducting an inventory of available physical resources in the surrounding environment as well as physical resources within the possession of the group, such as equipment. It also includes human resources—knowledge, experience, and expertise—both within and outside of the group. This inventory helps ascertain the resources that are available to you in making a decision or choosing a certain course of action.

Teaching and Facilitation

Three areas make up this competency, the first of which is *facilitation skills*. A common approach to facilitation in the early days of outdoor leadership was to let the experience speak for itself. Outdoor leaders took a hands-off approach when it came to the broader lessons that participants might gain from an experience. However, outdoor leaders eventually began to realize that they were forgoing an opportunity to make a difference in the lives of their participants. They eventually began to frame experiences in ways that would help participants gain as much as possible from an experience in a process now known as facilitation. Facilitation is intended to enhance the quality of experiences by assisting groups in gaining insights from an experience that they may not gain on their own.

Outdoor leaders commonly find themselves in situations where they must exercise *teaching skills*. Whether they are teaching participants basic wilderness living skills, climbing or paddling techniques, or safety and rescue skills, outdoor leaders are instructors. To become an effective instructor, outdoor leaders must learn how to teach. This means learning how to create lesson plans and learning activities. It entails developing an understanding of the various instructional and learning styles. It also entails learning how to model effective technique and how to coach others in developing effective technique.

Finally, outdoor leaders place a great deal of emphasis on *teaching experientially* and learning by doing. Experiential education is the method by which outdoor leaders deliver their educational content. Every lesson should involve a degree of explanation, a degree of demonstration, and a greater degree of practice. This means giving participants an opportunity to learn skills in a hands-on manner. In teaching a group how to operate camp stoves, for instance, an outdoor leader should explain the process of operating a camp stove, demonstrate the process, and then give the students a chance to actually practice operating camp stoves. The same is true for any other skill or lesson.

Environmental Stewardship

This competency embodies three areas, with *environmental ethics* as the first. Ethics are a moral code or rules of conduct, and environmental ethics are the moral code or rules of conduct that we follow in our relationship with the natural environment. Outdoor leaders typically follow the principles of Leave No Trace as the basis of their interactions with the natural environment. These principles are aimed at environmental preservation.

Ecological literacy is an important attribute of a good environmental educator. The goal of

An outdoor leader's classroom is the outdoors.

environmental education is to develop environmental or ecological literacy in participants so that they can engage in intelligent action regarding their relationship with the natural environment. Ecological literacy entails thinking and acting critically in an environmental context, especially when making decisions and exercising judgment concerning environmental problems.

An understanding of *natural resource management* is the last critical area. An outdoor leader's classroom is the outdoors. We rely on natural areas as a setting for teaching and programming. Many of the areas that we use are managed by national, state, and municipal agencies. In using these areas, it is important to know the rules and regulations under which these areas are managed. It is important to know the management principles and practices of the agencies that manage these areas. It is also important to know issues that are of particular importance to the areas into which we travel for outdoor education and recreation experiences.

Program Management

This competency consists of three areas. First, *planning skills* are applied in developing a program design or structure. Program design includes program goals and objectives, program procedures and operations, and program activities and services. Planning skills are also applied in developing trip, activity, and lesson plans. Trip plans include emergency management plans, contingency plans, time control plans, energy control plans, and so forth. Proper planning is essential to effective outdoor leadership.

Once a plan has been established, the ability to implement the plan is largely contingent on the *organizational skills* of a leader. This refers to creating a system under which to get things done, or the ability to orchestrate various components in a plan that comes together to create a unified, harmonious whole.

Finally, *management skills* refer primarily to the ability to direct the collective efforts of people in accomplishing program goals and objectives. It involves supervision and administration skills.

Safety and Risk Management

Safety and risk management is composed of four areas. First, we will look at *participant safety*. A primary goal of outdoor leadership is to ensure the safety of participants, including both their physical and psychological safety.

Next, *preparation and planning* are two important practices. One of the reasons program planning is considered a core competency in outdoor leadership is the severe consequences of improper planning. Poorly planned programs are more prone to mishaps than well-planned trips. Many times, accidents and injuries can be traced back to poor planning.

Legal aspects of safety and risk management make up the third area. Safety and risk management in outdoor leadership must be considered from a legal perspective as well as a practical perspective. Outdoor leaders can potentially be held liable for any injury or loss that befalls a program participant. To be held liable, the outdoor leader and program for which the outdoor leader works must be proven to have been negligent in their duty to provide a certain standard of care to the program participant. In addition, the participant must show that the injury or loss was a result of the leader's failure to provide that standard of care. In any case, a leader or a program that is shown to be negligent can be held financially responsible for the injury or loss. Program planning is as much about assuring that participants engage in a safe and quality experience as it is about ensuring that you as a leader are adhering to the standard of care in the industry.

Assessing abilities and limitations is the final piece of safety and risk management. The ability to accurately self-assess as a leader is significant not only in determining your own limitations but also in determining the limitations of your followers. As an outdoor leader, the safety of your followers is often in your hands. Knowing your limitations and those of your followers is crucial to ensuring overall safety.

Technical Ability

Technical ability involves three components. *Proficiency in particular outdoor activities* is the first. Outdoor leaders must possess technical competency in a variety of areas. The most basic of these areas is backcountry living skills. These skills include stove operation and use, cooking, navigation using a map and compass, prevention of animal encounters, latrine construction and use, and so forth. In addition to backcountry living skills, outdoor leaders should develop expertise in specific activity areas or modes of travel. These may include canoeing, kayaking, rafting, sailing, technical rock climbing, mountaineering, backcountry skiing or snowboarding, challenge course facilitation, and mountain biking.

Experience-based competency equates to technical proficiency in outdoor activities and is typically gained through experience. The more experience people gain, the more competent they generally become. Outdoor leaders who fall out of practice in a given technical activity should refresh themselves before leading participants in those activities. A common practice among white-water rafting companies is to have their guides perform at least two refresher runs at the beginning of each rafting season on the rivers on which they will be guiding. Outdoor leaders should do their best to stay in practice and seek continuing education in the areas in which they lead others.

Finally, *professional certification* is another indicator of competence in different areas of expertise. Certifications signify only a minimal level of competence; nonetheless, they do indicate competence. Certifications also typically represent the industry norm or standard of care in various technical activities. Examples of professional certifications in the field of outdoor education and recreation include the instructor and guide certifications of the American Mountain Guide Association (AMGA) in rock climbing and mountaineering, the instructor certifications of the American Canoe Association (ACA) in canoeing and kayaking, and so forth.

Current Status of Outdoor Leadership

Before discussing the current status of outdoor leadership, a look at our past deserves attention. The history of adventure programming and outdoor leadership share the same set of key events discussed in chapter 1. Modern-day outdoor leaders draw much of their methods and curricula from the Outward Bound movement. However, other events and people also influenced the development of contemporary outdoor leaders (Drury et al. 2005).

The 1800s marked the beginning of the organized camping movement in the United States. When Mr. and Mrs. Gunn founded the Gunnery School in Connecticut, they integrated camping as part of their school programming. The first professional guides in the early 1800s practiced their profession in the woods of Maine and New York. The Boy Scouts of America was incorporated in 1910, and Ernest Seton was appointed as the first Scout Chief. He was also a naturalist and an author and created a youth organization called Woodcraft Indians that emphasized outdoor skill development.

Outdoor leaders must maintain technical expertise in a variety of outdoor pursuits.

During the 1920s and 1930s, L.B. Sharpe integrated education into organized camping. He was first director of Life Camps for underprivileged youth and began using the term *outdoor education* synonymously with *public school camping*. The combined effect of these organizations, individuals, and other events influenced the template for the modern outdoor leader found in the United States.

From a historical perspective, the success of Outward Bound served as the catalyst that merged the adventure programmer and outdoor leader into the professional described in this text. At this time, no universal national certification or operating standards exist among outdoor professionals. A number of organizations have implemented activity-specific certifications, leader certifications, and program accreditations, as described later in this chapter. It is important to understand that outdoor leadership is a relatively young profession that continues to evolve. Aspiring professionals must become active in professional organizations in order to foster healthy growth and development within the entire profession. Some of these organizations include the Association for Experiential Education (www.aee.org), the Wilderness Education Association (www.weainfo.org), and the Association of Outdoor Recreation and Education (www.aore.org).

Leading Trips

Leading extended outdoor trips or expeditions is a critical skill that typically separates outdoor leaders from other adventure programmers. The art of leading trips deserves special attention as aspiring adventure programmers develop their professional résumé. Extended trips or expeditions are adventure experiences held in wilderness environments for more than three days. This chapter introduces only a small portion of the knowledge and skills required to lead extended trips. It is not feasible to cover the extensive body of knowledge associated with trip leading in this chapter; therefore, trip planning and the process of orienting and monitoring groups serve as two foundational skills discussed in the next two sections. Armed with this knowledge, aspiring professionals have a place to start as they develop the essential outdoor leadership competencies.

Planning Trips

The old saying that proper planning prevents poor performance holds especially true when planning an expedition. Most incidents, accidents, and injuries can be traced back to problems in the planning process. Good trip planning requires a systematic process to ensure a safe, quality, and environmentally sound outdoor experience. The **GO PREPARED system** of trip planning serves as a convenient guide to planning extended trips (Martin et al. 2006). The foundation of an effective trip plan is well-defined program goals and objectives (GO). The time taken to create specific, measurable, attainable, realistic, and time-bound, or SMART, goals and objectives sets the stage for a sound plan.

Once outdoor leaders establish trip goals and objectives, they must next prepare for the expedition by engaging in a formal planning process. The PREPARED system includes the consideration of participants, resources, equipment and clothing, plan, access, rationing, emergency plan, and don't forget about logistics! Addressing these areas will prevent many problems during the trip. These components are not listed in order of importance; seasoned leaders execute planning tasks simultaneously to bring the entire plan together. See figure 11.1 for a brief explanation of the GO PREPARED system.

Orienting and Monitoring Groups

Orienting and monitoring groups is another important leadership function in leading trips. Orienting a group will have significant ramifications on the quality of the experience, safety, and care for the environment. Monitoring a group's process along the way ensures that trip goals and objectives are met. Much of the knowledge and skills associated with orienting and monitoring mirror adventure programming techniques explained throughout this text. However, keep in mind that these skills are practiced over an extended period of time in a context where group members are traveling and living together 24 hours a day. This situation requires the outdoor leader to be diligent and adhere to a certain process in order to ensure quality. The concepts behind monitoring and orienting are challenging to execute. Therefore, beginning outdoor leaders must seek experience to master the skill.

Orienting

Orientation usually occurs before or during the initial stages of a trip. The process consists of four overall elements that a leader should include while preparing a group for an extended outdoor experience.

GO PREPARED System of Trip Planning

GO

GO = Goals and Objectives (What are the goals and objectives of the trip?)

Outdoor leaders must take the time to craft quality goals and objectives when developing their trip plans. Well-written goals and objectives serve the same purpose as a good map—leaders are able to focus on a specific path or direction as they create and execute a trip. If leaders are forced to make tough programming decisions during the trip, goals and objectives will assist in the decision-making process. The entire trip plan is based on the goals and objectives.

PREPARED

P = Participants (Who are the participants?)

Outdoor leaders know the age, gender, abilities, motivations, and health of their participants.

R = Resources (What resources are available to support an expedition?)

Outdoor leaders create and work from a budget and are aware of available resources to execute a trip.

E = Equipment and clothing (What equipment and clothing will be needed?)

Outdoor leaders develop equipment and clothing inventories appropriate for the trip. This includes individual as well as group equipment needs.

P = Plan (What is the itinerary and the time control plan?)

Outdoor leaders create detailed itineraries of events and activities. Also, time control plans are developed that include daily travel information such as distance, time, elevation gained and lost, break time, campsite locations, and so on.

A = Access (How does the group obtain proper access?)

Outdoor leaders obtain proper permits and permission to use trip areas and are aware of local rules and regulations.

R = Rationing (How will the menu be determined and food packed?)

Outdoor leaders use a menu or bulk-rationing system that meets the nutritional needs of the participants.

E = Emergency plan (What is the emergency plan?)

Outdoor leaders develop an emergency plan to deal with accidents and injuries that corresponds with an overall risk management plan.

D = Don't forget about logistics (Don't forget about trip logistics!)

An outdoor leader organizes a system to transport equipment, food, and participants throughout the experience.

FIGURE 11.1 The GO PREPARED system.

- **Setting the tone**—Leaders must create an atmosphere of trust and mutual respect from the very beginning. They can conduct initial activities such as icebreakers or initiatives to promote a positive tone. Leaders also model appropriate behavior by demonstrating a caring, respectful attitude.

- **Establishing group structure and group norms**—Leaders must take the time to establish acceptable standards of group and individual behavior. Leaders must share and emphasize static rules or norms such as organizational policies and safety protocol, and they must also help the group establish dynamic norms. Dynamic norms include the behaviors established within the group such as respect, support, trust, and good communication. One way to establish dynamic norms is through a full-value contract (see chapter 3).

- **Establishing goals**—Leaders must create common vision and purpose within the group. It is important to address all levels of goals: leader goals, participant goals, group goals, and goals of the sponsoring organization. Leaders must carefully facilitate a process to establish commonalities among the various individual agendas and goals. Time must be taken through activities and discussions to establish a common group vision.

- **Logistical tasks**—Finally, leaders must ensure that group members are prepared to go into the field. This includes obtaining the proper equipment and food. For example, leaders plan the time to inspect each group member's equipment for appropriateness. Many times the leader uses the first part of an extended trip to facilitate a shakedown. The shakedown allows members to test equipment and practice basic skills before heading into the wilderness. Leaders can also assess physical abilities and limitations during this time. For an overview of the orienting process, see figure 11.2.

Monitoring

The monitoring process occurs once the trip is under way. It is the leader's responsibility to monitor the group at all times. Leaders must focus their observations on key areas, which will be discussed next. Much of the monitoring process discussed here focuses on specific skills. The ability to observe

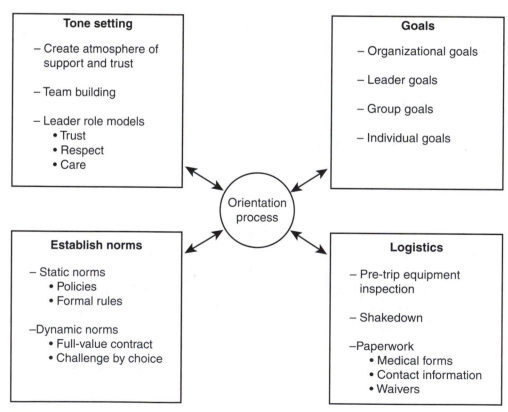

FIGURE 11.2 Process for orienting groups for an expedition.

Wagstaff, Attarian, and Drury

CAREERS IN ADVENTURE

NAME: Brian Murphy
POSITION: Field Instructor, NOLS (Lander, Wyoming)
BACKGROUND: BS in leisure services, outdoor recreation and education option from Radford University (RU); recreation specialist for the Department of the Army; manager of the RU Outdoors Outdoor Recreation Programming Service; outdoor education instructor; director of Boulder Valley School District's Youth Empowerment and Self-Esteem Program; teen coordinator for the Parks and Recreation Department of Lafayette, Colorado; raft guide; white-water kayak instructor; honorably discharged combat veteran of the U.S. Marines

WHAT'S YOUR JOB LIKE? I provide technical skill development and leadership curriculum delivery for NOLS. The primary focus of the curriculum is the NOLS seven leadership skills (expedition behavior, competency, communication skills, risk assessment and management, tolerance for adversity and uncertainty, self-awareness, and vision and action) and decision-making styles. All of this is delivered while on a multiweek wilderness expedition.

Currently I am a full-time field instructor for NOLS, working 25-plus weeks a year. My schedule generally sees me in the field from February until the first week of December. I work mostly white-water contracts for the school, so I am preparing for a course (briefing with other instructors, pulling boats and prepping gear, developing classes, and so on), working a river course, or getting off a river contract (debriefing a course, cleaning and putting away gear, and so on). I do enjoy a few days off in between contracts and generally do not have to work at all from December to February.

I love what NOLS offers students—easily transferable leadership skills from the wilderness setting to their lives back at home.

Mostly I like working with the people at NOLS. They're dedicated and passionate employees who are incredibly skilled and professional. Also, like I have always said, the view from the office is pretty sweet, too. The biggest challenge I face in my life is not seeing my family enough. There is never a day that I do not absolutely love my job, but I do miss my brothers, my nephews, my niece, and my grandmother. I make a focused effort every year to spend time at home in Virginia during my off-season. Sending digital photos, postcards, and e-mails helps a lot, but it isn't the same as being there. I also miss having a dog.

There are three skills that stand out most to me in my work. First is the ability to give and receive critical feedback. To master this communication skill, people need to let go of their ego and look at feedback as a means of improving as a leader or instructor. Second, the ability to teach to various learning styles is important. I think that the only way to develop this skill is through experience. And finally, humor in the face of adversity is necessary. I cannot help but smile as I am pelted with hail in a headwind of 40 miles per hour (64 kilometers per hour) while rowing an 18-foot (5-meter) oar rig down the Green River. Laughing goes a long way to making a miserable situation bearable. If you are passionate about the outdoors and want to work in the field of outdoor recreation, go for it. Do not listen to the people in our culture who maintain that you must be chained to a desk from 9 to 5. Do what you love in the wilderness and you will never work a day in your life. You will probably never be a millionaire, but you don't need money where you are going anyway if you live simply and within your means. Oh, and don't forget to wear sunscreen!

behaviors and react appropriately to those behaviors constitutes the monitoring process. A leader is constantly on duty as an observer.

Observation is a skill that must be learned and practiced. Many times novice leaders are so involved in the process (i.e., activities, group dynamics, taking care of personal needs) that they cannot step back and observe with an objective eye. To observe objectively, the leader must be able to take a backseat and watch the entire process, just like exercising a third eye that serves as a video camera. The leader records individual behaviors and group actions based on four categories. Observations will be played back to (shared with) the group during meetings and debriefings. A leader must observe the following key items:

- The group process: How group members are communicating (i.e., how well the group makes decisions)

- Task function: How the group accomplishes tasks (i.e., how they canoe from point A to B, how efficiently they break camp in the morning, or how well they negotiate an off-trail hike)

- Attention to safety: Does the group keep safety at the forefront of decision making?

- Attention to environmental stewardship: Does the group always take the environment into consideration and practice Leave No Trace ethics?

In order to observe and address these four categories, several suggestions are described in the following sections, which include observing member roles, observing motivation levels, and group check-ins.

Observing Roles   Observing member roles will dictate the effectiveness of the group process, task accomplishment, safety, and protecting the environment. During the group process, a leader can monitor relationships and task productivity by recognizing group roles and then reinforcing positive roles and confronting negative roles. Leaders should monitor member roles to help the group reach its goals. Positive roles would include individual behaviors that support the process. For example, people who willingly help others, openly share ideas and opinions, or exercise productive communication skills model positive roles. Negative roles might include undermining good communication, not doing their fair share of camp work, or acting selfishly in a group setting.

Observing Motivation and Competence   Levels of motivation fluctuate during an extended trip. Motivation can be affected by factors such as physical exhaustion, hunger, or fatigue. Leaders also need to monitor motivation through levels of participation in specific activities. Lack of participation or low levels of participation may mean the participant perceives the activity to have too little or too much challenge. Or, it may mean that the participant cannot envision the purpose or intended outcome of the activity, for example, if the participant's focus is on the actual climbing as opposed to staying focused during a comprehensive ground school to safely prepare to rock climb. As leaders monitor motivation levels, they should keep in mind the participant's level of commitment to the overall goal process.

Group and individual competence involve effective communication, skill level, and abilities. Some group members may have great ideas for getting the job done but their ideas are not heard or are disregarded due to power struggles within the group. If the group is having a difficult time accomplishing tasks, pay attention to skill level. Not being able to paddle at an appropriate level is dangerous and may breed frustration or fear, which takes away from enjoyment. Also monitor ability levels of the group. Based on the maturity of participants, they may deal with situations and conflict inappropriately. For example, if you are witnessing a lot of conflict, rather than stepping in and dictating a solution you might teach conflict resolution skills. This empowers groups to solve their problems in a mature way.

Group Check-In   An important part of the monitoring process is periodic check-ins with the group. You should conduct check-ins both formally and informally for several reasons. First, it is important to assess the physical health of the group and individuals. Continually monitor aches, pains, water intake, and food intake to avoid problems. You should also consistently monitor group functioning and development. For example, during a morning or evening debriefing, have group members share concerns. An open forum of this nature is effective in defusing situations that may grow and result in a major conflict.

In addition, an outdoor leader must continually assess goal accomplishment. Check-ins can be used to assess goal accomplishment individually or during a group meeting. Finally, if leaders have established a positive, supportive environment, they can use check-ins to assess their effectiveness. Group members should be given the opportunity to provide the leader with feedback. This is a tough thing for many leaders to do, but a leader who is open to feedback and acts on that feedback is modeling healthy communication skills. For an overview of the monitoring process, see figure 11.3.

Teaching Outdoor Pursuits

A competent outdoor leader embodies the characteristics and skills of an effective teacher. In this portion of the chapter, specific teaching methods are discussed to assist the novice adventure programmer in the art of teaching. First, the discussion will introduce the SPEC method of instruction and learning (Drury et al. 2005). We will compare traditional teaching approaches with the SPEC model, and we will focus on the creation of formal learning challenges in order to foster an inspiring learning experience, challenging the aspiring outdoor leader to avoid the pitfalls of traditional educational approaches. However, readers should realize that this chapter provides a limited explanation of the SPEC model. The goal is to introduce the broader concepts that define effective teaching and to highlight the development of challenges as a teaching tool.

In addition to the SPEC approach, outdoor leaders who facilitate extended trips must also be aware of other common teaching techniques. The grasshopper method and teachable moments are two such techniques. The **grasshopper method** is the process of covering an entire curriculum in a systematic way during an extended expedition. **Teachable moments** represent those instances during a trip when unexpected learning opportunities present themselves. This section concludes with specific examples to clarify the use of the teaching methods. A combined understanding of SPEC, the grasshopper method, and teachable moments will assist the novice adventure programmer in the development of critical teaching skills. In this section, outdoor leaders will be referred to as teachers and trip participants will be referred to as students.

SPEC Approach to Teaching and Learning

The SPEC approach differs dramatically from traditional methods. Outdoor leaders have a chance to meet the learning needs of a greater range of students by implementing strategies that are more student centered as opposed to teacher centered, problem centered as opposed to content based, experiential as opposed to theoretical, and collaborative as opposed to an individual. We'll take a

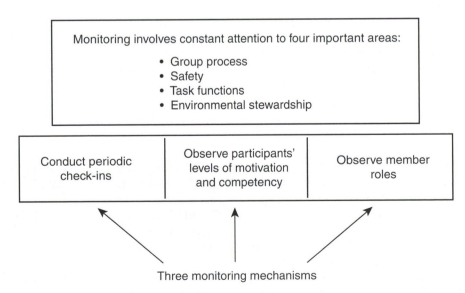

FIGURE 11.3 **Process for monitoring groups during an expedition.**

look at each of these approaches as adapted from Drury et al. (2005).

In **student-centered learning,** students learn by talking, listening, writing, reading, creating, and reflecting on content, ideas, and concerns as they work in small groups or individually to engage the curriculum. Authority is shared with the teacher in many ways. Students have direct access to knowledge. They are encouraged to develop their own questions and arrive at some of their own conclusions with teacher guidance. It is presumed that students have preexisting knowledge and skill that they can contribute to the learning. Students may learn from each other as much as they learn from the teacher.

The opposite of student-centered learning is teacher-centered learning, where the teacher is the center of authority. In the teacher-centered approach, the teacher transmits most information and all knowledge to the learner. It is presumed that the teacher will ask most of the important questions and that these questions have a correct answer that must be validated by the teacher. Students are empty vessels, and teachers are the experts who fill the vessels with appropriate knowledge.

In **problem-based learning,** teachers design complex and increasingly authentic problems for students to solve individually or in teams. Students must grapple with information (the content) as well as use skills (social, intellectual, emotional) to solve the problems successfully. Feedback and assessment is an integral and ongoing part of the process. Successful learning is assessed on multiple levels: content understanding, group process, individual skill development, and so on. Students receive personalized narrative feedback regarding their performance from several sources: peers, teacher, and self-assessment. The teacher serves as a facilitator, guide, colearner, mentor, and coach who helps students through the learning process.

The counterpart to problem-based learning is content-based learning, which is typically found in the more traditional classroom. Here the coverage of content is the focus of the learning. Teachers create structured lessons designed to help students understand and recall important facts, concepts, and processes that they will be expected to recall on tests and examinations. Concern for skill development is often tied directly only to those skills that are required for improved mastery of the content. Assessment often comes at the end of a unit of study and is frequently evaluated in terms of percentages of correct answers or expressions of understanding as shown on pencil-and-paper tests. The teacher may have little or no opportunity to share personalized, narrative feedback with each student to provide direction for future improvement.

In experiential learning, students learn by doing. All learning occurs within the context of firsthand experiences. Students participate, make choices, and accept responsibility for their role in the learning process. The interactive nature of this approach creates a wealth of physical, intellectual, emotional, and social experiences. Learners construct their own meaning by reflecting on all these experiences. They are prompted to make connections to their own lives, larger contexts, and theory during this reflective stage.

Experiential learning is contrasted with theoretical learning, where students generally learn by listening, reading, writing, or following tightly scripted activities related to the curriculum. Students have very few choices of consequence. The curriculum exists in and of itself, and passing exams is the primary motivation. Curricular content is often prepackaged in discrete bundles of information to be learned in a prescribed, often linear, sequence. Students may or may not recognize any connection between the content and their own lives.

Collaborative learning, the fourth approach, is where learning takes place in a social context. Working as an individual or as part of a team, students consistently function as part of a larger community. While competition has its place, collaboration is the fundamental value. All learners are expected to work with and show respect for others. Through multiple experiences, reflection, and a conscious attention to the emotional health of the group members, students learn to value (rather than merely tolerate) the differences among them. Success for both individuals and the group is recognized and rewarded.

The opposite of the collaborative approach to learning is the individual approach. In the individual approach, personal performance is the primary measure of success. Competition is encouraged as a predominant value. Individual accountability and achievement are recognized and rewarded, while group accountability and achievement may go unrecognized or may be actively discouraged. Little emphasis is placed on the development of social skills or group decision-making, management, or leadership skills. The emotional health of the group members is not as important as individual grades on exams.

Choosing a teaching approach that is suitable to the students and instructor involves a number of factors. Taking into consideration such factors as time, depth and breadth of understanding required, and amount of student ownership necessary can dictate what strategies will maximize learning. We firmly believe that the SPEC approach has distinct advantages over traditional approaches but that each has its time and place. Table 11.1 explores the issues associated with SPEC and traditional teaching approaches.

Designing SPEC Experiences

Many outdoor leaders view themselves as technical experts and their learners as empty vessels. They see their task as that of filling the vessels with their expertise by transferring information in the most efficient and effective way possible. Instructors who understand the SPEC approach see their role differently. They see themselves as designers of powerful learning experiences who coach learners rather than lecture them. Of course, mastery of content by the instructor is extremely valuable yet not absolutely necessary. More important is being able to differentiate between essential and nonessential knowledge and skills.

The SPEC approach generally takes more time than traditional approaches, so instructors must determine which knowledge and skills are important enough to take the time and energy to engage students. Ultimately the decision may come down to determining which parts of the curriculum should be taught in a more traditional manner and which are important enough to present as a SPEC challenge (lesson). The decision should be based on the factors in table 11.1 as well as the dependency of the learner on the instructor's expertise. In other words, if the learner has no knowledge or understanding of the topic and the instructor is a world-renowned expert on the topic, then the learner is dependent on the instructor and more traditional methodologies might be appropriate.

Consistently powerful learning experiences should be designed. They can and will occur with gratifying regularity if certain principles

TABLE 11.1

SPEC Method Versus Traditional Learning Approaches

SPEC approach	Traditional approach
Not confined by the teacher's agenda and schedule; tends to take more time	Lessons are designed within a specific time constraint; the instructor controls flow of the lesson
Provides greater depth of learning among a diverse group of learners; meets diverse learning styles	Tends to facilitate depth of understanding for a specific learning style; rarely meets the needs of all learners
Learners are able to synthesize diverse information and process diverse experiences; not as efficient if instructor requires students to recall a large amount of information in the short term	Instructors can present significant amounts of information in a short amount of time; tends to reinforce memorization for short-term memory
Student participation creates ownership in the process and frequently affects the learner on multiple levels (i.e., intellectually, emotionally, socially, physically, spiritually)	Students are supplied with information, resulting in passive participation; ownership and personal investment is minimal
Instructors must be comfortable handing over control and pace of learning to the learners	Instructors have mastery over the subject and control the pace and method of learning
Instructors are comfortable with chaos and with not knowing all the answers, and are prepared to let the students fail; they are equipped to support and redirect learning to facilitate success	Instructors manage the group as they deem appropriate and must be mature enough to put the needs of the learner first as they exercise their power

are followed. Outdoor leaders are designers of compelling learning events that immerse the participant in the essential knowledge and skills associated with the topic. The essence of the SPEC approach involves the creation of activity-based lessons known as *challenges*. Challenges consist of carefully constructed learning activities that meet specified learning outcomes. Participants engaged in a challenge will find themselves immersed in a student-centered, problem-solving, experiential, and collaborative learning activity.

There are three fundamental reasons to use challenges: They provide multiple chances to work with both basic and more advanced content, they allow learners to practice real-life cognitive and technical skills, and they provide more authentic learning experiences that allow learners to take more ownership and become emotionally involved in the learning experience. In adventure programming, whether it is summiting a mountain, paddling a difficult stretch of river, or performing the more mundane tasks of setting up camp and cooking dinner, these activities are all grounded in reality and practical application.

The challenge for outdoor leaders is to integrate these creative activities into their instructional methods. The sample challenge in figure 11.4, Different Strokes, provides a template for the design of challenges. In the example, a group of students in a canoeing class are challenged to apply new knowledge and skills related to canoe strokes.

In his landmark book *The Seven Habits of Highly Effective People* (1990), Stephen Covey states in habit 2 that you should "start with the end in mind." We use this as a driving principle in designing challenges, which means that we must determine what learning outcome or course objective we want learners to know as the first step. Put another way, a clear vision of the destination helps the student and teacher to stay on track throughout the learning process. Not only will having clear outcomes increase the odds for successful learning, but it will also help when it comes to assessment. Once you have clear outcomes, you can then determine what will be acceptable evidence of learning.

In the sample challenge, Different Strokes, there are three knowledge outcomes:

1. Participants can describe the three types of canoe strokes, the parts of a stroke, and the various p\rinciples that affect stroke execution and the canoe.

2. Participants can describe eight tandem canoe strokes and explain where and when they should use the strokes.

3. Participants can describe basic canoe safety as it relates to entering, exiting, and paddling a canoe.

What skill or disposition do you want them to practice? This needs to be expressed in terms that are observable. In the Different Strokes challenge, the skill is this: Participants can properly use eight different tandem canoe strokes at the appropriate moment in the appropriate circumstances.

It is important to ask what the essential question is that drives the challenge. One of the great benefits of outdoor pursuits is that, unlike in the traditional classroom, students rarely ask the question, "Why are we doing this?" Nonetheless, it is necessary to address the essential question in challenge design. When instructors grapple with the essential question, it frequently helps them determine whether the challenge is worthwhile. If the students and sometimes even the instructor are confused and not sure where the task is going, the essential question allows them to see the task clearly and adjust accordingly.

The essential question drives the exploration of the subject, and it is frequently difficult to answer. For example, consider the essential question, "How can we consistently develop quality rock-climbing instructors?" This is a complex and meaningful essential question. Addressing this question requires learners to struggle with a variety of issues associated with rock climbing and with leadership, decision making, and outdoor leadership in general. If the learners tackle this question earnestly, they will have learned a great deal about the topic.

Tackling a good essential question requires the use of Bloom's higher-order thinking skills such as analysis, synthesis, and evaluation. Beginning the question with "How?", "Why?", or "Which?" requires the participants to thoroughly research the topic, evaluate the various resources, and apply their new knowledge in a variety of ways. A good essential question is quite intricate. The more the question is explored, the more complex it becomes. Upon examination it quickly becomes evident that a good question may on the surface appear simple but in reality is multifaceted. In the Different Strokes challenge, the essential question is, "What canoe strokes and related stroke information must a tandem paddler have mastery of in order to be a competent paddler who can conduct

Different Strokes Canoe Challenge

Knowledge Outcome

1. Participants can describe the types of canoe strokes, the parts of a stroke, and the various principles that affect the canoe and stroke execution.

2. Participants can describe eight different tandem canoe strokes and explain where and when they should be used.

3. Participants can describe basic canoe safety as it relates to entering, exiting, and paddling a canoe.

Skill Outcome

Participants can properly use eight different tandem canoe strokes at the appropriate moment in the appropriate circumstances.

Essential Question

What canoe strokes and related stroke information must a competent tandem paddler master to conduct safe, enjoyable, and environmentally sound flat-water canoe trips?

Description of Challenge (Task)

Your Outdoor Pursuits Canoeing class has been asked to prepare a series of three hour-long lessons on canoeing for 12- to 14-year-olds at the local YMCA children's camp starting two weeks from today. Your class is to work as a single team in preparing the lessons but will work in teams of two during the actual instruction.

It is expected that you will introduce the participants to safe canoe use, present creative and enjoyable lessons on the eight basic flat-water tandem canoe strokes (forward and reverse power, draw, push-away or pry, forward and reverse quarter sweeps, J stroke, and rudder), and information necessary for participants to understand the principles that influence what stroke you need to use in various circumstances.

It is my desire for you *all* to have a common understanding and ability. To encourage that understanding, once you have decided the sequence and duration of various topics (two people to a topic), I will put the names of teaching pairs in a hat. The day of the class I will draw one pair from the hat for each topic to be taught that day. The pairs selected will teach the classes for that day.

As a final class exercise, we will go on a half-day canoe trip and I will observe your use of the canoe strokes and individually quiz you on the topics. The class will receive a collective pass–fail grade.

Good luck!

Criteria for Assessment and Feedback

Form:

- ✦ Instruction is appropriate for the age group.
- ✦ Information presented is accurate.
- ✦ Instruction is creative and enjoyable.
- ✦ Instruction covers the topics at an appropriate level.

Content:

- ✦ The eight basic flat-water tandem canoe strokes are accurately learned.
- ✦ The information necessary for participants to understand the principles that influence what strokes are needed in various circumstances is learned.

FIGURE 11.4 Sample challenge template.

Developed by Leading EDGE, LLC (www.realworldlearning.info).

safe, enjoyable, and environmentally sound canoe trips on flat water?"

Effective outdoor leaders enhance practical learning experiences by engaging participants in challenges. Challenges push learners deeper into the subject and stimulate higher-order learning skills that enhance mastery of the subject. Whenever creating a challenge, it is also a good idea to think about assessment, including assessment during the challenge. In the case of the Different Strokes challenge, a product quality checklist (table 11.2) has been provided to help leaders assess the product. The product in this case is a series of one-hour lessons for a YMCA group of 12- to 14-year-olds. Product quality checklists are an excellent way to provide feedback in SPEC challenges.

Teachable Moments

Teachable moments are spontaneous lessons stimulated by a specific situation or event (Drury et al. 2005). Teachable moments surface constantly during an outdoor experience. As groups encounter unknown situations, outdoor leaders have the opportunity to relay information and skills related to the situation. For example, let's say a group hikes down a trail and discovers a snake. While participant interest is at a peak, the leader takes the opportunity to do a brief presentation on snakes by identifying the snake, its characteristics, and its habitat and discusses the snake's place in the ecosystem. Another teachable moment finds a participant struggling with a rain tarp. A knot has been cinched so tightly that it is impossible to untie. Frustrated, the participant asks for the leader's help. The leader takes the opportunity to teach a more appropriate knot that requires minimal effort to untie (Martin et al. 2006).

As mentioned, teachable moments are numerous during an outdoor experience. The leader must carefully select appropriate situations to address as *formal teachable moments*. Leaders who address every situation are asking for trouble. Participants tend to disengage if the action is constantly halted for a lesson. If the lesson requires the entire group's attention, time must be taken to round up and organize the group to ensure everyone hears the message. *Informal teachable moments* include those situations when individuals or small groups within the larger group encounter a learning opportunity (Drury et al. 2005). The leader may choose to informally present a message or skill as part of a casual discussion. Both types of teachable moments are powerful learning opportunities because the timing is immediate and pertinent to the situation. In other words, formal and informal teachable moments take advantage of the participant's desire and motivation to learn (Martin et al. 2006).

Grasshopper Method

Paul Petzoldt (1984) coined the term *grasshopper method* as a colorful analogy to explain the expedition teaching process. Small grasshoppers travel by hopping from one point to the next in search of food or cover. Outdoor leaders also hop from one subject to the next during an expedition in order to reach a final destination. They break topics into small parts throughout a trip and cover content and skills in what may look like a random manner but in reality is a systematic approach that ensures the entire curriculum is covered.

Petzoldt cautioned leaders about their first attempt to use the grasshopper method. Most outdoor leaders come from traditional education systems where information is given by one source, the teacher, for memorization and then regurgitated for a grade. In the outdoors, this type of education does not lend itself to effective learning. Outdoor leaders are unknowingly conditioned in traditional settings to teach in limited ways. Petzoldt believes that the grasshopper method should be carefully presented to the outdoor leader so that teaching does not occur haphazardly (Wagstaff and Cashel 2001).

To effectively execute the grasshopper method, leaders must plan ahead. Remember, the fundamental concept of grasshopper teaching is to systematically link a series of topics to cover an entire curriculum. The outdoor leader must hop from topic to topic as opportunities present themselves (Martin et al. 2006).

Teaching opportunities naturally arise during an outdoor experience. The seasoned outdoor leader exercises the ability to predict that certain opportunities will naturally arise, whereas the teachable moment is unpredictable. Knowledge of future situations allows the leader to systematically cover a topic in fragments. By the end of an experience, the fragments come together to form a complete topic. The grasshopper method has many advantages. Topics can be covered in small pieces so that information and skills can be easily introduced, processed, and practiced before more content is introduced. Grasshopper teaching allows leaders to manage time effectively during a trip. Flexibility

TABLE 11.2

Product Quality Checklist

PRODUCT AUTHORS	PRODUCT TITLE *Different Strokes Canoe Challenge*	EVALUATOR NAMES

Observed	Criteria	Possible points	Rating
	Instruction is appropriate for the age group.		
	Information presented is accurate.		
	Instruction is creative and enjoyable.		
	Instruction covers topics at an appropriate level.		
	The eight basic flat-water tandem canoe strokes are accurately learned.		
	The information necessary for participants to understand the principles concerning what stroke should be used in various circumstances is learned.		
	Basic canoe safety, including entering and exiting a canoe, is learned.		
		Total:	Total:

Observations
Elements of questionable quality	Elements of exceptional quality

Developed by Leading EDGE, LLC (www.realworldlearning.info).

CAREERS IN ADVENTURE

NAME: Jason Smith

JOB: Retail manager, program and event coordinator, facility manager, instructor, and artist, Adirondack Lakes and Trails Outfitters (full-service canoe and kayak retail store and outfitter in the spring, summer, and fall) and Dewey Mountain XC Ski and Snowshoe Center (in the winter months); owner of a small graphic arts business (Saranac Lake, New York)

BACKGROUND: AS in wilderness recreation leadership, North Country Community College, Saranac Lake, New York; ACA-trained coastal kayak instructor and canoe instructor

WHAT'S YOUR JOB LIKE? My responsibilities are divided into three fields during paddling season: rentals and outfitting, guiding and instruction, and sales and merchandising. In the winter I am responsible for the day-to-day operations of our local cross-country ski area. This includes managing ski and snowshoe rentals, grooming trails, and marketing. Additionally I coordinate events, programs, and XC ski and snowshoe races. Dewey Mountain is managed by Adirondack Lakes and Trails Outfitters and is owned by the Town of Harrietstown. Therefore we actively solicit donors and other funding sources. As a graphic artist, I provide all marketing materials and Web site design for the businesses.

I'm certain I would not be happy in a career that I didn't have an interest in and that did not offer a variety of responsibilities. In any given week during the summer I may repair a canoe, plan a backcountry itinerary for clients, lead a kayak instruction course, develop new canoe or kayak programs, promote a sale or event, or help customers decide what canoe or kayak is right for them. Also, I develop brochures, advertisements, and Web site material to promote both the outfitting business and the ski area. I enjoy bringing in a creative aspect to my work in this way. Overall, I believe that to be successful and happy in this field, you need good communication skills and a desire to interact with the public. My advice to someone interested in the outdoor recreation field is to find your niche and get out and enjoy the activities you are selling. For instance, I paddle or ski with my family in my free time. The biggest challenge I face is finding that free time. It's a demanding business but extremely rewarding.

and control over the length of a lesson allow leaders to schedule other, necessary activities into a daily routine. A larger curriculum tends to be much more manageable during extended trips if it is broken down into small topics. The grasshopper method is conducive to the overall experiential learning process. Leaders can easily implement a variety of teaching tools so that all phases of the experiential learning cycle are touched.

Of course, the danger of the grasshopper approach is not meeting curriculum goals. The possibility exists that portions of topics will not be covered due to oversight or time constraints. This is why outdoor leaders must be systematic in their approach. Overall program planning plays a huge role in this process. The following example portrays the planning and thought process an outdoor leader uses to facilitate the grasshopper method based on a tentative schedule.

Some leaders are faced with the task of teaching land navigation, among many other skills, on a six-day wilderness trip. As they review the schedule before the trip, the leaders tentatively plan their method of covering the entire topic. The following is discussed:

- Day 1: Schedule is full—there's no appropriate opportunity to address navigation.
- Day 2: Only map-reading skills will be taught—the potential campsite is conducive to clearly viewing surrounding topography so that map-reading skills can be taught using the actual terrain (no more than 30 minutes).
- Day 3: No particular setting or environment needed—teach basic compass-reading skills at some point during the day (no more than 20 minutes). During hiking, encourage participants to use map-reading skills to find the route with instructor assistance.
- Day 4: Many dramatic overlooks of mountainous terrain exist along the hiking trail—use a break during the hike to teach use of map and compass in combination (no more than 30 minutes).
- Day 5: Schedule an off-trail hike and empower the group to find the route to the next campsite.
- Day 6: Present SPEC challenge to test and reinforce participants' knowledge and skills.

This example represents a formal thought process that novice leaders may undergo to systematically plan the coverage of a topic based on anticipated situations. As outdoor leaders mature, this process becomes intuitive. Seasoned outdoor leaders with knowledge of terrain, environmental conditions, group abilities, and so on can predict when, where, and how topic fragments will be covered. The amount of time needed to formally plan a program decreases as leadership experience increases. Imagine the amount of work it would take to create a tentative schedule for 30 days that covers more than 20 topics in depth. Even if this monstrous schedule could be planned, unforeseen challenges and changes would make the plan obsolete in the first few days. Aspiring outdoor leaders are encouraged to obtain field experience under the mentorship of seasoned instructors in order to develop their ability to use this teaching technique. In the beginning, novice leaders should at least attempt to outline an overall teaching plan, realizing flexibility is the key. At the very least, a tentative teaching plan broken down into fragments serves as a guide to ensure topic coverage (Martin et al. 2006).

Common Outdoor Pursuits

Outdoor adventure pursuits, a subset of outdoor recreation, are physical, low-impact activities and experiences that direct people toward sensory and muscular coordination and development. Non-mechanized, human-powered activities are preferable because they provide long-lasting physical benefits. Examples of these activities include land-based pursuits (backpacking, rock climbing, caving, mountain biking), water-based pursuits (canoeing, sea and white-water kayaking, rafting), and snow and ice pursuits (mountaineering, ice climbing, cross-country skiing, snowshoeing).

These experiences also have emotional implications such as fear, anxiety, accomplishment, and ecstasy, as well as possibilities for planning, seeking, and attaining highly personalized experiences. Participation in outdoor adventure pursuits is also mentally meaningful as it helps people cope with changes and live, work, and grow in a natural environment. Finally, participants can enhance and practice leadership and decision-making skills within a supportive group environment (Miles and Priest 1999; Priest and Gass 2005; Hilbert and Grimm 1973).

The following section presents a selection of outdoor adventure pursuits based on land, water, and snow and ice. The activities are briefly described and course content highlighted by identifying the primary technical, safety, and environmental skills associated with each activity. Technical skills create the foundation for each activity and provide a conduit for personal growth. Safety skills are those skills that protect participants from harm and create an awareness of the risks inherent in the activity. Environmental skills are introduced to minimize the ecological and social effects of traveling, camping, and participating in these activities (Priest and Gass 2005).

Land-Based Outdoor Pursuits

Some common land-based outdoor pursuits are backpacking, rock climbing, caving, and mountain biking. Some or all of these activities provide the basis for many outdoor adventure programs, as resources to conduct these activities are found nationwide. Both natural and human-made resources such as trails, cliffs, and caves are required for the conduct of these activities.

Backpacking

Backpacking can be defined as an outing that requires one or more overnight stays in a backcountry area. Participants should be able to plan and conduct a safe, low-impact multiday outing; plan and prepare a menu for a multiday outing; demonstrate competence in the care and use of packs, tents, stoves, and other major items of equipment; describe the various agencies responsible for managing lands that offer backpacking opportunities; interpret a topographical map; use a map and compass; demonstrate Leave No Trace traveling skills and practices; and identify the major health, safety, and first aid concerns associated with backpacking.

Rock Climbing

Rock climbing is a popular outdoor adventure pursuit that uses specialized techniques and equipment to climb steep rock faces. Participants should be able to demonstrate appropriate methods for the care and safe use of rock-climbing equipment (e.g., harness, rope, helmet, shoes, assorted hardware, software); exhibit knowledge of and respect for the potential hazards inherent in the activity; recognize, tie, and use the knots introduced for rock climbing (figure-eight follow-through, figure-eight on a bight, water knot, bowline, double fisherman's), including the proper coiling of rope; belay using at least two different techniques or devices; move with confidence on rock and in rappelling; construct the appropriate climbing anchors; demonstrate Leave No Trace climbing practices; and show awareness of safety through proper equipment use and practice.

Caving

Caving will take students into remarkable underground environments that include unusual formations, unknown passages, and unique and delicate ecosystems. Participants should be able to demonstrate proficiency with personal caving equipment; move carefully and efficiently underground; exhibit confidence with route finding and cave map reading; identify various speleotherms and cave formations; demonstrate Leave No Trace traveling skills and practices; and articulate some of the environmental and social problems associated with cave management.

Mountain Biking

Participants in mountain biking should be able to understand the fitness requirements, hazards, and risks associated with the sport; recognize the parts and proper use and care of the bike and equipment; appreciate and understand the spirit, history, and etiquette of mountain biking; distinguish among the various types of mountain bikes; describe the role that bicycle geometry plays in climbing, descending, and touring capabilities; describe how to properly fit a mountain bike; execute proper shifting techniques while pedaling over varied terrain; execute proper climbing and descending techniques; maintain and make minor repairs to a mountain bike; demonstrate an understanding of the environmental concerns related to pedaling in the backcountry; plan for and execute a safe, enjoyable all-day mountain bike tour; and appreciate the health-related fitness associated with effective mountain biking.

Water-Based Outdoor Pursuits

Water-based outdoor pursuits share similar foundational skills and consist of canoeing, whitewater kayaking, whitewater rafting, and sea kayaking. An abundance of aquatic resources nationwide make these activities popular with outdoor adventure programs.

Canoeing

Canoeing includes both flat and white-water skills. Participants should be able to gather the necessary equipment and clothing for an outing; demonstrate the loading and unloading of canoes onto a car top or trailer; outfit a canoe; demonstrate

Caving will take students into remarkable underground environments.

the primary paddle strokes (forward, back, sweep, reverse sweep, brace); paddle in a straight line; perform eddy turns, peel-outs, and ferries; swim a boat to shore; demonstrate swimming a rapid; demonstrate individual, group, and boat-assisted rescues; demonstrate knowledge of boating safety; work cooperatively with a partner to maneuver a canoe to a predetermined location; communicate effectively with group members about river hazards and features; demonstrate Leave No Trace practices; and articulate the International Scale of River Difficulty. Many of these topics can be presented in the following water-based activities.

White-Water Kayaking

Participants in white-water kayaking should be able to gather the necessary equipment for a river outing and outfit a kayak; demonstrate the loading and unloading of kayaks on a car top or trailer; demonstrate the fundamental paddle strokes (forward, back, sweep, reverse sweep, brace) and paddle in a straight line; perform eddy turns, peel-outs, and ferries; execute a wet exit; swim a kayak to shore; assist in a t-rescue and helping-hand rescue; demonstrate knowledge of boating safety; exhibit decision-making skills and responsibilities to one-self and one's group; communicate effectively with group members about river hazards and features; understand the basic concepts of river hydrology and the effects of moving water; demonstrate Leave No Trace practices; and articulate the International Scale of River Difficulty.

White-Water Rafting

White-water rafting requires mastery of the fundamentals of paddle rafting. Participants should be able to gather the necessary equipment for a river outing and outfit a paddle raft; demonstrate the fundamental paddle strokes (forward, back, draw, brace) and paddle in a straight line; perform eddy turns, peel-outs, and ferries; right a capsized raft; demonstrate knowledge of rafting safety; demonstrate decision-making skills and responsibilities to oneself and one's group; communicate effectively with group members about river hazards and features; articulate the International Scale of River Difficulty; describe the basic concepts of river hydrology and the effects of moving water; paddle class III or IV white water safely; perform self-rescue and respond to emergencies; plan and organize a safe white-water rafting trip; gain basic guiding experience; demonstrate Leave No Trace practices;

Learning to canoe requires participants to learn basic paddle strokes and to cooperate with a partner.

and appreciate the rewards of lifetime participation in paddle rafting on white water.

Sea Kayaking

The sea kayak was developed for paddling on the open waters of oceans or lakes. Participants should be able to understand and describe the differences in sea kayak equipment and designs; understand the spirit, history, safety, and etiquette of sea kayaking; demonstrate basic kayaking skills, including basic stroke and entry and exit techniques; demonstrate the proper use and care of sea kayaking equipment; discuss the concepts of hazard recognition and avoidance in sea kayaking; discuss hazards and the unique characteristics of coastal camping; discuss the intricacies of trip planning unique to sea kayaking; identify local resources and areas for sea kayaking, including their attributes and hazards; and demonstrate understanding of the major types of environmental damage that can occur during sea kayaking and practice ways to reduce or eliminate such damage.

Ice- and Snow-Based Outdoor Pursuits

While not as popular as land- and water-based outdoor pursuits, programs offering snow- and ice-based activities, such as mountaineering, ice climbing, snowshoeing, and cross-country skiing are highly technical activities that are both seasonally and regionally dependent.

Mountaineering

Mountaineering is the collective term used to describe alpine activities and includes many types of climbing, expedition planning, backpacking, navigation, and other wilderness travel skills and knowledge. Participants should be able to understand the role that careful planning and preparation play in determining the success of a mountaineering expedition; plan a three-day mountaineering expedition; understand the basic equipment requirements necessary for a safe and comfortable mountaineering outing; identify the hazards inherent to the mountain environment; understand the theories of safe travel in avalanche terrain; demonstrate a working knowledge of selected knots and slings suitable for mountaineering; demonstrate proficient rope handling and coiling techniques; demonstrate a sitting hip belay; demonstrate a working knowledge of map and compass techniques; describe the effects of the mountain environment on the human organism and the techniques for the prevention and care of environmental injuries (hypothermia, frostbite, snow blindness, altitude illness); and demonstrate Leave No Trace practices.

Ice Climbing

Ice climbing is the practice of climbing ice formations such as icefalls on glaciers, frozen waterfalls, and other frozen features. Participants should be able to demonstrate an understanding of ice and the ice environment; demonstrate an understanding of the care, strengths, and weaknesses of ice-climbing equipment (ice tools, ice protection, crampons); tie the appropriate knots used in ice climbing; demonstrate the basics of French (low angle) and American ice-climbing techniques; demonstrate the ability to place ice screws and construct anchors for top roping; articulate the objective and subjective hazards associated with ice climbing; demonstrate Leave No Trace practices; and belay using at least two different techniques or devices.

Cross-Country Skiing

Cross-country skiing is an adventure pursuit that involves traveling great distances on narrow skis over relatively flat terrain. Participants should be able to discuss the benefits of participating in cross-country skiing as a lifelong physical activity; demonstrate basic cross-country skiing skills; apply safety rules and concepts as they relate to participating in cross-country skiing; choose and maintain proper equipment and clothing; demonstrate the appropriate social skills by following all rules related to trail etiquette; discuss the hazards inherent in the activity and ways of reducing these risks; describe the appropriate prevention and treatment for hypothermia, frostbite, and other cold-related conditions; and demonstrate Leave No Trace practices.

Snowshoeing

Easy accessibility, inexpensive equipment, and its attraction as a lifelong activity have made snowshoeing one of the fastest-growing snow sports of the past decade. Snowshoeing is a great way to extend the hiking season into winter.

Participants should be able to choose the proper equipment and clothing for snowshoeing; put on and use a snowshoe and binding combination (including maintenance, adjustment, and field repair); perform basic and advanced snowshoeing skills (walking efficiently, kick steps, traversing, stem turns, kick turns, and descending); travel efficiently on snowshoes; describe the prevention and treatment of hypothermia, frostbite, and other cold-related conditions; develop an awareness of the hazards inherent in the activity and ways of reducing these risks; demonstrate Leave No Trace practices; and discuss the benefits of snowshoeing as a lifelong physical activity.

Summary

Adventure programming includes a wide variety of outdoor adventure pursuits. This chapter emphasized that professional adventure programmers also serve as professional outdoor leaders. Outdoor leadership is the practice of leading individuals and groups into natural settings via various modes of transportation, including backpacking, biking, canoeing, kayaking, climbing, and other outdoor pursuits. Outdoor leadership constitutes a rich tradition of leading extended outdoor experiences (more than three days) focused on safety, quality, and environmental stewardship. Aspiring adventure programmers would do well to take a critical look at the core competencies of outdoor leadership. Well-rounded outdoor leaders must possess knowledge and skills in a variety of areas in order to be effective. Proper training, extensive experience, ongoing professional development, certifications, and involvement in professional associations are all necessary to be successful professional outdoor leaders.

Review Questions

1. Define *outdoor leadership* and explain its relationship to adventure programming.

2. What are the core competencies of outdoor leadership that are necessary to execute safe, enjoyable, and environmentally sound wilderness trips?

3. You're leading a 10-day expedition. Outline the orienting and monitoring process you would facilitate to ensure a quality experience.

4. Define a challenge in the context of the SPEC learning environment and describe how creating challenges ensures a quality experience.

5. Explain the differences between the grasshopper method and teachable moments when instructing during an extended trip.

6. Discuss two different outdoor pursuits and the fundamental skills and knowledge needed to execute these activities in a safe, enjoyable, and environment-friendly manner.

Student Learning Activities

1. Using the eight competencies outlined in this chapter, schedule a meeting with an adventure programming professional to assess your potential as an outdoor leader. Have the professional provide you with feedback in each of the competency areas. If you don't have experience in certain areas, determine how you would obtain experience.

2. Using the Internet, find advertisements for at least three professional outdoor leadership positions and review the job responsibilities for each position. Discuss your findings in a group setting with other students.

3. Using the SPEC method of instruction, create a challenge for a certain population. Pick the outdoor pursuit in which you have the most familiarity. Choose a population with specific abilities and limitations in order to create a realistic outcome.

Adventure Education Programming and Career Paths

Steven Guthrie and Rita Yerkes

" Adventure connotes participation and active involvement in life. . . . An attitude that permits a person to seek adventure in life feeds upon itself and renews itself. Any life worth living is worth living with the advent of a venture. "

—**William Quinn**

© Getty Images

Chapter Concepts

✦ Adventure programs can operate under a variety of leadership philosophies. Five leadership models have been identified: guided, instructional, adventure education, cooperative adventure, and common adventure. These have been placed on a continuum of leadership control from a leaderless philosophy (common adventure), with trip participants being the decision makers, to a strong leader model (guided), with the leader making all the decisions.

✦ Adventure programming occurs in diverse settings, including kindergarten through grade 12, colleges, adventure clubs, outdoor schools, for-profit programs, not-for-profit programs, municipal and county organizations, military training, youth camps, corporate programs, and adult programs.

✦ Inclusive programming involves the philosophy that programs should meet the needs of all persons, regardless of physical, cognitive, or social differences. Although all adventure programming should be inclusive, some programs focus on providing opportunities for those with differences.

✦ Much adventure programming is based on the programming philosophy initiated by Outward Bound, the progenitor of adventure education.

✦ Many programs have been developed to provide training for outdoor leadership. Some of the best known are NOLS and the WEA.

✦ Numerous wilderness medicine and rescue organizations have started since 1990, and certification in wilderness first aid has become a standard for professionals.

✦ Most employment in adventure programming is seasonal. Those who do not have a college degree in adventure education or a related field generally must work several seasons before they can obtain full-time employment.

✦ A college degree related to adventure programming is becoming more important. Those with a degree in experiential education, physical education, recreation administration with a focus on adventure education, or outdoor leadership are much more employable and will obtain full-time employment sooner.

✦ As a professional, in order to keep up with changes in this rapidly developing field, you should belong to a professional organization and attend conferences. Four professional associations with a major focus on adventure programming include the AEE, ACCT, AORE, and WEA.

Adventure education takes place with many different age groups in diverse settings including schools, after-school programs, adventure clubs, outdoor schools, for-profit programs, not-for-profit programs, municipal and county organizations, military training, youth camps, corporate programs, and adult programs. These schools and agencies use a variety of leadership models for adventure programming and provide opportunities for careers in adventure education.

Basic Models for Adventure Programming

Most **programs** use a leader-led model for their adventure programs. However, in practice, adventure programs function under a continuum of leadership philosophies, ranging from "leaderless" adventure programs to highly directive guided programs (Guthrie 1999; Rennie 1985; Watters 1987). This continuum is helpful in understanding the range and scope of programs.

Under this continuum, five program models have been identified: common adventure, cooperative adventure, adventure education, instructional or school, and guided or packaged. As shown in figure 12.1, the least organizational and leader control is exhibited through the common adventure model, a leaderless model relying on participants to make all decisions, and the most control is exhibited in the guided or packaged model. Within adventure programming, the most frequently used models are probably the instructional or school and the

Least organizational control				Most organizational control

Common adventure	Cooperative adventure	Adventure education	Instructional/ school	Guided/ packaged

FIGURE 12.1 The five adventure program models.

Adapted, by permission, from R. Watters, 1987, A model theory of outdoor programming approaches. In *High-adventure outdoor pursuits,* 2nd ed. Eds. J.F. Meier, T.W. Morash, and G.E. Welton (Columbus, OH: Publishing Horizons), 221.

guided or packaged models, both of which may be characterized as leader led. Many people tend to think those are the ideal or only viable leadership models.

We will first discuss the five models, including advantages and disadvantages. The boundaries between these models are not necessarily clear (Watters 1987); nevertheless, an understanding of the model types is useful. In the later discussion of various programs in different settings, we will identify types of programs that use a common adventure or cooperative adventure philosophy.

For any group to function well, it must have people who perform leadership actions. In a **well-functioning group,** these actions are distributed among or taken on by various group members rather than fulfilled by only one or two people who are the formally designated leaders (Johnson and Johnson 2002). A well-functioning group thus relies on **informal leaders** in addition to **formally designated leaders.** The leadership roles of informal leaders are greatest in a common adventure program and least in an autocratic guided program.

Common Adventure

Started at the University of Oregon in the 1960s as an alternative to traditional authoritarian leader-led models, the **common adventure program** model was adopted by a number of programs in the western and midwestern United States, including Idaho State University and Illinois State University. This model is based on the adventure education ideals of group cooperation and acceptance of individual self-responsibility. If people go backpacking with a group of friends, they are common adventurers.

A common adventure program promotes and facilitates common adventure trips. Under this model, the **outdoor program** provides a trip board to help people come together to create their own outdoor experiences. Trip initiators post a trip on the board and invite others to join them. The trip initiator is not the leader and is not vetted, trained, or paid by the outdoor program, and anyone can be a trip initiator. The common adventure outdoor program does not provide trip initiators with finan-

cial benefits or with any form of leadership, supervision, or leadership training, but it does provide meeting space, resources and information, and a program philosophy emphasizing self-responsibility and group cooperation. Participants make all decisions cooperatively, share all expenses equally, and are expected to accept responsibility for themselves, including their preparedness and their involvement in group decisions.

For example, to be a trip initiator at the University of Oregon, the only qualification for initiators is that they attend a clinic to learn about the common adventure philosophy and to get oriented to the program's resource rooms. Initiators have no responsibility for pretrip logistics or for making decisions before the trip; their job is merely to get the ball rolling. Similarly, on the trip itself they have no more responsibility than any other trip member. The University of Oregon Outdoor Program rents vans, rafts, kayaks, camping equipment, snow gear, clothing, bikes, safety and rescue gear, and many other items that participants may not be able to afford. Their resource room also has an extensive collection of maps, guidebooks, videos, DVDs, and other information for trip planning.

In a common adventure trip, because there are no designated leaders, leadership emerges as necessary; the group functions well because members take on varying leadership actions and responsibilities. Although this model has been called *leaderless,* that term is a misnomer—it refers to the fact there are no *formally designated* leaders. As with any well-functioning group, many group members are, in effect, leaders (Johnson and Johnson 2002).

Advantages of this program model are that it requires and teaches group work and **cooperative leadership.** Further, because there are no formal leaders or training, it is inexpensive. Finally, because no duty of care is assumed by the organization, it absolves the organization of legal responsibility, and without leaders, no leaders can be sued. Over its 40 years of existence, this has been a very workable program model (Chernaik 1991; University of Oregon Outdoor Program 2005). This model is used by a number of university outdoor programs and many club programs. Several university outdoor programs, including the University of Oregon's, provide both a common adventure program and an instructional program that follows the leader-led model.

The success of the common adventure model depends on everyone involved (program administrators, trip initiators, and participants) understanding the program philosophy so that new participants don't confuse it with a leader-led model and expect a **directive leadership style.** A common adventure program requires a pool of experienced participants who regularly go on the trips to share their knowledge, skills, and experience with new people. The program will be less successful if most participants are unfamiliar with functioning in cooperative groups. In areas without this pool of regular participants, a program may need to modify the common adventure concept to a cooperative adventure concept or use an instructional or guided model. A final drawback is that, since many administrators tend to be directive leaders and are unfamiliar with the common adventure concept, they may be unwilling to accept common adventure as a viable option.

Cooperative Adventure

In 1985, Rennie noted that a number of so-called common adventure programs should have been distinguished as cooperative adventure because they were providing various incentives (payment, free use of equipment) to obtain trip initiators; in essence, they were recruiting and providing leaders. Unlike common adventure, the **cooperative adventure** model uses formally designated leaders. These leaders, however, are called *facilitators* or *coordinators* to indicate that their leadership role is nonautocratic. Trip coordinators may be selected and trained; typically they are volunteer leaders who must meet some standards.

The cooperative adventure model is used by programs that do not have the pool of experienced participants needed for a successful common adventure program and by adventure organizations desiring to exert some institutional controls over the common adventure model. The program exerts control over trip conduct through established policies and procedures. However, participants are asked and expected to be very involved in the decision-making process and not to rely on the coordinators. Typically, although these volunteer leaders have less expertise than leaders under the instructional or guided model, participants enter into the program knowing the leaders are not highly trained professionals, and participants are willing to participate in judgment and decision making. In addition, they knowingly assume the risks associated with having nonprofessional leaders. Watters (1999) has disagreed with using the term *coop-*

erative adventure, preferring to distinguish between pure, unassisted common adventure, and assisted common adventure, because some programs which had evolved toward a cooperative adventure model were still being called *common adventure.* However, the term *cooperative adventure* can refer more broadly to noninstructional programs which vet, train, and pay leaders, yet function cooperatively, as well as programs that use volunteer leaders.

One significant advantage of this program model is lower costs (less training, volunteer labor). A significant learning outcome is that participants learn and practice cooperation and participative decision making. With more participant involvement, the formally designated leaders may be less likely to make serious mistakes in judgment. From a liability perspective, this model is more risky because volunteer leaders can be held to the same standard of care as paid leaders. However, these programs do use waivers and rely upon informed consent as legal protection. In practice, it works because the activities are typically less risky, and participants are involved in decision making and are informed of the risks (Guthrie 1999).

As with the common adventure model, it is imperative that leaders and participants know, understand, and buy into the program philosophy. Unfortunately, many students do not know how to work cooperatively. If most participants go on a trip expecting a directive leadership style and they don't understand the nature of cooperative groups, there may be dissatisfied participants, tension, or group dysfunction. As with common adventure programs, this program model is more effective when a large part of the trip membership is composed of several regular participants who understand the program philosophy and can help set the group tone and model appropriate group behaviors.

Most club programs (of which there are several hundred) and a number of university outdoor programs use either a common adventure or cooperative adventure program. For example, the American Canoe Association (ACA), although not using the terms, implicitly suggests a cooperative or common adventure model for clubs.

Adventure Education

Important goals of an adventure education program, especially one such as Outward Bound, Project Adventure, or NOLS, are to help participants become more self-sufficient, responsible, knowledgeable, sensitive to others, and attuned to group process and working effectively as a group.

Essentially, an adventure education program starts from a leader-led model (instructional or

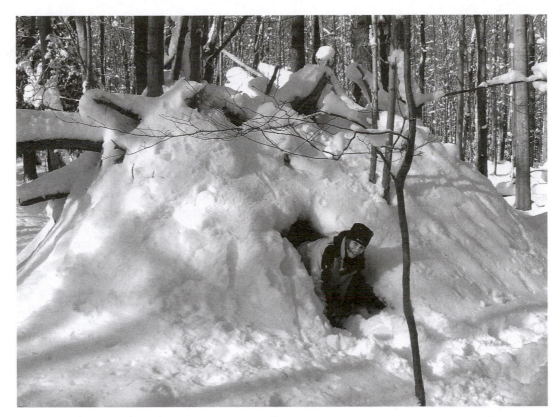

The range of settings for adventure programs is diverse.

guided) and, as members become more knowledgeable and mature as a group, the formally designated leaders turn leadership and decision-making responsibilities over to the group and function under a cooperative adventure model, and then under a common adventure model. Since this transition is best attained through a longer expedition and is unlikely to be attained through one or two ropes course or weekend experiences, we'll use an expedition model of 24 to 30 days as an example.

Unlike common adventure or cooperative adventure programs, this program uses well-trained, paid staff as leaders. In the beginning stages of an expedition, the job of the leader is to begin the process of teaching group members both technical skills and intrapersonal group process skills. In the beginning, the leadership style is highly directive and structured, and students are closely monitored. As the students acquire skills and knowledge, the formal leaders become less directive, providing less guidance and supervision as the students take on more responsibilities, become apt at group process, and acquire better judgment and decision-making skills. The end of the expedition is characterized by a final expedition unaccompanied by the leaders. If the group is functioning well, this final expedition should be like a common adventure trip, with leadership responsibilities distributed among the group members.

An advantage of this program format is that students acquire technical and intrapersonal skills under the tutelage of competent leaders who wean the students off reliance on the formal leaders. However, the total change process takes time. It is not practical to expect major, long-lasting development in shorter programs. Consequently, the adventure education expedition program model is the paradigm that shorter or more condensed adventure education programs try to achieve. Compared with common and cooperative adventure programs, significant disadvantages are that the expenses for leader salary, training, and supervision are higher, and administrative complexity is increased.

Instructional or School Model

The instructional or school model is far more practical than the adventure education model for most programs because instructional programs are shorter and more people can participate. Some instructional programs may be based on technical skills, while others may attempt to teach **intrapersonal** or **interpersonal skills.** Most people are familiar with this program model. Under the model, which is also leader led, the participant is perhaps more involved in decision making, but the experience is more or less structured and controlled by the instructor.

Outfitter or guide services and school programs that provide instruction in technical skills typify this philosophy. Outing clubs often have an educational component to club activities, and they use this model for their instructional component. Many people take ski, canoeing, or climbing lessons lasting from a one-hour lesson to a five-day workshop. In a school setting, this could be part of a physical education class. In college, this model is represented by a for-credit class or a noncredit outdoor program. In any case, the students come to learn a set of skills, and the course instructors have a fairly standard curriculum they follow to help their students attain those skills.

Challenge course or other adventure education programs, in which the purpose of the program is to teach team building, are instructional (educational) in nature. As Dewey said, it is the job of the educator "to direct the experience . . . without engaging in imposition" (1938, 40). Though the learning experience is determined ultimately by the student, it is the job of the educator to draw the student toward learning. Much of the education in these programs is learning how to work cooperatively.

This school model can also refer to recreational trips typical of high school or university cocurricular outdoor programs, the purpose of which is primarily fun. The school provides trained leaders who are responsible for the safety of the group members and who provide strong leader guidance. The program leaders strive to provide a nonautocratic, participative leadership style, but ultimately responsibility lies with the leaders. Often these programs have many beginners who rely heavily upon the leaders for structure.

The instructional or school model is best suited to programs with youth participants, large numbers of beginners, or participants unfamiliar with working in cooperative groups. It is also most appropriate for people who want to learn technical skills. Experienced participants and those used to working in cooperative groups tend to prefer a cooperative adventure format. As with the adventure education model, due to the level of expertise needed from leaders and due to leader wages and training expenses, this program model is more expensive than a common or cooperative adventure model. In addition, it, too, is administratively more complex. Finally, as the leaders assume more responsibility, the standards of care become higher and potential liability correspondingly increases.

Guided or Packaged Model

Under a typical guided or packaged (i.e., leader-led) model, the leader's role is to guide participants through a goal-oriented experience, typically one day or weekend spent floating or rafting a river or climbing a mountain. This program model is for those who want the security of a professional leader and do not want to be involved in making decisions. In this model, the participants turn over responsibilities to the guide. On more luxurious trips, the guide will cook the meals, pitch the tents, and pack and carry the food and equipment. Only basic skills are taught. In rafting, for example, it may be four basic paddle commands—right turn, left turn, forward, and back. In climbing, the skills may be limited to putting on a harness, attaching a rope to a harness, and using belay signals.

In adventure education, the terms **outdoor guide** and **outdoor leader** are often distinguished. *Guide* connotes a highly directive leadership style; *leader* connotes a person who uses a multifaceted style of leadership, including facilitative, collaborative, directive, coaching, teaching, and delegating styles, each determined by the situation. Given this distinction, *guide* well describes the leadership style in the guided program model. The guide's role is to guide, but not to educate or merely facilitate.

Just as an organization with a common adventure program might also have an instructional program, so too do many guide services have an instructional program. In an instructional program, the guide becomes an instructor or educator.

The guided program model is most suitable for those who want a structured experience without responsibility and for beginners. In high-risk activities (e.g., climbing), this generally is a preferred model for climbing club trips, especially when beginners are included. It works well when there is an agreed-upon goal that is clear yet challenging and is to be attained in a short time (e.g., the summit of Mount Rainier). Even the adventure education program model may begin as a guided model; however, it will soon emphasize teaching and less structure.

Due to total participant reliance upon the guide, guides have a higher duty of care. Because closer supervision is required, in some cases a smaller guide-to-client ratio is necessary, which raises the cost to participants.

Adventure Programming in Different Settings

The range of settings for adventure programming is diverse, as illustrated in figure 12.2. Following is a brief description of the various settings.

K Through 12 Schools

Colleges and Universities

    Academic degree programs

    College outing clubs

    Outdoor programs (nonacademic)

    New-student orientation

    Leadership programs

Not-for-Profit Organizations

    Environmental and outdoor education

    Environmental protection and advocacy

    Recreation centers (e.g., the YMCA, Boys and Girls Clubs)

Local Government Agencies

Federal and State Agencies

    U.S. Forest Service

    Morale, Welfare, and Recreation (MWR)

    State fish and game, or DNR, agencies

Adventure Clubs

Commercial Programs

    Outdoor stores

    Outfitters

    Guide services

    Ecotourism and adventure travel

Health and Human Services

    Adventure-based counseling

    Adventure therapy

    At-risk and adjudicated youth

Youth Camps and Programs

Corporate Group Training

Inclusive Adventure Programming

Single-Gender Programming

Outdoor School

Leader and Instructor Training and Certification

FIGURE 12.2   Range of adventure program settings.

CAREERS IN ADVENTURE

NAME: Kenneth Johnson

JOB: General Director and owner, EcoColors (Cancún, Mexico)

BACKGROUND: BS in marine biology; MBA in business administration; courses on archeology and Mexican history

WHAT'S YOUR JOB LIKE? My job includes marketing and sales, supervising administrative operations and staff, developing new trips and experiences, supervising quality of programs, identifying appropriate sites, and occasional guiding.

I am a Mexican citizen with an American father and have lived in Mexico for most of my life. I have a great job, which is trying to promote conservation through ecotourism. My wife and I cofounded our company in 1997.

Our company, EcoColors, gets its name from the array of colors that nature displays in the forests, meadows, lagoons, and seas of tropical America. EcoColors designs and delivers ecotours in the Maya world, biologically and culturally one of the richest areas of the world. Our tours incorporate outstanding natural, cultural, and adventure attractions of the region. Learners from ages 8 to 80 have slept in small lodges and ranches in the outback, in Mayan village cabanas, and in our tent camps, settings where we provide cultural and environmental interpretation and adventure activities while we realize our objective—to increase people's ecological understanding.

The guides of EcoColors are biologists who participate in research and protection projects in the Maya world. This gives visitors the unique opportunity to experience a solid interpretation of what nature shows us. As a business committed to sustainability, EcoColors works with local Mayan communities and promotes conservation projects in the Maya area. In addition to environmental and cultural interpretation, our guides must be able to safely lead snorkeling, kayaking, rappelling and caving, and mountain biking activities. They must also be fluent in English and Spanish. Because adventure programming and ecotourism is relatively small and new in Mexico, a big challenge is finding guides who meet our qualifications.

We are a small company that strives to work locally to provide good employment to Mexicans. Besides finding guides, we have other challenges; the most difficult one is to generate enough groups and tourists to survive. There is much competition, especially from larger companies that are less interested in the environment. Putting ourselves in front of those who are interested in our programs is quite difficult with our limited budget.

Our daily challenge is to provide unique experiences for travelers in the Maya area. Part of my daily job has me checking sales and e-mails, coordinating with guides on trips to be run, acquiring and producing interesting information to share with tourists, exploring new sites, and guiding trips.

Despite the challenges, I love this job because it gives me the opportunity to influence people, to conserve nature, and at the same time to generate employment within local Mayan communities, who then are able to keep their rituals, lifestyle, and cultural identity.

I believe that being self-motivated and energetic is essential in my position. In addition, having a service attitude toward generating interesting and satisfying experiences is essential. Public relations skills and maintaining integrity with nature and Mayan communities are quite important. It is difficult to reach a balance where nature, communities, and a private company benefit all.

My advice for someone who wants to enter our field is to be patient. Things do not happen as fast as we would like, and having patience and realistic goals is very important. In addition, realize that considerable research is essential to develop unique programs that can produce unique experiences.

Kindergarten Through Grade 12

Schools offer a wide variety of adventure education programs. These include facilities-based Project Adventure–style offerings in kindergarten and physical education, adventure-based counseling, and academic offerings through outdoor or **wilderness** expedition trips.

Adventure playgrounds in parks and preschools are examples of kindergarten adventure education. For example, many Montessori schools feature adventure playgrounds where children can explore and discover through adventure play. In Europe, these playgrounds have been very popular with school-aged groups (Yerkes 1980; City of Berkeley 2004). As European children move into the older grade levels, they often experience adventure education at outdoor centers that contract with the school districts for this purpose. Many schools, particularly independent schools, have their own dedicated outdoor trip programs, staffed by either a professional outdoor leader or teachers with an interest in outdoor education.

In the United States, elementary students experience adventure programming in physical education, structured after-school programs, structured recess programs, and academic classrooms that use an adventure education paradigm. Often these programs use initiative games; low-element challenge courses; and, less frequently, belayed climbing walls and challenge courses. More advanced adventure programming happens in the middle school through high school years as the same range of academic and physical education offerings are given with greater intensity. Facilities-based programs are the rule, with challenge courses and climbing walls proliferating. There are Project Adventure–style physical education programs in all 50 states, with a growing volume of new programming occurring thanks to recent federal grants. Public schools in Milwaukee, for example, have a long-standing physical education adventure program.

Often students receive adventure programming at outdoor education centers or outdoor recreation centers that are used as peak experiences for academic classes or as club offerings. One example is the Outdoors Wisconsin Leadership Synergies program at George Williams College of Aurora University in Williams Bay, Wisconsin.

A number of high schools around the country, both public and private, especially in New England and the West, have wilderness experience programs. Although the AEE publishes a limited directory of these programs, it is safe to say that at least 500 programs exist.

Colleges and Universities

Many community colleges and universities offer adventure education programming as for-credit academic programming and as noncredit recreational programming.

Academic Programming

Many colleges offer courses in adventure education, and some offer complete degree programs. As classes, these fall under the instructional or school program model. Some have been able to incorporate expeditionary adventure education into their curriculum. Examples of professional degree programs in outdoor leadership and outdoor leadership administration in universities include programs at Aurora University, Georgia College, Indiana University, Mankato State University, Oregon State University, and the University of New Hampshire. Experiential education, physical education, and recreation administration are some of the academic departments in which such degree programs are housed. A number of small liberal arts colleges offer specialized wilderness-based degrees, including Brevard, Green Mountain, Prescott, and Unity colleges. Two-year community college degree programs are found in several states, including California, Colorado, Massachusetts, Maine, Maryland, and Oregon.

Nonacademic Programming

Colleges and universities also offer noncredit adventure education in three general formats: a club program, an outdoor program, and a new-student orientation program. Historically, outing clubs are the earliest format (Webb 2001); they primarily rely on students developing, running, and administering the program. In the 1960s and 1970s, the outdoor program format emerged, using professional staff to administer the programs while relying on students as trip leaders and support staff. In the 1980s, adventure-based, new-student orientation programs developed.

Outing club programs   Currently, one of the largest collegiate outing clubs in the United States is the Wisconsin Hoofers at the University of Wisconsin–Madison, with more than 100,000 annual **participations.** Generally, outing clubs are run by students with little professional oversight, using a common adventure or cooperative adventure format. For example, to lead a trip for the Wisconsin Hoofers, the requirement is merely that the leader be a member of the Hoofers (although there are stricter requirements for climbing leaders). This

Adventure programming occurs in many different settings, such as this ascent from a cave in the Yucatan Peninsula, Mexico.

Campus recreation units or the student union typically house these programs. The primary purpose of a campus recreation or student union outdoor program is to provide recreational trips and activities for the college's students. Faculty and staff are usually encouraged to participate. Many programs are also open to the general public. In addition to a trip program, most campus programs offer rentals and informational resources. Some also provide a retail service. Student fees and fees for trips and services provide the primary financial support for these programs.

The major purpose of these outdoor programs is recreational; a secondary purpose is educational. Most trips are one day or weekend, with longer one- to two-week trips in the summer or between semesters. Many trips have an educational thrust, generally toward basic outdoor skills, environmental awareness, and ethics. Because the trips are group trips and many programs rely on student leaders, the trips will secondarily teach leadership and cooperative group living.

The majority of collegiate outdoor programs follow the instructional or guided model of leadership guides. Many large college programs function like a well-organized guide service, with good training and pay for staff. A number of programs value the educational component and consider it to be a form of experiential or adventure education. A sampling of universities with well-developed nonacademic leadership training programs include Colorado State, Cornell, Miami University of Ohio, University of Minnesota Duluth, University of Nebraska at Omaha, Princeton, San Diego State, and UCLA (Association for Experiential Education [AEE] 2001; Webb 2002).

Although the majority of outdoor programs use the instructional or guided model, a number of programs follow a cooperative program model. A few, notably Idaho State University and the University of Oregon, are common adventure programs.

New-student orientation programs   A number of colleges and universities provide adventure-based new-student orientation experiences. At some smaller colleges, such as Unity College in Maine, the experience is required of all incoming students. Most often, the wilderness-based experience is voluntary for the students. Usually, the experience happens during the week before college begins.

The use of wilderness programs for new-student experiences is growing. In some cases, the new-student orientation program is separate from the

program is essentially a cooperative adventure program because the club has a list of policies and procedures for leaders to follow and a safety review procedure if participants feel a trip might be poorly led or planned (Wisconsin Hoofers Outing Club 2005).

Outdoor programs   Since the 1970s, collegiate adventure programming has moved from clubs toward the creation of outdoor programs. Well-developed club systems are found in the northeastern United States; however, the primary vehicle for collegiate adventure programming in the remainder of the country is the outdoor program. Although hard data are unavailable, an estimated 450 collegiate noncredit outdoor programs exist in the United States, with more being created each year.

outing club or outdoor program. As more colleges create outdoor programs, they use the expertise of the outdoor program to provide new-student wilderness programs. A trend is to combine a new-student experience and a club or outdoor program under one administrative roof.

At many colleges, an adventure education professional supervises the adventure-based new-student orientation. This person generally has other responsibilities throughout the year, such as supervising clubs or other student activities. Finding a large number of capable leaders for a one-week adventure education orientation experience can be a challenge. Therefore, at colleges without ongoing outdoor programs, successful new-student orientation programs provide leadership training and experience throughout the school year to develop teamwork and camaraderie in its group of leaders. Universities with year-round outdoor programs can rely on a core group of leaders from which to recruit leaders for the outdoor portion of the new-student experience.

Because these colleges and university outdoor programs seek safety in an uncertain environment and rely on student leaders, they must provide leadership training programs, which are excellent training grounds for future leaders. Since many large state universities have outdoor programs and leadership training, these can be a source of leaders for an adventure-based orientation. Adventure-based orientation programs follow an instructional or guided model.

Not-for-Profit Organizations

Many not-for-profit organizations have used adventure education to work on team building, leadership development, and problem solving. A number of **environmental education** programs offer expeditionary challenges as part of their environmental education. For example, each summer the Penobscot River Keepers paddle more than 100 miles (161 kilometers) down the Penobscot River in Maine, stopping at communities along the way to teach outdoor education. The Chewonki environmental education center, also in Maine, provides three- to five-week expeditions in backpacking, canoeing, sea kayaking, sailing, and other activities, in some cases traveling as far as Labrador. Many organizations, such as the YMCA or Boys and Girls Clubs, offer challenge course experiences. In addition, these same organizations and many not-for-profits offer adventure programming through their camp programs.

Some not-for-profit organizations focus only on adventure programming and may function much like a commercial operation. For example, the Women's Wilderness Institute in Colorado provides trips for women and girls in Colorado and Utah. Of legal necessity, youth programs must follow an instructional or guided model, as do most of the other not-for-profit programs in this category.

Local Government Agencies

Many municipal, special district, and county park and recreation agencies provide adventure programming. The programs may be offered by their own staff, or by contracting with individuals or adventure activity companies in the area. For example, the Bureau of Parks and Recreation in Portland, Oregon, offers programs in mountaineering (on the high volcanoes of the Pacific Northwest), rock climbing and glacier ice climbing, backpacking and hiking, hang gliding, white-water and sea kayaking, white-water rafting, river canoeing, fly fishing, clam and edible sea-food digging, wild foods in wilderness survival, canyoneering in Utah, map and compass use, and cross-country skiing in places such as Glacier and Yellowstone national parks and the North Cascades.

Charleston County Parks and Recreation in South Carolina similarly offers an in-depth program. Their recreation programming focuses on environmental education and outdoor recreation. James Island Park houses their adventure recreation programs, including a challenge course and climbing wall. Adventure programs include canoeing and kayaking, mountain biking, hiking and backpacking, climbing, summer camps, and youth programs. Both their Surf Kayak Rodeo and East Coast Canoe and Kayak Festival have received nationwide recognition. Local government programs follow an instructional or guided model.

Federal and State Agencies

For the most part, U.S. federal and state agencies are not active in the business of providing adventure programming. For example, the National Park Service (NPS) contracts with concessionaires (such as guide services) to provide adventure programs. However, since 1995 the U.S. Congress has been encouraging federal agencies to provide profit-producing programs. In response, some national forests have begun to provide a variety of adventure recreation programs. For example, in 2005, Lolo National Forest in Montana offered a three-day backcountry survival course; and Willamette National Forest offered a variety of hiking trips combining hiking with historical and cultural interpretation. These programs are generally instructional, but some may follow a guided model.

At the federal level, the biggest provider of adventure programming is the Armed Forces, through their Morale, Welfare, and Recreation (MWR) programs. The navy, air force, and army all include adventure programming in the recreation they offer to soldiers and their families at their bases. For example, Fort Carson, in Colorado, offers the same activities as college or municipal outdoor programs—rock climbing, backpacking, white-water rafting, mountain biking, skiing, and so forth. The MWRs use civilian employees to provide their services.

Just as at the federal level, state land managers are being asked to seek alternative income sources. For example, in Pennsylvania, state parks have been asked to provide adventure activities to raise money for operating budget expenses. And most state fish and wildlife agencies, or departments of natural resources, offer a program called Becoming an Outdoor Woman (BOW). These programs for women focus on such activities as horse packing, wilderness camping, map and compass use, fishing, shooting (shotgun, archery, and rifle), hiking, and camp cooking. Some go beyond these basics to include kayaking, mountain biking, canoeing, and so forth. These are generally instructional programs.

Adventure Clubs

Adventure clubs provide a variety of activities in hiking, mountaineering, canoeing and kayaking, skiing, conservation, and trail work, and are growing in popularity. Some large clubs, such as the Appalachian Mountain Club or Seattle Mountaineers, provide instruction and outings in several disciplines; most clubs that specialize in one activity will offer a variety of other options. In general, outdoor clubs offer instruction and trips, promote conservation, and provide service opportunities.

The earliest clubs, founded in the late 1800s and early 1900s, were devoted to alpine exploration and preservation. These include the Alpine Club at Williams College (1863) (Webb 2001), the Appalachian Mountain Club (1876), the Sierra Club (1892), the Portland (Oregon) Mazamas (1893), the American Alpine Club (1902), and the Colorado Mountain Club (1912). Environmentalism is still important to their missions, but they also were leaders in providing adventure programming. Though led by

volunteers, climbing clubs tend to use instructional or guided models of leadership, with fairly rigorous standards for becoming a technical climb leader. In less risky pursuits (e.g., hiking), they may use a more informal cooperative adventure model.

In the United States, more than 185 paddling clubs are found in about 45 states. Larger mountain clubs (e.g., Sierra, Appalachian) also have special paddling chapters. Some of the largest and most active clubs are in the Midwest, with the Minnesota Canoe Association (1,100 members) and the Chicago Whitewater Association, and the Southeast, with the Georgia Canoe Association (2,000 members). In general, instructional programs use ACA-certified instructors. In contrast, although not identified as such, most often their trips are run under a common adventure or cooperative adventure format. The Western Carolina Paddlers is one club that clearly states their trips are under a common adventure format (2005).

Skiing clubs were significant in the development of skiing at the beginning of the 20th century. Many clubs own their own ski hill; others, such as the Atlanta Ski Club—one of the largest ski clubs in the world—focus on providing trips to ski resorts. Many ski clubs, such as the Farmington Ski Club in Maine, provide both cross-country and downhill skiing opportunities, with a focus on family skiing and training for racing.

Outside of colleges, there are at least 200 hiking clubs in the United States. As with the other types of clubs, hiking clubs tend to provide social opportunities, basic instruction, and conservation education. One significant difference between hiking clubs and other clubs is that the primary focus of many hiking clubs is trail maintenance.

Commercial Programs

Commercial (for-profit) programs, including outdoor stores, **outfitters,** and guide services, provide adventure programming under an instructional or guided format. For example, in the northeastern United States, several EMS (Eastern Mountain Sports) stores offer rock climbing, mountaineering, ice climbing and kayaking, plus international adventure trips. REI (Recreational Equipment Incorporated), with stores around the country, offers a range of outdoor adventures and workshops. In addition to the large national or regional chains offering adventures, many local outdoor stores supplement their sales by providing adventure program workshops and local trips. For example, Rock River and Trail in Lock Haven, Pennsylvania, is a small store that uses a few part-time trip leaders in the summer.

In contrast to stores, outfitters and guide services specialize in providing adventure recreation opportunities, which they supplement with in-store sales. Outfitters and guide services provide climbing, rafting, lake or white-water canoe and kayak instruction and trips, and cross-country skiing and snowshoeing trips. One of the largest is the Nantahala Outdoor Center in North Carolina, founded in 1972. Originally focusing on canoe-ing, kayaking, and rafting, they have expanded into challenge course programming, international adventure travel, special events, and leadership development, employing more than 500 guides and leaders in the summer. Most commercial programs are much smaller. For example, the Wild Institute in Minnesota, which focuses on trips for women, is a small, one-person operation.

A number of **ecotourism** or **adventure tour-ism** businesses have developed to provide adventure activities abroad. In addition, because so much adventure recreation is seasonal, many outfitters and guide services have expanded their services to Latin and South America to provide warm-weather adventure programming year round. Popular activities include coastal kayaking, white-water rafting and kayaking, mountaineering, hiking, and general adventure travel. Of concern to the adventure education professional is how closely these programs stick to green (environmental) principles, or whether they are just examples of ecotourism lite—green language without green practice (Honey 1999).

Health and Human Services Programs

Adventure programming for counseling or thera-peutic uses, especially involving challenge courses, has been a hallmark of the profession since the 1970s. In the 1990s, this trend accelerated. Today, many private and public agencies provide **adventure-based counseling,** therapeutic adven-ture, outdoor behavioral health care, and **adven-ture therapy.** Meanings of these four terms are still in flux; however, the main philosophical difference between programs lies in whether the program is primarily behavioral, focusing on behaviors only, or

Ecotourism combines environmental education with an appreciation of other cultures. Here, ecotourists explore the Cobá archeological site in Quintana Roo, Mexico.

whether it uses diagnostic assessment coupled with treatment for an underlying cause (Itin 2001).

In general, agencies use adventure programming to challenge participants and develop skills, provide reflection, and plan for a successful return to their communities. Adventure can be used therapeutically for most people with counseling needs, regardless of age. Although not-for-profit programs provide much of the therapeutic adventure programming currently available, One Step at a Time in Seattle is an example of a mountaineering club that supports persons involved in Alcoholics Anonymous.

Many programs have been established, especially for adjudicated youth and **youth at risk.** About 100 of these programs have been identified in the United States. The range of programming is extremely varied, including both residential and nonresidential programs. Various formats for nonresidential programs have emerged (Russell 2003). Some programs take a self-contained group into the wilderness for an extended period up to four weeks. Some rotate staff and leaders into and out of the field every week or so. A third model involves a three- to eight-week base camp in a natural setting, from which clients go on one- to two-week expeditions.

Residential models have clients at long-term treatment centers, which provide a variety of outdoor and wilderness treatments. In a residential model, therapeutic adventure may be only one of many therapeutic and educational opportunities for residents. Nonresidential programs provide an expeditionary adventure education model, although stopping short of the final common adventure phase. Residential programs, depending upon the length of the outdoor component, may use an expeditionary adventure education philosophy, but more often they will use an instructional model.

For 25 years, Hurricane Island Outward Bound in Florida has provided therapeutic adventure programs for the Florida Department of Juvenile Justice. The Santa Fe Mountain Center in New Mexico is another excellent example of adventure programming that works with young people and their families. Other examples include Outback Therapeutic Expeditions in Utah, Eckerd Youth Alternatives in Florida and seven other states, and SUWS programs in Idaho.

The use of facilities-based programming, including challenge course activities, in health and human service agencies is continuing to grow. Project Adventure is the leading provider of training and professional development in this growing sector

of adventure education. There are facilities-based, adventure counseling programs in all 50 states, with the number of agencies totaling at least 1,000. Generally, they use an instructional model.

Youth Camps and Programs

There are approximately 12,000 camps in the United States. Of these, two-thirds are private not-for-profit camps run by organizations such as the YMCA and YWCA, Boy and Girl Scouts, and religious organizations. Most camps (7,000) are residential and the remainder are day camps; however, many camps offer both a residential and a day program. Slightly more than half of the camps are coed; the remainder are single gender—either for girls or for boys.

The aspect of camps that has seen the biggest growth in the past several years has been adventure programming. Approximately one-third of camps offer trips of three days or more away from their camps—22 percent of these are wilderness programs. In addition, more than 50 percent of camps have adventure or challenge facilities such as a challenge course or climb wall (American Camp Association [ACA] 2005a). Generally, these camp programs follow an instructional philosophy.

Many youth programs do not operate out of a camp, instead choosing to operate in a travel format using vans to move campers to different locales for a variety of outdoor pursuits. For example, Longacre Expeditions provides 14- to 28-day coed expeditions for teens in several states around the United States, as well as in Canada, the Virgin Islands, and the British Isles, and many of their programs move participants to several locales. Other programs, such as Deer Hill Expeditions in Colorado, offer a base camp only as a staging group to outfit participants for a variety of expeditions in the American Southwest. As expeditionary programs, these tend to follow an adventure education model. However, the focus of some travel programs is a variety of outdoor experiences rather than teamwork; these tend to follow an instructional model.

Corporate Groups

During the past 20 years, corporations have either developed their own adventure education training sites, such as the Q Center owned by the Accenture Corporation in St. Charles, Illinois, or contracted with outdoor centers for this type of programming, such as Camp Tecumseh YMCA Corporate Programs in Indiana. They also contract with private consultants to deliver this programming, such as Goal

CAREERS IN ADVENTURE

NAME: Jen Ryan

JOB: Associate Director, Outdoor Pursuit Center, Miami University (Oxford, Ohio)

BACKGROUND: BA in psychology, Miami University; MS in recreation administration, Aurora University; focus area is outdoor pursuits

WHAT'S YOUR JOB LIKE? I'm responsible for the administration and management of all programming aspects of the domestic trip program and the low and high ropes course program. This position has significant responsibility to ensure the health and well-being of all staff and patrons due to the off-site nature of the programming. I also provide program staff management, facility coverage, and supervision of special events as needed.

My essential responsibilities include the following:

- Assisting with the supervision and management of subordinate full-time staff, graduate assistants, interns, and outdoor instructors
- Researching, planning, developing, and administering all trip and ropes course programs
- Assisting with the development of policies and procedures for the domestic trip program and ropes course program
- Planning and executing August student staff training and weekly in-service training
- Conducting regular safety assessments of facilities, vehicles, and equipment and taking appropriate action
- Recruiting, hiring, training, supervising, and evaluating staff (30-40 students)
- Assisting in the management of student payroll for all Outdoor Pursuit Center (OPC) staff

- Assisting in the development of OPC strategic plans, goals, and objectives and program assessments
- Assisting with coverage of the climbing wall and rental and retail programs as needed
- Assisting with the management and evaluation of all OPC special events (e.g., climbing competitions, end-of-the-year sale)
- Purchasing and maintaining inventories for all program equipment and supplies
- Providing the director with reports on program participation, activities, and budget and providing documented justification for program protocols and budget or personnel adjustments
- Establishing working relationships with individuals, agencies, and groups that further enhance the OPC mission
- Attending regional and national conferences regularly

I enjoy the fact that my position provides me with a good balance between administrative duties and program facilitation. I balance my time behind the desk and out in the field on a regular basis. I love that my days are filled with variety and are never the same. On a weekly basis I work with a variety of people from other departments across campus, from other employees of the Recreational Sports Center to the OPC student employees. I delight in working with the student population and playing a role in their development as leaders. Along with that, one of my greatest challenges is student staff turnover. Due to the fact that students work with us for a maximum of four years, I must constantly focus on hiring new staff and training them. Skills essential to my position as associate director are time management, flexibility, effective communication skills, and interpersonal skills.

Consulting in Wisconsin, Peak Performance in California, and Team Leadership in Texas. In addition, NOLS, Outward Bound, and Project Adventure each offer direct programming to the corporate sector. Typically these use an instructional format.

Inclusive Adventure Programming

Inclusive adventure programs emphasize providing everyone with opportunities for participation, regardless of physical skill. Skiing and canoeing are especially amenable to adaptation for people with physical disabilities. For example, the National Sports Center for the Disabled, located in Winter Park, Colorado, is a leader in providing skiing for the disabled, but they also provide many other activities, such as snowshoeing, therapeutic horseback riding, canoeing, mountain biking, and camping.

Increases in inclusive adventure education have been documented.

Approximately 10 percent of organized camps are dedicated to special needs (ACA 2005a). Indiana University's Bradford Woods Outdoor Center hosts many camps for young people with disabilities, including Camp Riley for people with cognitive disabilities and Camp About Face for people with craniofacial injuries. One Step at a Time Foundation camps, out of Chicago, are for children with terminal cancer and leukemia and their families. Easter Seals, a well-known national organization for people with disabilities, offers approximately 140 camps in most states and in Canada. Wilderness Inquiry in Minnesota and Idaho State University's Cooperative Wilderness Handicapped Outdoor Group (CW HOG) have been providing adult wilderness trips for many years, primarily for people with physical disabilities.

Single-Gender Programming

People in single-gender programs often feel freer to express or assert themselves, and they can learn better at their own pace; consequently, single-gender adventure programming has expanded. There continues to be a need for single-gender youth programs, which is why nearly half of all organized camp programs are single-gender programs. For example, both the Boy Scouts and Girl Scouts provide adventure and leadership programs and camps limited to one gender. Other single-gender camps include Camp High Rocks for boys in North Carolina and Camp Thunderbird for girls in Minnesota. As youth programs, they generally follow an instructional model.

Adult coed organizations have similarly found a niche for single-gender adventure programming. In addition, a number of private businesses, both for-profit and not-for-profit, specialize in single-gender programming. Two examples include the Women's Wilderness Institute and Adventures in Good Company. Finally, men's and women's groups have found that they need time with their own gender to reflect on their personal development, and they have sought this type of programming at outdoor retreat centers and private outdoor businesses. These programs tend to follow both the instructional model and the cooperative model of leadership.

Blindness need not prevent an individual from enjoying skiing, as this skier at Winter Park, Colorado, can attest.

Photo courtesy of National Sports Center for the Disabled

Outdoor Schools

Outdoor schools, also known as wilderness experience programs (WEPs), focus on education during a wilderness expedition. Outward Bound and National Outdoor Leadership School (NOLS) are exemplars for the adventure programming profession. The first U.S. Outward Bound Program was founded in Colorado in 1961. A few years later, in 1965, NOLS was formed to train leaders for Outward Bound. The original education model for those two programs was an extended (three- to four-week) wilderness expedition.

Since then, many organizations have ventured into adventure programming, with most programs modeled on the standards and practices set by Outward Bound and NOLS. Most outdoor schools, however, use shorter expeditions or other forms of adventure programming to achieve their outcomes. It is not clear how many such schools exist, but a 1996 survey suggested that there were at least 530 such programs (Friese, Hendee, and Kinzinger 1998), and probably more exist now. Outward Bound, NOLS, and the Wilderness Education Association (WEA) are paradigmatic examples of the expeditionary adventure education model. Insofar as other outdoor schools emulate those programs, they will follow an adventure education model. However, many outdoor schools may have shorter experiences, and these follow an instructional model.

Leader and Instructor Training

In addition to programs offering adventure trips, several organizations provide training or certification to instructors and leaders. One of the early organizations was the American Canoe Association (ACA), which originated in 1880. Today it provides curriculum and certification of instructors (but not leaders) in canoeing and sea and white-water kayaking and in white-water rescue. Another organization, Rescue 3 International, also provides white-water rescue training, primarily to firefighters and other rescue professionals.

In 1961, the Professional Ski Instructors of America was formed to promote ski instruction. Today it certifies instructors in downhill and cross-country skiing, and, through a sister organization, in snowboarding. A separate organization, the National Ski Patrol, provides training and certification of ski patrollers.

The WEA, established in 1977, works in universities to develop curricula for training and certifying outdoor leaders. In the early 1980s, the American Guides Association (AMGA) was formed. It provides training and certification of rock, ice, and mountaineering instructors and guides.

In the 1990s, wilderness medicine and rescue developed. Today, a variety of organizations provide certifications in wilderness first aid and rescue. Unlike other certifications, some form of certification in wilderness medicine, either wilderness first aid (WFA) or wilderness first responder (WFR), has become a standard requirement for outdoor leaders. Some of the more established organizations are Wilderness Medical Associates, Wilderness Medicine Institute, and Stonehearth Open Learning Opportunities (SOLO). In addition, there are innumerable newer, less established organizations.

When in remote areas, leaders need expertise in wilderness medicine.

Career Paths in Adventure Programming

As there is diversity in adventure programming settings, there is also diversity in adventure education careers. Positions include teacher of adventure education in schools, director of adventure education programs for colleges and universities, camp adventure program director, therapeutic outdoor counselor for special populations, outdoor recreation center director, and course instructor for an outdoor school such as NOLS or Outward Bound. Other career opportunities include adventure program director for social agencies and corporate adventure education consultant.

Regardless of which path you take in adventure education programming, consider carefully what kind of personal future you desire. For most adventure settings described in this chapter and for those who seek adventure programming as a career, a college education is needed. Your own education is an investment in you. Many in the field may indicate that you do not need a college degree, but life changes and education brings many opportunities that lack of a degree precludes. A community college may be the place to start, followed by a four-year institution.

Adventure programming falls under many majors. Look for regionally or nationally known faculty who have expertise in this area and who will assist you in determining where the courses and degree programs are housed in the college and university. Degrees will be available in experiential education, physical education, social work, recreation administration, wilderness studies, and others.

A mark of a professional is active involvement in professional associations, including membership, attendance at conferences, and using the association to keep up with trends and professional developments. The three **professional associations** with a major focus on adventure programming are the Association for Experiential Education (AEE), the Association of Outdoor Recreation and Education (AORE), and the Wilderness Education Association (WEA). In addition, the Association for Challenge Course Technology (ACCT) focuses on challenge course building and developing standards for challenge course facilitators.

Seasonal Employment

There are opportunities to work as a seasonal employee and a business owner without a college degree. However, for seasonal employees, the employment is short term and requires outdoor technical and facilitation training and some certifications. One must enjoy a lifestyle of moving from employer to employer each season. For professionals just starting out, seasonal employment might be a way to gain excellent experience.

Business Ownership

For the business owner, it takes vision, personal or public capital investment, and a market of participants to get started. The business owner should be prepared to both administer and deliver adventure programming in order to be successful. Examples are the wilderness trip outfitter who delivers adventure education to schools and the adventure education consultant who works as a corporate trainer to increase employee teamwork. Their portfolio would include both adventure education technical skills and adventure education or recreation management and business coursework or experience.

Administration

Qualifications for managerial and administrative adventure programming positions are varied. The candidate must have a foundation in adventure programming skills to know what kind of staff to hire for the programs offered. The adventure programming director needs to have good command of best practices for the field through understanding adventure education certifications and program accreditation. The administrator needs to exhibit business skills such as financial planning and budget management, public relations and fund-raising, personnel management, and program evaluation and assessment (Gass 1998).

Therapeutic Adventure

Directors of therapeutic adventure programs must address staff certification and training in client medical concerns. The populations served and regulatory bodies may demand higher education such as a master's degree in counseling, outdoor leadership administration, social work, or therapeutic recreation. Directors and staff in therapeutic adventure programs need adventure programming and technical skills and both coursework and experience with the populations they will be working with.

Summary

This chapter has provided an overview of adventure program settings, programs, and professional career paths. Adventure programming continues to be a dynamic methodology for human growth and development. The diversity of settings and opportunities for both participants and professionals provide us with ways to make a difference in the lives of others and our communities. We invite you to share in the adventure!

Review Questions

1. Adventure programs can operate under a variety of leadership philosophies. Explain the differences between two leadership models.

2. Adventure programming occurs in diverse settings, including kindergarten through grade 12, colleges, adventure clubs, outdoor schools, for-profit programs, not-for-profit programs, municipal and county organizations, military training, youth camps, corporate programs, and adult programs. Choose two of these settings, describe a program that is typically offered, and give examples.

3. Inclusive adventure programming is based on the philosophy that programs should meet the needs of all persons, regardless of physical, cognitive, or social differences. What qualifications would a director of this program type need?

4. Many programs, both for-profit and not-for-profit, have been developed to provide training for outdoor leadership. Describe a nationally recognized educational program and its program mission and philosophy on outdoor leadership training.

5. The issue of certification has been hotly debated in the professional community of adventure leadership. However, one type of certification has become generally accepted as important and a minimum requirement. What is it? Also discuss why this certification has been accepted as important, yet not others.

6. Describe the general qualifications for a seasonal adventure education instructor.

7. Describe the pros and cons of having a college degree when it comes to finding full-time employment in adventure programming.

8. Compare and contrast degrees in experiential education, physical education, and recreation administration for employment in adventure programming.

9. Describe why a professional in adventure education should belong to professional associations and attend conferences.

10. Describe the membership and mission of the following professional organizations: the AEE, ACCT, AORE, and WEA.

Student Learning Activities

1. Write a summary of three different adventure education programs and discuss their program missions and leadership philosophies. Make a brief presentation to the class.

2. Visit a local or regional adventure education program, write a paper, and prepare a presentation for class that answers the following questions:
   - What is the setting and where is the program conducted?
   - How many employees are there and what are their positions and qualifications?
   - What type of programming is offered and to whom?
   - What are the stated program outcomes?
   - What are some ways the program offers inclusive programming?
   - Is the program reviewed or accredited and if so, by whom?

3. Interview an adventure education program director and address the following:
   - How did you get involved in adventure education?
   - What are the professional qualifications for your current position?
   - What types of programs do you offer and to whom?
   - What do you look for in hiring staff?
   - What are your greatest challenges as a professional?
   - What are the greatest challenges to your personal life as a professional in this field?

4. Prepare a professional résumé for employment in adventure education.

5. Attend a professional adventure education conference and write a summary of the sessions you attended. What were your impressions of, or insights from, the professionals you met?

Overview of the Accreditation Standards of the Association for Experiential Education

Since the inception of the Association for Experiential Education (AEE) Accreditation Program in 1992, the AEE Accreditation Council has been charged with the task of developing standards for adventure programming. The Accreditation Council publishes the criteria in the *Manual of Accreditation Standards for Adventure Programs*. All the criteria for accreditation are contained in the manual. Approved applicants are provided with a current copy of the *Manual of Accreditation Standards for Adventure Programs* and the *Self-Assessment Study Workbook* on disk. The Council grants or denies accreditation on the basis of standards compliance.

The standards are not a prescriptive list that dictates how to function. Instead, they are broad in scope and are designed to be applicable to most, if not all, adventure-based education systems. As such, preapproved AEE reviewers and personnel are used to help interpret the standards, to compare the standards to a program's self-study, and to determine whether or not the program's practices indeed meet the intent of each standard.

The standards found in AEE's *Manual of Accreditation Standards, Fourth Edition,* are considered elements of effective and professional operations. They address philosophical, educational, and ethical practices; program management and program oversight; and most land- and water-based adventure activities. There is rarely one correct way to do something, especially given the diversity of outdoor adventure organizations. Instead, a program seeking accreditation is expected to explain in its self-study how it goes about meeting the intent of

each standard and provide documentation that is confirmed during a site review by AEE Accreditation Program reviewers.

Organization and Design of the Manual

The 2005 *Manual of Accreditation Standards for Adventure Programs, Fourth Edition,* is organized into the following five chapters:

• **Chapter 1—Philosophical, Educational, and Ethical Principles** contains standards applicable to the educational design of a program's activities. A program needs to demonstrate that its activities are experiential in nature, are based on sound goals and objectives, are sequential in nature, and are conducted ethically.

• **Chapter 2—Program Governance** contains standards applicable to a program's stability and soundness. A program needs to demonstrate that its mission is in alignment with the program's activities, that its business license and incorporation documents are in place, and that the organization's board of directors is familiar with the adventure activities the program conducts.

• **Chapter 3—Program Management, Operations, and Oversight** contains standards applicable to the organization's management, operations, and oversight of its adventure program. A program needs to demonstrate that it has an appropriate system in place for hiring and training

This appendix is adapted from the introduction to *Manual of Accreditation Standards for Adventure Programs, Fourth Edition,* by the Association for Experiential Education (Drew Leemon, Steve Pace, Deb Ajango, and Henry Wood, Eds.).

its staff, selecting venues, selecting and maintaining equipment, transporting participants, and objectively evaluating its operations on an ongoing basis through the use of a risk management committee and periodic reviews.

The standards in chapters 1 through 3 help organizations understand what the review team and Accreditation Council will expect regarding a program's operating systems and foundation. *Regardless of which or how many activities a program conducts, that program is required to demonstrate compliance with all standards in chapters 1 through 3.*

• **Chapters 4 and 5—Technical Skills, Land-Based and Technical Skills, Water-Based** contain standards applicable to the facilitation of specific adventure activities (e.g., climbing, rafting, service projects, solos). A program must demonstrate that it has qualified staff and appropriate policies, procedures, and safety systems specific to each activity it facilitates. A program is not required to demonstrate compliance with all standards in chapters 4 and 5. *However, a program is required to demonstrate compliance with all standards in chapters 4 and 5 that are applicable to its programming.* For example, if a program conducts only top-rope rock climbing and canoeing activities, it must demonstrate compliance with the standards in sections 12 and 40, respectively. On the other hand, if a program offers a variety of activities, it must demonstrate compliance with all of the standards associated with those activities, regardless of how infrequently the activities are conducted.

Accreditation Process

Starting with the initial application for accreditation, the average program spends one to two years working toward accreditation. A significant portion of time is spent completing the self-study. After the self-study is completed and approved, a site visit is scheduled and conducted. The program seeking accreditation receives spoken and written feedback from the review team and has a chance to respond to and correct any problem areas. Once a corrective action report is finalized, it is reviewed at the next scheduled Accreditation Council meeting.

Programs that complete the accreditation process find it educational and beneficial, and most claim that their risk management systems are improved greatly. While accreditation is, to some degree, an endorsement of the quality of an organization's programming and risk management system, the endorsement does have its limits. Accreditation is an endorsement that an organization has met, or appears to have met, specific minimal requirements or standards at a given time. While many AEE standards focus on risk management practices and safety, accreditation is not a guarantee that clients or staff of accredited programs will be free from harm.

To learn more about AEE accreditation or to order a copy of the *Manual of Accreditation Standards* or the *AEE Accreditation Program Policies and Procedures Manual*, go to www.aee.org, or contact AEE's accreditation program manager at accreditation@aee.org.

GLOSSARY

This glossary is a compilation of terms and definitions from the contributors to this text and does not reflect one particular point of view. The editors hope that this approach promotes both diversity and dialogue.

accessible approach—Elements that are designed to accommodate the physical needs of all individuals by eliminating physical barriers.

accessible design—Refers to the elimination of physical barriers or the construction of barrier-free environments.

action plan—Written plan of action created by participants that details the changes participants are committing to make based on what they learned during the program.

adventure education—Direct, active, and engaging learning experiences that involve the whole person and have real consequences. Educational activities and experiences, usually involving close interaction with the natural environment and within a small group setting that contain elements of real or perceived risk. The outcome, while uncertain, focuses on the intrapersonal and interpersonal development of the individual or group.

adventure recreation—Risk-oriented recreation usually intended to test the physical and mental capabilities of participants, such as rock climbing, white-water rafting, and hang gliding. See also *outdoor pursuits.*

adventure therapy—Relatively new field that currently has no set definition but in general is the use of adventure-based practices and therapeutic techniques to effect behavioral changes. Some argue that a distinction can be made between adventure therapy and therapeutic adventure, with adventure therapy involving diagnostic assessment and treatment and therapeutic adventure focusing on behavioral change.

adventure tourism—Travel to far-off destinations. The travel may itself be the adventure, or people may do adventurous activities in those places.

adventure-based counseling—The use of adventure activities to assist in personal psychological growth (e.g., self-esteem, self-concept, confidence), or to achieve counseling goals. It differs from adventure therapy in that it is not therapeutically based and does not use clinical diagnosis.

alternative reflection methods—These methods include art, drama, music, dance, poetry, writing, storytelling, photography, presentations, client-selected readings, or even repeating the same activity.

assessment—The process of gathering information about a student's abilities and understandings; gathering evidence of achievement and making inferences based on that evidence for a variety of purposes (NASPE 2004).

Association for Challenge Course Technology (ACCT)—The ACCT is a trade organization serving challenge course professionals all over the world. The purpose of the association is to promote the use of challenge courses and to set minimum standards for challenge course installation, operation, and inspection. Originally founded by vendors, ACCT members are now predominantly challenge course managers and facilitators, in addition to installers and trainers.

Association for Experiential Education (AEE)—The AEE is an international organization that promotes experiential education by helping practitioners connect to others in the field, helping organizations create and follow standards, and helping the field develop and access quality resources.

backward design—Intentional program planning where the instructor or leader begins with the desired exit outcomes and designs instruction and learning activities toward them.

belay—The securing of a person at height in order to prevent falls. A belay is a critical part of the high-element challenge course safety system and uses a belay device, a forged metal device of various configurations through which a climbing rope is threaded and then linked to a carabiner in order to provide friction to control a participant's fall or descent off a high element.

belay transfer—The exchange of one belay to another belay while the participant is on an element. One example is when a participant climbs to height on a dynamic belay and transfers to a static lanyard to ride down the Zip Wire.

briefing—A component of setting the stage for a particular experience and can take the form of a simple story to engage the learner in an initiative or can be a thorough briefing of a final, culminating expedition during a wilderness program.

carabiner—Forged aluminum or steel devices of various shapes (e.g., oval, D, pear) with a locking sleeve and spring-loaded gate through which a climbing rope can be threaded. They are used for such activities as belaying, rappelling, and clipping into safety anchors.

certification—Credentialing process, usually for individuals, in which competency is confirmed or attested to; used to verify certain competencies.

challenge by choice—A tool or concept that provides the individual with the right to choose the level of challenge that best supports their learning goals.

challenge course—Series of elements that provide challenging experiences to individuals or groups. Most modern challenge courses use a variety of construction materials, including lumber, rope, wire cable, tires, bolts, and other fasteners. Some elements are low and require spotting for safety, while others are high and use a belay for safety. *Ropes course* is an older designation for a challenge course.

circuit course—A challenge course layout that allows for the continuation of movement by the participant from one high element to the next high element until the complete course is finished. It may employ a dynamic or static belay or both as its safety system.

client-centered reflection—Using facilitation strategies designed to place learners in a situation where they are actively engaged in posing questions, investigating, experimenting, being curious, solving problems, assuming responsibility, being creative, and constructing meaning (AEE 2004b).

collaborative learning—All learning takes place in a social context. Working as an individual or as part of a team, students consistently function as part of a larger community.

common adventure program—Model in which leadership responsibilities are shared among group members. A common adventure trip has no formally designated leaders, only participants functioning as informal leaders. A common adventure program facilitates and promotes common adventure trips by providing a trip board for participants to initiate a trip, a resource room, and rental equipment.

cooperative adventure—Modified from the common adventure concept, this program model has designated leaders who function as trip coordinators or facilitators. Leaders typically receive some guidance (through formal policies and procedures) and oversight from the organization; they may receive training. Leaders are typically volunteers and employ a cooperative, nondirective leadership style that involves participants in decision making.

cooperative leadership—Leadership roles are distributed among group members rather than only a few members. In a fully cooperative group, such as common adventure group, no single leader is in charge. A cooperative adventure program model may employ cooperative leadership but have a designated leader.

cubic feet per second (cfs)—How river flow is calculated. One cubic foot per second is equal to the discharge of a stream of rectangular cross section, 1 foot wide and 1 foot deep, flowing at an average velocity of 1 foot per second.

curriculum—The subject matter or content provided to learners or participants in a program.

debriefing—Verbal discussion that takes place after an adventure experience in order to facilitate clients' learning and transfer to life beyond the adventure program.

design-down curriculum—Planning by starting with the end in mind (i.e., the desired outcomes, goals, or standards) and then deriving the curriculum or programming that these intents call for. See also *backward design*.

directive leadership style—Style of leadership in which the leader provides considerable direction, giving instructions, asking questions, seeking ideas, making suggestions, and supervising closely.

distributed leadership—When many group members, not just the formally designated leaders, assume leadership responsibilities and perform various leadership actions. In less effective groups, leadership actions are not distributed and are assumed to be the responsibility of the formally designated leaders (Johnson and Johnson 2002).

dynamic belay—Style of belaying where a rope attached to a climber is secured by a belayer. The belay rope runs from the climber's harness to an overhead belay anchor and back down to the belayer. A fall is usually limited to just the stretch in the rope.

ecotourism—Travel that minimally affects the local natural environment and culture, supports local business, and improves the welfare of local people. Such trips typically include a nature component, along with interaction with and appreciation of local culture.

edutainment—Leisure programs that educate as well as entertain.

effective leader—Person who makes sure things get done and also may be the one who does those things. The effective leader gives direction, and the direction is most likely followed.

emergency action plan (EAP)—Operational plan that specifically addresses the steps that will be necessary if an emergency occurs.

environmental education—One definition is developing a "population that is aware of, and concerned about [environmental problems] . . . and has the knowledge, skills, and [disposition] . . . to work towards solutions" (UNESCO-UNEP 1976, p. 2). Environmental education focuses on understanding environmental problems and on advocacy, developing a disposition to work toward solutions.

experiential education—The process of actively engaging students in an authentic experience that has benefits and consequences. Students make discoveries and experiment with knowledge themselves instead of hearing or reading about the experiences of others. Students also reflect on their experiences, thus developing new skills, attitudes, theories, and ways of thinking.

facilitation—To smooth the progress of and guide a group toward achieving their goals during an adventure program. The process of facilitation covers everything the leader does before, during, and after the experience to enhance clients' reflection, integration, and continuation of lasting change that occurs through the adventure experience (Priest, Gass, and Gillis 2000).

formally designated leader—Person who has been formally designated as a leader through administrative fiat, voting, or some other formal process. Contrast with informal leaders, who are not formally designated as a leader but who perform leadership actions.

framing—Facilitative process of engaging a group in an activity before the activity begins. This can be done by telling a story, building a metaphor, or telling a group what the task is in a straightforward way. Also called *briefing*.

frontloading—In direct frontloading, the adventure facilitator directs the clients to address one or more of the five functions (revisiting, objectives, motivation, function, and dysfunction) before the activity begins so the clients can make connections and learn both during and after the experience.

funneling—Guiding participants through a six-stage process that mimics the way people make cognitive connections between what happened to them and what it means.

GO PREPARED system—Formal process for planning extended trips that addresses the following: goals, objectives, participants, resources, equipment and clothing, plan, access, rationing, emergency plan, and don't forget about logistics.

grasshopper method—Systematic approach to teaching a curriculum over an extended period of time during a wilderness trip.

group cohesion—A group's commitment to a common set of values and a shared idea of goals. High group cohesion can bring both positive and negative consequences for group members.

group process—What is going on in a group, including the individual and collective emotions, the behaviors of the group members, who is saying what, and how the group is interacting concerning relationships and tasks.

hazards—Aspects that might cause harm, including the condition of the course; the competency of staff; the screening, training, and supervision of the participants; the general morale, or emotional state, of the participants; and the environment, including weather and the surrounding premises.

high element—A physical structure anchored at height, designed to challenge individuals and groups. A belay system provides for safe participation.

icebreakers—Activities that are designed to do just that—break the ice. Sometimes called *convening activities,* icebreakers set a positive tone and make participants feel comfortable.

idiographic—Explanations resulting from examination of the patterns, occurrences, or events of one case.

informal leader—Person not formally designated as a leader who takes on leadership responsibilities and performs leadership actions. An effective group has many members accepting responsibility and acting informally as leaders.

initiatives—Activities that require the initiative of the group to solve a problem.

instruction—The manner in which content is delivered to the learner; the delivery system.

intentional design—Designing a program that is based on the organization's mission and takes into account the needs of individuals and the group.

interpersonal skills—Ability to work with others and the awareness and acceptance of individual differences.

intrapersonal skills—Internal abilities such as self-awareness, self-concept, motivation, positive attitude, nonimposition of values, and so forth.

Kolb's experiential learning cycle—A four-phase model that describes how individuals absorb and apply information that they are given or that they experience. Commonly referred to in debriefing after an experience using "what," "so what," "now what."

leadership—The abilities, characteristics, qualities, and behavior associated with the role of being a self-leader or group leader. This role may be conferred on one by others on the basis of tradition, expediency, experience, or position.

leadership action—An action initiated by any group member to help the group make decisions either toward meeting its goals or toward being cohesive as a group. Examples include asking questions, noticing the need to make a decision, presenting ideas or feelings, supportive actions, observing and facilitating group process (Johnson and Johnson 2002).

learning styles—The combination of how an individual takes in information and how he or she applies that information. Kolb suggests four primary styles that include diverging, assimilating, converging, and accommodating.

local operating procedure (LOP)—Standard operating procedures often provide the basis for LOPs; however, the LOP must reflect the specific needs of the local challenge course's elements and activities. LOPs are dictated by the specific design of the element or activity, the environment around it, the competency of the staff running it, and the populations served by that program.

low element—Apparatus used in an adventure context that requires participants (either individually or as a group) to be off of the ground anywhere from 1 inch (2 centimeters) to 12 feet (4 meters).

negligence—The failure to act as a reasonable person would have acted under the same or similar circumstances.

nomothetic—Identification of a relatively few patterns or considerations that provide a partial explanation of many cases or examples.

orchestrated immersion—Curriculum design that immerses students in powerful and compelling learning experiences that use the whole brain in meaningful, evocative, challenging, and coherent ways.

outcomes approach—A curriculum or program that is developed by looking at specific outcomes or educational standards, identifying the skills, knowledge, and dispositions that participants should demonstrate to meet the desired outcomes, and then identifying the activities which will allow participants to reach the outcomes stated.

outdoor adventure pursuits—A subset of outdoor recreation, outdoor pursuits are physical, low-impact experiences that direct people toward sensory and muscular coordination and development. Non-mechanized, human-powered activities are preferable because they provide long-lasting physical benefits. Examples of these activities include land-based pursuits (backpacking, rock climbing, caving, mountain biking), water-based pursuits (canoeing, sea and white-water kayaking, rafting), and snow and ice pursuits (mountaineering, ice climbing, cross-country skiing, snowshoeing).

outdoor guides—Outdoor recreation leaders who have a leader-focused, directive style and usually work with small groups of one to four clients; typically found in commercial programs. Examples include hunting and climbing guides. Compare with outdoor leaders.

outdoor leaders—Outdoor recreation leaders who allow more participant involvement in decision making and have a less directive, more facilitative attitude, typically found in not-for-profit organizations and organized camping.

outdoor leadership—The practice of leading individuals and groups into natural settings via various modes of transportation, including backpacking, biking, canoeing, caving, rock climbing, mountaineering, sailing, kayaking, and horseback riding.

outdoor program—An organization, usually not-for-profit, that focuses on providing outdoor pursuit, adventure recreation, or challenge activities. Outdoor programs usually use outdoor leaders rather than outdoor guides.

outdoor pursuits—Human-powered (nonmotorized) nonconsumptive activities occurring in the outdoors. Excludes sporting events and includes backpacking, wilderness camping, canoeing, white-water and sea kayaking, and cross-country and downhill skiing (Phipps 1991).

outfitter—Commercial operation that sells or rents outdoor equipment and services, especially for camping, hunting, fishing, and boating. Outfitters may also provide guide services.

parallel process—Occurs when participants replay an interaction they had with a leader with other people. For example, if the participant came to the leader with a question and the leader took the time to caringly respond to the question, the participant is likely to respond to questions with care.

participation—One person participating in an event one time. One person participating five different times equals five participations.

portable adventure activities—Opportunities for people to interact, learn, solve problems, and laugh together via facilitated activities that are not based on the outdoors.

primary assumption of risks—Applies to injuries or losses arising from aspects of a sport or other recreational activity that might be dangerous but are such a part of the activity that to eliminate the risk would discourage vigorous participation.

problem-based learning—Teachers design complex and increasingly authentic tasks requiring students to solve problems individually or in collaborative teams.

professional association—Not-for-profit organization for members of a given profession interested in professional networking, advancement of standards and practices, promotion of professionalism, education and research in the profession, dissemination of the profession's knowledge, and advocacy for the profession. They typically offer an annual conference, a newsletter, and a professional magazine or journal.

program—Used in three different senses regarding recreation programming: as a recreation program event in which people participate (e.g., an instructional workshop); an agency program offering a schedule of program events (e.g., park district classes or events); or a program of actions or implementations to be undertaken by an agency to effect an outcome (e.g., a conservation easement program). Programming is the action of developing a program.

psychological leader—Person who helps create group morale and attends to other relationship considerations.

release—A means by which a program and usually its owners and staff are forgiven in advance for acts or omissions, including negligence, that might cause harm.

responsible leader—Person who has the ultimate responsibility for maintaining the safety and goal of the trip or program. This is the person who, if anything goes wrong, is called into account by higher authority.

risk—The potential for loss, including psychological, social, monetary, and physical harm.

risk management plan—An analysis of what the program is doing, why it is doing it, and how it expects to manage the risks of what it is doing.

rogue outfitting—Leading an adventure activity on government land without obtaining the necessary permits. Rogue outfitting is illegal.

ropes course—Older designation for a challenge course. Many of the early courses were made entirely of ropes and rope obstacles tied to trees or utility poles.

safety—Being free from harm or risk.

self-belayed climbing—Process whereby a facilitator uses a fall-protection lanyard to safely access high elements and climbing structures.

self-facilitation—Training clients to use techniques such as funneling to guide their own reflection processes during and after an adventure program.

SPEC approach—An instructional approach that involves creating a student-centered, problem-based, experiential, and collaborative learning environment.

spotting—The act of physically protecting group members who are on a low element. Spotting involves learning proper technique and applying it in a variety of settings.

standard operating procedures (SOPs)—General guidelines widely used and accepted in the field by reputable challenge course operators and providers that outline the minimum safety requirements for use of a challenge course element.

static belay—A climber negotiating a series of interconnected elements often uses this style of belay, which involves the use of a safety lanyard with two separate tethers attached to the climber's harness. While negotiating the elements, the climber remains clipped into secure belay cables. The second tether affords the ability to remain connected to the current belay cable while transferring the other tether to the new element belay cable.

stretch-zone experiences—An experience that is neither too easy nor too demanding to support an individual's readiness to gain new knowledge or insights.

student-centered learning—Participants learn by talking, listening, writing, reading, creating, and reflecting on content, ideas, and concerns as they work in small groups or individually to engage the curriculum.

teachable moment—Taking advantage of an unexpected opportunity to teach a topic of relevance.

therapeutic adventure—See *adventure therapy.*

trust activities—Activities that help not only to establish trust, but also to gauge the level of trust that exists in a group.

universal approach—A holistic and inclusive approach to course and program design that moves beyond the idea of accessible design; it is a framework for the design of places, things, and information to be usable by the widest range of people operating in the widest range of situations without special or separate design.

universal design—Universal design moves beyond the idea of accessible design. It is a framework for the design of places, things, and information to be usable by the widest range of people operating in the widest range of situations without special or separate design. In a universally designed program it is not evident that modifications have been made for a specific user or group.

well-functioning group—A well-functioning, or effective, group has several characteristics, including clear purpose, high morale, good communication, recognition of each other's contributions, distributed leadership, equality of power, consensus decision making, valuing of differences in style and ideas, and ability to work through disagreements (Johnson and Johnson 2002).

wilderness—Refers to a relatively undeveloped area. The term is a source of confusion because it is used in a variety of senses, including (1) a legally designated area (a wilderness area); (2) a roadless area that could be designated as a wilderness area and may be temporarily protected as such; or (3) any relatively undeveloped area with only primitive roads, cabins, and few amenities.

youth at risk—Troubled youth who are not doing well socially or academically; they may be at risk for becoming part of the juvenile court system as adjudicated youth.

REFERENCES

Ajzen, I., and M. Fishbein. 1980. *Understanding attitudes and predicting social behavior.* Englewood Cliffs, NJ: Prentice Hall.

American Camp Association (ACA). 2005a. Trend fact sheet. Retrieved November 2005 from www.acacamps.org/media_center/camp_trends/fact.php.

American Camp Association. 2005b. *Directions: Youth development outcomes of the camp experience.* [Brochure]. Martinsville, IN: Author.

Association for Challenge Course Technology (ACCT). 2004. *Challenge course standards,* 6th ed. Martin, MI: Author.

Association for Experiential Education (AEE). 2001. *Schools and colleges directory.* Boulder, CO: Author.

Association for Experiential Education (AEE). 2004a. *Accreditation self-assessment standards.* Boulder, CO: Author.

Association for Experiential Education (AEE). 2004b. What is experiential education? Retrieved September 7, 2004b, from www.aee2.org/customer/pages.php?pageid=47.

Babbie, E. 1998. *The practice of social research,* 8th ed. Belmont, CA: Wadsworth.

Bacon, S. 1987. *The evolution of the Outward Bound process.* Greenwich, CT: Outward Bound USA.

Barth, R. 1990. *Improving schools from within.* San Francisco: Jossey-Bass.

Barton, P.E. 2005. *One third of a nation: Rising dropout rates and declining opportunities.* Princeton, NJ: Education Testing Service.

Berne, E. 1963. *The structure and dynamics of groups.* New York: Grove Press.

Bernstein, P. 1996. *Against the gods.* New York: Wiley.

Blanchard, K.H., and P. Hersey. 1996. Great ideas revisited. *Training and Development* 50(1): 42-47.

Bobbitt, F. 1918. *The curriculum.* Boston: Houghton Mifflin.

Bohm, D. 1987. *Unfolding meaning: A weekend of dialogue with David Bohm.* London: Ark Paperbacks.

Borton, T. 1970. *Reach, touch, and teach.* New York: McGraw-Hill.

Buell, L.H. 1983. *Outdoor leadership competency.* Greenfield, MA: Environmental Awareness.

Butler, S. 2000. Creating your own adventure activities. *ZipLines* 40: 13-19.

Caine, R.N., and G. Caine. 1994. *Making connections: Teaching and the human brain.* Rev. ed. Menlo Park, CA: Addison-Wesley.

Carson, D., and H.L. Gillis. 1994. A meta-analysis of outdoor adventure programming with adolescents. *Journal of Experiential Education* 17: 40-47.

Chernaik, M. 1991. *Tort liability and the University of Oregon outdoor program.* Unpublished manuscript.

City of Berkeley. July 2004. Adventure playground's 25th birthday celebration. Retrieved November 2005 from www.cityofberkeley.info/news/2004/07jul/070604Adventureplaygrounds.html.

Clarke, J.I. 1984. *Who, me lead a group?* San Francisco: Harper & Row.

Conrad, D., and Hedin, D. 1981. *Executive summary of the final report of the experiential education evaluation project.* St. Paul, MN: University of Minnesota, Center for Youth Development and Research.

Covey, S. 1990. *The seven habits of highly effective people.* West Valley City, UT: Franklin Covey.

Cross, J.G., and M.J. Guyer. 1980. *Social traps.* Ann Arbor, MI: University of Michigan Press.

Csikszentmihalyi, M. 1991. *Flow: The source of optimal experience.* New York: Harper and Row.

Csikszentmihalyi, M. 1993. *The evolving self.* New York: HarperCollins.

Danforth, W.H. 1931. *I dare you!* St. Louis: Author.

Danziger, A. 1982. The effects of adventure activities on the self-concept of elementary school children. *Dissertation Abstracts, 43*(08A), 2594. (UMI No. AAT8300234).

Darst, P.W., and G.P. Armstrong. 1980. *Outdoor adventure activities for school and recreation programs.* Prospect Heights, IL: Waveland.

Davies, R. 1990. *The Deptford trilogy.* New York: Penguin.

Dewey, J. 1938. *Experience and education.* New York: McMillan.

DeZeeuw, J. 2002. *An examination of the impact of experiential education methodologies used in cross-cultural programs on the moral reasoning of high school students.* Master's thesis, University of New Hampshire.

Dimock, H.S., and C.E. Hendry. 1929. *Camping and character.* New York: Association Press.

Doughty, S. 1991. Three generations of development training. *Adventure Education and Outdoor Leadership* 7(4): 7-9.

Drury, J.K., B.F. Bonney, D. Berman, and M.C. Wagstaff. 2005. *Backcountry classroom: Lessons, tools and activities for teaching outdoor leaders,* 2nd ed. Guilford, CT: Globe Pequot.

Duckworth, E. 1987. *The having of wonderful ideas and other essays on teaching and learning.* Willison, VT: Teachers College Press.

Estes, C.A. 2004. Promoting student-centered learning in experiential education. *Journal of Experiential Education* 27(2): 141-160.

Ewert, A. 1986. Fear: Uses and abuses in outdoor adventure activities. *Underseas Journal* (first quarter): 44-48.

Ewert, A.W. 1989. *Outdoor adventure pursuits: Foundations, models, and theories.* Scottsdale, AZ: Publishing Horizons.

Expedition learning at NOLS (brochure). 2004. Lander, WY: National Outdoor Leadership School.

Flavin, M.J. 1996. *Kurt Hahn's schools and legacy.* Wilmington, DE: Middle Atlantic Press.

Fluegelman, A. 1981. *More new games.* New York: Dolphin Doubleday.

Fluegelman, A., and Tembeck, S., eds. 1976. *The new games book.* New York: Dolphin Doubleday.

Ford, P., and J. Blanchard. 1985. *Leadership and administration of outdoor pursuits.* State College, PA: Venture.

Friese, G., J.C. Hendee, and M. Kinziger. 1998. The wilderness experience program industry in the United States: Characteristics and dynamics. *Journal of Experiential Education* 21(1): 40-45.

Fullan, M. 2005. *Leadership and sustainability: System thinkers in action.* Thousand Oaks, CA: Corwin Press.

Furlong, L., A. Jillings, M. LaRhette, and B. Ryan. 1995. *20-year safety study.* Hamilton, MA: Project Adventure.

Garvey, D. 1991. *The effects of cross-cultural experiences on the moral development of a select group of college students.* PhD diss., University of Colorado.

Garvey, D. 1999a. The history of experiential education. In *Adventure programming,* ed. J. Miles and S. Priest. State College, PA: Venture.

Garvey, D. 1999b. Outdoor adventure programming and moral development. In *Adventure programming,* ed. J. Miles and S. Priest. State College, PA: Venture.

Gass, M. 1998. *Administrative practices in accredited adventure programs.* Needham Heights, MA: Simon and Schuster.

Giampietro, P.J. 2001. *The moral reasoning of undergraduate outdoor education majors.* Master's thesis, University of New Hampshire.

Gibbons, M. 1974. Walkabout: Searching for the right passage from childhood and school. *Phi Delta Kappan* 55: 596-602.

Glovich, T. 1991. *How we know what isn't so.* New York: Free Press.

Green, P. 1981. *The content of a college-level outdoor leadership course for land-based outdoor pursuits in the Pacific Northwest: A delphi consensus.* PhD diss., University of Oregon, Portland.

Greenaway, R. 1993. *Playback: A guide to reviewing activities.* Edinburgh, Scotland: Award Scheme Ltd., The Duke of Edinburgh's Award and Endeavour.

Guthrie, S.P. 1999. Outdoor program models: Placing cooperative adventure and adventure education models on the continuum. In *Proceedings of the 13th Annual International Conference on Outdoor Recreation and Education,* ed. R. Harwell and K. Emmons, 227-234. Boulder, CO: Association of Outdoor Recreation and Education.

Hall, M., and S. Raudenbush. 2005. *Wisdom teachings: Lessons learned from gathering of elders.* Gallup, New Mexico: National Indian Youth Leadership Program.

Hammerman, D., and W. Hammerman. 1968. *Outdoor education.* Minneapolis, MN: Burgess.

Hattie, J., H.W. Marsh, J.T. Neill, and G.E. Richards. 1997. Adventure education and Outward Bound out-of-class experiences that make a lasting difference. *Review of Educational Research* 67: 43-87.

Hazelworth, M.S., and B.E. Wilson. 1990. The effects of an outdoor adventure camp experience on self-concept. *Journal of Environmental Education* 21: 33-37.

Hilbert, H., and G.O. Grimm. 1973. *An operational definition and description of college outdoor programs.* Retrieved July 5, 2005, from www.isu.edu/outdoor/great.htm.

Hirsch, J. 1999. Developmental adventure programs. In *Adventure programming,* ed. J.C. Miles and S. Priest, 13-26. State College, PA: Venture.

Holbrook v. McCraken, 2004 WL 1402695 (Ohio App. 8 Dist. 2004).

Holman, T., L. McAvoy, M. Goldenberg, and D. Klenosky. 2004. *Outcomes and personal values associated with participation in an inclusive adventure program.* Paper presented at the biennial meeting of the Coalition for Education in the Outdoors Research Symposium, Martinsville, IN, January.

Honey, M. 1999. *Ecotourism and sustainable development: Who owns paradise?* Washington, D.C.: Island Press.

Hopkins, D., and R. Putnam. 1993. *Personal growth through adventure.* London: David Fulton.

Hunt, J. 1999. Philosophy of adventure education. In *Adventure programming,* ed. J.C. Miles and S. Priest, 115-122. State College, PA: Venture.

Hunt, J.S. 1998. Ethically tolerable accidents. *1998 Wilderness Risk Management Conference Proceedings,* National Outdoor Leadership School, Lander, Wyoming.

Hunt, J.S. 2002. *Ethical issues in experiential education,* 4th ed. Boulder, CO: Association for Experiential Education.

Hurricane island instructor manual. 1989. Rockland, ME: Outward Bound USA.

Iso-Ahola, S.E. 1980. *The social-psychology of leisure and recreation*. Dubuque, IA: Brown.

Itin, C. 1995. Utilizing hypnotic language in adventure therapy. *Journal of Experiential Education* 18(2): 70-75.

Itin, C., and S. Bandoroff. 2001. *Facilitation on the edge: Developing professional skills and competence to facilitate therapeutic change*. Workshop presented at the 29th Annual International Conference of the Association for Experiential Education, Charleston, WV, November.

Itin, C.M. 2001. Adventure therapy: Critical questions. *Journal of Experiential Education* 24(2): 80-84.

Janis, I. 1982. *Groupthink*, 2nd ed. Boston: Houghton Mifflin.

Jensen, M., and A. Young. 1981. Alternative for outdoor education programming. *Journal of Physical Education, Recreation and Dance* (October) 52: 64-67.

Jernstedt, C.G., and B.T. Johnson. 1983. *The effects of long-term experiential programs on their participants*. (ERIC Document Reproduction Service No. ED 238-625)

Johnson, D.W., and F.P. Johnson. 2002. *Joining together: Group theory and group skills*, 8th ed. Boston, MA: Allyn & Bacon.

Jones v. Three Rivers Management, 394 A.2d 546 (Pennsylvania, 1978).

Kaly, P.W., and M. Heesacker. 2003. Effects of a ship-based adventure program on adolescent self-esteem and ego-identity development. *Journal of Experiential Education* 26(2): 97-104.

Kerr, P., and M. Gass. 1987. A group development model for adventure education. *Journal of Experiential Education* 19(3): 39-46.

Kilty, K. 2006. *Creating healthy habits: An adventure guide to teaching health and wellness*. Beverly, MA: Project Adventure.

Knapp, C. 1990. Processing experiences. In J.C. Miles and S. Priest (Eds.), *Adventure education* (pp. 189-198). State College, PA: Venture.

Kolb, D.A. 1984. *Experiential learning: Experience as the source of learning and development*. Englewood Cliffs, NJ: Prentice Hall.

Kraft, D., and M.M. Sakofs, eds. 1988. *The theory of experiential education*. Boulder, CO: Association of Experiential Education.

Lambert, L. 1999. *Standards-based assessment of student learning: A comprehensive approach*. Reston, VA: AAHPERD.

Lambert, L. 2003. Standards-based program design: Creating a congruent guide for student learning. In *Student learning in physical education: Applying research to enhance instruction*, ed. S.J. Silverman and C.A. Ennis, 129-146. Champaign, IL: Human Kinetics.

Lehmann, K. 1991. Connecting ethics and group leadership: A case study. *Journal of Experiential Education* 14(3): 45-51.

Loughmiller, C. 1965. *Wilderness road*. Austin, TX: University of Texas Press.

Luckner, J.L., and R.S. Nadler. 1997. *Processing the experience: Strategies to enhance and generalize learning*. Dubuque, IA: Kendall/Hunt.

Martin, B., C. Cashel, M. Wagstaff, and M. Breunig. 2006. *Outdoor leadership: Theory and practice*. Champaign, IL: Human Kinetics.

McAvoy, L. 1978. Outdoor leadership training. *Journal of Physical Education and Recreation* 49(4): 42-43.

McBride, D.L. 1984. *The behaviors of adolescent boys in a residential treatment center during a high ropes course experience*. PhD diss., Ohio State University.

Meyer, B.B., and M.S. Wengler. 1998. Athletes and adventure education: An empirical investigation. *International Journal of Sports Psychology* 29: 243-266.

Miles, J. and S. Priest, eds. 1999. *Adventure programming*. State College, PA: Venture.

Miner, J.L., and Boldt, J. 1981. *Outward Bound USA: Learning through experience in adventure-based education*. New York: William Morrow.

Miner, J.L., and J. Boldt. 2002. *Crew not passengers*, 2nd ed. Seattle: Mountaineer Books.

Mitten, D. 1985. A philosophical basis for a women's outdoor adventure program. *Journal of Experiential Education* 8(2): 20-24.

Mitten, D. 1999. Leadership for community building. In *Adventure programming*, ed. J. Miles and S. Priest. State College, PA: Venture.

Mitten, D. 2003. An analysis of outdoor leaders' ethics guiding decision making. UMI Number: 3087775.

NASPE. 2004. *Moving into the future: National standards for physical education*. St. Louis: McGraw-Hill.

Nemarnik v. Los Angeles Kings (2002) 103 Cal. App. 4th 631.

North Carolina Outward Bound. 1981. *Book of readings*. North Carolina Outward Bound.

North Carolina Outward Bound. 2006. History: Kurt Hahn and Outward Bound. Retrieved July 9, 2006, from www.ncobs.org/about_us/history/kurt_hahn_outward_bound.php.

North Carolina State University. 2005. *Department of Physical Education: Courses*. Retrieved June 28, 2005, from www.ncsu.edu/pe/courses.html.

O'Connell, T. 2002. Self concept: A study of outdoor adventure education with adolescents. *Dissertation Abstracts International, 62*(7A), 2568. (UMI No. AAT 3022157).

Orlick, T. *Cooperative games and sports*, 2nd ed. Champaign, IL: Human Kinetics.

Panicucci, J., L. Faulkingham Hunt, A. Rheingold, and A. Kohut. 2003. *Adventure curricula for physical education: High school, middle school, elementary school*. Beverly, MA: Project Adventure.

Pann, J.M. 2000. The effects of an adventure education intervention of self-concept and verbal academic achievement in inner city adolescents. *Dissertation Abstracts International, 60*(10A), 3606. (UMI No. AAT 9948781)

Panowitsch, H.R. 1975. *Change and stability in the Defining Issues Test.* PhD diss., University of Minnesota.

Parker, M., and J. Stiehl. 2005. Personal and social responsibility. In *Standards-based physical education curriculum development,* ed. J. Lund and D. Tannehill, 130-153. Sudbury, MA: Jones and Bartlett.

Penn, W.Y., Jr. 1990. Teaching ethics: A direct approach. *Journal of Moral Education* 19(2): 124-138.

Petzoldt, P. July 6, 1983. Personal communication, Caribou-Targhgee National Forest, WY.

Petzoldt, P.K. 1984. *The new wilderness handbook.* New York: Norton.

Phipps, M. 1991. Definitions of outdoor recreation and other associated terminology. In *Employee preparation toward 2001: 1990 conference proceedings of national conference for outdoor leaders,* ed. M. Phipps and R.G. Cash. Gunnison, CO: Western State College.

Priest, S. 1984. Outdoor leadership down under. *Journal of Experiential Education* 8: 13-15.

Priest, S. 1999. Introduction: Experientia. In *Adventure programming,* ed. J.C. Miles and S. Priest, xiii-xiv. State College, PA: Venture.

Priest, S., and M.A. Gass. 2005. *Effective leadership in adventure programming,* 2nd ed. Champaign, IL: Human Kinetics.

Priest, S., M. Gass, and K. Fitzpatrick, 1999. Training corporate managers to facilitate: The next generation of facilitating experiential methodologies. *Journal of Experiential Education* 22(1): 50-53.

Priest, S., M. Gass, and L. Gillis, 2000. *The essential elements of facilitation.* Dubuque, IA: Kendall/Hunt.

Priest, S., and M.A. Lesperance, 1994. Time series trend analysis in corporate team development. *Journal of Experiential Education* 17(1): 34-39.

Project Adventure. 2005. *Adventure program management training manual.* Beverly, MA: Project Adventure.

Project Adventure. 2002. *Adventure programming training manual.* Beverly, MA: Project Adventure.

Quinn, B. 1990. The essence of adventure. In *Adventure programming,* ed. J.C. Miles and S. Priest. State College, PA: Venture.

Rachels, J. 1999. *The elements of moral philosophy.* 3rd ed. Boston: McGraw-Hill.

Rennie, J. 1985. An uncommon adventure. In *Proceedings of the 1984 Conference on Outdoor Recreation: A landmark conference in the outdoor recreation field,* ed. J.C. Miles and R. Watters. Pocatello, ID: Idaho State University Press.

Rest, J., S. Thoma, and L. Edwards. 1997. Designing and validating a measure of moral judgment: Stage preference and stage consistency approaches. *Journal of Educational Psychology* 89(1): 5-28.

Richards, A. 1999. Outdoor adventure programming and moral development. In *Adventure programming,* ed. J. Miles and S. Priest. State College, PA: Venture.

Robbins, T. 1976. *Even cowgirls get the blues.* New York: Bantam.

Rogers, D. 2000. Future challenge courses offer access for persons with disabilities. *Parks and Recreation* (March): 5 (online version).

Rohnke, K. 1977. *Cowstails and cobras.* Hamilton, MA: Project Adventure (out of print).

Rohnke, K. 1989a. *Cowstails and cobras II.* Hamilton, MA: Project Adventure.

Rohnke, K. 1989b. The ropes course: A constructed adventure environment. *Zip Lines* (4): 3.

Rohnke, K., J. Wall, C. Tait, and D. Rogers. 2003. *The complete ropes course manual.* Dubuque, IA: Kendall/Hunt.

Russell, K.C. 2003. A nationwide survey of outdoor behavioral healthcare programs for adolescents with problem behaviors. *Journal of Experiential Education* 25(3): 322-331.

Ryan, B. 2005. *The guide for challenge course operations: An essential reference for challenge course practitioners.* Beverly, MA: Project Adventure.

Schoel, J. 2005. Personal conversation, September 20, 2005.

Schoel, J. 2005. Personal conversation, July 12, 2005.

Schoel, J. and R. Maizell. 2002. *Exploring islands of healing.* Beverly, MA: Project Adventure.

Schoel, J., D. Prouty, and P. Radcliffe. 1988. *Islands of healing: A guide to adventure-based counseling.* Hamilton, MA: Project Adventure.

Senge, P. 1990. *The fifth discipline.* New York: Doubleday.

Shaffer, D.R. 1988. *Social and personality development.* 2nd ed. Belmont, CA: Wadsworth.

Smith, J.W., R.E. Carlson, G.W. Donaldson, and H.B. Masters. 1972. *Outdoor education,* 2nd ed. Englewood Cliffs, NJ: Prentice Hall.

Smolowe, A., S. Butler, M. Murray, and J. Smolowe. 1999. *Adventure in business: An IMMERSION approach to training and consulting.* Hamilton, MA: Project Adventure.

Spady, W.G., and K. Marshall. 1991. Beyond traditional outcome-based education. *Educational Leadership* 49(2): 67-72.

Steger, W. 2000. The spirit of adventure. In *The greatest adventures of all time,* ed. R. Sullivan and R. Andreas. Des Moines: LIFE Books.

Stiehl, J., and M. Parker. 2005. Outdoor education. In *Standards-based physical education curriculum development,* ed. J. Lund and D. Tannehill, 176-197. Sudbury, MA: Jones and Bartlett.

Sugerman, D.A., K.L. Doherty, D.E. Garvey, and M.A. Gass. 2000. *Reflective learning: Theory and practice.* Dubuque, IA: Kendall/Hunt.

Swiderski, M. 1981. *Outdoor leadership competencies identified by outdoor leaders in five western regions.* PhD. diss., University of Oregon.

Tannehill, D., and J. Lund. 2005. Building a quality physical education program. In *Standards-based physical education curriculum development,* ed. J. Lund and D. Tannehill, 16-45. Sudbury, MA: Jones and Bartlett.

Tuckman, B. 1965. Developmental sequence in small groups. *Psychological Bulletin* 63: 384-399.

Tuckman, B.W., and M.A. Jensen. 1977. Stages of small group development revisited. *Group and Organization Studies* 2(4): 419-427.

UNESCO-UNEP. 1976. The Belgrade charter: A global framework for environmental education. *UNESCO-UNEP Environmental Newsletter* 1(1): 1-2.

University of Oregon. 2005. *Physical activity and recreation services: Courses.* Retrieved June 29, 2005, from www.uoregon.edu/~opp/.

University of Oregon Outdoor Program. 2005. University of Oregon outdoor program philosophy. Retrieved September 2005 from http://outdoorprogram.uorcgon.edu/about/about.html.

Urban Freeflow. George Hébert and the Natural Method of physical culture. Retrieved July 9, 2006, from www.urbanfreeflow.com/the_core_level/pages/archives/methode_naturelle.htm.

Wagstaff, M. 2003. History and philosophy of challenge courses. In *Developing challenge course programs for schools,* ed. S. Wurdinger and J. Steffen, 3-16. Dubuque, IA: Kendall/Hunt.

Wagstaff, M., and C. Cashel. 2001. Paul Petzoldt's perspective: The final 20 years. *Journal of Experiential Education* 24: 160-165.

Waltzlawick, P. 1978. *The language of change.* New York: Norton.

Watters, R. 1987. A model theory of outdoor programming approaches. In *High-adventure outdoor pursuits,* 2nd ed. Eds. J.F. Meier, T.W. Morash, and G.E. Welton, 213-225. Columbus, OH: Publishing Horizons.

Watters, R. 1999. Revisiting the common adventure concept: An annotated review of the literature, misconceptions and contemporary perspective. In R. Harwell & K. Emmons (Eds.), *Proceedings of the 13th annual International Conference on Outdoor Recreation and Education,* (pp. 82-94). Boulder, CO: Association of Outdoor Recreation and Education.

Webb, B.J. 1993. The use of a three-day therapeutic wilderness adjunct by the Colorado Outward Bound School with survivors of violence. In *Adventure therapy: Therapeutic applications of adventure programming,* ed. M.A. Gass. Dubuque, IA: Kendall/Hunt.

Webb, D.J. 1999. Recreational outdoor adventure programs. In *Adventure programming,* ed. J.C. Miles and S. Priest, 3-8. State College, PA: Venture.

Webb, D.J. 2001. The emergence and evolution of outdoor adventure programs, 1863-2000: A history of student initiated outing programs. Unpublished manuscript.

Webb, D.J. 2002. *Outdoor recreation program directory and data/resource guide,* 3rd ed. Bowling Green, KY: Raymond Poff.

Weimer, M. 2002. *Learner-centered teaching.* San Francisco: Jossey-Bass.

Western Carolina Paddlers. 2005. Welcome to the Western Carolina Paddlers! Retrieved September 2005 from www.boatingbeta.com/-wcp.

Wheatley, M. 1993. *Leadership and the new science: Learning about organization from an orderly universe.* San Francisco: Berrett-Koehler.

Wiggins, G., and J. McTighe. 1998. *Understanding by design.* Alexandria, VA: Association of Supervision and Curriculum Development.

Wisconsin Hoofers Outing Club. 2005. Policies and procedures. Retrieved September 20, 2005, from www.hooferouting.org/modules/icontent/index.php?page=%2Fabout%2Fpolicies%2index.php.

Yace v. Dushano, 2003 WL 22953762 (Cal. App. 2 Dist. 2003).

Yerkes, R. 1980. The effects of creative-adventure playground participation on school readiness of young children. PhD diss., Northern Illinois University.

Yerkes, R. 1988. What about the young child? *Journal of Experiential Education* 11(2): 21-25.

Young, A., and M. Parker. 1987. Building human relations through instructional design. *Camping Magazine* 59(5): 46-49.

Zull, J. 2002. *The art of changing the brain.* Sterling, VA: Stylus.

INDEX

Note: The italicized *f* or *t* following page numbers indicates a figure or table, respectively.

ABOUT THE EDITORS

Dick Prouty, AB, is Project Adventure's president, executive director, and CEO. With Project Adventure since 1980, he facilitated the structure of PA as a 501(c)3 nonprofit organization. In 1982, he became director and led the strategic planning and organizational development of PA as it became the premier organization of facilities-based adventure learning. Coauthor of PA's classic text on adventure-based counseling, *Islands of Healing*, Prouty has become a leading proponent of the unique place and theory of adventure-based experiential education. He has also served as founder of the Association for Experiential Education's (AEE) accreditation committee, founder of the board of directors of Association for Challenge Course Technology (ACCT), and chair of the board of the Waring School. Prouty's current responsibilities at PA include strategic planning, partnering and development planning, directing new publications, and leading the senior executive team.

Jane Panicucci, MAEd, is currently Project Adventure's chief operations officer. Her adventure background includes 11 years as a course director at Outward Bound. In the mid-1980s, as a public school physical educator, Panicucci designed an adventure curriculum that is still going strong. Her current consulting specialties involve working with teachers and administrators to generate positive change in their schools and to create high-performing teams for both nonprofit and for-profit organizations. She is the lead author of PA's series of adventure curricula for physical education and is currently working on a fitness program curriculum.

Rufus (Ruthanne) Collinson has been working in the adventure field for 18 years as manager of communications, editor, and book developer for Project Adventure (PA). She is responsible for editing and developing all PA publications. Rufus is also a published poet. She and her daughter Suzanna have conducted experiential writing workshops, called Words from the Wild, at several field conferences. In 2001, Rufus received the Association for Experiential Education's (AEE) Karl Rohnke Creativity Award.

ABOUT THE CONTRIBUTORS

Aram Attarian, PhD, is an associate professor in the department of parks, recreation, and tourism management at North Carolina State University, where his teaching focuses on adventure recreation, outdoor leadership, and park and recreation facility management. His research centers on Leave No Trace behavior with a specialized interest on climbing resource education and management (CREaM), outdoor leadership and adventure programming, and risk assessment. With more than 30 years as a professional in outdoor leadership, Attarian has worked for a variety of programs, including Outward Bound and programs for adjudicated youth. In addition to writing curriculum for outdoor leadership programs, Attarian has been published in a variety of periodicals and books. He also designed and implemented an academic minor in outdoor leadership and created the outdoor pursuits program at North Carolina State University. Attarian has received five awards for excellence in teaching.

Kent Clement, PhD, is professor of outdoor recreation leadership at Colorado Mountain College. He has over 300 weeks of field experience in outdoor leadership and has taught outdoor leadership and technical skills, including rock climbing, mountaineering, sea kayaking, canyoneering, and orienteering for 27 years. Clement is in the process of writing another book for Human Kinetics titled *Decision Making: Judgment Training for Outdoor Leaders* as well as two chapters in the new *Boy Scout Fieldbook* and several papers on judgment and environmental ethics. Clement is a member of the Wilderness Risk Managers Committee and is a former executive director of the Wilderness Education Association.

Christopher J. Damboise, BS, is director of credentialing services and technical training for Project Adventure. In that role, he oversees the management of practitioner certification and program accreditation. He was the director of design and installation of challenge courses for Project Adventure and course director for the Hurricane Island Outward Bound School. He continues in his role as senior trainer at Project Adventure and is responsible for new technical content and oversees PA's internal trainer certification. Damboise is also a professionally trained mountain guide with high-angle rescue skills. He is a member of the Association for Challenge Course Technology and the American Mountain Guides Association.

Jack K. Drury, MS, is vice president of Leading EDGE, an education development and consulting firm, and exclusive provider of Education by Design training in New York State. He has been an Education by Design institute coordinator since 1992 and has facilitated experiential learning experiences at an international level for more than 25 years. Drury is past president of the Wilderness Education Association (WEA) and coauthor and editor of the definitive wilderness leadership text *The Backcountry Classroom: Lesson Plans for Teaching in the Wilderness* and *The Camper's Guide to Outdoor Pursuits: Finding Safe, Nature-Friendly and Comfortable Passage Through Wild Places*. Drury is a winner of the WEA's Frank Lupton Service Award as well as the Adirondack Council's 1989 Outstanding Adirondack Educator Award.

Cheryl A. Stevens, PhD, is an associate professor in the department of recreation and leisure studies at East Carolina University. With 20-plus years of experience in outdoor adventure education, Stevens has worked with Ohio State University's adventure education center and program of outdoor pursuits, Outward Bound, and SUNY Cortland's outdoor leadership program. Stevens has received five excellence in teaching awards throughout her 13 years of university teaching. She has been published in the *Journal of Experiential Education* and is an active member of the Association for Experiential Education and the Society of Park and Recreation Educators. Stevens currently pursues sailing and sea kayaking in eastern North Carolina.

Alan Ewert, PhD, is professor and graduate coordinator in the department of recreation, parks, and tourism studies at Indiana University. He holds the Patricia and Joel Meier endowed chair in outdoor leadership and serves as the editor of the *Journal of Experiential Education*. Ewert has served as an editor and author for a variety of journals and books related to outdoor leadership and recreation. He continues his professional service in a variety of capacities, including board member of the American Alliance of Leisure Research (AALR), fellow of the Research Consortium, and guest editor of *JOPERD* and *Leisure Today*. In addition, he serves as an instructor and course director for Outward Bound Wilderness. Ewert was the recipient of the 2005 Julian W. Smith Award presented by the Council for Adventure and Outdoor Education/Recreation.

Dan Garvey, PhD, is president of Prescott College in Prescott, Arizona. Author of more than 25 books and articles on adventure-based programming and education, Garvey has worked in the field for more than 30 years. Garvey served as president and executive director of the Association for Experiential Education and was a faculty member in the outdoor education department at the University of New Hampshire. He was a recipient of the Kurt Hahn Award in 1997 and the Julian W. Smith Award in 2000. He is also a trustee of the National Outdoor Leadership School in Wyoming and Project Adventure in Massachusetts.

Michael A. Gass, **PhD**, is a professor and chair of the department of kinesiology in the School of Health and Human Services at the University of New Hampshire (UNH). He is one of the creators of the Browne Center, a program development and research center at UNH. Gass has produced more than 100 publications and 200 professional presentations in the adventure programming field. He currently directs research programs for Project Adventure. He served as president of the Association for Experiential Education (AEE) in 1990 and in 1994 was chair of the Council for Outdoor Education in the American Alliance for Health, Physical Education, Recreation and Dance. Gass is currently editor of the *Journal of Therapeutic Schools and Programs* and serves on the advisory board for the *Journal of Experiential Education*.

Charles R. Gregg, LLB, is a licensed attorney in Houston, Texas. He is an active author and lecturer in the field of legal liability of outdoor education and recreation programs. Gregg served as chair and board member of the National Outdoor Leadership School and has been its legal counsel since 1978. He serves as legal counsel to many other leading programs and organizations in the fields of outdoor and experiential education, including the Association for Challenge Course Technology. Gregg also serves on the accreditation council of the Association for Experiential Education and is a member of the Wilderness Risk Managers Committee. He has written numerous articles for the Wilderness Risk Managers Conference and written chapters for other publications dealing with issues of legal liability.

Steven Guthrie, **PhD,** is assistant professor of outdoor recreation management at Lock Haven University of Pennsylvania. Instructor and leader of outdoor recreation and adventure education activities for 33 years, Guthrie was a founding member and president of the Association of Outdoor Recreation and Education. Coauthor of *Outdoor Recreation in America, Sixth Edition*, he also served as peer reviewer for the *Journal of Experiential Education* for 12 years. Formerly faculty member and program coordinator of the outdoor recreation leadership program at Unity College in Unity, Maine, Guthrie received the Jim Rennie leadership award from the Association of Outdoor Recreation and Education in 2003.

Lisa Faulkingham Hunt, BA, is a senior trainer and consultant for Project Adventure. She has 15 years of experience using adventure activities directly with diverse populations, from youth at camp to college leadership groups. She also has 6 years of experience training teachers to use adventure games and activities in their own venues. Hunt was a contributing author for Project Adventure's series *Adventure Curricula for Physical Education* and has managed PA's New Product/New Activities initiative.

Denise Mitten, PhD, is associate professor at Ferris State University in the department of recreation, leisure services, and wellness. For the past 30 years she has worked in adventure, experiential, outdoor, and environmental education with many populations, including youth, women, nuns, homeless people, and men in prison. Mitten, an experienced adventure guide, has led trips involving scuba diving, mountaineering, rafting, kayaking, rock climbing, and skiing. For 10 years, she was the executive director of Woodswomen, an educational and adventure travel organization for women. In 1992, she received the Excellence in Teaching Award from Metropolitan State University and was selected as Entrepreneur of the Year by the National Association of Professional Saleswomen in 1993. As a writer and consultant, Mitten addresses nature and wellness, ethics, group dynamics, and gender issues.

For the past 8 years, **Jim Stiehl** and **Melissa Parker** have taught together at the University of Northern Colorado; however, their professional relationship spans almost 20 years. They became acquainted through a shared interest in promoting children's well-being through physical activity. After working together, Stiehl and Parker discovered a mutual interest in outdoor and adventure education. Both have taught a variety of outdoor and adventure courses and led wilderness expeditions with adults and children. Jim has supervised UNC's challenge ropes course for over 15 years, and Melissa has continually explored ways to incorporate adventure concepts and philosophy into physical education curriculum and teacher education.

Alison Rheingold, MEd, is coordinator of school-based implementations at Project Adventure. In her current role, she leads adventure-based professional development for teachers. This includes the process of integrating adventure into academic content and physical education as well as the whole school environment. Before working with Project Adventure, Rheingold used experiential teaching methods as a special education teacher, an environmental educator, and a wilderness instructor for Outward Bound. Additionally, she was one of the authors of Project Adventure's *Adventure Curriculum for Physical Education*. Rheingold is a member of the Association for Experiential Education and the American Alliance of Health, Physical Education, Recreation and Dance; she has presented workshops at both associations' international conferences.

Mark Wagstaff, EdD, has taught outdoor leadership and adventure education in the college setting for 13 years. Mark currently serves as an associate professor at Radford University, where he teaches in the recreation, parks, and tourism department. He worked as a professional river guide for over 10 years, served as an instructor for the North Carolina Outward Bound School, developed curriculum and instructed for the Wilderness Education Association for 19 years, managed the outdoor program at Oklahoma State University, and is a master instructor trainer for Leave No Trace, Center for Outdoor Ethics. Wagstaff recently coauthored a textbook for Human Kinetics titled *Outdoor Leadership: Theory and Practice* and also coauthored *The Backcountry Classroom: Lessons, Tools, and Activities for Teaching Outdoor Leaders, Second Edition,* a lesson plan manual for training and developing outdoor leaders.

Rita Yerkes, EdD, is dean and professor at the school of experiential leadership at George Williams College of Aurora University in Wisconsin. She is a cofounder of the Coalition of Education in the Outdoors, past president of the Council on Outdoor Education, and past board member, president, volunteer interim executive director, and accreditation council chair for the Association for Experiential Education (AEE). Yerkes received the Outstanding Service Award from the Wisconsin Parks and Recreation Association in 2005, the Reynold E. Carlson Lecturer Award from Indiana University in 2000, the Kurt Hahn Award in 1998, and the Julian Smith Award for Outstanding Contributions to Outdoor Education in 1990. She has served on the editorial boards of *Camping* magazine and the *Journal of Experiential Education*. She has written book chapters, numerous journal articles, and presentations.